REGIONAL DYNAMICS

TITLES OF RELATED INTEREST

REGIONAL DYNAMICS

Studies in adjustment theory

GORDON L. CLARK
Carnegie-Mellon University

MERIC S. GERTLER
The University of Toronto

JOHN E. M. WHITEMAN
Harvard University

Boston
ALLEN & UNWIN
London   Sydney

Allen & Unwin Inc.,
8 Winchester Place, Winchester, Mass. 01890, USA

Allen & Unwin (Publishers) Ltd,
40 Museum Street, London WC1A 1LU, UK

Allen & Unwin (Publishers) Ltd,
Park Lane, Hemel Hempstead, Herts HP2 4TE, UK

Allen & Unwin (Australia) Ltd,
8 Napier Street, North Sydney, NSW 2060, Australia

First published in 1986

British Library Cataloguing in Publication Data

Clark, Gordon L.
    Regional dynamics: studies in adjustment theory.
1. Regional economics
I. Title   II. Gertler, Meric S.
III. Whiteman, John E. M.
330.9   HT391
ISBN 0-04-330353-6
ISBN 0-04-330354-4 Pbk

Library of Congress Cataloging in Publication Data

Clark, Gordon L.
    Regional dynamics.
Bibliography: p.
Includes index.
1. Regional economics   2. Space in economics.
3. United States—Economic conditions—1945–
Regional disparities.   I. Gertler, Meric S.
II. Whiteman, John E. M.   III. Title.
HT391.C493   1986   330.973   85-22998
ISBN 0-04-330353-6
ISBN 0-04-330354-4 (pbk.)

Set in 10 on 12 point Bembo by Paston Press, Norwich
and printed in Great Britain by Mackays of Chatham

For our families

Preface

The aim of this book is to introduce a different approach to the study of regional economic systems. Throughout the book, our analytical method is termed the "adjustment" approach because of our concern with how regional economies adapt and respond to changing circumstances. We are concerned with the structure of the spatial system and the processes of restructuring. Adjustment theory is dynamic and historical, being based upon the passage of time and events. While economic events may be anticipated or unanticipated, from an adjustment perspective we are most interested in the spatial patterns of response and the consequences of adjustment for the regional economic system as a whole. Thus, regional adjustment theory is about the spatial context of economic behavior.

Our adjustment theory does not assume perfect information, nor does it necessarily assume a known future. Rather, we deal with the reality of uncertainty and spatially heterogeneous information in circumstances where social agents are unable to "sit-out" events. In this environment, transactions are costly and imply significant risks; distributional issues are also of vital importance. Inevitably, our adjustment theory is fundamentally concerned with disequilibrium, rather than equilibrium. In this respect, our goal is to provide an analytical framework relevant for the study of the dynamics of advanced capitalist economies.

This book is also about the structure and performance of the United States regional economy since the early 1950s. Tremendous changes have occurred over the past thirty years in the structure and relative economic prosperity of US regions. For instance, twenty years ago – even ten years ago – most commentators on the regional economic system believed that the New England region was destined for further economic misfortune. There seemed to be little possibility of regional transformation; further job losses and lower incomes seemed inevitable. Yet, in recent years, this region has been so successful in "restructuring" itself that it is now used by politicians and others as a model for regional transformation. As a consequence, many other regions are attempting to replicate the "success" of New England by encouraging growth in their local high-technology sectors. On the other hand, regions dominated by heavy industries such as autos, steel, chemicals, and the like have seen their relative economic prosperity slip away. The "success" regions of the early postwar era have been profoundly affected by all kinds of events: import competition, oil

ix

price shocks, the escalating value of the US dollar, and the very severe
recession of 1982. Simultaneous regional growth and decline has created a
new geography of prosperity. Understanding the dynamics of the US
regional system is a major focus of this book.

By virtue of our methodological commitment to adjustment theory,
our analysis of the US regional system constitutes a fundamental departure
from conventional regional economic theory. In terms of temporal adjustment, so much of regional theory depends upon neoclassical equilibrium-
based competitive models of economic processes. These models are deliberately static in nature, and have little interest (and no ability) in specifying the processes whereby economic systems move from one spatial
configuration to another. These kinds of models assume perfect information over space and time, or at least a stable probability distribution covering
all possible events. The extreme version of this model is the so-called
rational expectations theory, in which all agents are assumed to know how
the system is structured, even its formal parameter representation. While
few regional economic models are so extreme, most are only one step
removed from conventional static neoclassical macroeconomic theory.

A second point of departure which marks our approach as being
different from conventional regional theory has to do with our treatment
of space. Most models of regional growth and decline are concerned with
demonstrating, theoretically and empirically, the logic of spatial
homogeneity. That is, they are typically employed to derive the conditions
necessary for spatial economic equilibrium. In this type of ideal world,
spatial variations in price disappear, as do variations in wage rates, profit
rates, and the working conditions of labor, to name just a few dimensions
of regional economic structure. This is entirely consistent with neoclassical
economic theory, which presumes equilibrium at a point in time and
space, rather than continuous disequilibrium adjustment over space and
time. Generally, neoclassical theory is a theory of instantaneous adjustment; the texture of history and location have no significance which is
endogenous to the structure of the theory itself.

By contrast, in this book we argue for a methodological stance that takes
time and space seriously. Instead of rationalizing time by assuming all
possible contingencies to be known, we are directly concerned with the
processes of adjustment to temporal discontinuities. And instead of
homogenizing space we are concerned with the adjustment processes that
produce and reproduce spatial differentiation. Throughout the book, we
deal with the spatial processes and patterns of disequilibrium and thus this
book is basically concerned with the dynamics of regional economies. One
consequence of this methodological stance is the significance we attach to
questions of distribution. We return throughout the book to how and why
the costs of local adjustment are distributed across the landscape and
between contracting parties.

This book collects in one place our previous research on the empirical dimensions of regional economic adjustment as well as articulating our theoretical perspective on the nature of regional economic adjustment. We have resisted the temptation to make massive revisions to the empirical studies but have, nevertheless, made some revisions as appropriate, especially in terms of the organization of our empirical results. Large tables and very detailed discussion of results are generally avoided; the interested reader is referred to the original papers. The book should be read as a series of related studies, each aimed at explicating the logic of adjustment theory in relation to a particular facet of regional structure. Few of the chapters in this book are strictly theoretical. Most combine aspects of the theory of adjustment with more practical issues of empirical analysis in the regional context. The data, methods of dynamic analysis, and results of analyzing the US regional system since the early 1950s are all of importance in developing the logic of adjustment theory. We hope the combination of these modes of inquiry have demonstrated the virtues of adjustment theory as a practical mode of discourse.

In designing the book, we have attempted to link in sequence the most important facets of regional economic structure. Thus, we in turn deal with employment, wages, prices, migration, and capital investment in the regional context. Essentially, we have tried to cover the crucial elements of regional economies, stressing their own particular dimensions as well as their connections with the larger theoretical framework. Readers should recognize that each part of the book concentrates on one particular dimension of regional adjustment. For example, Part I concentrates on the theory of regional adjustment and, like all parts to the book, has its own overview and summary. In each part, a sequence of related studies are presented focusing upon the empirical aspects, theoretical logic, and distributive consequences of the particular element of regional adjustment under study.

By this sequential mode of organization, the book accumulates evidence for our theoretical conception of regional differentiation. As the table of contents indicates, the book has 15 chapters and 5 parts. Part I introduces the reader to recent debates in the regional economic literature, while also establishing the theoretical logic of adjustment. Chapter 1 is a critique of current neoclassical and related models of regional transition. We argue here that these kinds of models have no true dynamic structure and depend upon logical devices to generate change in the spatial economic system. This argument is followed in Chapter 2 by a conceptual treatment of adjustment theory, and in Chapter 3 by a more empirical treatment of the same topic. Contrasts are drawn between what we propose and how current theories treat the same issue. These chapters are especially important in this regard since we develop a decision framework for firms located in space and time which we then return to in later chapters. Chapter 3 deals in particular with firms' production decisions and spatial heterogeneity.

Part II of the book considers issues of local labour market structure. Not only are the determinants of the demand for labor considered, but the whole issue of the spatial division of labor is dealt with at this point. In Chapters 4 and 5 the dimensions of local labor market differentiation are analyzed in depth. Chapter 4 examines the question of how firms adjust their labor needs over space and time. Notions of contract, bargaining, and spatial–industrial differentiation are introduced at this point to provide an empirical perspective on the arguments introduced in the previous theoretical chapters. Chapter 5 considers alternative specifications of local labor demand functions within an adjustment context. Empirical evidence is introduced, and various models of labor demand are related to the framework introduced in the previous section. Chapter 6 considers the issue of allocating the costs of employment adjustment at the local level in the context of economic change over the past decade.

Having established the logic of regional production and employment in the first two parts of the book, we consider then the dynamics of local price and money wage inflation. Part III has three chapters. Chapter 7 deals with the empirical dimensions of local price inflation, in particular its degree of similarity to national inflation. This chapter also analyzes the temporal properties of local price adjustment, paying close attention to the rigidities of local prices. Following up on this analysis is Chapter 8, which analyzes the significance of the various components of aggregate price indices. Variations in local housing, energy, and rent components are amongst the components of total prices analyzed in this chapter. In Chapter 9, a model of regional real-wage indexation is proposed and empirically evaluated. This chapter is also concerned with the temporal patterns of causality between local wages and national prices, as well as with who bears the burden of uncertainty regarding the likely patterns of local price inflation.

Moving on to Part IV, we then deal with the temporal and spatial structure of labor migration. Chapter 10 provides a detailed analysis of the temporal patterns of migration, especially the relative volatility of in- and out-migration to fast- and slow-growth regions. Chapter 11 takes the inquiry a step further by analyzing the temporal and spatial links between regional capital investment and labor migration. Here we consider not only how synchronized these processes are, but also the patterns of causality between them. The analyses presented in this part of the book lead us to surmise that interregional economic adjustment is frequently an investment-led process. In Chapter 12, labor migration is analyzed in terms of the distribution of uncertainty and transaction costs. Our argument is that labor migration involves tremendous risks, partly the product of the spatial configuration of production, but more especially the result of established property rights. This argument extends our empirical analysis of inter-state migration patterns by considering once again the distributive consequences of regional adjustment.

Chapter 11 is also the prelude to a more detailed treatment of the dynamics of regional capital accumulation. Part V is devoted to this topic and is composed of three chapters. Chapter 13 tackles the literature on this topic by evaluating how the various theories of regional growth conceptualize capital dynamics. We move from simple accelerator models of local capital investment to more complex regional restructuring theories. This chapter is followed by an empirical analysis of the space–time patterns of investment. In Chapter 14, the focus is on how observed patterns in local investment do or do not conform to theoretical expectations derived from a variety of theories. For example, it is found that these patterns are not consistent with catastrophe models of regional dynamics. Chapter 15 ends the empirical portion of Part V, and the book, by concentrating on the interrelations between local investment, technological change, income distribution, and labor relations. This last empirical essay returns to many of the issues raised earlier in the book regarding spatial differentiation and its reproduction over time.

Throughout the book, our analysis operates at a variety of spatial and temporal levels. Often state-level data are used, while at other times city-level data are employed. Similarly, we vary the precise time frame, sometimes using data from the early 1950s, and at other times using more recent data. The choice of empirical frame was typically decided by the issue at hand and the data available. All regional economic theorists who wish to ground their models in a real context face such choices. And for this we make no apology. If, as a consequence of this book, more theoretically and empirically consistent data bases are assembled, we would have no quarrel with a refined version of our adjustment theory. Nevertheless, a move must be made to develop more plausible theories of regional dynamics; to that end we hope that the studies developed in this book will indicate the way forward.

Gordon L. Clark
Meric S. Gertler
John E. M. Whiteman

Acknowledgements

Our research program was supported by many people and institutions. Very important in this regard was Professor Carl Steinitz, chairman of Harvard University's Ph.D. Committee on Urban Planning. He provided a supportive and accommodating institutional environment for our study, and the resources for empirical analysis. We would also like to extend our sincere thanks to Dean Brian J. L. Berry of Carnegie-Mellon University's School of Urban and Public Affairs, the previous chairman of the Ph.D. Committee. Because of their commitment to our collective enterprise, we were able to pursue a research agenda which ultimately led to the work produced here. We are most grateful for their support and encouragement.

Meric Gertler and John Whiteman both benefited from the scholarship fund of the Ph.D. Committee on Urban Planning. Meric Gertler was also supported by a Fellowship from the Social Sciences and Humanities Research Council of Canada. Gordon Clark's research was supported by grants from the W. F. Milton Fund, the MB Fund, the National Academy of Sciences and the National Science Foundation. Concurrently, John Whiteman has been supported by a grant from the Graham Foundation for Advanced Studies in the Fine Arts. Finally, Roger Jones of Allen and Unwin provided the necessary financial support in developing the book from conception to reality.

We wish also to acknowledge the help and advice of many of our colleagues. Takatoshi Tabuchi was very generous with his time and expertise. Not only was he the co-author of the study which provides the basis of Chapter 9, but he provided tremendous help in the collection and analysis of the data which are at the heart of the book. Others who contributed to the book with advice and insight include Ron Martin, Victor Solo and Ron McQuaid, and Gordon Mulligan, Kenneth Warren and Nancy Obermeyer who read and commented on the entire draft. Michael Childs helped to create the bibliography, and Paul Mathes helped prepare the index. We are grateful for all their critical comments and help in clarifying our arguments.

We also wish to acknowledge the following publishers for their permission to use portions of previously published papers by the authors:

The Association of American Geographers for "Dynamics of interstate labor migration," *Annals* **72** (1982), 297–313 and "Migration and capital," *Annals* **73** (1983), 18–34; Clark University for "The dynamics of regional capital accumulation," *Economic Geography* **60** (1984), 150–74; Edward Arnold for "Regional capital theory," *Progress in Human Geography* **8** (1984), 50–81; Ohio University Press for "Regional wage and price dynamics," *Geographical Analysis* **16** (1984), 223–43; Pion Ltd. for "Fluctuations and rigidities in local labor markets part I: theory and evidence," *Environment and Planning A* **15** (1983), 165–85, "Spatial labor markets and the distribution of transaction costs," *Society and Space* **1** (1983), 305–22, "Discontinuities in regional development," *Society and Space* **4** (1986), in press, "Labor demand and economic development policy," *Government and Policy* **2** (1984), 45–55, "Does inflation vary between cities?" *Environment and Planning A* **16** (1984), 513–27, "Price shocks and the components of urban inflation," *Environment and Planning A* **16** (1984), 1633–48, and "An adjustment model of regional production," *Environment and Planning A* **17** (1985), 231–52; and Rowman and Allanheld for permission to publish excerpts from *Interregional migration, national policy, and social justice* (1983).

This book is dedicated to our families, for their patience, dedication, and love.

Contents

List of figures

List of tables

PART I

A theory of
regional adjustment

PART I *A theory of regional adjustment*

In the first part of the book we introduce our central theoretical and empirical concepts emphasizing our notion of "adjustment theory." This theory of regional economic structure is both conceptualized and empirically investigated, and serves as a first way of articulating the geographical and temporal structure of the economy. More substantively, we are concerned to model the strategic organization of production and the uncertainties which this process generates. Essentially, we seek an explanation of how economic uncertainty is absorbed by the spatial organization of production and show the implications of such organization for the structure and dynamics of regional economies. The empirical context of our work is the transformation of the US regional economic system since about 1950.

In Chapter 1, we demonstrate the necessity for adjustment theory. We show how, within the strict neoclassical paradigm of the regional economy, theory and evidence are at odds with one another. Dramatic changes in regional economic fortunes which characterized the study period are shown to have confounded accepted theories of regional growth and change, including neoclassical growth theories, more dynamic theories of circular and cumulative causation, and the so-called catastrophe theories of regional reversal. In a systematic critique of neoclassical economic theory as applied to regions, we show how certain key aspects of the adjustment problem persistently plague any equilibrium theory of regional growth. We show how the speed of adjustment, the durability of investments, the income effects on households, and speculation due to the existence of money remain as conceptual stumbling blocks for the neoclassical theorist. We also note that general equilibrium theory contains a major internal inconsistency of argument in that it essentially assumes real prices to be fixed once and for all.

We then articulate our own version of adjustment theory. In doing so we are anxious to avoid the idealizing devices of neoclassical theory which attempt to recharacterize the passage of time and the nature of economic uncertainty. Instead, we seek a more realistic vision of how the strategies and actions of individual workers, firms, and investors combine to produce the aggregate landscape and vice versa. Our goal is to show how the actual means and institutions of economic adjustment, the strategies and decisions concerning economic fluctuation and change are very important in determining the long-run economic fortunes of different regions.

Given this view of economic adjustment, certain aspects of economic organization are crucial, even though conventional neoclassical theorists would otherwise tend to find them irrelevant. Conceptually, it becomes very important to describe the "local" situations in which economic

2

adjustment actually takes place. The "scene" (structure) and interests (variables) of adjustment decisions must be articulated. This means that, on the one hand, we must be more specific in our depiction of the local institutional context (institutions *per se*, as something other than mere conduits of discrete exchange, are largely eschewed by a neoclassical analysis). This institutional picture must portray the strategic relations and interests of the parties involved. On the other hand, we also must be more specific in our empirical analysis of economic variables, instead of automatically clumping them together according to a preconceived view of economic growth. For example, it is often assumed that as investment produces output, output produces employment. But the empirical version of this theoretical chain of logic turns out to be much more complex than neoclassical growth theory would have us believe.

Finally, an interest in economic adjustment (as opposed to equilibrium) focuses our attention not on ahistorically conceived cross-sectional analyses, but on time-series analyses of data, where we can see more clearly the historical traces of particular adjustment decisions, events and responses.

From this first outline of the adjustment problem in conceptual terms (Ch. 1), we then provide a theoretical account of economic structure and adjustment in regional economies in Chapter 2. The central thesis is that the invested structure of firms and industries exists to manage a distribution of economic uncertainty between labor and capital, a distribution of uncertainty which is inevitably generated for investment capital by the nature of the productive process. This means that the economic landscape itself can be depicted as a landscape of uncertainty. The goal of our second chapter is to provide a theory of economic locations which is derived out of an understanding of local production arrangements and the way they distribute economic uncertainty.

Our argument proceeds in two parts. First, we present a characteriza-tion of the economic landscape from an aggregate point of view, showing how the arrangement of uncertainty has dramatically changed with the equally dramatic shifts in the nature of industrial organization. Secondly, a counterpart argument is advanced showing how industries and firms secure and manage their labor supply with respect to economic fluctuations and uncertainties. We then combine the two aspects of our theory (macro and micro respectively) within the single structural notion of the spatial division of labor. The spatial division of labor, it is argued, exists to structure the social and spatial distribution of economic uncertainty.

In Chapter 3 we develop a preliminary empirical evaluation of our adjustment theory of regional economies. Here, an adjustment model of regional production is presented. A crucial feature of this model is that it distinguishes between decisions concerning production quantities and decisions concerning employment. (Most neoclassical models use the latter as a proxy for the former.) The distinction is important because from the strategic perspective of the firm, the two variables can be manipulated within a series of short-run decisions concerning production, sales and receipts, and employment (levels and costs). The crucial variable for the firm is the flow of funds, since most production is financed by retained earnings. The pattern of money flows, with all its inherent fluctuations, forces the firm into a zero-sum distribution of economic uncertainty between labor, on the one hand, and capital and its product (inventory) on the other. The firm, in our theory, is constantly engaged in calculations about how much to produce and how to finance that production. The firm, in our theory, is anxious that its capital should not be forced to bear the costs of its own unemployment. In this way the long-run, aggregate profiles of regional employment, and indeed the time path of technological change in the firm, are seen as nothing but the continual accumulation of short-run production decisions.

A simple mathematical formulation of this model of regional production is then tested for two industries, textiles and electronics, across the various states and regions of the USA. We find that changes in output can be explained by changes in the ratio of disposable profits to labor costs. We also find that the performance of our model varies with the rate of regional capital growth, but more especially with the geography of unionization and "right-to-work" laws which dramatically alter the power of the firm to affect the distribution of economic uncertainty between labor and capital.

1   *The adjustment problem*

Introduction

In this book we are concerned to describe and explain the economic dynamics of the US regional system for the post World War II period. Thus, we are concerned with the patterns of regional change over time. To date, studies of the dynamics of contemporary regional economic systems have sprung from two distinct, but irreconcilable, traditions. On the one hand, there exists a set of propositions, derived from neoclassical economic theory, which aims to understand how the regional economic system behaves in the context of assumptions which promote spatial equilibrium. On the other hand, there is a body of empirical evidence whose categories and concepts seek to record how the regional system, and individuals and spatial units in it, actually behave in practice. In the first instance, equilibrium models aim at establishing the ideal conditions for stability – typically regional full-employment equilibrium – while in the second instance, the practice of regional analysis presumes disequilibrium (see Richardson 1973).

Regional economic theory is similarly affected by the internal strife within the neoclassical paradigm, particularly since it is this body of economic theory which has dominated the field (see Borts & Stein 1964). Few would disagree that dynamic economic theory is in drastic disarray. One has only to note recent analyses of this issue in macroeconomic theory by Hahn (1970, 1984), Leontief (1981), Fisher (1983) and Radner (1982) to recognize that even its practitioners agree with this proposition. The ideal propositions of pure theory are not easily reconciled with the stubborn facts (or regularities) of the real world. But, in regional analysis, there are a couple of other problems of an epistemological nature which have further limited progress. Foremost among these problems is the practice of adopting theories and conceptions from other disciplines in an uncritical manner (adopting without adapting). A second problem, closely related to the first, is the habit of developing theory for regional economic systems by making analogies with the characteristics and behavior of physical systems. Thus, while many theorists have proposed "new" or modified theories of regional dynamics, most have used physically based analogies to drive their models. The most recent of such models of

5

regional dynamics is the phenomenon of catastrophe theory, or the theory of "structural stability and morphogenesis," as developed by Thom (1975) and further elaborated by Zeeman (1977). A much-publicized development within mathematics, it has recently been applied to the analysis of regional economic change (see, for example, Casetti 1981a, b, Thrall & Erol 1983) as well as other areas in geography (Wilson 1981).

We begin our discussion of regional dynamics by analyzing the relevance and theoretical appropriateness of the catastrophe approach to understanding the processes of regional change. In doing so, our intent is to offer a point of departure from contemporary debates in regional economic theory, as well as a critique of a specific theory. We then turn to an analysis and critique of neoclassical equilibrium theory in general as a means of identifying the adjustment problem which forms the basis of our book. Our critique aims at how abstract economies of pure theory are supposed to move from one condition to another over time and space. This chapter serves as our introduction to the problem of regional economic analysis, and our own perspective in particular.

A binary theory of regional change

In order to embark upon a useful analysis of catastrophe theory (hereafter CT) as applied to regional economics it is necessary first to sketch its fundamentals. For this purpose we shall focus on the model proposed by Casetti (1981a), presenting and analyzing in turn its key attributes. This model was originally proposed by Casetti as a way of understanding what was perceived by many to be a sudden reversal of the relative economic performance and fortunes of regions in the United States during the mid to late 1970s. As Casetti noted, these events appeared to be at odds with stock-in-trade theories of regional change – notably the cumulative causation and growth pole theories, "since these theories imply that the more developed areas will grow comparatively more, and will induce growth in the territories around them" (p. 572). His attraction to CT as an heuristic device for better explaining recent events stems apparently from its emphasis on the dynamics of discontinuous systems.

Casetti began by limiting his analysis to those situations in which capital formation within a region (and the jobs thereby created) is responsible for inducing subsequent immigration of population to regions undergoing net capital accumulation, and outmigration from regions experiencing net decline in capital stocks. Then, assuming perfectly mobile capital (an assumption which is implicit rather than explicit in Casetti's exposition), he constructed a model of net regional capital formation which depended primarily on differences between the marginal productivity of a region's capital base and the marginal productivity of capital in the rest of a country's regions. When the former exceeds the latter, according to Casetti, capital will flow to the region in question. When capital's marginal product is greater outside the region, capital will emigrate to those other regions. With equivalent marginal productivities inside and outside the region there will be no net interregional capital flow.

Thus far, the model is indistinguishable from the standard neoclassical equilibrium conception of regional investment (see, for example, Romans 1965, Engle 1974), given its assumed perfect capital mobility and emphasis on relative regional marginal productivities. However, Casetti departed from the neoclassical norm by making some very particular assertions about how one might expect the marginal productivity of regional capital (MPRC) to change over time. In seeking to understand the case of regions such as the US northeast (up until recently, a declining region), Casetti presumed that MPRC initially increases as the scale of regional production grows, to a peak at some point in the region's historical development (corresponding to the scale of production attained at that point), and will then decline as development continues beyond this point (and reaches higher scales of output). The result is an era of capital growth and influx followed by a reversal involving capital flight when regional relative productivity begins to decline. Basically, Casetti believed that regional production (output) eventually reaches a level which induces a reversal in MPRC and, hence a catastrophic interregional shift in capital investment and job creation.

Clearly, the catastrophic nature of the system's development as portrayed above hinges on the central assumption of first increasing, then decreasing MPRC with increasing scale of regional output (a point later emphasized in an exchange between Vining 1982 and Casetti 1982). Casetti justified the initial increasing phase by characterizing it as an era of regional growth of a cumulatively causative nature. Citing Kaldor (1970) and Richardson (1973), Casetti invoked both internal and external economies of scale in production, which he believed create and nurture self-reinforcing growth. However, the switch to declining MPRC is attributed to a range of somewhat vague and sketchy processes. Regional capital apparently is diverted by government regulation away from "strictly productive" uses in order to redress "the negative consequences of past economic activities, such as toxic wastes and those deriving from the spatial concentration of economic activities," Casetti (1981a). The result is a lowering of local MPRC. Fixed capital, embodying older technology, is assumed to be both less productive and a drag on the marginal productivity of new capital in the region, although this process is never fully explained by Casetti. Finally, Casetti contended (ibid.) that "more than proportional coordinative and integrative functions, governmental or otherwise" are required in the older, more developed region.

In this sketchy rationale, there is no fully developed argument as to why the self-reinforcing regional growth which dominated Kaldor's and Richardson's thinking ought to be terminated, and indeed reversed, simply because of the attainment of greater levels of regional output or the passage of time. Nevertheless, the little explanation offered by Casetti is highly reminiscent of the kinds of arguments posited in the previous debates over the economics of urban size (Gertler 1984b). While Casetti did not wish to suggest that diseconomies of production will arise at any one particular scale of regional output, his qualitative assertion that marginal returns to production eventually will decline, once regional output passes a particular level, amounts to an espousal of the inevitability of regional scale diseconomies. It is evident that the relevance and usefulness of the CT approach in this context depends on two key assertions: first, that the empirical phenomenon being modeled does represent a fundamentally discontinuous process characterized by abrupt change or reversal and, secondly, that this apparent discontinuity may be accurately modeled in catastrophe terms, whereby slow changes in one or more key system parameters brings about an eventual rapid shift in the state of the overall spatial system.

A critique of catastrophe theory

How discontinuous is regional change? More specifically, given that Casetti's operative variable was capital investment, what kind of discontinuity does this variable actually exhibit over time and space? There is little doubt that, in answering this question, we have few avenues open to us because of the overall scarcity of work on these topics in regional theory. In the realm of traditional theory, one is confronted with two opposing views. One view, associated with the work of Richardson (1973), stresses the perceived spatiotemporal "stickiness" of capital accumulation, as realized in the dependence of current and future investment on the previous distribution of capital in space. Indeed this approach finds its roots in the writings of Kaldor (1970), Myrdal (1957) and Hirschman (1958), who stressed the positive feedback between "inherited" and "expected" geographies of capital accumulation and production. It is also, of course, precisely this perspective which Casetti believed is unable to offer an adequate accounting of US regional economic events over the past decade or so.

A second approach, at the opposite end of the spectrum, sees capital as an economic entity capable of almost continuous spatial relocation. This perspective is shared by neoclassical economic theorists and even some radical theorists. Neoclassical theorists assume perfect mobility of productive factors such as capital through a timeless and costless adjustment process (Romans 1965). Some radical theorists, however, emphasize the *potential* mobility of capital afforded by basic property rights, the logic of a spatial division of labor, and a multilocational organization of production (see Clark 1981a, Walker & Storper 1981, Storper & Walker 1984). Recent empirical investigations informed by this later perspective have found indirect evidence of an increasing "hypermobility" of capital between places and sectors, although the support for this contention derives mainly from an examination of locational shifts in employment rather than capital *per se* (Bluestone & Harrison 1982). While discovery of a heightened mobility of production could be construed as evidence of a "catastrophic shift" of productive resources between regions, it is not the interpretation which is lent to these events by Bluestone and Harrison or others sharing their perspective.

As for direct evidence on regional capital movements, there is a marked and well known paucity of data which goes beyond individual case studies. Nevertheless, one recent analysis of the changing spatial distribution of manufacturing capital in the United States found little evidence of the catastrophic transformation which Casetti perceived as having gripped the USA during the 1960s and 1970s (Gertler 1983). Based on an analysis of annual state-level capital stock estimates for the period 1954 to 1976, Gertler found a steady and continuous increase in the share of US fixed capital which was located in the southern and western portions of the country. This study suggested that the "sunbelt" regions of the country have been gaining relative to the "snowbelt" regions from the earliest point in the sample time frame, and indeed it would not be surprising to find that this trend began before 1954, were such data available (see also our analysis in this book). It was also evident that the rate of relative decline of the capital stocks of northeast and northcentral states was somewhat higher toward the end of the study time period, as was the rate of improvement in the south's relative position.

Hence, it is rather difficult to find regional economic catastrophes when observing the changing geography of capital itself. Indeed, the picture obtained from these data includes a much earlier decentralization of production from the northeast and northcentral regions than is evident from analyses of employment or migration alone. The implication is that southern and western investment has been relatively more capital-intensive than that in the rest of the nation, and this has been borne out by empirical investigations of regional capital–labor ratios over this time period (see later chapters). Thus, the spatial realignment of productive forces within the American economy does not appear to have demonstrated the "abrupt transition" which Casetti presupposed as the initial premise for his catastrophe interpretation of regional economic dynamics (for a related argument see Perry & Watkins 1978). Now that we have cast some doubt on the empirical relevance of this approach, let us now shift our attention to the second key assertion identified earlier concerning the process which generates regional shifts in productive capital over time.

As noted earlier, Casetti's model of regional production relied crucially on the assumption of first increasing, then decreasing marginal returns to regional capital (MPRC), in order to produce a discontinuity in regional capital accumulation. Empirical irrelevance notwithstanding, there are a number of theoretical reasons why Casetti's conception of the recent process of regional growth, decline and qualitative change is fundamentally flawed. Recalling our review of his model from previous pages, we note that at the heart of Casetti's inverted U-shaped MPRC function is an essentially Kaldorian growth process which obtains over the early phases of a region's ascendance, perhaps slowing down as a stage of "maturity" is reached, and ultimately undoing itself and breaking down as late maturity and economic decline set in. Given Casetti's reliance on arguments found in Kaldor (1970), it is instructive to return to that now classical statement of regional growth for a re-examination of its own internal logic.

According to Kaldor, financial capital, once invested to comprise fixed capital (machines, equipment and plant) in a particular location, will exhibit a characteristic "profile" of potential physical productivity over its ensuing lifetime. This profile typically consists of a period of relatively constant potential output followed by a period of gradual depreciation during which physical decline and technological obsolescence combine eventually to reduce the productivity of capital to zero (see Varaiya & Wiseman 1981). The precise nature of this profile will, of course, vary depending on the type of capital (plant or machines) and the sector of production being considered. Nevertheless, for any given sector and type of capital, the same general shape of depreciation ought to be evident *a priori* in any location. In his treatise justifying the need for regional policies in Britain in the late 1960s and early 1970s, Kaldor pointed out that production was not equally profitable at all locations because of a number of important factors which effectively increased the productivity of otherwise similar capital in particular *core* locations.

Kaldor argued that the core's locational advantage stemmed primarily from the phenomenon of increasing returns to scale in production, present both within and external to the individual firm in core regions. His argument took the following tack. Because of accidents of history and initial advantage, the early development of sizable markets in a few locations provides local producers with sufficient demand for them to develop and expand local production of goods. By the time other regions might have grown to a level which would support their own indigenous production, initially established regions will have attained local population sizes of sufficient magnitude to sustain local levels of demand which offer local producers greater efficiencies of production at that higher level of output. The existence of these scale economies of production (not to mention the development of innovations in process technology) creates a cumulative spiral of growth in the productive capacities of core firms since their lower average costs of production enable them to undercut actual or would-be producers in peripheral regions.

Accompanying these developments *within* individual core firms are a series of developments in the relations *between* firms in the core region. Foremost among these is increasing specialization of firms within this region, producing within the context of a more developed inter-firm (or intra-corporate) division of labor, thus enjoying all of the efficiencies of production likely to flow, in Smithian fashion, from this integrated arrangement of local production. This, combined with the sheer size of urban concentrations in the core, is supposed to produce all of the well known localization and urbanization economies believed to characterize such agglomerations. The result is presumably a large number of specialized producers located close to one another in order to facilitate their interlinkage and interdependence in production relations. Among the benefits they may reap from this spatial organization of production is the sharing of a large and easily accessible pool of skilled and unskilled labor, which further reduces production costs, especially those related to labor acquisition and training.

Hence, by invoking the existence of internal and external economies of scale, Kaldor believed he had captured the basic forces behind the seemingly self-perpetuating growth of core regions in the developed countries, as well as offering an explanation for the persistent depression of peripheral regions in these same countries. He also contended that his view was consistent with an empirical regularity first noticed by Verdoorn (1949) – now known as "Verdoorn's Law" – that the marginal productivity of factors in production is a direct function of the rate of growth of output in the recent past, a nationally observed relationship which Kaldor also felt to be relevant to the scale of individual regions.

From the outset, one must be clear about the basic assumptions which are implicit in Kaldor's analysis. First, he presumed that the kinds of efficiency benefits deriving from conventional agglomeration economies require or depend upon the spatial proximity of individual producers to other producers (with whom they are interlinked) and a large concentration of consumer demand (which provides them with internal scale economies). Furthermore, he implicitly presumed a predominately unilocational organization of production coupled with interregional trade (or "spread") effects. In sum, Kaldor assumed a geography of production marked by spatial concentration and contiguity. In such a setting his arguments and theoretical development carry considerable force. However, laid bare in this manner, the assumptions upon which Kaldor's model was based now appear to be somewhat out of date in light of recent trends in the spatial organization of production and consumption in countries such as the United States. To begin with, firms are increasingly able to avail themselves of a scale-generating market on a nationwide level, with the improvement and cheapening of transportation technologies for the distribution of their product, along with the trend to smaller, lighter, and higher-valued industrial products (Norcliffe 1975).

Secondly, the organization of production has undergone profound changes, including the vertical integration of sequential functions within single firms and, more recently, a multilocational arrangement of production (Pred 1977), which is frequently characterized by an accompanying spatial division of labor (Clark 1981a, Storper & Walker 1984, Massey 1984). These latter developments have been facilitated or enabled by the adoption of sophisticated telecommunication technologies, but have more likely been driven by other imperatives. Among these is the desire to seek spatially isolated and vulnerable pools of local labor so as to overcome demonstration effects which aid the diffusion of wage demands between spatially contiguous labor organizations and individual workers (Clark 1981a). Other imperatives include the matching of specific labor demands of particular industrial functions (characterized by such dimensions as skill, cost, degree of militance or organization, and "captivity") with the particular supplies of labor in different communities, or the desire to seek workers unaccustomed to established work patterns or rules so as to implement new production technologies (Storper & Walker 1984).

The American semiconductor industry serves as an interesting case in point. Its history of development in California's Santa Clara county has been recently documented by Saxenian (1984), who noted that the original era of growth was based on strong local external economies – including a large supply of highly skilled workers, an environment in which frequent innovations diffused rapidly, locally available specialized services and other inputs, the ready access to local finance capital, and nearby "braintrust" establishments such as Stanford University, plus (and by no means least) a highly concentrated regional market which was largely defense related.

With development of this industry over time, however, particular phases of the production process were relocated elsewhere. The first departure was of the final assembly of semiconductors (a labor-intensive production phase requiring little in the way of skills) to low-wage sites in Asia and Mexico beginning as early as 1961. However, this was followed several years later by another spatial restructuring of the industry which saw the relocation of high-skilled phases of the production process (largely wafer fabrication, which requires a mix of engineers, technicians and unskilled workers) to other places within the USA such as Pocatello in Idaho, Tucson and Chandler in Arizona, Aloha, Oregon and Albuquerque in New Mexico, which offered not only an adequate supply of unskilled labor, but also sufficient environmental, cultural and social amenities and affordable housing to appeal to engineers and technicians.

Saxenian noted that these changes have shifted all but the highest-order product development functions out of Santa Clara county, and she attributed the latter episode of spatial restructuring to a number of specific factors. Among these were the skyrocketing costs associated with the reproduction of the labor force (an extremely tight housing market and high commuting costs) which made it difficult for firms to attract and retain all but the most highly paid forms of labor to this area. Equally important however, was the changing nature of organization and production within the industry itself. The 1970s saw a flurry of mergers and acquisitions as dramatic sophistication of semiconductor technologies produced much higher research and development, design, and fabrication costs. These expanding capital requirements created entry barriers to new, small firms, as well as conferring a distinct advantage upon larger firms among those already in existence. At the same time, the expansion of consumer applications of semiconductor technology has produced a growing national and international market for the industry's output, reducing its dependence on previously localized demand as well as offering the prospect of scale economies in production and marketing.

This descriptive analysis supports our earlier contention that recent changes in the organization of production and its relation to consumption have wrought a spatial transformation of industry, which finds new economies of production in spatially discontiguous configurations that defy the old agglomerative forces, while still offering the benefits of large firm scale, specialization and division of labor. Yet such considerations are entirely absent from Casetti's catastrophe model of capital shifts. In addition, his reliance on vague notions of the diseconomies of mature large-scale regional production as the switching mechanism for inducing a spatial reallocation of capital may well be misplaced. The evidence seems to suggest that it is the capital movements themselves which create the lion's share of social costs in the disenfranchised communities of "mature" regional economies (Bluestone & Harrison 1982). A return to first principles, as set forth in the seminal work by Kaldor (1970), revealed that the forces which generated economic growth in the original core regions are still at work in the present era but in a spatially discontinuous way. Hence, both the external form and inferred processes presumed by Casetti's model appear to be erroneous. We now need to re-examine the logic of regional dynamics and regional discontinuities from a theoretical perspective. We believe that older traditions in regional economic analysis are no longer relevant. Yet we also acknowledge that our new perspective requires a good deal of introduction.

The necessity for adjustment theory

In the realm of abstract economic theory, the process by which an economy moves through time from one state to another is referred to as the "adjustment process" (see Hahn 1984 from which the following discussion is largely drawn). We are concerned in this section to set out the critical issues concerning adjustment which have been developed in recent years through the analysis of abstract economies. To begin, we must acknowledge that there seems to be little or no support for the traditional view that the responses of individual agents in their economic environment make the "invisible hand" perform as it is supposed to do. To believe that this vision of economic adjustment is relevant to the real world, one must also take faith in the Marshallian vision of a tendency to equilibrium over space and time. The purpose of adjustment theory is to examine the logic of claims for such a position, and to examine alternative visions of the adjustment process.

Even in the most pure and abstract versions of an economy, knowledge of the exact form of the adjustment process is still of vital importance. Consider a Walrasian economy with its supposed process of *tâtonnement* based on recontracting or no exchange (see Walras 1874). In order for such an economy to possess a stable and unique equilibrium, a number of further strict conditions must be set. For example, we might suppose that all goods are gross substitutes. Even if we then follow a purely mechanical approach to adjustment, as suggested by Samuelson (1947), we must get around the income effects of households (see Hicks 1965), perhaps by assuming that all households are alike. But even then, the *speed* of adjustment is conceptually important. While convergence on a stable equilibrium might be demonstrated in theory, the speed of convergence may in fact be slow, forcing individual agents to respond to the "wrong signals." See, for example, the lucid description of how a Walrasian conception of the urban economy may collapse and unravel in Harvey (1973: 55–6). Even with the heroic assumptions of general equilibrium analysis, the effects of time and lags in adjustment remain as conceptual stumbling blocks (Hahn 1984).

Such a picture of the economy also neglects the logic of production decisions, and the devastating effects which these decisions may have on our abstract Walrasian economy. Consider a pure exchange economy (i.e. no production). Let the pricing rule be Samuelsonian, but allow exchange at all prices. Assume that two individuals exchange if, and only if, neither suffers a utility loss and one gains. Almost by definition such an economy will converge on a pareto-optimal allocation. Furthermore, such an economy will always follow a linear or gradient expansion of utility (again, by definition). In this abstract economy, "we have one of the few constructions where the invisible hand can be analyzed under the grand unifying principle of maximization" (Hahn 1970: 3).

But this is a fragile world which cannot withstand the existence of production and its associated decisions. Two critical problems arise. If production decisions are allowed at any set of prices, profits will not be normal, in the sense defined by the assumptions of a neoclassical equilibrium. Production decisions may in fact lead to simultaneous losses and gains in the "utility" of economic agents. Additionally, if production requires the investment of capital in concrete and durable objects, then a theoretical neoclassical maximization will be constrained by the actual form of investment. Producers will then make the wrong (equilibrium-oriented) decisions, and the path of the system at any time will be strewn with the history of past mistakes. Note that our consideration of a pure exchange economy implies that general equilibrium theory founders upon the nature of production. A *tâtonnement* analysis would suggest the reverse: that general equilibrium theory founders upon the income effects of households. As a matter of empirical reality we know that binding decisions are made at all prices. So it seems that neither a Walrasian equilibrium nor a "pure exchange" equilibrium are appropriate simplifications for analyzing the real economy (see Robinson 1971: 3–15).

There is yet a further complication: that of the existence of money. In contemporary capitalism, virtually all transactions involve money. If an individual economic agent is constrained to use a medium of exchange, then s/he may be willing to exchange one good (like labor) for money on the supposition that the money so acquired can be used in exchange for some other good. But should the second part of the transaction fail to materialize, the first transaction will be associated with a fall in utility. A speculative element is therefore introduced into the economy by the very existence of money, and one can no longer be certain that the simple linear qualities of a pure exchange economy would hold.

Even if we set all these problems aside, there is still a major internal inconsistency of logic in general equilibrium analysis with which we must deal. Suppose we interpret the economy in an Arrow–Debreu fashion, so that we are concerned not only with current markets for current goods, but also with current markets for all future goods (see Arrow & Hahn 1971). The attainment of equilibrium (if it is attained) must be taken as *working once and for all*. So as the future unfolds, changing spot prices would not be "signals" suggesting the correction of an error, rather simply prices *already agreed to in the past*. Obviously this is a caricature of general equilibrium theory, but it is instructive to see how the annihilation of time, production and exchange sequences, and history in pure neoclassical theory provokes a tremendous dissonance between this theory and the actual workings of a capitalist economy.

This strict view of a Walrasian system might be relaxed so that it deals with current markets for only a small number of future or primary goods. This would mean that changing spot prices in unfolding future markets must be recursively linked to previous values of the primary goods. Thus, we would have a *sequence* of markets. In this abstract economy of a sequence of states, the "invisible hand" must do two things. First, it must establish an equilibrium at each stage of the sequence. But, secondly, it must generate a sequence of prices which will ensure the continuity or sequencing of these momentary equilibria. Just how such an abstract sequence of economies relates to a real economy of places, people, prices, and expectations remains unknown. But even if we suppose that all people form expectations in a similar way, and even if we also neglect all the problems of uncertainty which make the expectations problem difficult to formalize, there remains one further problem. Convergence on a sequence of equilibria still requires the assumption that goods are gross substitutes, but also, in addition, the further assumption that expectations are universally formed in a conservative way. The gross substitute assumption is restrictive, but so is the expectation formation hypothesis. There are good reasons to suppose that expectations are not formed in such a conservative manner, but are often formed in quite radical anticipation of future price changes.

Finally, even if the economy is conceived as a sequence of equilibria, we are still left with the problem of the speed of adjustment. The issue is conceptually important because if recontracting occurs at the "wrong prices," the sequence of equilibria which was supposed above would lose its meaning entirely. These brief but critical excursions into theoretical general equilibrium states are intended to do just one thing: to show how *within the body of pure theory* (let alone real capitalist economies) there is a fundamental need to tell plausible stories about how adjustment occurs. By definition, adjustment theory provides a framework for discussing more fully the issues of how the economy actually functions in time and space. Given that the abstractions of neoclassical analysis repeatedly imply temporal and spatial absurdities, it is then crucial to shift the task of theorizing regional growth and decline to the notion of adjustment, as opposed to static equilibrium.

The adjustment problem

The above exercises in theory also help to set out the main dimensions of adjustment theory and the tasks which it must seek to accomplish. The problems which we encountered above are not entirely fictitious, and do indeed reflect genuine problems in the organization and management of regional economies over time. The actual dynamics of any decentralized economy are the result of how individual economic agents can and do form plans, and how these plans (which may actually conflict) are worked out in practice. The task of regional adjustment theory is to analyze how this process happens in space and how space and time enter into the very fabric of adjustment itself.

By reducing all plans, claims, and interests to mere preferences, by idealizing the grasp that individuals have on their situation, and also by abstracting individuals from their circumstances, neoclassical theory does not resolve the practical problems of the formation and reconciliation of plans. Rather, it achieves a recharacterization of the problem at hand and avoids the issue altogether (see Sen & Williams 1982: 1–2). We would contend that individual consumers are often faced with the problem of forming expectations about the future and making plans. They must necessarily involve themselves in the kind of speculation that money provokes. Furthermore, they must do so in situations of relative ignorance. Producers also face a problem of similar structure. They too must form expectations about the future, make plans, and commit themselves to binding decisions in a speculative way. The multitude of plans thus generated must be worked out in space and time, and a new spatial configuration formed as a result.

This is the proper terrain for a genuinely dynamic theory of regional adjustment: to theorize the temporal structure of plans and the spatial consequences of the attempts to realize them. The trouble with neoclassical theory, including Casetti's catastrophe theory of regional switching, is that it employs a number of devices which so recharacterize time that the processes of plan formation and reconciliation are fundamentally ahistorical. By collapsing the future into the present in an idealized form of rational calculation, the very structure and history of regional change is smoothed out and reconceived as a theory of equilibrium, not change. And, by collapsing the future into the present, theorists recharacterize the nature and consequences of uncertainty in the space economy. We contend that it is *normal* for individual economic agents to *have to make* choices in the face of genuine uncertainty, even ignorance. That is, the person may not be aware of the very possibilities which are available to him/her, let alone their relative probabilities.

Standard analyses of risk and uncertainty in economic theory are inadequate for dealing with the predicament of partial ignorance, as described here. They essentially try to modify a theory based on the assumption of perfect knowledge. "Risk" analysis assumes that the decision maker is equipped with a complete listing of all possible outcomes and with a probability distribution fully defined over that set. On the basis of this information s/he is then thought to compute not only every possible outcome of each choice, but also the expected value of each device. Thus, it is necessary only to substitute those expected values for the known values of the simple model, and everything can proceed as before. In risk analysis, both the set of outcomes and their probabilities are regarded as pure, or objective knowledge. This is crucial, for otherwise the individual maximizer may not share the analyst's definition of the situation. But the notion of an objective probability distribution carries a strong (but unstated) implication about the nature of the world; namely, that it generates all the necessary (and quite unambiguous) frequency distributions from a stable (spatial) set of events. This is clearly implausible.

"Uncertainty" analysis is another search for determinate solutions. By supposing the decision maker's criteria (optimism, pessimism, etc.), the theorist can then predict the individual's unique choice. Uncertainty analysis still requires a full listing of outcomes (but not of their probabilities). However, such listings are not available. When someone says s/he is uncertain, s/he can mean that s/he does not know what outcomes are possible; not just their chances. S/he may not even know the structure of the problem s/he faces. A state of ignorance is simply not defined in the analysis of uncertainty, and consequently "uncertainty" takes on an esoteric meaning (Webber 1972). This change of meaning serves to hide from observers the fact that theorists, faced with an awkward problem, succeed not in solving it but in denying the legitimacy of its existence. In its insistence on a framework which cannot accept ignorance, general equilibrium theory is very specific to a highly idealized situation: it is inevitably conditional. The posited equilibrium may be general but the theory is not.

The attractiveness of general equilibrium theory rests on its seeming ability to finesse all these practical problems. Prices in neoclassical theory are supposed to play a crucial role in ensuring the correct adjustment. Individual agents in this kind of decentralized economy apparently do not need to know the structure of their own circumstances. They need merely to respond in a self-interested way to price signals; it is thus supposed that the spatial economy will be self-organizing.

Regional adjustment theory, when properly construed out of the shadow of equilibrium theory, must avoid such mischaracterizations. A genuinely dynamic theory should analyze situations in ways which make it possible to see more clearly how "individual" actions of economic agents combine to produce aggregate results *and* vice versa! The regional adjustments problem is therefore characterized by a number of concerns which so far have tended to elude formal economic analysis. First, the actual mechanisms of how regional economic changes are wrought over time are *conceptually* fundamental. No longer can it be assumed that the adjustment process will automatically establish the "correct" equilibrium, as supposed by the Arrow–Debreu version of the economy. Instead, the actual institutions of the spatial economy (and the adjustments which they permit) must be examined in understanding the implications which they hold for the aggregate path of regional economic change. The precise form of adjustment is then a crucial part of our analysis, whereas in neoclassical analysis questions concerning the form of the adjustment process are conceptually unimportant.

The perception that the form of adjustment is important in determining the path of regional change validates areas of inquiry which would make little sense to pursue in a neoclassical framework. Perhaps the most important implication of adjustment theory so construed is the idea that the relations between individual economic agents do not comply with the ideas of discrete exchange which are embodied in neoclassical theory. Instead, the relations between economic agents are less fluid, and are more durable over time. The very durability of economic relations sets a pattern or custom in which expectations of the other party and notions of principles and rights come to be formed. Furthermore, expectations so formed may come to be set in codes contained in formal or informal contracts. Notice that the idea of a structured and durable relation between economic agents is contained within the very notion of an institution. Thus the form and purpose of an economic relation is instrumental in determining the shape of regional economic change over time.

Many of the troublesome adjustment questions, such as the information question, the formation of expectations, or the speed of adjustment, which have been given a slightly fictitious form by neoclassical theory, may now be seen in a new light. For example, one neoclassical way of seeing a spatial imbalance in employment (a labor shortage here but unemployment there, *ceteris paribus*) is to assume that labor is immobile because of a failure of information. The neoclassical response is to institute a "job-clearing house" which "lubricates the workings" of the labor market by speeding up the adjustment process of matching labor to jobs. The resulting labor mobility is argued to increase national efficiency (see Clark 1983a). But this ignores the localized pattern of adjustments and their underlying institutions. The neoclassical view binds together what may be two quite distinct events in the economy in a superficially ubiquitous logic. In this way "information" becomes the problem, and the question of local expectations and customs are submerged or lost.

In the subsequent chapters these ideas are explored in more detail, moving from immediate questions of theory to actual empirical examples. Generally, we deal with the spatial and temporal structure of adjustment, focusing upon local labor market relations. In no sense should this mode of analysis be construed as a *complete* inquiry into US regional structure. After all, if we do take seriously the critique mounted above concerning current macro-theoretical practices, whether in the spatial domain or not, it must be obvious that there can be no *general* theory of regional adjustment. Instead, adjustment in time and space must be a partial and incomplete process.

2 Contemporary regional economic structure

Introduction

This chapter introduces our theory of regional structure and adjustment. The theory seeks to explain how industries and their firms are organized to construct and manage a distribution of economic uncertainty, producing an economic landscape which itself is *organized* to absorb fluctuations in economic activity. This theory, which is largely specific to contemporary spatial patterns of capital investment, is based upon a logic of labor domination: securing a labor supply within a particular geographical form of economic organization. The argument presented here is therefore twofold. First, a characterization of the economic landscape is presented, depicting how uncertainty is channeled and distributed from an aggregate point of view. Secondly, a counterpart argument is advanced to suggest how industries and firms secure and manage a labor supply with respect to economic fluctuations and uncertainties. Finally, the two sides of the argument are used to show the implications of location for the patterns of change and fluctuation in regional and urban employment. It is argued that regional economic adjustment is best explained as a process by which a particular social and spatial distribution of uncertainty is created through production.

Our argument runs counter to much of received regional economic opinion. It is often assumed that profiles of regional employment result from external forces acting upon areas, which can best be explained by factors which are intrinsic to those areas (for example, factor prices and changes therein). The theory presented here advances the idea that regional employment profiles, for instance, can only be properly understood extrinsically; that is, when seen also within the context of the wider form of economic organization. In the previous chapter, we discussed this issue within the context of contemporary regional economic theory. There we argued that the principal difference between the two approaches lies in their (often implicit) treatment of time and their consequent characterizations of the passage of change. Before proceeding with our argument, we summarize the theoretical terrain of adjustment

20

theory against which the competing notions of regional fluctuation and change must be evaluated.

Adjustment theory in general

In the realm of economic theory, the process by which an economy moves through time from one state or condition to another is referred to as the "adjustment process." The artificial characterization of how successive economic states are actually realized over time is the counterpart in theory to the empirical profiles described by the data for our study. However, the issues raised by the theory and examination of adjustment are moot, if one believes the economy to be in a stable equilibrium state, or to be successively reproducing in a stable fashion a series of equilibrium states over time (see, for example, Samuelson 1947: Ch. 9; and, for a more critical view, Hicks 1965: 14–27). However, the question of adjustment and the need for providing satisfactory explanations of the economy as an actual process *in time* are not moot issues at all, from the moment that disequilibrium is an admitted possibility (see the critical review by Hahn 1970). In fact, not only is disequilibrium possible, it is very likely given the restrictive assumptions of equilibrium states.

In the previous chapter, we have seen also that the theoretical literature which typically deals with regional economies over time does not adequately discuss the process of individual decision making in disequilibrium states. Consequently, regional theory cannot yet obtain a dynamic description of what individual decisions would imply for the stability of the spatial economic system as a whole – a description which is actually required by economic theory to substantiate itself. Instead, economic theory assesses the stability of an economy by taking a final equilibrium position – in most cases a neoclassical equilibrium – and by subsequently obtaining sufficient conditions, in terms of supply and demand, to ensure the stability of such an *a priori* defined equilibrium. The sufficient conditions known to date are purely mathematical restrictions, and bear little or no relation to plausible economic restrictions. In other words, no known, reasonable, economic behavior by optimizing individuals has been shown to lead to the restrictions needed for the stability of neoclassical equilibrium (Hahn 1984). Hicks' fear that the neoclassical, "mechanical" approach to adjustment may not refer back to the economic problem (as formulated by Marshall and his contemporaries) appears justified. The need for a theory of adjustment remains as great as ever.

The unsatisfactory state of pure theory concerning the adjustment problem means that we must adopt an altered method of inquiry. If formal theory is at a loss to come to grips with the real world, then regional researchers have two available alternatives. First, they might take recourse to more qualitative (less reductive) forms of inquiry. These may be either at the detailed level of case studies, or at a more generalized (but nonetheless qualitative) level (see Piore 1979a). Secondly, they might look to the available empirical evidence. In either case, the abstractions of theory are pitted against the particularities of the real world. As Hahn (1970: 1) sardonically noted, "to discuss and analyze how the economy actually works, it may be necessary to go and look."

One final introductory distinction must be made. The patterns of adjustment which we are attempting to theorize are local patterns of economic adjustment. Specifically, we are concerned here with the temporal profiles of such indicators as employment and wages in different areas. When considering the issues of adjustment, this distinction of local patterns as opposed to national ones becomes important for good theoretical reasons. The task of regional adjustment theory is to be explicit about how the economy works as a process in space and time. This means that we are not only concerned with theorizing how individuals "respond to signals" in decentralized situations (Spence 1973), but we are also necessarily concerned with the actual structure and design of the decentralized system itself (Rothschild 1973: 1283–6). The supposed process of adjustment is no longer an abstraction, but now must somehow encompass real events and places. In this depiction of things, there is a world of difference between the existence, coordination, and management of a decentralized regional economy and a centralized national one (given a particular aggregate economic organization in the first place). Because of the individual position of an area *in* the overall economic organization, and because the structure and performance of a local economy is more subject to direct decisions beyond its control, it is no longer appropriate to develop theory for a local economy as though it were the economy of a small nation–state (cf. Thompson 1975). The local economy must be embedded in the wider spatial system.

Local economic structure

The economic landscape of this century is very different from that of the last. Indeed, the patterns of economic location are so different that geographical events now seem to outstrip the abilities of spatial economic theory to describe, explain, and predict them. Trusted concepts and methodologies from the spatial analysis of 19th-century economies seem to flounder in the complexities of the present. The principal reason for this is that there is a qualitative difference in the geographical organization of the contemporary economy, when compared to that of the previous century.

The crucial difference between then and now lies in a completely different form of what Massey (1984) has called a "spatial division of labor." In the 19th century, the economies of leading nations were based on geographical specialization, which was also predominantly a sectoral specialization. In the United States, major industries such as steel, textiles, automobile manufacturing, and so on formed the basis of growth. In establishing their spatial configuration of production within the USA, these industries were not faced with an undifferentiated geography of opportunities. They also faced important geographical variations, including access to transport, raw materials, skilled labor, and markets. In very general terms, key industries put their stamp on the economic geography of the USA simply by concentrating all their capacity in the areas most propitious in terms of their requirements for production. Moreover, since these industries were the nationally dominant industries, in terms of new investment and growth in output and employment, they were the structuring element in the new pattern of regional differentiation: a geographical pattern of sectoral specialization. Thus Pittsburgh meant steel, Lowell meant textiles, and Detroit meant automobiles.

The economic landscape today, however, contains a spatial division of labor which is new. The spatial division of labor is no longer a sectoral one. Instead, it is an *intra*-sectoral one: one within the overall process of production of individual firms. As this book argues, this means that in the future, places will not be known (as they were in the 19th century) by *what* they produce so much as by *who* is employed there at certain stages of specific production processes. Because of their size and organizational power, corporations can now construct locational hierarchies that place their production functions, which are separable within the firm, at different places in the economic landscape. This kind of power gives rise to an altered form of the economic geography of employment, where skills, wages, and the uncertainty of employment play a new and fundamental role in the spatial division of labor.

The new spatial division of labor reflects the changing requirements and characteristics of modern production practices. Such characteristics and requirements include the changing size distribution of individual firms where economic power is concentrated into the hands of a few large firms and variable demand is allocated to a periphery of small firms; the decreasing size of individual plants (see Dunford 1977); the separation and hierarchization of technical, control, and management functions (see Westaway 1974, Clark 1981a, *inter alia*); and the increasing division, even within production, into separately functioning stages (Massey 1975, Lipietz 1977).

Within the production process itself there have also been considerable changes. On the one hand, growing intensity of competition from overseas sources has, in recent years, led to increased pressure to cut labor costs and to increase productivity. This in turn has produced an apparent acceleration of the processes of standardization of the commodities produced (thus reducing both the number of workers for any given level of output, *and* the levels of skill required of them), of automation (with effects similar to those of standardization), and of the introduction of systems such as numerical-control machine tools (again reducing the number and skill requirements of the direct labor force, but also needing a small number of more qualified technicians). In terms of the bulk of workers, then, a de-skilling process of some magnitude has been in operation. At the other end of the scale, both the changing balance between sectors of the economy, and the nature of competition (particularly the reliance on fast rates of technological change) in the newly emerging sectors such as electronics, have increased the importance within the national employment structure of research and development activities.

The above arguments are only intended as introduction and are not new. Aspects of these arguments have been presented elsewhere by other authors including, among others, Pred (1977), Massey (1978b, 1984), Clark (1981a), Walker and Storper (1981), and Bluestone and Harrison (1982). However, the implications of such an overall economic landscape for specific places remain largely unexplored. Of the many implications which follow from this reconfiguration of the economic landscape, three deserve particular emphasis: first, the nature of indices of geographical differentiation; secondly, the nature of local economic problems; and thirdly, the structure of local economies and the economic volatility which is implied for each locale.

Clearly, the indices by which regional differentiation and geographic inequalities are measured must be reconsidered. In an economic landscape based on sectoral specialization, appropriate indices of local economic health include the amount of manufacturing employment, rates of (usually male) unemployment, per capita earnings, and in- and outmigration. But locational patterns have so changed that manufacturing employment, for example, is no longer a reliable indicator of economic vitality. Indeed, under the new scheme of things, manufacturing employment may be a mixed blessing, being located in a place precisely because of the failing economy found there.

Indeed, the meanings of employment and of unemployment are changing. It is the nature of contemporary production to organize its own labor supply (Piore 1981). Usually this involves calling forth into the labor force people who by virtue of occupying a particular social/institutional position do not think of themselves as belonging to an industrial workforce (see Berger & Piore 1980: Ch. 2). Consequently, the loss of manufacturing employment and the increase in unemployment in the nation is paralleled by an increase in the size of the labor force, even after accounting for demographic influences. The twin increase in unemployment and labor force participation runs counter to the neoclassical intuition, reflecting structural changes in the organization and nature of employment and unemployment.

These kinds of changes reflect a new economic geography, and pose crucial problems for indices that would describe the new situation. For example, as new dimensions of geographical variation arise, such as geographical variations in labor's skill and wages, new indices become necessary. Yet to identify and recognize *new* indices of spatial variation is itself problematic for existing theory. Similarly, old indices recording geographical differentiation can take on new and different meanings. For example, the spatial distribution of occupations may no longer reflect the sectoral specialization of particular locales so much as the location of different strata from within a single organization. Again, the identification of such changes and their significance is problematic for existing theories designed primarily to explain a predominantly sectoral division of labor across space.

In the new geographical differentiation of the economy, the nature of regional and urban economic "problems" changes. It is important to note that a process of sectoral specialization between places produces geographical differentia which are not necessarily problems in themselves, and indeed may be signs of economic vitality. So, for example, in the 19th century, occupational differentia between places simply reflected the nature of local specialization (and presumably constituted a national benefit). Regional or urban problems under such a scheme were of a very different nature than contemporary problems in the spatial economy. Regional problems were usually just the reflection of wider national (or even international) problems in specific industries. Changes in the international competition for a given industry often provoked severe crises in very localized economies specializing in the production of a particular commodity. That is, sectoral decline often brought with it specific regional decline. Even today, lingering economic problems of particular locations still can be of this kind.

However, a fundamentally new kind of local economic problem is arising. In an economic landscape where geographical specialization is not intersectoral but rather intrasectoral, a qualitative change in the organization and responsiveness of the local economy occurs. Most importantly, and perhaps most ominously, geographical inequalities in this new spatial division of labor appear not only at its demise, but are integral to the structure of the spatial system itself. That is, regional problems and their concomitant geography of inequality were previously the result of prior collapse or failure of an economic system (or part of it). The problem for recovery was to restore the economy to working order, causing regional problems to disappear, or so it was thought. This is not the case under the new spatial division of labor. Now, localized inequalities in skill and income, for example, form the very basis of the geographical organization of the corporate economy. Large corporations by their nature possess considerable power in the modern economy which they can use to bolster their strategic organizational advantage. Corporations construct locational hierarchies which are aimed at achieving a particular distribution of economic uncertainty between labor and capital. In this way, spatial inequalities become a part of the normal working order of the economy, and no longer a sign of its failure or demise.

An important implication of the above is that the evolution of local economies and their short-run fluctuations do not now depend only on the ups and downs of whole sectors of the economy (as in an export-base model, a fundamentally 19th-century construct). Instead, the evolution and performance of local economies also result from conscious adjustment decisions by organizations within sectors and firms.

The locational implications of the new spatial division of labor are as follows. Taking the "bottom end" of the locational hierarchy first, the mass production and assembly stages of production are now increasingly located in areas not only where unskilled labor and semi-skilled labor are available but also where wages are low, and where there is little tradition of organization and militancy among the workers. Very frequently this means location in areas where there are workers with very little previous experience of wage work. These may be areas suffering from collapse of a previously dominant industrial sector, such as in Pittsburgh and its steel industry, or in Massachusetts and its textile industry. In such cases, labor drawn upon in the new industry will not be mainly that which was employed in the former specialization, but more typically the women of the area. Other areas favored for this stage of production include those where workers (again often women) do not become totally dependent upon, nor organized around, wage work. Seasonal resorts with annual fluctuations in employment, places of high immigration (Piore 1979b), and ethnic enclaves are also typical of this second type of area.

Note that this opportunistic management of labor supply does not provide a tidy geography of production facilities. There is no massive geographical scheme at this level. Instead, firms (or rather corporations) seem to be taking advantage of "incidental" opportunities in the landscape which are offered to them by economic events as they unfold.

There is also a second stage of production consisting of processes which are not yet automated, reduced to assembly work, or producing standardized products. This stage is typically located in old centers of skilled labor – primarily 19th-century industrial towns and cities. The critical characteristic of this stage, however, is its decreasing quantitative importance. More and more, the acceleration of technological change and the processes of de-skilling enable industry to be locationally freed from its old ties to skilled and organized labor. The effect of the relationship between such changes in the production process and the possibilities open to industry as a result of the spatial differentiation of labor is one component of the present industrial decline of the inner cities.

Finally, at the "top" of the locational hierarchy, the central metropolises are typified by the presence of control functions (including the allocation of production to other regions), product research, design and development, and technical and managerial strata. It is the presence of these elements, rather than the absence of manual work, which is distinctive.

As noted above, the new spatial division of labor does not produce a neat, compartmentalized economic geography. Indeed, the structuring of spatial compartments in the economy is a problematic feature of economic organization. The geographical reflection of this organization is considerably more complex and incidental than a simple projection or mapping. Evidence of spatial economic structuring will not be readily reflected in the neat accounting categories of data collection. The same general process can operate at a variety of spatial scales. In fact, the scale of effects is a result of a particular process at work, and not itself a cause. Even so, it is possible to introduce some propositions about the structure of local economies and their short-run economic performance.

Again, consider the "bottom" end of the locational hierarchy. New investment into production facilities in such (frequently depressed) areas is often hailed as beneficial, but its effects may be few. Wages and skills remain low, and it is not always the case that much new employment will result. One of the major characteristics of such factories is that they have few "links" with the local economy and consequently stimulate little in terms of associated local production. Such investment will not significantly expand the local technical, research, or managerial strata (by definition), and consequently will reinforce the geographical differentiation of labor. Additionally, given the currently dominant nature of the formation of new companies, the lack of associated research and development will also reduce the likelihood of the local (internal) generation of new firms. The major implication of these arguments is that this "bottom end" of the spatial division of labor will express itself in terms of a very "open" local economy, with a high degree of integration with other economic systems.

There are a number of further implications of this openness. First, the local economy is at the mercy of external economic changes. This is often argued to be a new effect, but in fact internally controlled sectoral specialization has a similar effect. Nevertheless, the "openness" of the local economy serves a very different purpose in the new scheme. Secondly, remission of interest, profits, and dividends is likely to go to a parent company *outside* the locality. Thus local income generation may be minimal, and may function contrary to conventional export-base model expectations. Thirdly, new investment will consequently not provide much associated or linked employment locally, and its multiplier effects through additional local spending likewise will be minimal.

However, the most important implication is that certain types of local economies are now subject to external control. This has further implications for both the path of local development and the patterns of short-run fluctuations. The local economy is now subject to deliberate adjustment decisions by corporations in a way it previously had not experienced. True, the firm or corporation still faces an external economic environment – including, for example, the pressures of international competition. However, the corporation now has a degree of decision available to it which it did not have before. That is, the corporation can choose *where* to allocate the fluctuations and the uncertainties of demand and the path of technological change which comes its way. Furthermore, the corporation can now organize its own economic geography to considerable advantage. It can devise locational hierarchies which by virtue of their locational characteristics become effective means for channeling economic adjustment. The costs implied are then shifted away from the corporation's account, and become part of the "vicissitudes of economic life" in that locale.

The management of labor supply

So far in this chapter we have considered the processes of economic restructuring from an aggregate perspective. We have emphasized the overall geography of the economy, and we have speculated about the implications for the structure and performance of local economies within the new spatial division of labor. However, these aggregate arguments have their atomistic counterparts. It is to these detailed arguments that we turn in this section. The principal line of argument to be developed in this and the subsequent section is that the new economic geography, with its fundamental locational hierarchies, is *at root* connected to the variability and uncertainty inherent in modern industrial economies. This argument is developed through a consideration of the individual employment relation in specific social and spatial economic settings.

Piore (see Berger & Piore 1980: 23–35) identified three different notions of the way in which the workforce has been used to absorb the fluctuations and uncertainties which industrial economies generate in the production process. First, Piore argued that the workforce can be compelled to bear the costs of economic fluctuations because "labor is the variable factor of production and, as such, can be freely hired and fired as productive activity fluctuates" (p. 23). This is true in a fundamental sense in that, despite the reforms made by unionism, the basic right *under the law* to provide employment or not resides with the employer. Thus the process of hiring and firing, although often highly circumscribed by the rights of employees, provides the simplest of mechanisms for transferring the costs of economic uncertainties (Johnston 1986). Labor, then, is a variable in a way that contrasts directly with capital "which cannot be made to bear the costs of its own unemployment" (Berger & Piore: 23).

Secondly, Piore argued that the sequential nature of production planning implies another sense in which labor is a residual variable. The planning and design of production processes is neither a simultaneous nor an iterative process. It is sequential: one aspect of a production plan or engineering design is completed before an attempt is made to resolve the next. Thus, "the labor component is generally the last factor which is taken into account, virtually forcing the labor force to adjust to other aspects of the economic system, rather than the other way round" (ibid.).

Finally, Piore argued that labor may constitute a residual factor of production in still a third sense. Technological progress, Piore suggested, "consists in dividing up the productive process into its component parts, and then attaching those components one by one to a different and presumably more efficient logic" (p. 25). This process produces a residue of older tasks which cannot (yet) be reassigned. As more and more of the component tasks of earlier production processes are gradually reassigned, the residual components become progressively more diffuse. This creates a "left-over" class of employees, who, either by rote or by instruction, perform a number of essential tasks which capital cannot yet incorporate into its own logic. These jobs may be essential, even highly paid (relatively), but their future is insecure.

Piore then argued that dualism arises in the labor market when certain portions of the labor force, for whatever reason, begin to be insulated from the variability in demand, and their requirements begin to be anticipated in the planning of production: "they become at this point like capital" (p. 24). Consequently, the original dualism between labor and capital becomes translated into a dualism between those workers who share in the security and rewards of capital and those who continue to absorb the full brunt of economic fluctuations. This accounts, Piore claimed, for the observation that in the labor market duality occurs largely between privileged and underprivileged positions in the socioeconomic structure. Of course, corporations do not limit their organizational planning to those workers whom they wish to retain and shield from economic uncertainty (the "primary" sector). Indeed, an equal if not greater amount of planning effort and economic organization goes into identifying and securing a labor force which can/will accept a high degree of volatility in employment (the "secondary" sector).

A distinguishing, if not *the* definitive, feature of the secondary labor market is that the employment which it offers is very volatile (see Doeringer & Piore 1971, Edwards *et al.* 1975, Berger & Piore 1980).

Insecurity of income and employment is a crucial aspect of a "bad" job, and contributes significantly to the perception of the low status attached to such jobs. Because of their inferior structure of rewards, security and status, the supply of labor for "secondary" jobs is *not* self-organizing (as neoclassical economics would suggest), but instead requires a logic of economic management in which location plays a fundamental role. Briefly, the logic is as follows. The process of technological change creates an imperative for labor of a particular kind. The demand for labor then "creates its own supply" – that is, the supply of labor is *deliberately created*.

More fully, the logic of technical development in production creates, for example, the need for standardized, routine jobs which can also be made to absorb variation in demand. The "setting up" of this kind of employment requires careful planning. The most vital requirement is to find a labor force that does *not* have a prior conception of itself as being dependent upon an industrial economy. At this point in our logic, social categories come into play. Being something other than "a worker" (such as being a recent immigrant, being a farmer's wife, or being old, young, female, or black) provides individuals with an identity which is not drawn solely from work. Furthermore, such categories often signify that their incumbents belong to another network of economic support (although that source of support may itself be failing). This point is crucial, because it means that such individuals have something to fall back on; a network of support, or just welfare, upon which to rely in hard times. For the employer these social institutions act as a form of unemployment insurance for the workers, but one to which the employer does not have to contribute.

Finding this kind of labor supply clearly satisfies the employer's demands. Because of their marginal attachment to the industrial labor force, such people are most likely to accept the volatile, low-wage employment which the firm has to offer. The employer's remaining problems are twofold: first, how to induce such people to take work; and secondly, how to keep the situation steady over time, so that the firm can continually pass the costs of economic fluctuations on to the labor force.

Instigating a flow of labor is accomplished in such a way as to manage local economic fluctuations in a stable form. But the whole situation is inherently unstable. As potential labor is drawn into the labor force, its self-conception begins to change. What starts as a casual and intermittent source of income becomes an essential part of the new worker's economic life. Consequently, new demands begin to be placed upon the stream of income initially offered by the employer. These demands take the form of agitation for higher wages, more stable wages over time, associated benefits, improving prospects, and better conditions at work – in fact, all the trappings of a permanent worker.

The employer can forestall this process by any of a number of practices.

For example, the firm may limit the duration of employment of any one worker to, say, two years, and subsequently hire only those without prior experience of wage work. But this solution, like many others, shares the unfortunate attribute of accelerating the rate at which the labor pool is used up, and consequently acts only to postpone the employer's problem, not to cure it. In time, the situation will become untenable, forcing the employer to reorganize both production and labor supply.

However, for the duration of its early reorganization, the firm will have achieved a more or less stable form for the management of economic variability. The solution depends critically on the social categories which can be made to generate a labor supply. Because of their diverse and idiosyncratic nature, the utilization of social categories to yield a labor supply will *not* result in a neatly organized geography of employment structuring. Instead, the economic landscape of employment will be more variegated. This will seem to be largely a geography of historical "accidents" which the economy makes use of, but does not itself create. Nevertheless, ethnicity, age, sex roles, racism, and the like are categories which, if not actually created by employers, have been largely strengthened and manipulated by them in order to stabilize and legitimize existing local economic structures (Clark 1980a).

Location and adjustment strategies

Location plays a complex but important role in the processes of labor supply outlined above. This is not to argue that the spatial configuration of the economy determines economic behavior in any simple way (see Castells 1977, and Massey 1978b, for critiques of the idea of space as a determinant of behavior *per se*). Nor does it mean that spatial structures are unimportant in economic organization. In fact, quite the contrary holds. Economies exist only in real geographies and real times (Giddens 1981). And the particular spatio-temporal forms which they take are among the most powerful structures conditioning human action.

The role played by location in the social distribution of economic fluctuations has two major aspects. First, there is a geography of employment which largely just reflects the *ad hoc* incidence of the social categories which are made to yield a labor supply. Secondly, there are the effects which arise solely because of location and spatial organization *given an already existing economic landscape of employment*. That is, given a pre-existing spatial division of labor, the manipulation of locational hierarchies gains instrumental value in its own right.

Initially, in merely reflecting the relevant social categories, the geography of employment may take many forms. For example, suburban locations provide access to a large female workforce, often more "willing" than white men to accept lower wages and poorer conditions of employment. Declining industrial areas often provide the same. Or again, border locations provide access to temporary migrant workers. Sometimes migration streams are organized to staff production in more "central" locations. Finally, we have argued that there are more idiosyncratic locations, like seasonal resorts, which provide access to labor which has other part-time employment, or inner suburban locations which may yield an elderly workforce wanting additional income. All these examples produce a geography of secondary employment, but since each is so particularistic, when taken together they do not produce a neat geography of economic fluctuations. Instead, they produce a variegated geography which reflects their *ad hoc* nature.

But firms must also find locations for workers whom they wish to insulate from the vicissitudes of economic uncertainty (the incumbents of "primary" jobs). In general, these are the employees who receive higher pay, enjoy a more stable job tenure, and face better promotion prospects. Their jobs are "privileged" and require a degree of institutional protection. The institutional protection of "primary" jobs can be provided in a number of ways. First, protection can be guaranteed by the institution of rigid hierarchies of promotion which are internal to the firm (usually based on seniority and age: see Doeringer & Piore 1971). Or, again, access to certain (primary) jobs may require "skills" and "education" which are not available to the ordinary production worker. In this way, a variety of economic conditions and differing prospects for different kinds of people may be created *in the same plant or location*. Although this is mainly an organizational form especially suited to the sectoral–geographical specialization of 19th-century economies, it could presumably function to structure the organization of small firms which lack the spatial command power that characterizes many 20th-century corporations.

The ability to organize production workers over a wider geography, itself largely a function of firm size, allows a second strategy for simultaneously insulating "primary" jobs and organizing "secondary" ones – that of physical separation. Given the new locational abilities of large firms, "secondary" jobs can simply be relocated far away from "primary" ones. Expectations of employment and the institutions of advancement internal to the branch plant can then be considerably modified and more easily controlled than in large single-plant firms. Additionally, the ability to exploit a larger spatial range allows the firm a greater flexibility in the organization of labor supply (Clark 1981a).

A further strategy, noted by Piore (see Berger & Piore 1980: 23–54), involves the provision of economic security to a segment of the production workers themselves. Firms can act to separate (via a subcontracting mechanism) stable and unstable portions of demand. That is, within a given industry, large firms can afford to retain a more permanent workforce if they subcontract the uncertain portion of demand to an array of smaller (usually more technologically primitive) firms. Thus, by utilizing a dualistic organization of firm sizes, a measure of economic security can be given to the employees of larger firms. Note, however, that this new power of firms provides a measured liberation from their dependence on more skilled, permanent labor. We would therefore expect this strategy to be of declining importance in the emergence of the new spatial division of labor.

Thus, while the geography of "secondary" employment may be *ad hoc* in pattern, it is nevertheless the case that individual corporations organize specific locational hierarchies which serve both to accommodate the changing requirements of production due to technological change (whatever its cause and motive), and also to manage the transmission of economic fluctuations into local economies. The implications for the structure and performance of local economies are drawn out in the final section of this chapter.

A typology of regional adjustment

When capital decides to "submit itself to the future" (Harcourt 1979), it does so in such a way as to attempt to off-load the costs of economic fluctuations on to its labor force. We have argued that the locational hierarchies of firms are aimed at creating and stabilizing a particular distribution of the costs of economic fluctuation and uncertainty. That is, in new patterns of investment, instead of qualitative divisions between kinds of jobs being policed by labor "markets" internal to a single firm *and* location, the spatial opportunities offered by an historically given economic landscape are exploited to do the same job more effectively. The internal labor market of the individual corporation is laid across the map, as it were.

This strategic organization of production has a number of advantages for firms. The sheer fact of spatial separation significantly alters the ability of different strata of labor within companies to bargain with reference to each other – either to preserve time-honored status differentials, to peg relative wages, or indeed to argue for narrower differentials. By sorting different kinds of labor across the economic landscape, firms are able to increase their control over the bargaining process. Notice that the geographical division of labor in this way provides employers with increased leverage over both "secondary" and "primary" labor. The fact of spatial separation prevents wage referencing and forces labor to operate within a set of *local* expectations. These localized expectations may be further manipulated by corporations using their new-found spatial freedom to secure "marginal" workforces. Similarly, firms also have potential bargaining advantages over their primary (and most expensive) labor. By eliminating the ability of labor to monitor and maintain the differentials of status and pay traditionally accorded to various strata within the firm, corporations now have an increased ability to manipulate primary labor in their own localized environment. Of course, their ability to exercise this power is more severely curtailed than in the case of secondary labor. This is because many primary jobs are skilled, and have not yet been routinized.

So, the first aspect of the argument involves the geographical division of labor into spatially discrete labor markets by the individual corporation. The spatial portioning of labor serves the purpose of securing for the employer the most favorable distribution possible of the costs of economic fluctuations. In other words, the geographical structuring of different kinds of labor serves to organize and exploit discrete sets of localized expectations. Or, put another way, the spatial division of labor within the individual firm is an active but surreptitious way of organizing the labor bargain or contract. Furthermore, given the "employment at will" rule and the legal requirements that *local* conditions dominate employment contracts, the spatial division of labor is an almost invisible exercise of power which labor finds hard either to oppose institutionally or to refute within the logic of contemporary discourse (see Ch. 12).

At this point, it seems worth noting the antithetical nature of this argument to neoclassical labor theory, especially as it regards the implications of spatial differentiation. In neoclassical arguments, spatial differences are treated in one of two ways. First, they may be simply explained away as an inevitable and beneficial product of the geographical specialization of the economy. That is, local economic differentia presumably reflect local specialization, and consequently are necessary for national efficiency. Or, if not explained in this manner, spatial differentia (now thought of as inequalities) are characterized as a geographical "mismatch" caused by an irrational and arbitrary "factor immobility." Solutions to geographical problems of the economy are therefore to be found in the movement of people and resources to new areas of economic opportunity. Presumably, increased mobility will redress the balance and promote national economic growth. Of course, neither of these views, framed as they are within a neoclassical logic, is capable of the structural kind of explanation of the geography of employment which we advanced above. In this view of local economic organization, spatial differentia are integral to the workings of the system. They are neither inevitable nor simply a sign of economic malfunctioning. Rather the new spatial division of labor is a new economic geography premised on spatial inequalities. Thus the depiction of economic reality is antithetical to the neoclassical argument.

The second aspect of the argument is that major changes in the organization of the economic landscape, apart from those wrought by technological progress, either originate from the inherent instability of these local economic arrangements or result from an attempt to restructure or improve the labor bargain which a particular location implies. The processes of industrial restructuring (investment, technological change, and capital mobility) therefore play a crucial role in altering the pattern of economic activity (see Bluestone & Harrison 1982, Markusen 1985).

So far, the logic which we have developed, while it may speak to the activities and locational strategies of individual corporations, does not yet speak to the aggregate structure and performance of local economies. Note, however, that any attempt at classifying such a scheme is necessarily an historical argument, and consequently deals with an economic landscape which is thought to be emerging and not necessarily complete. The typology which is advanced attempts, therefore, to embrace the salient characteristics of a new economic pattern and does not pretend to be a classification of all existing economic locales. The value of the typology consequently lies in the extent and importance of the patterns which it tries to reflect.

In historical terms, the geographical distribution of economic activity which results from the evolution of a new form of division of labor will be overlaid on, and combined with, the pattern produced in previous periods by different forms of division of labor. This combination of successive layers will produce effects which themselves vary over space, thus giving rise to a new form and spatial distribution of inequality in the conditions of production, as a basis for the next round of investment. The economy of any given local area will thus be a complex result of the combination of its succession of roles within the series of wider – national and international – spatial divisions of labor.

Local economies can then be differentiated along the basic dimension of economic uncertainty. Taken together as a structured set, local economies form a means for absorbing within the workforce the fluctuations and uncertainties which industrial economies generate for the productive process. Taken individually, each place, by virtue of its location within a spatial division of labor, represents a structured relation between capital and labor, which effectively sets a customary contract governing not only the level of local wages but also the pattern of how economic fluctuations are absorbed.

The first kind of local economy absorbs the most economic variation. Given our arguments above, the structural requirements for managing such a local economy are as follows. Clearly, the locale must yield a marginal workforce. Also, the location must allow a high degree of external control, which effectively partitions the labor market (whether literally in space, or by the use of social institutions, or both), but which also integrates the local economy into a system of product markets and possibly into the flows of intermediate goods. Thus, while certain aspects of the local economy become extremely open (the flow of goods in and products and profits out), other aspects (the labor market) simultaneously become geographically (or institutionally) segmented or partitioned. Into such a setting can be introduced the restructured jobs which are decentralized from corporations' research and development and early production centers. The crucial feature of these new locations are that they represent for the firm a restructured labor relation, a new and localized contract, as it were.

The second kind of local economy is afforded some measure of insulation from economic variation. It involves production via those processes not yet automated, reduced to assembly work or producing standardized products. Its crucial feature is its continued reliance on skilled or semi-skilled labor, since the point of technological development lies mid-way between early production routines (which require considerable on-the-job expertise on the part of labor as to the particularities of the production process) and, later, more standardized routines. The firm, therefore, is forced by circumstances to anticipate the requirements of labor in production planning. Notice again, however, that an important characteristic of this stage is its decreasing quantitative importance. This is because the combination of increased firm size and the development of fast rates of technological change obviates the need to rely on traditional skilled labor. Notice, also, that characteristic of these locations is a particular form of labor contract, one that involves some degree of insulation from economic uncertainty, a measure of "labor hoarding" (see Hicks 1932).

Finally, the third and most insulated kind of local economy involves the location of product research and development, early production facilities, and of course the presence of control functions. Because such labor is indispensable, its requirements are more fully anticipated in production planning (see Berger & Piore 1980: 24). Again, the location implies a particular form of contract, providing the greatest insulation from economic fluctuations.

It must be emphasized that this spatial division of labor only characterizes certain sectors, for instance electronics, plastics, and many "high-tech" industries. Nevertheless, these sectors are increasingly important in the present establishment of new aggregate geographical patterns of economic activity. Insofar as these sectors are absorbing large amounts of the available investment capital, they constitute the most recent round of new investment. Furthermore, such leading sectors must work within the context set by an already existing spatial division of labor. Consequently, the descriptions of local economies advanced above must be seen as ideal types – to be subjected to the vagaries of the space and time in which they find themselves.

How the above theory translates into a precise geography of economic locales now becomes an empirical issue. We may, however, make some further observations about the nature and logic of regional economic adjustment. Generally, we could contend that a simple core–periphery model (see Myrdal 1957, Hirschman 1958) is too naive about space to provide a plausible picture of contemporary geographical differentiation. The precise geographical definition of what is core and what is periphery goes largely unresolved in such models. Instead, periphery must be seen in the more abstract terms of a labor contract implied by location which structures relative wage levels and also sets a distribution of economic uncertainty. We noted that the most open and uncertain locations include not only international places providing an appropriate workforce, but also places nearer home – former agricultural communities, declining 19th-century centers, or, more subtly, suburbs or seasonal resorts. Locations for the most insulated locales obviously include the major central metropolises providing, as they do, a variety of immediate support functions, but also a range of more complex services, such as education and access to technical expertise. Often such places also provide pools of skilled and semi-skilled labor, suitable for our second type of economic locale.

One of the greater paradoxes of regional economic theory has been its inability to explain a number of simultaneously occurring convergences and divergences in spatial economic indices. For example, Syron (1978) noted that, while the industrial mix or composition of US cities and regions has been growing individually more diversified with time (meaning that the industrial composition of places has grown more similar), their reactions to economic fluctuations have become more variable and diverse. This is a paradox for those who believe that the search for the right kind of industrial mix will act as a local stabilization policy (see Thompson 1965, 1975, Bolton 1982). Within the logic of industrial diversification policies, spatial similarities in industrial composition should lead to similar local economic performance over business cycles. But this is premised on an assumption of the spatial homogeneity of industries. Intrasectoral variation or structuring is ignored.

Our theory can explain this paradox. For while the industrial composition of cities and regions may in fact nominally be converging with time, the structural changes within industries concerning the development of locational hierarchies and the redistribution of economic uncertainty may have become dominant in their effects on urban or regional accounts. If this is the case then it is the locational restructuring of labor contracts which is the important factor, not the composition of industrial categories in an individual region *per se* (see Clark 1986 for a related analysis of the US auto industry).

The empirical observations of convergence in industrial composition and divergence in cyclical performance carry an additional implication. This is that the locational strategies of individual sectors are in fact operating to produce a conjoint landscape of economic uncertainty. That is, certain locations are becoming popular with corporations precisely because they can absorb a high degree of economic uncertainty.

Conclusions

The major arguments of this chapter may be summarized as follows. First, location in the economic landscape is seen as a point which sets a particular social distribution of the costs of economic fluctuations and uncertainties. Secondly, the channeling and management of economic fluctuations are seen as dependent on the structuring and exploitation of *local* expectations, thus denying the existence of ubiquitous "rational expectations" (see Muth 1961, Grossman & Stiglitz 1980, Lucas 1981). Thirdly, the use of "local expectations" by companies plays a major role in determining the local wage bargain or contract. This local contract not only sets the wage to be paid, but (whether implicitly or explicitly) determines a local customary pattern for the absorption of economic fluctuations in the terms of how hours worked are varied, or in how employment totals are varied through hirings, firings, quits and temporary layoffs.

Fourthly, our analysis of the spatial division of labor is linked to "dual" theories of labor market segmentation. This is critical for an explanation of the geographical patterning of economic fluctuations, as evidenced in employment volatility. This is because insecurity of income and employment is a crucial feature of jobs in the "secondary" labor market (see Piore 1981). This can provide a new perspective on the spatial division of labor as we can now see how an individual firm attempts to lay the structure of its internal labor market across the landscape. Furthermore, we can see how to interpret such locational hierarchies in terms of a distribution of economic uncertainty, and begin to draw inferences about the geographical structure of economic fluctuations.

Finally, we have explained the instability of these local economic arrangements in terms of a theory of labor supply in which the workforce is called into economic activity by a pre-existing demand. Instability is caused by the desire to exploit "marginal" labor which does not have a prior conception of itself as belonging to an industrial workforce. Because the experience of employment changes this self-conception the situation is inherently unstable. Expectations change over time, and new, more permanent demands begin to be placed on a source of income which was once regarded as casual by the new employees. Crises of this kind prompt the migration of capital.

3 An adjustment model of regional production

Introduction

Most models of regional economic growth are based upon the logic of production. The structure and performance of local economies are measured by what is produced, how much is produced, and what is used in production. Performance indicators include the volume of local output, employment, capital invested, sales of finished goods, and profits on capital invested. From this standpoint, regional growth is a process of specialised commodity production linked to the rest of the economy through commodity exchange. As an example, neoclassical regional growth models like that of Borts and Stein (1964) start with a geographical pattern of comparative advantage, then add a specific production technology to derive the structure of local production. Comparative advantage and decreasing returns to scale, both production-based factors, are invoked by neoclassicists to generate spatial–economic equilibrium (Casetti 1981a). While Keynesian theorists do not share these spatial equilibrium-inducing assumptions, they do depend upon the configuration of production to "drive" local growth. For instance, economic base models trace through the impacts of export production income on local consumption, suggesting a process of cumulative growth which integrates export and local production to determine overall employment, income, and capital growth (see Kaldor's 1970 model of increasing returns to scale, labor productivity and income).

Behind these models of regional growth lies a surprise for anyone wishing to analyze the geographical and temporal patterns of production. There have been few attempts actually to model regional output, from any theoretical perspective. The only examples are to be found in the regional econometric literature, although these models seem more concerned with "counting" output than causally determining output (for a recent review see Bolton 1980; and for a recent example, see Ballard *et al.* 1981). Researchers have been more concerned with the local employment effects of production than in determining the volume of local output. Perhaps one reason for such emphasis has to do with the political importance of employment in local economic development planning. Perhaps another reason for concentrating on employment rather than production is the presumption that employment and output are so closely associated that nothing is gained by modeling them separately.

It is also true that levels of output and employment are not as strongly correlated as often assumed. Indeed, Clark (1984a) demonstrated that changes in the demand for labor are not statistically dependent upon changes in output. Similarly, it is shown elsewhere that there are many different regionally based short-run adjustment strategies used by firms which limit the volatility of employment relative to output (see Ch. 4). Employment changes are not adequate as proxies for changes in output, as assumed by neoclassical and Keynesian production theorists. How much to produce and how many workers to employ are quite different decisions, a point emphasized in the macroeconomic literature by contract theorists such as Baily (1977).

In this chapter, a production–oriented model of regional output is proposed which distinguishes between how much to produce and how many workers to employ. This model is adjustment oriented and argues that the flow of funds to capitalists is a crucial determinant of output. Our model is disequilibrium oriented, not equilibrium seeking as are most (if not all) neoclassical models. It is concerned with the spatial pattern of money flows and uncertainty. Notice also that it depends on Keynesian assumptions of quantity adjustment and price rigidity. In this manner the proposed production model aims to be relevant for short-run economic crises and long-run geographical discontinuities. Empirical evidence is presented in support of our model based on yearly data for some 28 US states and two industries: textiles (SIC 22) and electrical and electronic equipment (SIC 36). Time-series models are used to demonstrate the temporal relationships between regional output and income.

Traditional regional production models

Without doubt, the most widely employed model of regional economic growth is based on the neoclassical production function (NPF). Many contemporary theorists owe their model structures to the work of Borts and Stein (1964) on regional equilibrium, and Ohlin's (1933) much earlier study of interregional trade adjustment. Contemporary theorists use CES or VES production functions wherein they assume perfect factor markets, certainty, and some degree of substitution between factors of production (Carlino 1983). By also assuming competitive product markets, increasing and then decreasing returns to scale, and distance-related transportation costs, neoclassical theorists aim to generate a landscape of income equality, full employment and stability. In this model, output is derived from the most efficient combination of capital and labor, given their respective real prices and marginal productivities.

Of course, the NPF model has been subject to many criticisms. Richardson (1973) objected to the assumption of perfect factor markets and the implied negation of spatial differentiation. Indeed, NPF theorists rarely acknowledge spatial segmentation of product, labor and capital markets, believing that spatial monopoly pricing is irrelevant. It is remarkable to us that cross-sectional spatial data are so often used to estimate single-equation NPF models. Not only do NPF theorists have to assume perfect factor markets to estimate these models, they also have to assume spatially invariant production technologies and uniform employment practices (see Gertler 1984b for an extended review of this literature). NPF theorists start with a uniform homogeneous plane and then derive the necessary conditions for such homogeneity. The irony is that NPF theorists do not take spatial differentiation seriously and suppose at every turn that nominal spatial price differences are merely surface ripples covering underlying real-price equilibrium (Johnson 1983).

Any reading of Borts and Stein (1964) would show that their own NPF models lacked much empirical validity. Yet more recent NPF theorists have tended to invoke Borts and Stein as evidence for their equilibrium assumptions, even though Borts and Stein were forced to conclude that there is "no evidence which could sustain the wage equilibrium hypothesis." Similarly, recent trends in US interregional income convergence have been shown to provide little in the way of support for the neoclassical logic, despite the recent attempt by Newman (1984). Garnick and Friedenberg (1982) demonstrated that at least 75% of the reduction in interregional disparities in per capita personal income between 1929 and 1979 could be explained by interregional convergence in employment and industrial composition. And Garnick (1983: 12) concluded that "the relatively small contribution made by wage rate convergence [to per capita interregional income convergence] would seem to cast doubts on the appropriateness of neoclassical theory, with its focus on wage rates as the equilibrating mechanism."

What accounts for the continued popularity of NPF explanations of regional growth? One common answer from NPF theorists is that spatial economic equilibrium is a datum point from which to judge the performance of the economic system. At first sight, this proposion seems appealing, but it has many difficulties. For a start, focus upon equilibrium conditions may drastically mislead empirical inquiry. Instead of focusing upon the patterns of disequilibrium adjustment, the NPF theorist will continually look for equilibrium-oriented solutions. Instead of focusing upon the actual adjustment variables such as quantities, the NPF theorist will continue to measure price variations. And, instead of focusing upon the time-paths of economic change, the NPF theorist will remain with static, cross-sectional models of regional production.

A second, and more telling, criticism of this position was made by Fisher (1983). He suggested that the equilibrium-as-datum-point argument is plausible only if one assumes economic events to be fully anticipated and temporally continuous. That is, equilibrium is only plausible if economic agents know the future events, their spacing (temporal and spatial), and the ultimate equilibrium termination point. Individual responses to economic change must be consistent with the long-run steady state. Otherwise, short-period adjustment may act to shift the economy away from equilibrium. This is a restatement of Kalecki's (1971) point that the long run amounts to nothing more than the sum of short-run events. For Fisher (1983) this point was particularly important because it suggested that short-run responses to unanticipated shocks may swamp any tendencies to equilibrium to such an extent that the equilibrium-as-datum-point simply becomes irrelevant. His analytical discussion of this possibility forced him to conclude that we must study the adjustment of the economic system in disequilibrium rather than focusing on equilibrium behavior, for it is only this kind of analysis which can help us understand equilibrium itself.

Once we step out of the NPF world, a whole host of other issues rises to claim significance. First, if the crucial adjustment time frame is the short run, firms may be caught in quite dramatic liquidity crises. To illustrate, assume fixed short-run technical production coefficients (Oi 1962). With very limited substitution between capital and labor (in contrast to the usual NPF assumptions of perfect or near perfect substitution), all that could vary would be the labor input and capital utilization, not the absolute volume of fixed capital. In these circumstances, if the relative prices of capital and labor were to change (through, for example, a local wage increase), the rule that labor is paid the value of its marginal product would not be satisfied. If firms are takers of nationally determined prices they will not be able to accommodate local input-price increases through output-price changes; thus price adjustment is one adjustment strategy which is not available to producers. Also, with a limited capacity to substitute labor for capital, fixed costs will continue to rise and profits will decline. In these circumstances, labor and capital are involved in a zero-sum game for income distribution which will directly affect the revenue of firms, and ultimately their capacity to respond to unanticipated events.

Since short-run adjustment to changing circumstances is the decision-logic of this alternative kind of model, the distribution of revenue will also affect subsequent investment. Thus, a second implication is that short-run decisions will accumulate into long-run patterns of regional growth, income and employment. Both of these implications have a great deal of empirical merit. For instance, we show in the next chapter how important the flow of capitalists' revenue is in determining the demand for labor in many regions and industries of the USA. Neoclassical wage variables have little influence on the short-run labor adjustment patterns of firms, and it can be shown for a number of US regions that increasing demand for labor is associated with increasing real wages (Clark 1984a). Also Gertler (1983) demonstrated that regional investment is a volatile process, conditioned by immediately past economic events rather than some stable long-run equilibrium target. He was able to show that past changes in the stream of capitalists' disposable income determine current changes in regional investment; evidence which is consistent with our methodological position regarding the significance of short-run disequilibrium events structuring long-run regional patterns of output and employment.

A third implication which deserves emphasis has to do with the role of expectations in planning output. Here we assume, along with Fisher (1983) and Kalecki (1971), that expectations are formed by observing past outcomes. Rather than planning on the basis of a forecasted equilibrium target, we assume that firms plan output on the basis of past disequilibrium-oriented adjustment decisions. The crucial lesson to be drawn from the past is that unanticipated events occur which require immediate response. Uncertainty cannot be ignored in this kind of world; strategies must be conceived to deal with the future. If, as Fisher (1983) suggested, these unanticipated events occur without obvious periodicity and accumulate upon one another, thereby forcing continual revisions of plans and actions, firms must develop contingency strategies. Firms' actions are conceived in terms of the context in which firms find themselves, not some long-run equilibrium state. In this regard, rational expectations arguments, which presume long-run equilibrium adjustment, seem largely misplaced as do other risk or probability-uncertainty-equivalency modes of analysis.

These theoretical issues are developed in more depth in the subsequent sections of this chapter, and other chapters of the book. Our reasons for detailing the disequilibrium implications of short-run adjustment are twofold. First, we wish to demonstrate that the equilibrium-as-datum-point argument for retaining NPF theories of regional growth is untenable. But we wish also to demonstrate that there is a basis for an alternative model of firm behavior and economic dynamics which takes seriously disequilibrium and uncertainty. As indicated, this model owes much to Kalecki, Keynes, and more recently to Fisher. This is, then, our second reason for emphasizing the implications of short-run disequilibrium adjustment. It is not the case, as sometimes suggested by NPF theorists, that there is no alternative to neoclassical regional growth models based on equilibrium theory. Indeed, NPF equilibrium theory can be very misleading from both theoretical and empirical standpoints.

Given these points of departure, we now turn to specifying an adjustment model of production.

A production model of the firm

Begin by assuming that firms produce a single product over the period t to $t + n$, which is to be sold on the national market at time $t + n$. We assume that firms are price takers in an industry dominated by two or three firms. Firms are assumed to have a fixed capital stock in the short run, little chance of substitution between capital and labor, and increasing returns to scale (capital utilization). Firms attempt to maximize revenue at the date of sale, time $t + n$. This objective function is obviously conditional upon (1) expected prices ($p^\star$) for a planned volume of output ($q^\star$); (2) expected costs of production ($c^\star$) over the period t to $t + n$ for the planned volume of output $q^\star$; and (3) a targeted volume of profit, derived from subtracting expected production costs (t to $t + n$) from expected revenue ($r^\star$). This profit can be used to invest in more capital, replace old capital, plan for the future output, or even consume luxury items.

Firms are assumed to forecast expected prices $(p^\star)_{t+n}$ using past observations ($t - n$) of output prices, while weighing the most recent observation most heavily (a geometrically declining set of weights). These prices are fixed at time ($t + n$) in that firms face significant transaction costs in varying their prices once they have announced to the market their likely price regime (Iwai 1981). Actually, firms may follow a market leader in this regard, implying that $p^\star$ is likely to be realized although $q^\star$, planned output, may not all be sold at that price. Firms with different production technologies facing an expected price $p^\star$ will then offer planned output $q^\star$ so as to maximize revenue at time $t + n$. While we assume a transaction-cost model of price rigidity, other models are possible. For instance, Kalecki (1971) assumed an oligopolistic cost-plus mark-up model of commodity pricing. The implication of both types of models, nevertheless, are the same in the short run: quantity adjustment not price adjustment.

Next, it is assumed that production is a flow, not a stock. That is, we assume that output $q^\star$ is created in a sequential assembly process over the period t to $t + n$, even though at time $t + n$ it is sold as a stock of goods. This also implies the following conditions: (1) firms must pay for labor over the period t to $t + n$ although they receive no revenue during this time; and (2) firms must buy or be advanced credit to buy the raw materials to be used in production, at time t. Given a planned output $q^\star$, firms can then estimate labor requirements and average labor productivity. Estimated costs of production over the period t to $t + n$ depend on the stock of materials and the flow of labor needed to produce $q^\star$. It is also assumed that capital replacement (depreciation etc.) comes out of realized revenue (r) at time $t + n$. What is required in the first instance is a production fund for the period t to $t + n$ derived from previous realized revenue (r) at times $t, t - 1, t - 2, \ldots, t - n$. Basically we assume that production costs are paid for by internally generated flow-of-funds based on previously realized sales (Harris 1981). While such funds may be raised in public capital markets, we presume (in the manner suggested by Meyer & Kuh 1957, Kalecki 1971, L'Esperance 1981b) that firms would prefer retained earnings as the source of such funds because of the managerial freedom conferred by internal financing. Furthermore, all but the largest firms would encounter difficulty in raising market funds to provide working capital and would have to pay a significant risk premium to an outside lender (see Backus *et al.* 1979).

This fund is then a production fund; it is also a contingency fund since it is used by firms to adjust to unanticipated events over the period t to $t + n$. For instance, wages may increase at a greater rate than anticipated over the period t to $t + n$. Or, it may become obvious during the course of production that the firm could sell more output at $(p^\star)t + n$ than previously expected. Or, energy costs and material costs may increase faster than expected over the production period. This contingency fund is a stock of money held by firms to respond to unexpected events. Presumably, this fund may earn interest, although we assume here that the interest rate is never so high (once the corresponding uncertainty of return or risk is taken into account) that firms would abandon their production plans and simply play the short-term money market.

These assumptions provide us with the rudiments of a theory of production. Specifically, since production $(q^\star)$ is paid for out of past receipts (r), disposable profit (π) at time t is a function of planned output $(q^\star)_{t,t+n}$. Assuming that the cost of materials are known (m_t) and bought at time t for production over time t to $t + n$, the major unknown will be labor costs $(L^\star_{t,t+n})$. Therefore:

$$\pi_t = (r_t - m_t) - L^\star_{t,t+n} \tag{3.1}$$

or

$$\pi_t = r'_t - L^\star_{t,t+n}, \qquad \text{where} \qquad r'_t = r_t - m_t \tag{3.2}$$

and

$$\frac{\pi_t}{L^\star_{t,t+n}} = \frac{r'_t}{L^\star_{t,t+n}} - 1 \tag{3.3}$$

Since it is assumed that the contingency fund to pay $L^\star_{t,t+n}$ is drawn directly from r, at time t, actual disposable profit will be a function of expected returns given $q^\star$. Assuming firms desire a certain profit rate, output $q^\star_{i,t+n}$ will then depend on the flow of income to capital, and capital's relationship to labor. This situation arises primarily from our arguably realistic assumption of fixed technical coefficients in the short run. This means that the proportion of labor inputs to production will be constant (relative to other inputs) as $q^\star$ changes. The higher rate of profit arises because the firm is able to raise output while capital costs remain fixed (because of slack capacity). The result is a higher absolute net revenue over a constant quantity of fixed capital. However, since labor's share of output is fixed, average productivity must remain constant.

Notice what this relationship implies. First, previous high relative profits will encourage firms to plan further output, especially since *ceteris paribus* increasing output means higher returns on a given stock of capital. Higher rates of capital utilization will reap greater returns to capital as output (and hence profit flow) increases with total fixed capital constant. Secondly, this model also implies that unanticipated increases in labor costs will be vigorously resisted, since the end-of-period profit will depend on minimizing drawings upon the contingency fund. Indeed, if the contingency fund is not large enough, output would have to be scaled back over the balance of the period t to $t + n$. If this were to happen, the revenue stream at $t + n$ would be lower in absolute terms and lower in terms of return per worker (assuming that none are laid off, but all simply work fewer hours). Of course, output per man–hour would remain roughly constant if hours per worker could be reduced sufficiently. Consequently, disposable profit (π) at $t + n$ would also be lower relative to the stream of revenue. Thirdly, a lower income stream would force firms to cut back on production unless prices could be increased for the subsequent sale date to compensate for unexpected production cost increases. As Kalecki (1971) suggested, short-run output decisions depend upon the distribution of income between classes. Output will rise as profit's share of income rises, and will fall as wages' share increases.

The geography of output

So far, discussion has centered upon a firm without location. Here, we wish to extend our analysis to the economic landscape, assuming a set of two differentiated decentralized labor markets. Again, it is assumed that there is a national commodity market, an expected price $p^\star$ known to all firms regardless of output, and a standard production technology. Like Kaldor (1970), we assume increasing returns to scale and a standard beginning wage rate at time t. What makes these two labor markets different are differences in their labor practices, based on different legal conceptions of the proper relationships of workers *vis-à-vis* owners. For simplicity's sake, we denote the regional labor market dominated by conservative employment-at-will practices (wherein firms can fire workers at their own discretion) as the right-to-work (RTW) region. The other region is assumed to be dominated by "fair labor practices," that is, significant negotiated limits on the application of employment-at-will doctrine enforced by the courts. Although we do not believe unions to be necessary to sustain these agreements, for simplicity the label "union" will be used to indicate the differences between this region and the RTW region in their employment relations.

To understand the implications of what has been proposed, let us also assume a measure of national stagflation over the period t to $t + n$. This means that it becomes apparent during this period that all $q^\star$ produced will not be sold at $t + n$ because of an unanticipated fall in demand. It also means that inflation increases faster than expected (assuming national consumer price inflation approximately equals local inflation; see Ch. 7). Firms in both labor markets respond to the unanticipated fall in demand by cutting output, even though per unit costs of production increase as capacity utilization falls. But, as we shall see, there are marked differences between the firms in their abilities to externalize costs. For RTW firms, employment-at-will allows them to lay off excess labor, thereby forcing labor to bear a large portion of adjustment costs. But union firms are unable to lay off the same number of employees because of "fair employment" conditions negotiated at time t for the period t to $t + n$. The burden of adjustment in the union region is more equally spread; all that unionized firms can do is cut hours worked to the legal minimum (a reduction which is assumed less than that implied by declining output). In this situation, unionized firms will use much more of their contingency funds compared to RTW firms.

Let us also assume that a representative union firm agrees to a cost-of-living clause in its labor contract over the period t to $t + n$ such that the firm will cover all increases in the cost-of-living for all workers. In the RTW region, indexation is assumed limited to just a few workers. Unanticipated inflation will then be a double burden for the unionized firm. Not only will unanticipated inflation need to be covered from the contingency fund, but the firm cannot lay off its excess workers and avoid both the standard labor costs and the inflation costs. At the end of the period t to $t + n$ when output is sold and revenue recovered, an accountant would observe the following circumstances. First, the unionized firm will have exhausted its contingency fund, but will have received a much lower volume of revenue than anticipated, accumulating excess unsold output in the process. The unionized firm will have made a lower per unit profit, if any. Moreover, its ratio of disposable profit to labor costs will have shrunk dramatically. In contrast, the RTW firm may have reduced per-unit profit, but nevertheless will have saved much of its contingency fund so that even though output will have fallen dramatically, the ratio of disposable profits to labor costs will have remained relatively stable.

Secondly, an accountant appraising these circumstances would be forced to conclude the following. If the unionized firm is to continue production in the subsequent period, it must draw off some of its current profit to replenish its contingency fund. Inevitably, lower relative profit to labor costs in the previous period will mean lower planned output in the subsequent period, unless expectations appear so rosy that it would be a good risk to gamble on a large expansion in output. Notice that this is unlikely since expectations are formed on the basis of past experience. There are major risks in an expanded level of output, specifically the prospect that at the end of the subsequent production period all output would not be sold. The firm could attempt to renegotiate its labor contract and perhaps offer profit sharing or revenue enhancement if the union were to contribute to the contingency fund. While there are reasonable prospects for renegotiation, the damage has been done. Lower liquidity will limit subsequent output, thus reducing per-unit profit even further.

On the other hand, the RTW firm faces a more pleasant decision context. Despite previously reduced output, it was able to maintain its contingency fund, and even to maintain its planned disposable-profits-to-labor-costs ratio. Output will be less sensitive to this ratio, perhaps more dependent upon longer-term expectations of consumer demand. Not only would the RTW firm be willing to gamble on expanded output and perhaps even investment in the subsequent period, the costs of making a poor output decision are not borne by the firm as much as by labor. Assuming that labor is tied to the firm because of few other opportunities (local and interregional), the RTW firm could continue to juggle its output without dramatically impairing its liquidity. Of course, lower output will mean lower profits per unit of output and capital invested, but even so, the RTW firm will be more competitive than the unionized firm in attracting investors and orders. Plainly put, the adjustment potential of the RTW firm is paid for by its workers. The only limit of this advantage is if labor campaigns to change the conservative employment-at-will doctrine.

Ultimately, this scenario carries with it the seeds for further regional differentiation and inequality beyond the short run. To the extent that capital investment is paid out of disposable profit, then the RTW firm and the unionized firm will have markedly different investment potentials. Based on the fact that the flow of profits is a crucial determinant of capital investment across many US regions and industries (see Ch. 14), investment for the unionized firm, from one period to the next, will be a variable and problematic process. In the circumstances imagined above, the exhausted contingency fund will probably drain disposable profits, thereby leading to lower – even no – capital investment. Since the desire to invest is largely a function of recent past changes in profit levels (as suggested by acceleration theories of investment and confirmed at the regional scale by Gertler 1983), not only will the union firm be unable to assemble the necessary resources required for new investment, but the incentive to invest is unlikely to exist. Furthermore, if the firm must borrow to cover short-run operating costs, this will raise the firm's debt-to-equity ratio, making access to further external capital for new investment all the more difficult to obtain.

In contrast, capital investment for the RTW firm need not be threatened. Therefore, as each new event is adjusted to, as adjustment costs escalate, and as capital investment in the unionized firm lags behind the RTW firm, the actual production technologies in these two firms will begin to change. Indeed, the RTW firm could end up over a sequence of events and production to be more profitable per unit produced than the unionized firm. This would encourage disinvestment in the unionized firm and further enhance the profitability of the RTW firm.

There is considerable irony in the realization that, although the incentives to introduce labor-saving technological change through investment are likely to be stronger in the unionized environment, it is the unionized firm which is least able to introduce such changes in production. This inability stems not only from the impediments to investment discussed above, but also from the political difficulty of implementing technology which displaces labor or changes its deployment in a unionized environment. Hence, when the unionized firm does gain access to investable funds (including depreciation allowances and profit) it has a strong incentive to reinvest these in a new location – perhaps even in a new product sector (see Harrison & Bluestone 1984).

The limits of this process of short-run adjustment and regional differentiation are to be found in the nature of production. If, as is entirely plausible, the production process can be segmented so that portions of the unionized firm's production can be relocated to the RTW region, then the unionized firm may be able to recover its position. In this manner, the costs of "fair labor practices" would be borne (relocated) by workers in "right-to-work" circumstances, even workers in completely different countries. Thus we can imagine a geographical division of labor which would result from the assumptions and scenarios introduced in the previous discussion. Hence, our model offers a rationale for regional differentiation and technological change which springs directly from local short-run adjustment to disequilibrium. The economic landscape will be both produced and reproduced by short-term contingencies rather than by a desired long-run optimal spatial configuration of economic activity. Like Kaldor (1970), we can begin with similar regional production technologies, wages, and so on, and derive long-run regional variations in investment. However, unlike Kaldor, we are not forced to conclude that the rich get richer.

Specifically, our model suggests that output at time t is a function of previous relative shares of income between owners and workers (the ratio of disposable profits to labor costs). These variables can be measured either in simple nominal terms, or can be discounted by the sale price of output. But also suggested by our model are differential regional sensitivities in the relationship of output to the distribution of income. For instance, regions characterized by "fair labor practices" will be likely to have a stronger relationship between these variables than regions characterized by more conservative employment relations (RTW legislation, for example). Furthermore, we also hypothesize that RTW regions will experience higher rates of capital growth than unionized regions, even though the former regions' output may be less sensitive to changes in the ratio of disposable profits to labor costs. This sensitivity is a function of the level of control that owners may have over the production process and the distribution of adjustment costs.

Data and empirical methodology

In order to analyze the relationship between output and the distribution of income, data on value-added (the value of output, less the cost of material inputs) were derived from the Census and Annual Surveys of Manufactures. These data were used in nominal terms and real terms. The latter series were deflated to 1972 dollars using industry-specific producer price indexes supplied by the Bureau of Labor Statistics. Disposable profits were estimated using a method which has been employed by Alonso (1971), in which the total wage and salary bill for both production and nonproduction workers in a given state and industry is subtracted from value-added. This estimate is still gross of a number of minor charges to producers, such as certain payments for business services, equipment rental, depreciation and taxes. Thus, the profit measure used here is best interpreted as a flow of disposable funds, measured again in nominal and real terms. From these series, another measure was derived, this time for workers' income. The total wage bill was also measured in both nominal and real terms.

Two industries were used in our analysis (see Clark & Gertler 1985 for details): textiles (SIC 22) and the electrical and electronic equipment industry (SIC 36). Textiles' importance as an employer nationally declined substantially over our study period, from 6.9% of US manufacturing employment in 1954 to 4.1% in 1976. In 1981 its total employment stood at 792 400, a sum which has been declining in absolute terms at a compound annual rate of 2% since at least 1972. While generally regarded as a labor-intensive industry, its employment profile exhibits a number of interesting characteristics. Women currently comprise some 40% of all employees, compared to only 31% in total manufacturing. Minorities account for nearly 18% of textile employment, while in total manufacturing this figure stands at 11%. Also, hourly wage rates in this industry have always been relatively low, and in 1981 were 31% lower than the average wage in manufacturing (Department of Commerce 1981). Demand for textile products is largely cyclical, since consumer purchases of clothing and furniture are frequently delayed during economic downturns. Moreover, the automotive and construction industries are particularly cyclical themselves and, as Strong (1983) points out, the increasing importance of these markets within the industry has made the textile sector more sensitive to cyclical fluctuations in recent years.

The electrical and electronic equipment industry is composed of a number of major subsectors which can be divided into two broad groups: a high-technology complex and a somewhat more ordinary or "low" (in relative terms) technology group. The former includes electronic components, and telephone and telegraph equipment and elements of consumer electronics, such as television receivers, video disc players, radios, stereo components and microphones. At the lower end of the technological scale are products such as electric lighting and wiring equipment and transformers and switchgear. In recent years the low-tech end of this industry has experienced various difficulties. For example, electrical lighting and wiring is directly dependent on the construction industry and the growth of public and private utilities, both of which have been poor. Even the high-tech sectors of this industry have undergone considerable restructuring over the past 25 years, causing much flux and turmoil in the process. For example, while the electron tube reigned supreme in the late 1950s, it is scarcely in evidence today, producing only for a small and very specialized market. Moreover, much of the industry's demand is cyclical in nature and it suffered a substantial setback in the 1974–5 recession.

So as to provide a fine grain of detail to our analysis of the temporal dimensions of adjustment, we first sought to examine the degree of similarity in the timing and strength of annual fluctuations in output and the distribution of production income across the different states and two industry groups. To accomplish this, we employed a cross-correlation analysis of output and the distribution of income for each state and industry. This strategy was designed so as to compare the series of each individual state and industry to one another, and to measure the strength of association between the series at different leads and lags and at the same year (lag 0). The actual measure of association which we employed was derived from Box and Jenkins (1976: 373) and is reported in Clark and Gertler (1985).

We were also interested in causal relationships between output and the distribution of income, as discussed in the last section. Going beyond cross-correlational analysis, we required some form of multivariate modeling. A generalized least squares method was utilized to estimate a series of time-series regression models. This method was based on Beach and MacKinnon (1978) and was selected primarily for its directness and ease of application to the multivariate case. Its use is premised on the important assumption that the series of residuals resulting from the fitting of a multivariate OLS regression model to the variables concerned will exhibit first-order serial autocorrelation. Hence, this technique can be regarded as a restricted form of the more general Box–Jenkins multivariate techniques.

Regional output and the distribution of income

Figures 3.1a and b illustrate the temporal patterns of the ratio of disposable profits to wages for a small sample of states and the two selected industries, textiles and electronics, over the period 1954–76. Both figures demonstrate that the π/W ratio is quite volatile over the short run, and with respect to national peaks and troughs in economic activity. For textiles, it is apparent that there are geographical variations in the temporal volatility of the π/W ratio. On one hand, Maine's ratio ranges widely from a peak value of about 1.5 in 1958 (just before the national peak in economic activity) to a low value of about 0.4 in 1959 and then rises rapidly through the 1960s to fall again to 1969–70. This kind of volatility is not so obvious in North Carolina, which maintained a very steady upward trend over the entire period. In between these two extremes are Kentucky, which is more like North Carolina until the 1970s, and Ohio, which is more like Maine in that there are pronounced fluctuations in the π/W ratio over the business cycle. The amplitude of temporal variations in π/W ratios for electronics are not as pronounced. All state series exhibit a slow increase in their π/W ratios with distinct business cycle interruptions (compare Alabama and California).

Proceeding to a more direct evaluation of the correlation between the ratio π/W and output (Clark & Gertler 1985 summarize the results of a cross-correlation analysis), two measures of output were used; one was in nominal terms, the second was discounted by producer prices reflecting the real value of sales at the end of each year. Generally, the cross-correlations between output and the ratio π/W were quite strong for time-series data (see Granger & Newbold 1977), ranging from about 0.40 through to 0.90 across many different states and the two industries. Most often, the highest cross-correlations occurred at the zero lag, indicating that the two series were temporally synchronized (as far as we could

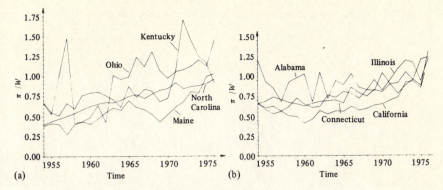

Figure 3.1   Ratio of disposable profits to wages (a, textiles, and b, electrical and electronic equipment).

discern from annual data). For the textile industry, it was difficult to isolate any geographical patterns in these results. Southern states did not consistently have lower or higher cross-correlations, although it is clear that no significant cross-correlation could be established for North Carolina. And, for the electronics industry, it was readily apparent that no significant cross-correlations could be established for most of the southern states.

While not too much can be made of these results, since they are simply descriptive of short-run cross-correlations, we are able to make some preliminary observations regarding the consistency of these results *vis-à-vis* Figure 3.1. It was noted above that the ratio π/W for North Carolina textiles exhibits little volatility over the study period, the variance being dominated by an upward sloping trend. This is consistent with our cross-correlation results (note that all series were differenced prior to cross-correlation). Similarly, it was noticed that Alabama's π/W ratio for electronics was volatile but inconsistent with respect to national peaks and troughs. And again it was found statistically that there were no significant cross-correlations between output and the ratio π/W for that state and industry. Notice also that it was very difficult to establish a temporally dependent causality structure. That is, no leads and lags could be identified, indicating that the direction of causality remains somewhat ambiguous (see Granger 1982 for more details on causality).

We also undertook a more direct test of the relationship of output to π/W (see Clark & Gertler 1985 for more details). The relationship, estimated via Beach and McKinnon's (1978) method, cast output at time t as a function of π/W at time t. Since the series were differenced, the model estimated was a dynamic adjustment process between changes in π/W and changes in output (nominal and real). The parameters a and b refer to the estimated intercept and the independent variable's coefficient or weight,

Table 3.1   Growth and distribution of capital in the textile industry.

		% distribution	
Region/state	% growth 1954–76	1954	1976
Northeast		41.5	18.8
Maine	−46.2	2.1	0.7
Massachusetts	−37.8	8.3	3.2
Connecticut	−36.5	3.2	1.2
New York	−18.0	9.8	4.8
New Jersey	−17.0	6.4	3.3
Pennsylvania	21.8	11.7	5.6
Northcentral		1.9	1.0
Ohio	−16.7	1.9	1.0
South		56.6	80.2
Virginia	88.8	4.6	5.3
North Carolina	154.7	20.5	31.8
South Carolina	120.7	13.6	18.1
Georgia	165.9	9.3	15.1
Kentucky	161.2	0.4	0.6
Tennessee	55.0	3.3	3.1
Alabama	105.7	3.9	4.9
Arkansas	364.9	0.2	0.5
Texas	52.4	0.8	0.8

respectively, while the parameter "p" was the estimate of first-order serial autoregressive autocorrelation. By considering the coefficient of determination (R^2) it was apparent that the relationship between output and the ratio π/W was significant and strong for many states in both industries. Moreover, the signs of the b coefficient were positive and thus consistent with our hypothesis that increasing π/W ratios are associated with increases in output. Although we should like to claim that increases in π/W cause increases in output, the temporal sequencing remained somewhat ambiguous.

The relationship was strongest amongst northern textile states as opposed to southern textile states. Indeed, the relationship was very weak for North Carolina, Tennessee and Arkansas, and weak (compared to northern states) for South Carolina, Georgia and Kentucky. It was also apparent that these southern states typically had significant intercept terms. When we considered the electronics industry, a slightly different picture emerged. First, it was apparent that a number of northeastern states had very low coefficients of determination, including New Hampshire and New York, as well as the midwestern states of Ohio, Michigan and Iowa. Secondly, however, it was found that the few southern states in our sample had relatively weak coefficients of determination and insignificant b coefficients on the π/W variable. Thirdly, all the estimated parameters had the expected sign, positive. In

Table 3.2 Growth and distribution of capital in the electrical and electronic equipment industry.

Region/state	% growth 1954–76	% distribution 1954	% distribution 1976
Northeast		46.5	35.6
New Hampshire	103.9	0.8	0.6
Rhode Island	88.8	0.4	0.3
Connecticut	71.4	3.7	2.5
New York	162.4	14.7	15.3
New Jersey	37.7	12.0	6.6
Pennsylvania	73.2	14.9	10.3
Northcentral		45.2	43.8
Ohio	133.4	11.0	10.2
Michigan	211.3	2.5	3.1
Indiana	167.0	8.4	8.9
Illinois	125.5	15.6	14.0
Wisconsin	113.0	4.4	3.7
Iowa	496.2	0.9	2.0
Missouri	99.6	2.4	1.9
South		2.1	4.2
Maryland	275.8	1.5	2.2
Alabama	632.9	0.3	0.9
Arkansas	1016.4	0.2	1.1
West		6.3	16.4
California	556.0	6.3	16.4

this industry, no easy north–south split could be made to order our results geographically, and it was apparent that there were wide variations in local output sensitivity to changes in their π/W ratios.

Without going into microeconomic studies of local firms' adjustment to changing macro variables, it is difficult to go much further in evaluating these results. After all, we found very much what was expected; changes in the distribution of income between classes matter a great deal for changes in the volume of local output. There remain, however, a number of questions which can be evaluated using other macro data. In particular, there is a question of whether or not local capital growth is associated with the sensitivity of local output to the distribution of income. As well, there is the question of whether or not those states with low adjustment sensitivities are those with right-to-work legislation. Granted, we can only associate patterns in this context. Nevertheless, we believe that there are some remarkable associations which should be given due recognition.

Beginning with the issue of local capital growth, Tables 3.1 and 3.2 summarize state capital growth patterns for the textiles and electronics industries over the period 1954–76. These data were derived from Gertler (1983) and Browne *et al.* (1980), and represent local investment in constant

(1972) dollars net of depreciation. From Table 3.1, it is obvious that those southern states which grew the most in terms of their textile capital stock were also the states which our previous analysis found to have the weakest relationship between output and the ratio π/W. And the reverse holds true; that is, northern states with low rates of capital growth (actually declines) were also those with strong output and π/W ratios. In this context, we feel that our theoretical speculations in the previous section may have been substantiated: long-run growth is closely related to short-run economic adjustment. Of course, the evidence is hardly complete or even unambiguous since the measured association is qualitative in nature. Nevertheless, when the patterns of state electronic capital growth are compared with output sensitivity to π/W, a similar picture emerges (see Table 3.2). In the northeast, those states with the highest rates of capital growth, New Hampshire and New York, are also states with very weak output–income distribution relationships. This is also apparent for the midwest and south. Again, there is good evidence for suggesting a link between short-run adjustment and long-run growth.

What then of institutional factors? Can any association be made between RTW legislation, unionization and the sensitivity of local output to the distribution of income? Table 3.3 summarizes rates of unionization and the pattern by states of RTW legislation in the USA over the period 1953–76 for our sample of states. Unionization declined over this period in all states except Rhode Island and New York. And those states with the highest levels of unionization in 1953 typically experienced the largest falls in percent unionized. Even so, as of 1976 there remained large differences between the states in their levels of unionization. The major northern industrial states recorded unionization rates of around 30%, southern states averaged about 15%, and the Carolinas averaged about 7%. States with RTW legislation were concentrated in the south. The year 1947, when most RTW legislation was passed, was apparently a very bad year for American labor! Unfortunately, no state and sectoral specific data are available on unionization, so we must be content with overall rates of unionization.

By now the reader, having remembered the pattern of results reported above regarding local output sensitivity to the distribution of income, will have also recognized that for textiles, at least, there maybe a positive relationship between low rates of unionization, the existence of RTW legislation, and weak output sensitivity to the ratio π/W. It is also clear that these institutional factors are associated with the geographical patterns of capital growth. A bivariate linear regression between percent change in state capital stock (1954–76) and the level of unionization in 1953 established a coefficient of determination of 0.50 and significant parameters for the intercept and the independent variable (at the 0.05 level). Moreover, the sign on the independent parameter was, as expected,

Table 3.3 Growth in unionization and right-to-work legislation by state, 1953–76.

State	Level of unionization[1]		Growth/ decline	Date RTW adopted[2]
	1953	1976		
Maine	21.4	17.9	−3.5	—
New Hampshire	24.6	13.7	−10.9	—
Massachusetts	30.1	24.6	−5.5	—
Rhode Island	27.4	31.1	+3.7	—
Connecticut	26.5	24.9	−1.6	—
New York	34.4	37.1	+2.7	—
New Jersey	35.2	25.3	−9.9	—
Pennsylvania	39.9	36.4	−3.5	—
Ohio	38.0	31.5	−6.5	—
Indiana	40.0	30.7	−9.3	1957*
Illinois	39.7	32.2	−7.5	—
Michigan	43.3	32.7	−10.6	—
Wisconsin	38.3	29.4	−8.9	—
Iowa	25.0	18.5	−6.5	1947
Missouri	39.7	31.8	−7.9	—
Virginia	17.4	13.6	−3.8	1947
North Carolina	8.2	6.8	−1.4	1947
South Carolina	9.3	6.6	−2.7	1954
Georgia	15.0	14.2	−0.8	1947
Kentucky	25.0	24.7	−0.3	—
Tennessee	22.6	18.3	−4.3	1947
Alabama	24.9	19.0	−5.9	1953
Arkansas	21.5	15.5	−6.0	1944
Texas	16.7	12.0	−4.7	1947
California	35.7	26.3	−9.4	—

[1]   Percent of nonagricultural employment, derived from Smith (1983: Table 1).
[2]   Derived from Farber (1983: Table 1).
 * Repealed in 1965.

negative, indicating that high capital growth is associated with low levels of unionization. Altogether, these associations suggest that the textile industry dramatically shifted its geographical and capital bases over the period 1954–76 from unionized to nonunionized RTW states. Those firms remaining in the north may be very vulnerable (in terms of output) to shifts in the local distribution of income between capital and labor. Indeed, this vulnerability may have itself induced a trend to capital intensity in the northeast even while the total capital stock in this industry has dwindled (Gertler 1983).

While this picture is entirely plausible for the textile industry, it is more difficult to construct a similar scenario for the electronics industry. High rates of capital growth are associated with weak sensitivities of output to changes in the π/W ratio. But strong capital growth has occurred in nonRTW states and even in states like New York which have actually gained in terms of unionization. Generally, the electronics industry grew in most states over this period of time, and faced market conditions very different from textiles. Perhaps a more complex scenario is required, one which can account for subtleties of product development and assembly, and the accompanying geographical division of labor which so characterizes firms in the electronics industry. An attempt is made along these lines in later chapters of this book. Even so, in general terms, the logic of our short-run model of disequilibrium adjustment has been demonstrated for both industries, even if there remain many other factors to be introduced.

Conclusions

This chapter began by observing that studies of regional production hardly ever model regional output directly, preferring instead to use employment as a proxy. But there are issues hidden by this approach, particularly relating to what determines output as opposed to employment. It was argued that firms' output decisions are different from, although related to, firms' employment decisions. For instance, it can be demonstrated that output plans may simply manipulate employment. Part of the difference between output plans and employment decisions has to do with the power relations between capital and labor. To demonstrate, a set of two differentiated decentralized labor markets were introduced, characterized by radically different labor relations: one region was assumed dominated by capital through right-to-work legislation and judicial enforcement of the employment-at-will doctrine, the other region was assumed dominated by union-oriented labor contracts. These two regional "types" were used to explicate the short-run adjustment and long-run structural implications of disequilibrium.

The model of adjustment developed here depends on assumptions relating to fixed short-run technical coefficients and quantity adjustments in production. The model emphasizes the interdependence between income distribution and planned output, and the accumulation of short-run adjustments into long-run regional economic differentiation (reflected in profitability, capital investment and technology). Like Kalecki (1971) and more recent macroeconomic theorists such as Fisher (1983), we argued that understanding the process of disequilibrium adjustment is necessary before we can understand structural change. Also implied, however, is a further proposition: we must be concerned with uncertainty and the short-run distribution of economic adjustment costs. The model introduced in this chapter depends on a flow-of-funds notion of economic planning, coupled with what was termed a contingency fund.

It was found that changes in output can be reasonably explained by changes in the ratio of disposable profits to labor costs measured in nominal and real terms. This was the case for the textile industry, in northern and midwestern states, as well as a number of states in the electronics industry. It was also shown that the performance of the proposed model is associated with the patterns of regional capital growth as well as with state levels of unionization and existence of right-to-work laws in the south. It remains to extend the implications of this model of regional production to employment, wages, unionization and investment.

PART II

Local employment profiles and labor demand

PART II *Local employment profiles and labor demand*

In this, the second part of the book, we develop our adjustment theory of the regional economy through what appears as its most fundamental aspect, the spatial division of labor. We argued, in Part I, that the spatial division of labor functions as the major structural element in the organization of production and the consequent distribution and absorption of economic uncertainty. We also provided an understanding (Ch. 2) of how the economic geography of the present time has been restructured to accommodate new production arrangements and their consequent uncertainties. The three chapters of the second part of the book explore empirical aspects of this basic theme.

Beginning with Chapter 4, we explore the patterns of adjustment of employment in regional labor markets. In isolation from other production variables, we examine the cycles, fluctuations, and rigidities of local employment profiles for three industries (apparel, electronics, and printing and publishing) in 11 US cities. The focus is on the three major variables of employment (total employment, weekly hours worked, and wages) for the period 1972–82.

Our first major finding is that the quantity adjustments of employment (total employment and hours worked) cannot be systematically related to their associated wage series. This observation holds true for all the industries and cities examined. In *all* the wage series examined, the upward trend of wages appears to be centered on an industry-oriented trend; and the deviations from this trend are small and essentially random. Wages, it appears, simply do not act as the price adjustment mechanism envisaged by neoclassical theory. And, on the basis of our empirical evidence, it becomes impossible to maintain that the spatial labor market system is an efficient, neoclassical bourse. It does not "clear" in the fury of discrete exchange between labor and capital as envisioned by Walrasian economic theorists.

Wages, being so rigid and dominated by trend patterns over time, do not contain enough variations or fluctuations to act as a significant adjustment variable. Variations in revenue must therefore be borne either as a cost to capital (by carrying inventories) or else are transposed into quantity adjustments of labor (by layoffs and changes in the length of the working week). And indeed, this is where the overwhelming proportion of adjustment in local employment is to be found. The pattern of employment adjustment varies from industry to industry and from city to city. Sometimes economic uncertainty is accommodated by layoffs (whether temporary or permanent), sometimes by changes in the length of the working week, and sometimes by changes in both adjustment levers. These quantity adjustments are so varied, both across industries and cities, that no easy geographical pattern can be advanced. Nevertheless, it is readily apparent that employment adjustment is geographically contingent, while wages appear temporally contingent.

We then advance a view of the labor–capital relation as being driven by contract. The contract mechanism (whether implicit or explicit) is the only institution, we argue, which is capable of explaining the empirical adjustment patterns that are evident in the local employment data. The contract is an agreement between employer and employee which sets the terms of employment, but most importantly sets a particular distribution of economic uncertainty among the variables of wages, weekly hours, and employment totals.

These three variables go to the heart of the employment relation in that it is capital, as a class, that owns the job and the commodities produced by labor. Thus we see that labor as opposed to capital will more readily compromise on wages and hours worked. The primary strategic goal of labor becomes employment security. But employers have the upper hand. As long as labor mobility is limited and costly, employers can exercise their unilateral power in determining how the costs of economic uncertainty are to be borne. This argument returns us to the theme of a spatial division of labor. By its structural arrangement, the geography of the economy comes to set and reflect a heterogeneous distribution of the costs of economic fluctuations.

In Chapter 5, we provide a more detailed and analytical test of the relation between wages and the demand for labor. Using state-level data for two industries, textiles and electronics, we evaluate the strength of the association between labor demand and wages. We test a series of models. First, we test neoclassical models which assume that price (wage) adjustment is the basic determinant of changes in labor demand (the "wages as prices" view in the strict neoclassical account of the labor market). The results of these tests are significant, because in no case can it be maintained that changes in wages drive changes in employment levels – a finding which is anathema to neoclassical theories of the labor market.

If changing wages have little relevance as signals for the allocation of labor, what then determines changes in employment demand? In this same chapter (Ch. 5) we test alternative hypotheses concerning the demand for labor. The flow of profits was found to be a very significant determinant of the local demand for labor in the electronics industry. This result was entirely consistent with our previously introduced (Ch. 3) model of regional production and adjustment. Otherwise, no significant determinants of local labor demand could be found, even though we analyzed variables such as the return on capital, the distribution of income between labor and capital, levels of capital intensity, the level of output or the level of labor productivity.

Our results carry important implications for local industrial policies. Contrary to popular wisdom, the demand for labor is little affected by changing wages. Therefore, local industrial policies which aim to provide cheap labor to industry are not likely to succeed. The battle between labor and capital is not so much fought over wages as over the conditions of employment and the status of labor in terms of economic security. Our findings provide some evidence in support of those development policies which are premised on the idea that profit opportunities beget employment growth. For the electronics industry, at least, this appears to be true, but to be effective for labor, these policies also imply public-sector initiatives of a distributional nature and this runs counter to their initial "pro-business" attitudes.

Finally, in the last chapter of this part (Ch. 6), we provide an empirical methodology and an analysis of economic uncertainty from the perspective of the individual worker. Most conventional analyses of labor demand simply assume that the experience of employment is derived through competition as a logical necessity from the imperatives of market efficiencies. In treating labor in such a residual way, these kinds of analyses effectively make the actual experience of labor "uninteresting." Whatever the pattern of variation in labor demand, it is derived by necessity from the iron laws of supply and demand. So in itself, says neoclassical theory, the experience of labor is not worthy of investigation; it is a phenomenon whose real sources of influence lie elsewhere.

But we show in Chapters 4 and 5 that the adjustments and fluctuations of employment *cannot* be causally linked to a combination of wages, output and productivity. Only the flow of profit can be said to influence the temporal structure of employment. The experience of labor is not, given our empirical evidence, determined as a passive link in a chain of necessity. We have suggested in Chapter 5 that employment profiles are the result of particular, local economic arrangements which act as contracts setting a specific distribution of economic uncertainties. In this view of the labor process, the actual experiences of labor become conceptually very important, for it is these experiences that form both the basis and result of the local (regional) organization of production.

In Chapter 6, we therefore provide a method of describing the labor experience in terms of economic uncertainty. Our methodology (explained more fully in Chapter 6 itself) provides a way of estimating the distribution of job "lives" as they are created and destroyed in an aggregate series. From this histogram of job durations we can compute (using a standard demographic analysis) a set of statistics which describe, in more personal terms, the labor experience implied by a particular aggregate series. While our results are of a preliminary nature, we do show that growth in a region tends not only to reduce the risk of job loss, but also to concentrate it within the first few months of job tenure. Regional decline, on the other hand, presents the worker with a more extended temporal pattern of job risk, involving recurrent phases of high risk over the tenure of employment. Given the preliminary nature of this investigation, we cannot draw firm conclusions, but we do note that, while most regional economic policies still focus on attracting manufacturing employment to the area, it is precisely this sector of the economy which presents the worker with the least favourable (stable) conditions of employment.

4 Fluctuations and rigidities in local labor markets

Introduction

Imagine that a firm is faced with a sudden and unanticipated decline in demand for its output. How would it be likely to respond? Conventional neoclassical models, based upon perfect competitive assumptions, suggest at least two possibilities. First, if the market price for its good could fall quickly enough, a compensating increase in demand could be induced via the bargain prices then faced by consumers. Secondly, if commodity prices did not adjust fully to compensate declining demand, or if there were lags in response, the firm would be forced to reduce output and lay off excess labor. As a consequence, with declining demand for labor relative to supply, wages should also fall. Only a minor modification to this second option is required if money wages are sticky downwards. Phillips (1958) argued that while wages do not decline absolutely, their rate of increase does.

What of workers' responses in this situation? Neoclassical models emphasize real wages as a key behavioral criterion. With declining commodity prices, a commensurate decline in money wages would be of little relevance if, as suggested by conventional theory, real wages would be maintained. A step further in this line of reasoning is to suggest that money wages vary according to workers' *expectations* of likely changes in prices and therefore their real wages (Grossman & Stiglitz 1980). Even if money wages are sticky downwards, neoclassical theory still expects a great deal of wage-rate inflation volatility over the short run. Studies of the dynamics of local labor markets depended to a large extent on these propositions regarding firms and workers (Clark 1980b). In these analyses, short-run patterns of employment are typically linked to industry-specific demand patterns and the location of those industries. Similarly, local wage inflation models typically depend upon the Phillips curve and its implied neoclassical quantity and price adjustment mechanisms. Essentially, the local labor market is treated just like any other commodity market, albeit with the appropriate cautions regarding the significance of flex versus fix-price adjustment arrangements.

Workers are not simply commodities. They can, and often do, enter into implicit and explicit contractual agreements with employers. Rather than supply and demand being the dominant means of setting wages, unionization, and collective wage bargaining are key institutional characteristics of the labor market (Ross 1948). In recent years Baily (1976) and Azariadis (1975) have also shown that implicit contracts can dominate decisions regarding wages and employment. Over the economic cycle, workers can expect to be laid off and their overall wages reduced according to the severity of demand shifts. One option is to spread the risks and benefits of association with a particular employer over a longer period than any one phase of the business cycle. For example, a worker could agree to moderate wage demands during a boom in return for a guaranteed wage during a recession. In doing so, the worker seeks to minimize disruptions to income with respect to the timing and duration of subsequent booms and recessions.

In this chapter, the cyclical sensitivity of local labor markets is explored over the period 1972–80 for three industries (apparel, electronics, and printing) and some 11 US cities. The next section details the familiar neoclassical discrete-exchange theory of labor markets. Notions such as individual choice, autonomy, and aggregate efficiency are considered as central elements of this paradigm. Newer implicit contract theory, which eschews discrete-exchange in favor of long-term continuous relationships, is also reviewed and considered in terms of commodity exchange. The subsequent sections then consider the empirical evidence, utilizing time-series techniques such as spectral analysis. Local sensitivity is measured in terms of three strategic variables: employment, hours worked, and wages. Rigidities consistent with implicit contract theory are in fact found (see Hall 1980). However, a critical assessment of this theory is provided utilizing neo-marxist notions of power and interdependence.

Labor as a commodity

Neoclassical economics is based upon two axioms: individual free choice and utility maximization. The decision to participate in the labor market (to suppy labor) is a decision taken by individuals with respect to their utility (income, leisure, and life-cycle characteristics). Labor can be described by dimensions such as skill, training, and education which may or may not be job specific (Williamson 1975). These dimensions are essentially the "human capital" of the worker. Whether or not individuals invest in human capital depends upon actual and expected returns, including expected income from future job opportunities. On the other hand, the demand for labor depends on the technical requirements of production. As Oi (1962) pointed out, labor skills often have particular and fixed technical relationships with capital in the short run. Basically, one can imagine the worker as a complementary machine, with "its" technical competence being determined by individual choice and utility maximization. Here, of course, the demand for labor is like that for any other commodity. When couched in terms of marginal productivity, labor is a divisible commodity arranged according to the most efficient mode of production (as noted in the previous chapter).

One way of representing the discrete-exchange (commodity) nature of the neoclassical labor market is to describe it as an auction. Labor is offered for sale by individuals at a minimum bid price (reservation wage) based upon their calculus of utility. Given that each individual can be valued in terms of his or her human capital, demand and supply for that particular individual (commodity) will set the market price. If there are no bids at or above the worker's reservation wages then labor will be withdrawn from sale (in essence the "discouraged worker" effect). Labor is sought between competing employers, and it is used to the point where its output is no longer required; or, more significantly, to the point where it can be replaced by a cheaper worker with the same skills somewhere else. Implied is a possibility that workers can be drawn from, and returned to, the auction at any point in time. An example that comes to mind are the day-laborer hiring halls that still exist in many American cities.

Auction models of labor exchange may not be efficient under conditions of less than perfect information. To illustrate, assume both that the total set of workers offering their labor at any time *and* their human capital dimensions are known. But also assume that their reservation wages are unknown. The order in which each individual comes up for auctioning is very important. Since it is not known whether or not the first worker's reservation wage is indicative of the overall distribution of reservation wages, one employer strategy would be to wait for more information (i.e. disclosure of others' reservation wages). However, if demand is strong relative to supply, employers could only afford to wait only through a portion of the auction before deciding what the wage distribution *might* look like. Of course this does not guarantee that succeeding offers will be similar to previous offers. It is also plausible that workers themselves would revise their reservation wages according to previous offers and bids, leading to further uncertainty on both sides of the auction.

Imagine a further example wherein there are many more workers than potential vacancies although, as before, the distribution of reservation wages is unknown. An employer could bid for a worker and employ him/her, but as other less expensive workers come up in the auction, the initial contract would be re-negotiated in favor of the employer or the employee would be replaced. The only means of counteracting the power of employers would be to unionize and standardize the reservation wage. Consequently, workers in the upper order of the auction would be employed first. Employment would be rationed on the basis of *order* in the auction queue. However, with no union and greater labor supply than demand, the auction model predicts tremendous instability in the length of job tenure and overall employment (Hall 1981). Depending upon changes in the demand for labor, the auction model also predicts rapid wage inflation at the onset of a boom. Thus wage and employment instability with respect to levels and rates of change are essential features of a neoclassical auction labor exchange.

The neoclassical labor market could also be characterized as a bourse. All commodities (in the case of labor, differentiated by skill and experience), with their quantities and prices, are listed in a central marketplace for a given period of time (like Hicks' 1965 "trading week"). As bids are made, prices are determined by supply and demand and there is an option of substitution between different commodities. For a bourse to operate efficiently there must be many buyers (employers) and sellers (labor), and there must also be a market coordinator. Under monopoly conditions, however, prices are unlikely to reflect the true dimensions of supply and demand, and without a coordinator the exchange process itself would collapse. Recontracting is a key feature of such an exchange system; as new bids are made, and quantities supplied are adjusted in accordance with bids, the "best" market allocation changes. Hence, within the exchange period, recontracting is the means of facilitating the optimal price–quantity combination.

In a system of local labor markets, we could imagine a set of bourses coordinated such that labor is allocated over time and space according to patterns of demand and supply. Given the recontracting process, prices and quantities are initially likely to be quite volatile but eventually to attain a stable equilibrium. Whether or not equilibrium is actually attained in reality is quite problematic. Frictions of distance and implied problems of market coordination and information may result in a less than efficient spatial allocation of labor (Ballard & Clark 1981). Migration is then a key mechanism in coordinating any spatial system of labor markets, and labor is assumed to respond to the spatial configuration of demand and supply, expressed in terms such as wages and unemployment (Lowry 1966). Flows and exchanges between and within local labor markets have then an equilibrating function, although the time-frame in which such flows adjust to changing prices is subject to some debate (Clark 1982a). Inevitably, the bourse model depends upon changes in prices and quantities as the signals for recontracting and allocating labor efficiently.

When expressed as an exchange commodity, labor can be conceptualized just like any other good. Standard principles of supply and demand apply, as do notions of marginal pricing and adjustment. The actual form of the neoclassical labor market does have important implications for understanding the roles of prices and quantities. For example, in an auction system, the distribution of reservation wages provides important clues for employers in bidding for labor. Also, in a bourse, prices (wages) are the signals for recontracting and exchange. Both types of market systems depend on assumptions of perfect or pure competition and atomistic individual behavior. Under uncertainty, both modes of exchange will not necessarily be efficient. For example, if the distribution of reservation wages is unknown, as in an auction, employers may be forced to bid on earlier offers in the queue, thus generating wage inflation and the possibility of nonclearing markets. Similarly, if prices do not truly reflect demand and supply conditions (perhaps because of time or space lags), false trading could occur, leading to problems of coordination and disequilibrium. Prices and quantities are required to be adaptive to changing conditions if the market for labor is to be efficient (Okun 1981).

Dunlop (1944) argued that "the labor market is not a bourse." He claimed that the "technical organization" of labor exchange does not conform to either an auction or a bourse. His argument concerned the structure of the labor market much more than its institutions. Dunlop observed that in capitalist labor markets there are many more sellers of labor (workers) than buyers (employers). Firms generally set the wage rate that they are willing to pay and then allow workers to sort themselves according to those who will offer services and those who will not work at the given wage rate. By varying the "quoted price" for labor, firms are then able to attract different types of labor (See Clark & Whiteman 1983). Unlike a bourse or even an auction, it is practically impossible for one worker to displace another by offering to work at a less than quoted price. A likely effect will be market segmentation by workers and employers alike, around different clusters of wage offers and skill types. Thus, the labor market is an exchange system that has inherent tendencies of segmentation, quantity rationing given quoted prices, and market power favoring employers (Piore 1979b).

Unions, according to Dunlop (1944), are actually a response by workers to the power of employers. However, it should be emphasized that for Dunlop the existence of unions is a result of the structure of capitalist labor markets, *not* their distinguishing feature. The quoted–price market will obviously favor the employer. Even if labor is scarce in the short run, labor has no direct means of forcing a change in its wage unless it switches to another employer. In essence, recontracting is unlikely because price determination is set by one side of the market. If a firm cannot hire labor after repeated offers at a certain quoted price, then an increase may be forced, although even the increase need not reflect overall supply and demand conditions. On the other hand, if labor is plentiful, repeated offers to work at a certain quoted price may encourage firms to change their quoted price. However, firms are rarely able to restructure their wage contours unilaterally, because new hires and quoted prices are typically made with reference to existing salary structures, and it is only after a quoted price draws many more potential employees than expected that firms are able to re-evaluate their quoted price for *future* new hires. In Dunlop's model, wages adapt only slowly to labor supply even though employers have significant power in the exchange system.

Dunlop (1944) severely criticized wage determination models based upon notions of power (e.g. Ross 1948), as being uneconomic. However, there are reasons to suppose that his critique was over-drawn. For example, it is clear that he considered that firms make price offers with reference to existing internal and external wage contours. Why should firms be so concerned with internal wage relativities given their power in the market? One answer is that the wage rate is more than a price: it classifies workers by prestige, status and even responsibility in the firm. Consequently, a change in the quoted price relative to existing standards will disrupt the internal social structure of firms' labor markets. A second answer, one also noted by Dunlop (1944), is that changes (especially increases) in the quoted price for a given class of worker will initiate claims by other workers who use such prices as reference points for wage bargaining. Whether or not unions exist is irrelevant; workers and employers depend upon complex implicit contracts that relate as much to standards such as "fairness" and "equity" as to a simple price quoted by firms for labor services (Wood 1978). Dunlop argued that this is the result of the technical organization of labor markets. However, the existence of wage relativities implies an important normative content.

Contracts and labor relations

The newer implicit contract literature is based to a large extent on Dunlop's pioneering studies of the economics of labor market exchange. Rather than viewing labor as a discrete-exchange commodity, these theories emphasize the pattern and determinants of long-term employment relationships. Moreover, they recognize that recontracting in the Walrasian sense is meaningless in labor markets. Agreements are made with significant time dimensions included that purposely preclude short-run market solutions. Like Dunlop, Azariadis (1975) and others have not been concerned with unions as the key institution of the labor market. They start from a commodity model of the labor market – both demand and supply – and then derive contractual solutions to problems such as uncertainty and risk, from the objective functions of those involved. To illustrate, assume that firms have specific labor requirements (skills) in their production processes and that labor efficiency is a function of years of experience on the job. A firm may hoard its labor over the short run, protecting itself from having to search for new labor, and perhaps pay extra for scarce supplies in a tighter market.

On the other hand, workers typically face two kinds of uncertainty: uncertainty with respect to the duration of job tenure and uncertainty with respect to the expected average flow of income (Grossman & Stiglitz 1980). Boom conditions mean higher wages, while busts mean greater unemployment and loss of income. If both workers' and employers' concern for such uncertainties coincide, one option is to draw up a contract. Essentially the risks implicit in a discrete-exchange commodity market for labor are shared through implicit or explicit contracts that bind both workers and employers over the business cycle. The key issues here, hardly addressed by auction models, are the interdependence between workers and employers and the longer-term employment relationships which are a function of the production process. Notice, however, that contracts could be interpreted as discrete exchange, but with time lags to cover the transaction costs implicit in risks (MacNeil 1981). Some kind of prior agreement on conditions and compensations is required if the contract is to have any validity over time.

Contracts may be explicit (i.e. described by law) or implicit (i.e. agreed to without any adjudicating third party; see MacNeil 1980). Contracts describe the obligations and penalties to which parties to any contract agree to, and are also promises that both parties will adhere to agreed conditions in the future (Fried 1981). If in a recession demand for a firm's output fails, the contract between a firm and its workers may call for reduced overtime and perhaps temporary layoffs of certain segments of the firm's workforce. Contracts specify a range of possible market situations and the appropriate response. However, in reality all possibilities may not be known, so contracts may specify average responses based on the past and promise that employers and workers will adhere to particular rules in the future. It is the uncertainty inherent in the discrete-exchange market that makes the promise to adhere to contractual obligations most important. Such promises result in built-in rigidities of response to short-run fluctuations. For example, when demand for labor is low, employment and wages may be maintained at previous levels. When demand is high, wage increases may be moderate, rather than reflecting "actual" labor market demand and supply conditions.

Baily (1976) argued that it is the mutual advantages inherent in any employment relation which bind the two parties (workers and employers) together over the short run: a joint decision is made concerning the nature and conditions of each contract. Thus, following Williamson (1979), the firm can be treated as a single maximizing unit which integrates the interests of both workers and employers. Obviously, this abstracts from the commodity exchange relationships which we argue above to be central to the neoclassical versions of how labor markets function. However, it should be emphasized that contracts are negotiated for specific lengths of time. Once the technical conditions which encourage what amounts to collusion have passed, then exchange in the market can resume. Theoretically, implicit contracts delay the exchange process, but they do not replace exchange.

Baily's (1977) model is analogous to a game of bridge. The partners (workers and employers) cooperate to maximize their joint winnings before deciding on their respective shares. Real income is of course the crucial variable in this instance. A further assumption is then made wherein workers are considered to be risk averse with respect to income fluctuations. On the other hand, firms are assumed to be either less risk averse or possibly risk neutral because management is able to diversify its portfolio (Azariadis 1981). The result is that firms offer a "joint product" – wages plus an insurance premium reflecting the likelihood of layoff. Thus, in the short run, workers are paid more than their marginal product, as firms attempt to reduce some portion of workers' risk. Each job offer contains an implicit insurance premium which can be traded in the labor market. In a competitive labor market, workers will sort themselves according to their risk averseness and firm-specific layoff probabilities. At the limit, competitive pressures will force firms to offer similar contract conditions, assuming of course that there is full information concerning competing implicit contract offers.

From these propositions it is then argued by Baily (1977) that a "good" implicit contract would make employees indifferent between being employed and being unemployed. As a consequence Baily argued *a priori* the likelihood of rigid wages and greater volatility of employment. For firms, implicit contracts that center upon wages have the advantage of stabilizing labor costs over the short run. As Azariadis (1981: 235) noted, "contracts are [a] combination [of] production plans and insurance policies." And the argument can be generalized to include situations wherein workers with specific and highly demanded skills are given larger premiums commensurate with their importance to firms (compare Oi 1962). Implicit contracts are then *efficient* to the extent that they can account for the costs of transactions and the risks associated with the chances of being laid off. Notice, however, that the wage bargain necessarily involves both workers' expectations of price changes *and* a known probability distribution of being laid off. Otherwise, over time, as new information becomes available, workers would claim for a renegotiation of the contract terms, and wage volatility would again become widespread.

An obvious question at this juncture is whether or not these assumptions of perfect knowledge are tenable. What would be implied if the future is unknown? It is immediately obvious that it would be virtually impossible to fashion a wage offer that makes workers indifferent between employment and unemployment in all but the most trivial circumstances. There would be a significant random element in trying to predict the "proper" risk (wage) premium. Under these conditions, workers could equally seek to maintain employment continuity and then compromise on wages and hours worked. Such an "insurance" policy would reverse Baily's (1976) order of rigidity so that employment becomes more stable than wages. Since workers cannot affect the aggregate price level and its future patterns (see subsequent chapters), a parallel argument could be made to the effect that real wages are of little relevance. With a large stochastic element inherent in money wages, why would workers be willing to gamble their jobs? The reality of modern capitalist economies implies that different orderings of the importance (rigidity) of wages and employment are quite likely, compared to the noncontextual orderings of implicit contract theorists.

To summarize, neoclassical auction and bourse models narrowly conceive of labor as a discrete-exchange commodity. Short-run variations in labors' price (wage) and quantity (employment) are predicted by both models as recontracting and bidding allocates (and reallocates) labor to firms. On the other hand, Dunlop (1944) predicted that with or without unions, wages will tend to be more stable than employment. The key concepts here are based upon the notion of a "quoted price" for labor and the inherent difficulty of changing internal wage contours when recontracting does not exist. More recent neoclassical theorists, following Dunlop's earlier analyses, suppose that the labor market is structured around more continuous employment relationships. Contract theorists maintain that because the objective function of workers and employers is centered around income, the crucial variable for workers is the real wage. To the extent that wages compensate for being laid off, workers are hypothesized to be indifferent to their employment status. Thus, contract theory predicts greater volatility in employment than in wages. However, it is less clear what the order of rigidity versus volatility should be with regard to employment levels and hours worked. Moreover, it is unclear whether or not contracts are contingent upon more general economic conditions. That is, would an excess supply of labour in a geographical or industry labor market affect the terms of a particular employer's contract? And, if real wages are so crucial for implicit contract theorists, how adaptive are money wages? Are there observable rigidities in money wages?

Adjustment scenarios by city and industry

In this section empirical evidence is presented as a partial demonstration of the relevance of implicit contract theory. Empirical studies of local labor market dynamics generally use economic aggregates such as total employment and the unemployment rate. Local responsiveness to short-run fluctuations has been analyzed via regression models, spectral-fourier transformations and Box and Jenkins (1976) autocorrelation (ARIMA) equations, all of which are modified for the structure of space–time lags (see Marchand 1981 for a recent example using a modified entropy-spectral analysis). Implicitly these analyses have assumed that labor markets are just like discrete-exchange commodity markets, and are in the main concerned with "bourse-like" quantity and price adjustment mechanisms (Clark 1980b). Explanations of different space–time adjustment patterns focus upon the frictions of labor market exchange and the location of industries. It is often assumed (wrongly, as was noted in the previous chapter) that changes in the demand for a firm's output should proportionally affect the level of employment. Local wage determination models also presume a very conventional labor demand and supply format, being dependent upon the Phillips curve. As such, rigidities are a minor element of the analytical paradigm. In contrast, contract theorists predict rigidities over the short run, and rigidities are thus central to the analytical framework.

The relative importance of these alternative claims of local labor-market adjustment were evaluated for a set of industries and cities in the United States over the period 1972–80 (Clark 1983a). In terms of aggregates, firms can adjust their workforce on three counts: the total number of employees, hours worked, and wages paid (Medoff 1979). Unpublished data for these variables were collected from the Bureau of Labor Statistics (BLS) for 3 industries and some 11 Standard Metropolitan Statistical Areas (SMSAs). The employment measure was quite straightforward: simply total monthly employees in the particular industry and city. Hours worked were measured through average weekly hours worked per employee for a given month in the industry and city. Following Dunlop (1944), wages were measured via the total monthly wage bill standardized by the number of employees. Thus, the wage rate is not simply the standard wage per hour, but reflects other important elements such as overtime penalty rates, bonuses and shifts of workers among different earning categories within firms. If, as Dunlop (1944) suggested, maximization of the total wage bill is the objective of unions (and minimization of the wage bill is the objective of firms), then the average hourly wage is a much better measure of compensation than the standard wage rate for a standard hour worked.

Studies of the patterns of local economic adjustment to national fluctuations have suggested that differential local response can be linked to local industrial structures (see King & Clark 1978). To account for such a possibility, data on employment, hours worked, and wages were collected at the two-digit SIC level for three industries: apparel and textiles, electronics and electrical equipment, and printing and publishing. Three considerations dictated the choice of these industry groups. First, these industries are *nationally* quite responsive to economic fluctuations. Secondly, these industries can be found in a variety of US regions, and thus comparisons can be made between the patterns of fluctuations and rigidities in northeastern and southern SMSAs, holding industry structure constant. Thirdly, these industries are highly competitive, dominated by smaller firms, and are not significantly unionized. Data availability helped dictate the period of analysis, although it should also be recognized that the 1970s were quite unusual, in terms of postwar economic history. There are two reasons for this. First, the standard Phillips' curve model apparently failed to predict persistent simultaneous high inflation and unemployment over the decade (Cagan 1979); and, secondly, economic growth in the south and relative decline in the northeast dominated the US spatial economy (Chinitz 1978).

The printing and publishing industry.   Four SMSAs, two from the south (Birmingham, Alabama, and Dallas, Texas) and two from the northeast (Boston, Massachusetts, and Rochester, New York), were selected to represent the diversity of local labor-market adjustment patterns in the printing and publishing industry. Figure 4.1 illustrates the patterns of local adjustment for the three key labor-market adjustment variables identified by Medoff (1979): total employment, average weekly hours worked per employee, and average hourly wages. Each series was smoothed using a running average with a span of five months. Extraneous month-to-month fluctuations were minimized and underlying business-cycle patterns highlighted. This was important for each SMSA's employment and hours series, with the latter series being, by far, the most volatile of the three key adjustment variables.

Periodograms were also estimated for these series, for all places and industries. Periodograms indicate the intensity of amplitude in each series over a range of frequencies (Box & Jenkins 1976). In the estimation procedure each series was de-trended, corrected for its mean and then tapered before being analyzed. First, differences were used to de-trend each series, assuming that this is simpler and easier to interpret than fitting a polynomial of unknown order (Granger & Newbold 1977). Correction for the series mean is a way of inducing stationarity, although shifts in the series variance are not accounted for in such a procedure. Not surprisingly, each series exhibited what Granger and Newbold (1977) have termed the "typical shape of an economic variable," that is, high intensity at very low frequencies with a falling-off in intensity over higher-order frequencies, coupled with evidence of white noise. In this instance, because of the limited length of the series (96 months), it is difficult to claim that any one frequency is *the* business-cycle component.

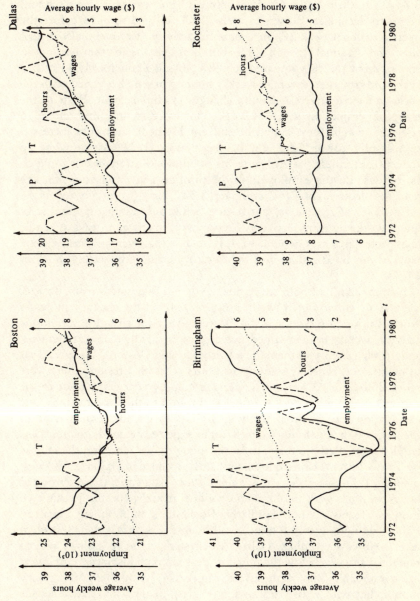

Figure 4.1 Local adjustment strategies (printing and publishing).

Although Strong (1983) argued that interregional differences in the cyclical sensitivity of the paper industry (of which printing and publishing are a smaller component) have declined since 1950, Figure 4.1 indicates that significant differences remain between the different SMSAs in their patterns of adjustment. For example, employment began to decline in Boston in early 1972, fully 18 months before the overall national peak (P) in economic activity. Recovery also began after the national trough (T), but was less than the decline in employment (6.2% compared to 8.8%, based upon locally identified peaks and troughs). Average weekly hours worked also varied with the cycle and were interrelated with changes in employment. Prior to the trough in employment, hours worked increased significantly, although after the trough they lagged behind employment, and only increased significantly toward the end of the period (1979). If we were to conceptualize these patterns in terms of employer strategies, it could be as follows: Boston employers in the printing and publishing industry tend to initiate layoffs (or terminate "new" hires) of employees in the early stages of recessions, but re-hire before increasing the number of hours worked during recovery. Presumably, overtime is used to handle unexpected increases in demand. It is notable that average weekly hours worked remained stable, near the statutory minimum, during much of 1975–7.

Birmingham had both similarities with and differences from Boston. Layoffs in employment were compensated for by changes in hours worked prior to recession, as in Boston. After the trough in economic activity, average hours worked increased more rapidly than employment, and then fell as employment grew further (unlike Boston). The effect was to maintain a relatively stable man–hours worked, although there were rapid shifts in each series. The peak in employment came prior to the national peak with a decline of 8.1% through to the local trough. One explanation could be that Birmingham employers adjust their requirements through both hours worked (for unexpected demand situations) *and* employment. Perhaps they are more willing to hire (and fire) than to use overtime. In contrast, employment hardly declined in Dallas (2.0%) and, over the 1972–80 period, grew dramatically. Adjustments were made in hours worked, with the local and national troughs coming within two months of one another. Similarly, Rochester's employment remained stable (without a growth trend), and hours worked was the adjustment lever. However, unlike Dallas, Rochester's average hours worked remained at levels below the previous peak. In both instances, employers had presumably *hoarded* employees, rather than laying them off, a policy more in line with a growth situation (Dallas), than with a relative decline (Rochester). The contrast with Birmingham is then quite remarkable, especially if total man–hours and adjustment strategies are compared.

What might at first glance appear to be similar local adjustment patterns in total man–hours are in fact quite different under the surface.

What of price adjustment? The patterns of wages shown in Figure 4.1 suggest autonomous growth rather than adjustment to changing labor demand conditions in the four SMSAs. Trend-line ordinary least squares (OLS) regression equations were fitted to each SMSA's wage series (see Clark 1983a). The slope of each regression line was taken to indicate the overall trend in wages over the 1972–80 period. It was apparent that Boston, Dallas, and Rochester had quantitatively very similar trends in their money wages, with coefficient values of 2.8, 2.8 and 2.7 respectively, despite marked differences in the patterns of employment and hours worked. Of the three cities, Boston experienced the largest cyclical change in employment, yet it also had the highest initial average wage and (marginally) the steepest trend-line. The parameter value for Birmingham was significantly smaller, but nevertheless indicated a marked upward shift in wages. High estimated R^2 and low standard errors suggested that not only did wages *not* fall, but there was also little evidence of change in the rate of increase that might reflect changes in employment or hours worked over the business cycle.

To test this hypothesis further, an analysis was conducted on the residuals from the regression equation. Using the Kolmogorov–Smirnov (K–S) test, which essentially tests for serial autocorrelation amongst the error terms, it was found that only Rochester had a significant (discernible) autocorrelation pattern. With Boston and Birmingham there was a problem with the regression model, in that it failed adequately to predict the up-turn in wages in late 1979. However, neither wage series was found to have residual patterns significantly different from white noise. The same was true for Dallas. In the other cities, the trend in wages dominated the series in relation to the general price level, *not* according to local labor-market conditions. Moreover, Dallas employment and wages were both maintained in the short run despite the effects (as evidenced in hours worked) of a minor slow-down. Overall, local labor-market rigidity was a fact of life in the printing and publishing industry with short-run adjustment being taken up principally through changes in hours worked, then employment, and not in money wages.

The apparel and textiles industry.   Following the methodology outlined above, Figure 4.2 describes the local adjustment patterns for the apparel and textile industry in three northeastern cities (Buffalo, New York; New Bedford, Massachusetts; Johnstown, Pennsylvania) and a southern city (Greensboro, North Carolina). In terms of total man–hours, it was found that there were closer parallels in behavior for these cities than those shown for the printing industry. The recession was clearly marked, and only Greensboro evidenced a significant growth trend in total man–hours

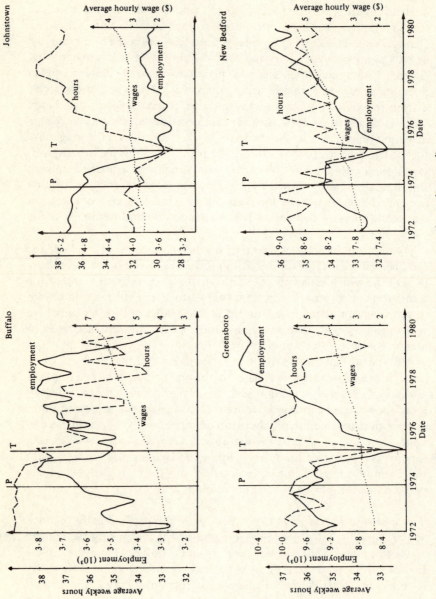

Figure 4.2 Local adjustment strategies (textiles and apparel).

for the apparel industry. However, unlike the previous set of cities, there was also a great deal of volatility in all cities' employment and hours worked. For example, from local peak to trough, Buffalo's employment declined by 34.7%. All cities exhibited a close timing with the national trough, although not as well synchronized with the national peak of economic activity (exceptions being Greensboro and New Buffalo).

When shifts in hours were included into our analysis, the following scenarios were plausible for Buffalo. Employers increase employment while maintaining very high levels of overtime in response to very strong (unanticipated) demand for output. In recession, however, employment is cut dramatically, and more than average hours worked. With recovery, employers hire before expanding output. Essentially there are two trends in the data: toward a larger workforce and away from reliance on overtime. Unlike all other cities analyzed here, Buffalo experienced a drastic slump in 1979. The scenario for Greensboro had similarities with the previous analysis of Birmingham. Employers used overtime to adjust to unexpected increases in demand in the short run, while in the long run, employment was expanded to cover labor requirements. A similar pattern was evident for New Bedford, although employment did not expand or contract at the same rate as Greensboro (in which employment grew 33.5% compared to New Bedford's 18.8%) or at the same time that hours worked changed. Johnstown was the real surprise. With the biggest decline in employment, it also had the smallest recovery increase. Prior to recession, average hours worked were very low and quite stable (in the 30–2 hours per week range): however, recovery saw average hours worked rise an amazing 41%. Extra overtime, rather than increased employment, was the major post-recession response by firms in Johnstown.

As with the previous industry example, average wages were analyzed for time-series patterns over the long and short run. It was apparent that the trends in wages for Buffalo and New Bedford (northeastern cities) were significantly greater than for Greensboro and, in particular, Johnstown. The sizes of the representative slope parameters for Buffalo and New Bedford were similar to those of Boston and Rochester's printing and publishing industry, analyzed above. Not only was Johnstown's employment significantly affected, but as well the rate of wage increases was quite slight when compared to other cities' wage trends. A test was also conducted for serial autocorrelation in the residuals derived from the trend equations. Only in the case of Buffalo could it be concluded that there was evidence of nonrandomness and serial autocorrelation in the pattern of residuals (at a fundamental frequency of 12 months). From this evidence, the following observations can be made. First, wage rigidity is a dominant characteristic of the apparel industry over a range of different cities, although the overall trends in wages are quite different and vary according to region. Secondly, in two instances

(New Bedford and Greensboro), hours worked was the principal short-run adjustment lever, although over time, employment changes dominated. In essence, price adjustments were very small, if not insignificant, and quantity adjustments were the norm.

The electrical and electronics equipment industry.   Figure 4.3 illustrates the patterns of local adjustment for four cities (Baltimore, Maryland; Little Rock, Arkansas; Rochester, New York; and Tampa, Florida) for the electronics and electrical equipment industry. Employment in this industry was clearly more volatile than was the case with the printing and publishing or apparel and textiles industries. The electronics and electrical equipment industry has been expanding and growing over the 1970s, relative to most other industries. This growth was evident in the employment profiles for Baltimore, Little Rock, and Tampa. As well, the industry closely matched the timing of national fluctuations. The exceptions were Baltimore, which declined much more rapidly (in terms of employment) than the nation, and Tampa, which lagged behind by about six months.

The largest decline in employment from local peak to trough was shown by Little Rock (24.9%), closely followed by Rochester (20.5%). However, there were marked similarities and differences between these two cities. Prior to recession, employers in both cities maintained high levels of overtime (as was the case in Baltimore and Tampa). In recovery, employers in Little Rock expanded both hours and employment. Employment increased in Little Rock by 42.9% but only by 11.1% in Rochester. In this regard, the latter city has some similarities to Johnstown in its printing and publishing industry performance. Employment in Baltimore's electronics and electrical equipment industry grew by 31.2% after the recession, just below that of Tampa (33.7%). As in previous cases, it is apparent that short-run, unexpected shifts in demand were filled through overtime (increased hours worked) rather than by immediately adding employment. It should also be recognized that layoffs were often quite sudden in all cities except Tampa. It is apparent from Figure 4.3 that prior to recession, hours worked declined significantly before changes in employment occurred. This pattern was less important in Rochester and insignificant for Baltimore and Little Rock.

By now, having analyzed wage trends in two other industries for different local labor markets, it would come as a surprise if there were a significant price adjustment in the electronic and electrical equipment industry. As expected, the trend again dominated the pattern of average wages. In this instance, however, the overall trend of increase evident in the estimates of the slope of the regression line was larger than in previous industries and cities. The steepest slope was Rochester's (4.8) and the shallowest slope was Tampa's (3.0). Notice that it was Rochester which

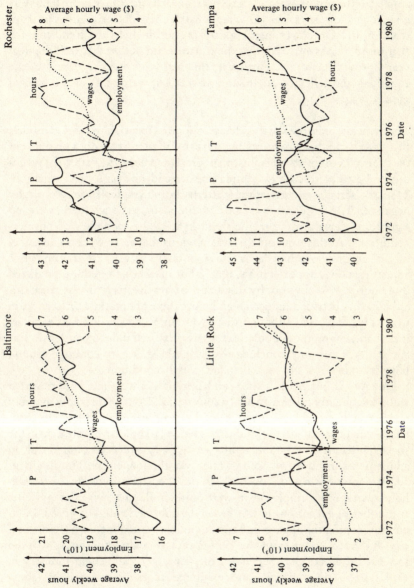

Figure 4.3 Local adjustment strategies (electrical and electronic equipment).

both experienced the largest decrease in employment during the recession *and* did not significantly recover after the recession. Rochester also had the largest initial average wage. A Kolmogorov–Smirnov test was again applied to the residuals from regression for each city. Once more there was no evidence of the residuals having a pattern significantly different from white noise. On closer inspection of the residuals of the trend-line for Baltimore, it was apparent that the equation did not predict well the final year's growth in wages. However, this was a problem for many of the equations and reflected an apparent overall upward shift in the path of money wages.

The evidence presented in this chapter supports local labor-market models that predict rigidities in prices and quantity adjustments, not volatility. In the examples of short-run adjustment presented here, the pattern of wages can be best described by a simple linear trend-line regression equation. Tests for serial autocorrelation (patterns in the residuals) were typically negative. The implication of our findings suggest that there were no significant deviations from the trend in response to phases of business conditions. At the same time, it was obvious that there were no instances of an absolute decline in average money wages. Short-run price adjustment does not exist in the local labor market – something predicted by Dunlop (1944) but not by implicit contract theorists. It was apparent, as well, that between industries and cities there are marked differences in overall wage trends, although there were more within-industry similarities than geographical similarities across different industry types. In this context, we can only conclude that wage bargains are contingent upon industry standards, not local demand–supply conditions.

Quantity adjustments in the local labor market were much more varied and consequently more difficult to summarize. In some instances, notably northern cities such as Boston, Buffalo, Baltimore, and New Bedford, employment across all three industries tended to be less volatile than in the south. Unanticipated rapid shifts in activity were accounted for in adjustments in hours worked, while over the longer run, employment adjustments dominated. For southern cities, business-cycle fluctuations in hours worked and employment were quite similar in terms of magnitude. A number of exceptions to this broad description should be noted. First, employment in the apparel and textiles industry of Johnstown (a northern city) did not recover from the 1974–5 recession although hours worked increased dramatically. Secondly, the paper and publishing industry in Dallas grew very rapidly and exhibited marked evidence of labor-hoarding despite business-cycle fluctuations. Rigidities in employment and emphasis upon hours worked as the key short-run adjustment mechanism indicated that implicit employment contracts may be important in some cities of both the south and the north of the USA. In contrast to the evidence for money wages, it was also apparent that adjustment strategies are quite variable across locations *within* the same industry. That is, employment contracts are geographically contingent.

Dunlop's (1944) union model, which predicted that wages are unaffected by business-cycle conditions, could be substantiated from the evidence presented in this chapter. However, money wage rigidity is also evident for cities and industries where unions are unimportant. One can only conclude, as implied by Dunlop, that it is not the existence of unions *per se* that creates rigidities; rather it is the unique character of capitalist labor markets that encourages continuous contractual relationships between employers and workers. With variations in levels of quantity adjustment across cities and industries, particularly those cities that trade off hours worked against the level of employment, one could also suggest the likelihood of contracts that "spread" the risks of employment across the business cycle.

Conclusions

Given a previous review of alternative notions of contract theory and the empirical results described above, an appropriate question at this point concerns the virtues of such notions of contract and local labor-market adjustment. Clearly, local labor-market rigidities which result from implicit or explicit employment contracts can be interpreted from a variety of perspectives. In fact, there are a variety of arguments which accept the existence of contracts, but at the same time depend upon a different logic. For instance, coercion instead of voluntarism, or duress instead of mutual collective agreement would give similar profiles (Clark 1983b). At the minimum, we must be cautious of the capacity of neoclassical implicit contract models to capture the reality of, in Dunlop's (1944) terms, the actual technical organization of capitalist labor markets. The neoclassical contract model idealizes reality, ignores the conflict and inequality inherent in capitalist labor relations, and treats as eternal the exchange roles of buyer and seller.

If local labor markets are fraught with more substantive disputes over the respective powers of employers and employees, what speculations could be made concerning the issue that set the context of this chapter? That is, given a choice between lowering wages, reducing hours of work, or reducing employment, what would be the strategies of labor and capital? These three variables go to the heart of employment relationships in that capital ultimately owns the job and commodities produced by labor. The fact is that workers depend upon employers for the sale of their labor power and income. In absolute terms they depend upon capital for sustenance. The only alternative is welfare supported by the state. Consequently, in a local labor market dominated by a small number of employers, one might expect worker strategies to involve compromises primarily on hours of work and wages rather than on employment itself. It is easier to compromise on the first two variables (up until the point where the total wage equals welfare) because workers ultimately depend on employers for the jobs themselves.

However, this suggests another implication. The objective function of workers must be the maintenance of employment continuity. Only if that is guaranteed are workers likely to focus upon wages, as suggested by Dunlop (1944). Employers who operate in small labor markets which can provide all their employment needs have enormous discretionary powers when negotiating implicit or explicit contracts. As long as labor mobility is limited (between other employers and between other labor markets), employers can exercise their full unilateral power – leading to high levels of instability in both employment *and* wages! Under these conditions, bilateral wage agreements are of minor importance in contract negotiations. Money wages can be increased in accordance with the rate of inflation because the total wage bill can be manipulated by changing the absolute stock of workers. As well, coercive force can be used to increase productivity per worker, with no fear of losing workers to another employer. Small labor markets dominated by few employers are the domain of capitalist unilateral power.

What then are the likely strategies of labor and capital in larger labor markets with many more employers? As long as employers do not act in collusion, bilateral negotiation is the key to contractual relations. To the extent that labor is specialized and in limited supply in the short run, bilateral contract negotiation could take place on a more even footing. Employment continuity is more likely to be a negotiable item as the pattern of money wages is likely to become a more contentious issue. Consequently, greater employment stability and continuity is likely up until the point where workers are in such short supply that they can significantly improve their wages and conditions by switching between employers (Clark 1981b). At that point, employment stability becomes a major goal for employers (not employees) and becomes interrelated with wages as negotiable items in terms of their employment contracts. Over the long run, however, employers operating in these conditions will tend toward capital intensification as a strategy of lessening their dependence upon labor (as we saw in Ch. 3).

These speculations are generally consistent with the patterns of local hours, wages, and employment shown in the previous part of this chapter. Notice as well that the pattern of rigidities and fluctuations can be deduced from the particular characteristics of each local labor market and the distribution of power (unilateral and bilateral) in society. Thus we can hypothesize specific patterns of interaction and adjustment between hours, employment, and wages, something which is virtually impossible in neoclassical implicit contract theory. A second implication is that we are not reduced to a marxian version of the Phillips curve (compare Rowthorn 1980) to understand the patterns of wages in different types of local labor market. Wages are obviously influenced by labor supply and turnover, but this issue is not the only determinant of wage changes. Price-competitive firms may raise their wage rates if their total wage bills can be manipulated with respect to other local firms and other parts of the country, according to notions such as "fairness", without compromising the competitive positions of such firms. The argument made here was that labor markets are not commodity markets since they implicitly involve nonexchange relations. The fundamental determinant of these relations is the distribution of power. Thus, the terms of contracts are structured by the local *context* in which workers and employers operate.

5   Regional demand for labor

Introduction

The High-Technology Industry Council of Massachusetts, an employer organization representing firms associated with the burgeoning semi-conductor industry, has complained in recent years about the cost and availability of labor. They contend that not only are skilled, highly educated workers difficult to find and retain, but even production workers are in limited supply. Digital, the multinational computer company with headquarters in Massachusetts, has also contended that labor is in short supply, arguing that the Boston area has become expensive compared to lower-wage regions in other parts of the USA. In response, Massachusetts state economic development agencies have sought to reduce the cost of labor through tax credits and wage subsidies. These policies take seriously the neoclassical notion that the demand for labor is a function of its relative price (relative, that is, to the market price of output and marginal productivity of labor). And, in many other states, economic development agencies obviously believe this conception, as is made evident by their advertising in the national media of the relative cost advantages of locating in their states.

Despite the apparent faith of local policy makers in the neoclassical labor demand model, and the claims of industry representatives, it is not clear that labor markets actually function according to theoretical expectations. Wages are quite inflexible in the short run, exhibiting little sensitivity to changing demand and supply conditions (see Ch. 4). Interregional wage patterns tend to be dominated by industry trends, not by local conditions that would give firms relative price advantages in the national market. Wage subsidies may be simple cash transfers between governments and business, with little real effect on the local demand for labor (Clark 1983a). If the price of labor is not the crucial determinant of labor demand, then what is? There are a number of possible answers. Kaldor (1970) contended that wage inflation can be offset by increased labor productivity and output, and thus wages can increase as the demand for labor increases. Others contend that profit is the crucial determinant; given a fixed wage, output and presumably employment are varied so as to attain a targeted profit rate. In these instances, quantity adjustment is the rule, not price adjustment, as assumed by local economic development agencies.

This chapter considers in detail the determinants of local labor demand. The neoclassical real-wage hypothesis is evaluated using data from two industries, textiles and electrical and electronics, in a set of southern, western, and northern US states over the period 1954–79. Analytically, the testing framework was based on a time-series methodology which is concerned with the paths of adjustment of labor demand to changes in various determinants. Since it is shown that the neoclassical model is of limited applicability, we also consider alternative models, premised upon fix-price assumptions, emphasizing quantity adjustment as opposed to price adjustment. Profit, output, and capital-to-labor ratios are considered in a sequence of alternative tests of theories and implied policies. Time-series labor demand equations were estimated in the context of regional and industrial growth and decline during the postwar era, using the autoregressive maximum likelihood estimation procedure developed by Beach and MacKinnon (1978).

Wages as prices

Neoclassical economic theory is so well known that we need not dwell for long upon its intricacies. Efficient allocation of scarce resources is the objective of neoclassical theory. The price of any good, be it labor or cheese, is both a signal that enables exchange and a means of valuation. Given a set of resources, tastes and preferences, the use of any good or factor of production will be determined by demand. And given a set of possible uses for resources, their specific use will be allocated to those willing to pay the highest price. Prices then effectively provide a relative measure of the value of any set of goods. Assuming marginal productivity conditions and perfect competition, neoclassical theory supposes that demand and supply will equilibrate at full employment. Again it is prices that make this result possible; they are assumed to be infinitely flexible, and are the means of allocating resources.

The price of labor, its wage, is similarly assumed to reflect its relative value, relative, that is, to other competing uses and other competing inputs, like capital. Three steps of logic are implied in this statement. First, it is assumed that firms are price takers, adjusting output and the demand for labor in accordance with market signals. Secondly, in such a competitive world, no firm would or could, given conditions of "normal" profit, pay labor more than the value of its marginal product. In this manner the price of labor is directly linked to the market price of firms' outputs. Labor is paid a real wage, its nominal wage weighted by the price of output. Differences between individuals in their productivity would allow for variations in wages, but not in the market price of output. A more productive individual would be paid more than a less productive individual; a tautological statement which is implied in the marginal productivity assumption. Thirdly, assuming a perfectly integrated commodity market, all goods would be produced at their least costs. The result should be pareto equilibrium, wherein no further exchanges would be made without making at least one person worse off.

For policy makers concerned with stimulating local economic development, the implications of this model are stark. For instance, given a national – even an international – commodity market, local agencies must ensure that local firms are competitive. A condition for competitive strength is that labor must be paid the value of its marginal product; that is, local wages must be standardized by the market price of output and labor productivity. It is also required that local firms must be as competitive as other firms in the industry, regardless of location. For regions dominated by older and less efficient firms, this means that the competitive strengths of other more efficient firms outside the region would directly affect the pricing behavior of local firms. Consequently, labor in the older region would be paid less than labor in other regions. It should not come as a surprise to see economic development agencies focus upon reducing the real costs of local production through subsidies and tax credits.

National policy makers have also taken this theory seriously, insisting that maximum national wealth is possible only if production and resources are sectorally and spatially allocated in accordance with their most efficient uses. The 1982 *President's national urban policy report* (US Department of Housing and Urban Development), for example, contended that national wealth has been compromised by past attempts to stimulate local economic development regardless of the best market solutions. Plant closing legislation, minimum wages, and local direct job creation programs have all been the targets of conservative critics of local development policies. Enterprise zones have been promoted by the federal government, and depend to a large extent on the real wage notion of neoclassical theory. The costs of production are reduced via reduced regulations, differential wage scales, and the like, *and* the demand for labor thereby stimulated. Again, competitive pricing is assumed and "institutional" forces that are thought to maintain artificially high wages are implicated as being the causes of higher local unemployment.

These arguments are familiar to many. The most immediate question, however, is whether or not empirical evidence supports the theory and its policy prescriptions. To evaluate the proposition that the demand for labor is a function of its real wage, data were collected from the US Census of Manufactures and the Federal Reserve Bank of Boston for two industries, textiles (a declining industry) and the electrical and electronics equipment industry (a growing industry), and a set of northern, southern and western US states. By choosing this set of industries and places, it was hoped that the geographical diversity and range of different employment conditions would be given fullest expression. For example, textiles in Kentucky and North Carolina is a growth industry when compared to textiles in Massachusetts and New York. On the other hand, the electrical and electronics equipment industry has been growing in many states since 1954, and has accelerated in recent years especially in California.

The relationships tested regarding the neoclassical "wages as prices" hypothesis were:

$$\text{MHOURS}_t^{i,j} = a + b\ \text{RWAGES}_{t-1}^{i,j} + \epsilon_t \tag{5.1}$$

and

$$\text{MHOURS}_t^{i,j} = a + b\ \text{RWAGES}_{t-1}^{i,j} + c\ \text{LPROD}_{t-1}^{i,j} + \epsilon_t \tag{5.2}$$

where the dependent variable MHOURS was the formal labor demand dependent variable for a point in time t, state i and industry j, and RWAGES and LPROD the relevant real wage and average labor productivity independent variables for state i and industry j lagged one time period $t - 1$. Real wages were measured by total compensation per year per production employee weighted by the national producer price index for the relevant industry. This index measures "average change in prices received in primary markets of the United States by producers of commodities in all states of production" (Bureau of Labor Statistics, 1982b: 166). In this context, the real wage is defined from the producers' perspective.

All variables in these, and subsequent, empirical tests were differenced so that instead of dealing with levels, we dealt with changes over time. Total man–hours, rather than employment, were chosen to represent labor demand, because there are a number of different strategies that can be used by employers to vary the quantity of their labor input. Actual changes in the level of employment is one strategy, but so too is overtime. Man–hours is the most general variable that indicates labor demand (Baily 1977). Since the estimated equations were based on yearly time-series, an estimation method sensitive to serial autocorrelation was required. Beach and MacKinnon's (1978) maximum likelihood regression procedure (MLRP) was used to account for possible biases that may result from the existence of first-order autoregressive autocorrelation.

Hazledine (1978) has noted that there have been few tests of dynamic labor demand functions that have used disaggregated sectoral data, let alone disaggregated spatial data. On these two counts we expected to see variations in parameter estimates, as well perhaps as variations in parameter signs and significance levels. It should also be acknowledged that the use of lagged independent variables also implies a number of assumptions. First, like Nickell (1978), we assume that a firm's demand for labor changes slowly in response to changes in determining variables. Transaction costs of hiring and firing workers as well as fixed technical production relationships between labor and capital all conspire to make labor demand a lagged adjustment process. Notice, however, that since the data are yearly we assumed the lag in adjustment to be captured by the previous years' observation. Secondly, and more technically, we would also argue that if we are to establish causality between the dependent and independent variables, the temporal sequence of change and response must be unambiguous. Thus, we use a time-series methodology that tests adjustment of the dependent variable to changes in the independent variables in the previous time period.

Results of analysis indicated that the "wages as prices" hypothesis is hardly tenable as a *general* explanation of the demand for labor. Assuming that labor demand is an inverse function of real wages, the results in Table 5.1a provide little systematic evidence for policies that seek to reduce the local cost of labor as a condition for further employment growth. For the sample states with electrical and electronics equipment industries, the signs on the wage parameter were positive, implying that increasing real wages are associated with increasing labor demand in the subsequent period. This is not the result predicted by neoclassical theory; the sign on the wage parameter should have been negative. For textiles, two states did in fact have significant negative parameters, Massachusetts and New York – two states that have been characterized as declining (absolutely and relatively) in terms of the national growth patterns of that industry. Yet for Kentucky and North Carolina, two relative growth states for textiles, the signs are positive, even though in the case of Kentucky the parameter is insignificant.

Table 5.1a Labor demand and real wages by state and industry.

Industry/state	a	b	DW	R^2	ρ
electrical and electronics					
Arkansas	−34500*	10200*	1.78	0.71*	0.67*
California	−50400	29600*	1.47	−0.01	0.74*
Indiana	74700	11000*	1.64	0.33*	0.66*
New York (d)	−4020	22200	1.87	0.17*	0.43
textiles					
Kentucky	3500	1160	1.50	0.01	0.60*
Massachusetts	171000*	−18000*	1.55	0.85*	0.47
New York	130000*	−6900*	1.52	0.69*	0.52*
North Carolina	311000*	29000*	1.70	0.76*	0.65*

* Significant at the 95% level.
(d) Double differenced.

Other writers have found positive and significant signs on real-wage parameters, particularly when modelling the short-run dynamics of labor demand. Hamermesh (1975) explained this result by what he termed the "interdependence effect." Essentially, workers are assumed to be very sensitive to changes in relative earnings, more so than to wage levels. The wages of one group of workers are the reference point for another so that, in general, there exists a high degree of interdependence between workers in their relative wages. As a consequence of increasing the wage of one group of workers (for example, in response to increasing labor productivity), a firm may have to adjust the wages of all workers. Otherwise, those workers not included in the wage increase may slacken their work effort. If this were to happen, according to Hamermesh (1975), firms may be required to increase the hours worked of all employees, or even hire extra employees to sustain targeted production levels. In this sense increasing wages would cause increasing labor demand.

Lack of theoretical consistency in sign and significance of the real-wage parameter is consistent with aggregate empirical macroeconomic studies that have found real wages to be of limited importance in explaining the demand for labor (Hazledine 1981). In response, some writers have included labor productivity variables on the assumption that real wages may not adequately reflect variations in labor productivity. Table 5.1b reports the results of a test of such an augmented neoclassical labor demand model. The results of this test are even more disheartening for those who would depend upon the veracity of the neoclassical model. There were few significant coefficients (and all were positive) found in the real-wage variable and the labor productivity coefficients were uniformly insignificant.

Table 5.1b Labor demand, real wages, and labor productivity by state and industry.

Industry/state	a	b	c	DW	R^2	ρ
electrical and electronics						
Arkansas	−34600*	10300*	−19	1.80	0.71*	0.67*
California (d)	2800	20100	827	1.83	0.06	0.11
Indiana	78100	9950	319	1.64	0.33*	0.67*
New York (d)	−4249	22300	294	1.86	0.76	0.21
textiles						
Kentucky (d)	385	−274	−112	1.88	0.02	0.08
Massachusetts	167000*	−15300	−1150	1.55	0.85*	0.49*
New York	−4640*	17000*	−316	1.83	0.52*	−0.19
North Carolina	276000*	47800*	−6430	1.75	0.78*	0.63*

* Significant at the 95% level.
(d) Double differenced.

Prices and profits

If changing wages have little relevance in the majority of states and industries studied here, as signals for allocating resources, what then determines changes in the demand for labor? And, if increasing real wages are related to employment and production restructuring, we still require an explanation of the demand for labor *per se*. One implication to be drawn from the fact that increases in real wages rarely have a negative effect on changes in the demand for labor relates to firm pricing practices in general. If production costs do not directly affect factor demand, then there is some question as to the general significance of commodity prices being the signals for final demand. Perhaps commodity prices are not set on the basis of cost but rather on the basis of profit. That is, if input costs are assumed given or predictable, then variations in product demand over the short run would be reflected in changing profit levels. A second implication is that some firms may price their products on a cost-plus (or mark-up) schedule that has as its objective function a certain expected profit (Kalecki 1971).

This scenario is not as neat as the neoclassical vision of competition in a flex-price world. The expected profit hypothesis depends upon a set of arguments that essentially deny the validity of neoclassical competitive market assumptions. For instance, lack of immediate importance of input cost constraints in setting commodity prices suggests that either demand for firms' commodities is relatively secure regardless of price, or that commodities are rationed in the market by quantity produced. In either event the price of the good is likely to be relatively stable, and less sensitive to every shift in demand than assumed by neoclassical theory. Gordon (1981) has noted, in fact, that commodity prices are sticky, like money wages, and that they are clearly less sensitive to demand than, for example, to output. Indeed, consumer prices adjust relatively slowly whether at the national or local levels (see Ch. 7).

There are three possible explanations for price insensitivity to demand. First, we could argue that with many industries which are dominated by few firms and are national, rather than local, commodity markets, oligopolistic practices obviously apply. With few sellers and many buyers, firms could operate to ration supply, thereby sustaining prices that cover production costs and assure a certain profit. With limited supply, prices would hardly vary to the extent predicted by neoclassical theory, and firms would adjust their production (and hence the demand for labor) according to changes in their profits. Secondly, it is also plausible that some industries are also able to ignore input prices because demand for their products is so strong. For instance, calculators were very popular and were in great demand in the 1970s throughout the USA. Revolutions in production technology, component parts, and very large-scale production drastically reduced per unit prices as demand accelerated. Again, under these conditions the demand for labor is hardly likely to be sensitive to real wages, and is more likely to be sensitive to the pattern of profits. Thirdly, Iwai (1981) has suggested that many firms write contracts precisely to avoid rapid fluctuations (and the costs associated) in input and commodity prices. As a consequence, prices change slowly and only after a protracted period of time.

Under these conditions, commodity prices are set in accordance with a cost-plus mark-up system. Thus the demand for labor is simply a function of profit. To test this hypothesis, the following two relationships were evaluated for the sample industries, states, and time period noted in the previous section:

$$\text{MHOURS}_t^{i,j} = a + b \text{ RPROFIT}_{t-1}^{i,j} + \epsilon_t \qquad (5.3)$$

and

$$\text{MHOURS}_t^{i,j} = a + b \text{ RPROFIT/K}_{t-1}^{i,j} + \epsilon_t \qquad (5.4)$$

where RPROFIT and RPROFIT/K were respectively the gross (before taxes) real profit of each industry–state combination and the real profit (again before taxes) on capital invested. Real profit was measured by gross profits, before tax, of firms in each state and industry, weighted by the producer price index. Profits were calculated by subtracting the total wage bill of all employees, and the cost of other inputs, from the total value-added of the industry and state. Real profit on capital invested measured real profits relative to the value of real net capital invested for each industry and state. Both series were standardized by 1972 producer prices. The sources for the capital data were the Federal Reserve Bank of Boston and Gertler (1983). Using the MLRP of Beach and MacKinnon (1978), equations 5.3 and 5.4 were transformed to adjustment modes so that changes in the demand for labor were functionally related to previous changes in gross real profit and gross real profit on capital invested. For interpretive purposes, we could imagine that equation 5.3 represents the managers' notion of profit; on the other hand, equation 5.4 could represent investors' or share-holders' notions of profit.

Real profit, the managers' version, was clearly an important determinant of the demand for labor in the electrical and electronics equipment industry (see Table 5.2a). Not only was the parameter of the correct sign (positive, implying that an increase in profit will increase the demand for labor and vice versa) and significant for the states of Arkansas, California, and Indiana, but the coefficients of determination were also very reasonable for a time-series methodology. However, it was also true that for the textile industry in general, real profit was not a significant determinant of the demand for labor. This was despite the fact that in some instances the coefficients of determination were quite strong. What is

Table 5.2a Labor demand and real profit by state and industry.

Industry/state	a	b	DW	R^2	ρ
electrical and electronics					
Arkansas	5550*	0.13*	1.88	0.66*	0.57*
California	149000*	0.60*	1.63	0.60*	0.91*
Indiana	110000*	0.07*	1.71	0.49*	0.50*
New York (d)	262	0.01	1.83	0.02	0.34
textiles					
Kentucky	7380*	0.04	1.68	0.03	0.61*
Massachusetts	80700*	−0.01	1.53	0.19	0.98*
New York	77200*	0.05	1.88	0.54*	0.94*
North Carolina	382000*	0.06	1.70	0.72*	0.60*

* Significant at the 95% level.
(d) Double differenced.

immediately apparent is that gross real profit is significant for southern, western and northern states in the electronics industry, a general result that cuts across geography, and something that was not the case when we considered the impacts of real wages on the demand for labor. When real profit from the investors' point of view is included as the independent variable a markedly different picture emerges (see Table 5.2b). This variable is not significant for any industry or state.

Thus far we have two broad conclusions. Real wages are only significant and of the correct sign in determining the demand for labor for two northern states with textile industries. Real profits, on the other hand, are significant and important determinants of the demand for labor in the electronics industry for states from a variety of US regions. This industry is one that has grown rapidly over the past two decades, and the observations made above concerning the "sticky" nature of prices may apply with some force. For instance, for many product lines, demand has expanded rapidly (as for electronic calculators and the like) and technology has transformed both the nature of production and the commodity itself (for example, portable radios). At the same time, the industry has become more concentrated, leading to a reduced importance for competitive pricing and an increased likelihood of the strategy of profit targeting being used.

For an economic development agency aiming to stimulate local employment, these results have two specific implications. First, the notion of cost efficiency seems much less relevant for growing industries compared to declining industries. In fact, given the relative insignificance of input prices as constraints for firms in the electronics industry, policies such as wage subsidies may simply be cash transfers to those firms rather than incentives to hire more labor. At the same time, it is also plausible that

Table 5.2b Labor demand and real profit on capital invested by state and industry.

Industry/state	a	b	DW	R^2	ρ
electrical and electronics					
Arkansas	16000	0.54	1.68	−0.24	0.96*
California	164000*	418.00	1.50	−0.20	0.93*
Indiana	141000*	17.60	1.66	0.28	0.75
New York (d)	−448	−0.54	1.85	−0.01	0.30
textiles					
Kentucky	7460*	1.47	1.73	0.04	0.66*
Massachusetts	83300*	−11.40	1.55	0.21	0.98*
New York	88300*	5.81	1.76	0.54*	0.93*
North Carolina	44000*	0.66	1.69	0.69*	0.79*

* Significant at the 95% level.
(d) Double differenced.

wage interdependence may lead to employment restructuring, so that in the longer run the whole local economy may itself be transformed (Clark 1981a). Secondly, it is also apparent that the demand for labor is quite sensitive to profit, albeit a quite specific definition of profit. Conventional accounting notions of profit relative to capital invested are not as relevant as the gross flow of profits. For firms that finance expansion internally (that is, generate their own funds by tapping revenue), the gross flow concept is obviously crucial. Profit begets profit or, as Kalecki (1971) once remarked, "capitalists get what they spend."

We must be careful, however, not to overplay the results found in this section. In particular, it is obvious that the gross-profits hypothesis did not work for New York, a state with quite a vibrant electronics industry. It is also apparent that for textiles, we still must explain labor demand for Kentucky, a state in which neither the real-wage nor the real-profits hypothesis succeeded in significantly explaining the demand for labor. North Carolina's textile industry also presents a slight problem in that, although the demand for labor increases with real wages, the real-profits variable was not significant. In the electronics industry, high wages and profits were associated; in textiles this may not be the case.

Output and labor adjustment

Keynesian economists often argue that price adjustment is rare in a modern economy, and that quantity adjustment is the rule. As demand changes in the short run, firms adapt by changing output, not the price of their goods nor the price of their inputs. As a consequence, prices are "sticky" in the short run and productive resources are allocated on the basis of quantity requirements. From this position it is then argued that, as output changes, so too does the demand for labor. Essentially, quantity adjustment brings forth further quantity adjustments. Presuming that prices do not vary in the short run, there should be a direct relationship between output and employment.

Indeed, many short-run labor demand models have no price or profit variables, preferring instead to link employment to output and lagged values of itself (see especially Ball & St. Cyr, 1966). In the absence of output measures, employment then becomes a lagged function of itself. Of course, theoretically, the supposed adjustment process is more complex than its empirical representation. Firms are assumed to have a desired level of employment, subject to planned output. In some instances, such as Peel and Walker (1978), scale variables are also included to account for particular production functions (for instance, CES formulations), and their implied labor demand schedules. Because employment fluctuates less than output in the short run, and because desired employment levels cannot be measured, the theoretical elegance of these models often degenerates into the empirical forms noted above.

Conventional regional econometric models, such as the economic base formulation, take this logic as an article of faith. Indeed, so well accepted is the supposed relationship between output and employment that few researchers bother to make the logic explicit, let alone test its veracity. Employment is taken as the proxy for output, and the derived economic base multiplier asserts (albeit implicitly) a one-to-one correspondence between employment and output. Debates rage over the proper time horizon for estimating employment multipliers, with some authors contending that the multiplier is relevant only for short-run situations, holding the stock of capital constant (see Gerking & Isserman 1981 for a recent re-examination of the evidence). For writers such as Kaldor (1970), however, this relationship is a central aspect for explaining continuing regional inequality. Over time (perhaps the long run in Kaldor's terms), given initial production and locational conditions, increase in the output and scale of production leads to greater demand for labor. Migration from depressed to rapidly growing regions sustains the increasing demand for labor, further impoverishing the periphery. The Verdoorn (1949) "effect" is essentially one based on a particular output–employment assumption.

Yet for all the apparent importance of this concept in the regional economic development literature, the evidence noted below hardly supports the notion of a direct relationship between changes in output and changes in the demand for labor. The following relationship was tested:

$$\text{MHOURS}_t^{i,j} = a + b\ \text{RPROFIT}_{t-1}^{i,j} + c\ \text{ROUTPUT}_{t-1}^{i,j} + \epsilon_t \quad (5.5)$$

where ROUTPUT was the variable representing the output hypothesis.

Real output measured the value of output, or value-added, based on the 1972 producer price index for the two industries and their states. Real profit was retained as an independent variable to hold constant revenue effects. Again, the whole relationship was transformed to be dynamic, concerned with changes, *not* levels.

In the previous section it was observed that changes in real profits are important determinants of changes in the demand for labor in the electronics industry, but not the textile industry. However, when we take output into account, it is obvious that neither real profit nor real output is a significant determinant of the demand for labor (Table 5.3). This was true for both industries and all states; there were no exceptions! For those models that have assumed employment to best represent output, for example, the economic base model, this result must be viewed with a great deal of alarm. It is agreed that these results are based on a dynamic time-series model, and it is true that, cross-sectionally, output and employment are highly correlated, yet these results also imply that the most conventional and widely used regional impact model may have little empirical veracity. Models utilized by authors such as Vernez *et al.* (1977), which deal explicitly with employment as an indicator of short-run demand shifts, may be prone to significant errors.

Lest the reader dismiss this result as an aberration, we should hasten to note its consistency with other recent macroeconomic and regional labor-market studies. Hall (1980), in a study of employment fluctuations at the national level, observed that output is clearly more volatile than employment in the short run. In fact, employment is quite sticky, adjusting much more slowly than output to consumer demand shifts. Elsewhere it has been observed that this is also the case in many local labor markets (see the previous chapter).

Table 5.3 Labor demand, real profit, and real output by state and industry.

Industry/state	a	b	c	DW	R^2	ρ
electrical and electronics						
Arkansas	5530*	0.08	0.03	1.87	0.69*	0.54*
California	132000*	0.56	0.01	1.65	−0.16	0.84*
Indiana	121000*	0.16	−0.05	1.72	0.51*	0.53*
New York (d)	−1700	−0.08	0.59	1.81	0.11	0.23
textiles						
Kentucky	4140*	−0.38	0.30	1.67	0.29*	0.40
Massachusetts	54200	−0.27	0.17	1.93	0.40*	0.96*
New York	63200*	−0.05	0.07	1.94	0.53*	0.94*
North Carolina	319000*	−0.32	0.20	1.82	0.76*	0.61*

* Significant at the 95% level.
(d) Double differenced.

Wages and profits

The final issue we wish to address regarding the determinants of the demand for labor relates to the relationships between capital and labor. In particular, the question considered in this section is whether or not changes in the distribution of income (in the form of wages and profits) affect changes in the demand for labor. Radicals have argued that in the short run, given total revenue, as labor exerts a stronger hold over capital (as, for example, in a boom period), wages should increase relative to profit, initiating a subsequent decline in the demand for labor (Rowthorn 1980). This argument is essentially premised upon a zero–sum conception of income distribution. All we need assume is that the stock of labor is relatively limited in the short run, albeit sometimes underemployed.

To investigate the relevance of this hypothesis, an empirical test was developed such that:

$$\text{MHOURS}_t^{i,j} = a + b\,\text{RJUST}_{t-1}^i + c\,\text{KIN}_{t-1}^{i,j} + \epsilon_t \qquad (5.6)$$

where RJUST was the ratio of real profits to real wages and KIN was the capital intensity of production. Income distribution was measured as the relative shares of gross real profit and the total real-wage bill as a ratio based on the variables noted above. Capital intensity was measured, and the amount of capital per production employee was standardized by the 1972 producer price index. So as to retain the concern with dynamic adjustment, these variables were also differenced.

The results of analyzing this relationship are shown in Table 5.4. In only one instance were changes in the distribution of income between capital and labor a significant determinant of changes in the demand for labor. For

Table 5.4 Labor demand, income distribution, and capital intensity by state and industry.

Industry/state	a	b	c	DW	R^2	ρ
electrical and electronics						
Arkansas	14100	230	447000	1.69	−0.24	0.96*
California (d)	17700	27800	-0.2×10^7	1.88	0.03	0.02
Indiana	51700	101000*	0.3×10^7	1.71	0.49*	0.69*
New York (d)	13000	−51600	-0.2×10^7	1.83	0.15	0.14
textiles						
Kentucky	9280*	−254	−137000	1.64	0.02	0.75*
Massachusetts	110000*	−22700	-1.2×10^7	1.84	0.46*	0.95*
New York	92900*	7470	-0.1×10^7	1.80	0.56*	0.91*
North Carolina	370000*	90600	0.1×10^7	1.63	0.72*	0.70*

* Significant at the 95% level.
(d) Double differenced.

Indiana's electronics industry an increase in profits relative to wages will cause an increase in the demand for labor in the subsequent time period. Otherwise, there was no apparent relationship between the distribution of income and the demand for labor, holding capital intensity constant for the other states and industries. This result should not come as too much of a surprise. After all, over the 1954–76 period, real wages *and* real profits generally increased for many sectors and geographical areas. Indeed, this period is dominated by the sustained postwar economic boom that extended through to the early 1970s. Only in the last couple of years of the period under study was there any apparent systematic shift in this pattern.

Even the significant parameter result for Indiana has some ambiguity. The positive sign on the estimated parameter indicates that as profits increase relative to wages, so does the demand for labor. Previously it was noted that real profits by themselves are significant determinants of the demand for labor both in the electronics industry and in Indiana. Thus both results may in fact measure the same phenomenon: the demand for labor is sensitive to the *flow of profits*. It is nevertheless striking that the relationship is significant for Indiana's electrical and electronics industry. This state and industry have in the past been dominated by the auto industry (principally as a component manufacturer), with many similar labor relations practices: *very* high wages, stable workforces and a great deal of union organizing.

Conclusions

Many state economic development agencies in the USA are significantly involved in stimulating the local demand for labor. Although the policies and practices vary from state to state, two types of policies can be identified. The first could be thought of as an input–cost subsidy approach, wherein the logic of conventional neoclassical theory is followed. Assuming that firms operate in a competitive price environment, any policy that reduces the costs of production – like wage subsidies – would presumably stimulate the demand for labor as firms' commodities become more competitive. The evidence presented here did not support this supposition, except in two cases, the textile industry in two states, Massachusetts and New York (which confirms Tannenwald's 1982 case-study findings). For states where textiles and electronics have been growing, it is apparent that the cost of labor is not the crucial constraint on labor demand. Furthermore, it is apparent that wage interdependence may exist in growth industries–states, leading to *short-run* increases in the demand for labor.

One explanation of this result could be that in many industries prices do not perform their allocative function as suggested by neoclassical theory.

In fact, prices of commodities and labor are quite sticky in the short run, implying that quantity adjustment is crucial. However, when we tested for the relationship between changes in output and changes in the demand for labor, no significant short-run relationship could be established. It is simply not the case that changes in output and employment are closely related in the short run, despite their cross-sectional correlation. The economic base multiplier is on very shaky ground as a predictive tool, let alone as an evaluative method. Thus, the input–cost type of policy cannot be sustained in its most obvious case (real wages as prices) or even in its modified quantity-adjustment case where, *given* real wages and commodity prices, output is the crucial lever.

The second general type of economic development policy is based on profits. In this chapter, evidence was presented that confirms the logic of this approach. For the electronics industry in three of the four states, it is gross real profits that determine the demand for labor. Notice, however, that profits were measured before taxes, and were significant only as a stream of revenue. When the demand for labor was related to profits on capital invested, no significant relationship was observed. A related test, that of the significance of changes in the distribution of income between capital and labor for changes in the demand for labor, was found to be generally insignificant. For an economic development agency contemplating these results, one thing stands clear. If gross profits can be stimulated, then so can the local demand for labor. But this implies quite stark public-sector distributional consequences which may not be politically palatable.

6 *The risks of local adjustment*

Introduction

Until now empirical analysis of employment in this book has been conducted at the aggregate scale. We have provided a detailed statistical analysis of the determinants of employment, and we also have provided an analytical account of how fluctuations in employment in localities affect the contractual structure of local employment relations. In this chapter we deal with two interrelated issues: the broad geography of economic fluctuations in American cities over the past decade, and how these fluctuations are translated into job risk at the local level. The former issue can provide us with a portrait of the geography of regional economic adjustment, although it still remains distant from the interests and fears of individual workers. But, of course, in many ways it is the questions which surround the local fortunes of the individual workers which are of crucial interest, given our stated concerns for the allocation of adjustment costs.

In this chapter, therefore, we provide preliminary answers to questions about the path of regional economic adjustment and its associated risks from the perspective of the individual worker. We assume individuals want to know how the broad spatial pattern of economic risk affects them in the most immediate of ways: how secure is their job? What are the chances that they might lose it? How is this risk distributed over time? Is a new job more risky than one held for a while? How do their chances of job loss vary from industry to industry? Or from place to place? Obviously a complete and systematic analysis of the geography of employment risk is well beyond the scope of this particular book.

The analysis presented in this chapter concerns a previous study by Whiteman (1985) on the geography of economic fluctuations, and is a pilot study of the allocation of employment risk at the local level. In this study we seek to establish two things. First, we postulate and develop an empirical methodology to answer the personal kinds of questions which have just been outlined. Secondly, a selected set of preliminary empirical results are developed from which we draw tentative conclusions regarding the local patterns of employment risk in Dallas and Pittsburgh.

Geographical profiles of employment dynamics

In Chapter 4 we described the adjustment paths of a group of cities and industries over the period 1972–80. It was shown for individual cities how national trends and cycles were played out over the economic landscape, emphasizing discontinuities of time and space. There were major variations between individual cities and industries: variations in growth and decline, variations in the severity of recessions and the extent and speed of recovery, and variations in the profile of adjustment between layoffs (and hirings), the length of the working week, and money wages. In this section we review, more generally, the patterns of employment change across metropolitan economies between two peaks of the business cycle, November 1973 to July 1981. This broad perspective will then be followed by a detailed analysis of employment risk in the cities over this period.

In a study of metropolitan employment dynamics, Whiteman (1985) described a geographical profile of employment which has some similarities to that found by other researchers (see, for example, Gertler 1983). Employment decline was heavily concentrated in the northcentral and northeast regions, although the northeast had a noticeably buoyant subregion, New England, centered on the Boston economy. Apart from Boston, growth in his sample was concentrated in the west and south, particularly in the west-southcentral region (which included Dallas). "Stable" city economies, outside of New England, were all to be found in the far midwest (west-northcentral) and in the south. In contrast to other studies of regional and metropolitan growth in capital stocks and job totals, Whiteman found a higher incidence of *absolute* decline. There were several reasons for this finding. First, the period 1972–82 was a particularly economically troubled and turbulent period. Secondly, the data presented were only for manufacturing employment, the slowest growing sector of the US economy.

A more complete picture emerges once we consider sectoral composition. Whiteman found that, with the single exception of mining, manufacturing employment grew at the lowest rate of all US SIC divisions over the period 1967–77, a growth in employment of only 1.7% in ten years. If the period 1977–82 (a period of pervasive decline) is included, it was found that manufacturing employment actually declined over the past ten years by 5%. National employment growth has been generally found in the retail, services, and government sectors. The wholesale trade sector and the financial, insurance and real estate offices sectors have also made a substantial contribution to employment growth. The slowest national sectors have been transportation, manufacturing and mining.

These national changes in employment growth and composition have had a remarkable, differential regional character. Considering all employment, not merely manufacturing employment, it was found by Whiteman that the northeast dramatically lagged behind the rest of the nation, and was the slowest growth region. The fastest growth region was, as expected, the south, which outstripped even the west. The northcentral region experienced moderate employment growth rate, midway between the fast and slow growth regions. In more detail, Whiteman (1985) found that while employment in the northeast grew comparatively slowly, it was the northeast that made the most radical transformation toward the "service economy." Of course, the national trend toward greater levels of service employment was evident in all regions; however, this trend was fastest in those regions where decline in manufacturing employment was highest.

Even though manufacturing activity in American cities may still be growing in the south and west, its relative importance within the urban economy is declining everywhere. The pride of place of manufacturing as the single largest economic sector in the city has been severely challenged by both the retail and service divisions and to a lesser extent by government. The importance of wholesaling and transportation is declining, as is that of construction. Employment growth in finance, insurance, and real estate is holding its own as a share of the urban economy. Regionally, the picture is more varied. The northcentral region appeared to be most "backward" of all regions in terms of the rate of increase in service sector employment. Whiteman noted that in northcentral cities, 32% of all economic activity is still in manufacturing. In the northeast the figure is only 27%, in the south 19%, and in the west 21%. Outside of the northcentral region the compositional profiles of urban economies have changed to be more service-oriented. This trend toward service employment is more marked in the south and west, and especially in the northeast, particularly in the New England subregion of the northeast.

The compositional changes in industrial sectors and in urban economies described above did not occur at a steady and even pace over the period 1972–82. In correspondence with business-cycle fluctuations there have been times when employment decline has been abrupt, growth curtailed or even reversed, and so on. Nationally, over the whole period, fully 90% of the new jobs created were in service industries – in distribution services, such as transportation, communication, wholesaling, and retailing; in producer services, in social services and in personal services. Only 10% of the employment increase came in the mining (3%), construction (2%), and manufacturing (4%) sectors. All industries at the division level showed an increase in employment totals, however slight. But the national job gains and job losses over each successive period of economic recovery and decline were quite varied. The only period of economic "bust" in two business cycles to show an absolute decline in employment totals was the November 1973 to March 1975 recession, when some 1 321 100 jobs were lost in the economy. The economic "bust" of 1980–82 was a period where employment growth slowed rather than absolutely declined. The two periods of economic recovery, 1970–4 and 1975–80, saw substantial net increases in national employment. Among the various industrial divisions the experience of the national business cycle was in many ways quite uniform. Only manufacturing employment stood out as being significantly more volatile or variable than the other divisions.

The temporal aspects of employment growth and change were not uniform across the country. Different cities had quite different structural and cyclical experiences over the decade 1972–82. In manufacturing industries, the recession of November 1973 to March 1975 struck individual cities quite unevenly. In the northeast and northcentral regions weekly man–hours declined anywhere from 12% to 22%. The hardest hit cities in New England were New Haven and Providence, and in the mid-Atlantic states the hardest hit cities included Utica, Erie, Philadelphia, and Reading. In the northcentral region, Ohio's cities were especially hard hit. However, the most serious losses in employment (weekly man–hours) occurred in the south. Asheville (North Carolina) and Greenville (South Carolina) both incurred losses of 30% or more. Southern cities experienced greater percentage losses in employment than northern ones, losses of 20% or over being relatively common. The Pacific states were the least affected in Whiteman's sample. Seattle (Washington) experienced the recession as a slowing in growth, as only a 10% loss in weekly man–hours.

Recovery from the March 1975 slump was slow but steady. The massive loss of manufacturing employment which took only 14 months to achieve would take 57 months to recover, and even then recoveries in individual cities were not always complete. In particular, all the mid-Atlantic cities (except Lancaster, Pennsylvania) and most of the south Atlantic cities failed to recover to their previous levels of employment. This was also true of all the SMSAs in Ohio. But, in contrast, New England, west-northcentral, west-southcentral and the west all exceeded their November 1973 levels of employment.

According to the National Bureau of Economic Research (NBER) there also was a mild recession from January 1980 to July 1980. This recession was most severe in the south, where in six months, employment levels fell by as much as 10% to 20%. Worst hit of all was Fort Smith, Arkansas, while Little Rock, Arkansas, its near neighbor, exhibited a similar if not quite so extreme profile. The mid-Atlantic SMSAs were also hard hit in this recession, with many cities losing 10% to 15% of their employment in six months. The NBER also reported a recovery from July 1980 to July 1981. In Whiteman's sample this appeared only as a slowing of the decline which continued through to November 1982. The recovery was most marked in the south, and least marked in New England and the mid-Atlantic states. Curiously, the Pacific states, which hitherto had managed to insulate themselves against recessions by sustaining a high rate of growth, suddenly found themselves in decline during what was supposed to be a recovery. After July 1981, a serious recession set in across the whole country. Fort Smith, Arkansas and Little Rock, Arkansas incurred their serious employment losses, but very serious and substantial losses in manufacturing employment were also incurred in cities in the mid-Atlantic states and in Ohio. Very serious losses were also incurred in the more buoyant urban economies of the south.

Risk and regional change

In this chapter we analyze the temporal structure of economic adjustment and its associated risks in two US cities (SMSAs) – one is a growing urban economy, the Dallas–Fort Worth SMSA (Texas); the other a declining one, the Pittsburgh SMSA (Pennsylvania). For each city we provide an analysis of economic risk for total nonagricultural employment and for each of the major industrial divisions. This analysis should prove particularly interesting because it has been noted elsewhere (Clark 1983a, Whiteman 1985) that long-run temporal profiles of regional growth and decline are essentially composites of a myriad of short-run adjustments. Indeed, this was the basis of our previous analysis in Chapter 3. It has been also observed that while the notion of a long-run profile as a composite of short-run changes is plausible as a general proposition, there are a number of distinctions to be made in the realm of short-run adjustments which seemed to produce or determine the longer-run path or the overall trajectory of regional change (Whiteman 1985). For example, it appears that both rapid regional growth and severe decline are characterized by a greater and more extenuated influence of past levels of employment on the levels of the present. The major distinction between the two seems to be that growing areas can either accumulate a series of positive shocks or "bounce back" quickly from negative ones. Declining areas, on the other hand, seem to accumulate a series of negative shocks, or never seem to be able to string two positive shocks together.

How do these observations translate into the more personal statistics of the risk of job loss? And how do these more personal statistics vary in the differing scenarios of growth and decline? In advance of an actual empirical investigation it is very hard to know what to expect in terms of results. The primary reason for this is that there is very little writing and research at all on the question of the geography of economic risk (for an exception see Bolton 1982). It has been suggested that regional growth depends on taking risks and "moving with the times." In other words, we should expect to find that high rates of regional employment growth are associated with high degrees of regional employment volatility. On the urban scene the work of David Birch (1979) at MIT suggests this kind of dynamic. Birch found that the firms which grow in the future are unequivocally the ones with "rocky" pasts, precisely those that an investor would shy away from. Extending Birch's argument somewhat (and anticipating our later results), we should expect that the path of regional growth be strewn with "ups and downs." There is also research on local job turnover which suggests that in good times the rate of local job switching increases while in bad times, job switching declines (Clark 1981b). The inference is that we should find that high rates of growth are associated with volatility in employment.

Both of the above arguments hold implications for the temporal structure of regional decline. Birch's arguments suggest that an unwillingness on behalf of individuals to take risks (to "hang on" to jobs, thereby valuing security of employment *too* highly) prevents aggregate growth. Decline, on the other hand, should therefore be smooth in its descent, although smooth periods may be interrupted by unanticipated periods of decline. Models of job turnover also suggest that decline or stagnation is a smoother process – although here we cannot judge the shape of the changes wrought by external influence which drive people to "hang on" to their current jobs.

However plausible those propositions, we can just as easily manufacture arguments which suggest precisely the opposite of the expectations which we have just outlined. For example, it is a clear inference from Kaldor's (1970) thesis of regional circular and cumulative causation that the upward path of growth is relatively smooth and free from the risk of job loss. Growth, in Kaldor's view, is a rising escalator, and any volatility in this process would be swamped by the progress of the upward trend. While it would not be impossible to marry Kaldor's thesis with the arguments put forward by the job turnover theorists that job switching is greatest in periods of boom, we should not expect this necessarily to produce significant volatility in our own analysis. The existence of volatility in our local employment series would, in this combined scenario, depend on the existence of a labor shortage in conditions of growth. In situations of plentiful labor supply, there should be no such volatility as firms can quickly replace workers who leave. The result would be a smooth set of employment series in a city that was growing.

From the above discussion it is plain that in advance of more precise empirical studies, we cannot decide which of our conflicting expectations would be the more correct. We therefore turn now to the issues of an appropriate empirical methodology.

A methodology for aggregate risk analysis

In order to obtain statistics which speak to the situations of individual workers, it is usually necessary to have data which are themselves records of individual case histories. From a collection of individual case histories on employment, it is sometimes possible to provide generalizations about the risk of job loss (and other recorded employment "events") according to previously known personal, sectoral, occupational and locational characteristics (for example). However, this common method has problems for those interested in the geography of employment risk. While it is true that individual work histories can provide a very thorough and systematic picture of employment changes along such dimensions as personal, sectoral and occupational lines, the same is not true of the geographical dimension. The reason for this is that the size of an appropriately stratified sample simply becomes large and unwieldy as we attempt to obtain a systematic geographical coverage.

Of course, we do not have the requisite data for this study either. While we have employment data which provide a very extensive geographical coverage, we do not have data which record individual work histories. Instead there are aggregate accounts of the number of persons employed in specific industry sectors in particular areas. What we require is a method which takes us from these aggregate data on employment totals to approximate information concerning individual job histories.

Clearly our method will have to be an approximation. From local employment data we can measure increases and decreases in employment over time. Any increase shall be counted as "new jobs." Thus, local employment series can then be scanned, counting all the "new jobs" which appear within it. Similarly, the number of jobs lost can also be counted over a given period of time by noting the decreases. What is needed is an assumption which will allow us to relate the timing of increases (new jobs created) to the timing of decreases (jobs lost). Then we can determine a complete count of jobs generated and lost, and we shall know the frequency distribution of their duration (how long they last).

One such assumption is a simple one: assume that "last hired is first fired." This is in fact a common employment practice or "rule," but is hardly the only practice which is behind the local employment series used in our analysis. We shall discuss the shortcomings of this assumption below, but for the moment continue explicating the methodology employed in this chapter. The rule "last hired first fired" allows us to relate increases in employment and their timing to decreases and their timing. If in local employment series we observe an increase of, say, one employee, then according to our assumption the very next decrease will imply firing or quitting of that very same worker. By keeping track of the timing of all increases and decreases, and by recording the duration of each new job (as implied by our assumption), we may then generate an employment count and a frequency distribution of job durations. This kind of data can be used to generate statistics which describe more than personal impacts of local economic fluctuations. A set of statistics on local job risk can then be generated using the methods of mathematical demography: "life-tables" are used wherein we simply substitute "job" for "person."

The count of job increases, decreases, and durations (produced by the method outlined above) are then fed into a standard demographic statistical package. Ordinarily these demographic packages are used to determine statistics relating to people and their chances of survival. Here we do the same for jobs instead of people. A life-table is a method of summarizing the results of a study by grouping the intervals of specified events (like death, or in our case, job loss or termination) into time intervals. For each time interval the life-table in our case will record the number of jobs which still exist at the start of the interval (here months), the number still existing at the end, and the number which are "withdrawn" during the interval – here meaning the number of layoffs and quits. From these numbers the probability of "response," termination of a job, in an interval is then estimated.

Two types of probabilities are of interest. One is the conditional probability of showing no response in an interval, a job surviving, given that it existed at the beginning of that interval. The second type of probability is the probability of showing response from the start of the study (in this instance, January 1972, or the date of job creation) to any specified interval. The latter probability distribution is known as the "survival function." These probabilities serve much the same purpose as a histogram or cumulative distribution function in describing data. From a "life-table" of jobs we can read a number of vital statistics for each interval. Notice that an "interval" (periods of one month, two months etc.) is treated ahistorically. That is, we are *not* concerned with a particular three-month period (as an example) in our study (a piece of real history, as it were), but instead make generalizations about *any* three-month period which could be specified from within the span of our study. And we can do this for four-month, five-month intervals, and so on. Intervals are denoted by the subscript "i" in the equations which follow.

From the counts for job creation, job loss, and duration, a life-table can compute the following statistics concerning the probabilities evident in the data. First, for each interval we may compute the number of jobs exposed to risk of termination during the interval. This is estimated by:

$$R_i = N_i - \tfrac{1}{2}C_i \qquad (6.1)$$

where R_i is the number of jobs exposed to risk. N_i is the number of jobs entering the interval, and C_i is the number of jobs lost during the interval.

We assume that job loss occurs randomly within the interval. Hence jobs which are lost are considered to be "at risk" for half the interval. Based on the number of jobs at risk we may compute the conditional probability of job loss or termination. This is given by:

$$Q_i = d_i/R_i \tag{6.2}$$

where Q_i is the conditional probability of job termination during an interval given that the job existed at the beginning of the interval, and d_i is the number of jobs which are lost or terminated during the interval. The conditional probability of job survival for an interval, P_i, is simply the inverse of the probability of job loss or termination, Q_i. That is,

$$P_i = (1 - Q_i) \tag{6.3}$$

We may then compute a cumulative survival function, cp_i, which is an estimate of the cumulative proportion surviving to the beginning of the ith interval. This is defined as:

$$cp_i = p_{i-1}(cp_{i-1}), \qquad \text{where} \qquad cp_1 = 1 \tag{6.4}$$

This estimate is based on the inevitable fact that survival to the ith interval requires that a job survive to the $(i - 1)$st interval, and is the usual life-table estimate. We may also calculate a hazard function, H_i (also called the "force of mortality" statistic), which describes the probability that a job which is i intervals old will be lost in the subsequent interval. This is given by:

$$H_i = [2Q_i/h_i(1 + p_i)] \tag{6.5}$$

where h_i is the ith of the interval. Similarly, we can calculate a probability density function (hereafter called a "job loss density function") which measures the probability of job loss per unit or interval of time. This is given by:

$$F_i = (cp_i - cp_{i+1}/h_i = (cp_i \times Q_i)/h_i \tag{6.6}$$

The hazard function and the job loss density function are two alternative ways of describing our job survival/loss data. Their estimates are useful for detecting patterns suggestive of parametric models that may describe the data.

Each of these statistics (described above) is computed for each interval (1 month to 129 months), and the results printed in a life-table. We have made such tables for the period January 1972 to December 1982, and for each major period of boom and bust in the national business cycle which occurred within this period. With this method we seek to learn the following:

(a)   How many local "new jobs" were created over the period of interest;
(b)   the number of local jobs created which lasted one month, two months, three months, etc.;
(c)   when and how many local jobs "died;"
(d)   all of the above expressed as a proportion of the total;
(e)   the proportion of local jobs surviving one month, two months, etc.;
(f)   the cumulative proportion of local jobs surviving one month, two months, etc.

Then the following can also be calculated:

(a)   The probability density function (the probability that a newly created local job will die in 1 month, 2 months etc.);
(b)   the hazard function (the probability of the death of a local job which is 1 month, . . ., X months old).

We may also calculate all of the above statistics not just for the series as a whole, but also for various episodes within it. In our analysis we computed statistics for the series as a whole and for each of the major periods of boom or bust in the business cycle (Whiteman 1985).

The assumption of "last hired first fired" will systematically bias all of these statistics. The cumulative effect of this bias will be to make it appear as though jobs only last for a very short while. In other words, this assumption will overemphasize the short-run volatile nature of job creation and loss. To attempt to counteract this bias, each local employment series was smoothed using a five-month moving average technique. This had the effect of weeding out excessive amounts of month-to-month variation, but did *not* alter the probability distributions for longer time intervals. Where appropriate, seasonal variation was also removed from the series, especially for construction, wholesale and retail, and services. This was achieved using a technique of first seasonal differencing (see Box & Jenkins 1976). We did this simply because we are interested only in national demand effects and the effects of structural change. In the above listed industries, demand effects are buried by very strong seasonal fluctuations.

Our restrictive assumption also poses us with a problem of interpretation. A "last hired first fired" policy implicitly assumes that all decreases in employment are layoffs (i.e. involuntary). We have ignored the effects of job quitting. There is little that we can do about this, except to modify our conclusions in the light of the literature on job turnover.

Job risk in two urban economies

Beginning with the results of our empirical analysis for total urban employment, Table 6.1 summarizes the results for Dallas, and Table 6.2 does the same for Pittsburgh. The column titled "Number of terminal events", and the column immediately adjacent, titled "Proportion terminating", describe in absolute and proportionate (of the total number of "new jobs" created) terms the distribution of job loss by interval. In other words, these columns tell us how many jobs were lost in the space of one month, two months and so on. In Dallas, it was found that *of the jobs that were in fact lost*, all of them were lost before they had lasted a year. The biggest losses came within intervals of one and two months. And yet not many jobs were lost at all, since nearly 74% of the "new jobs" created in the period lasted the remainder of the decade. So in Dallas most new jobs survived, although the relatively few jobs that did not survive were lost very quickly (within the space of a few months). The median survival time of a new job in Dallas was 10 years and 9 months. Of course, in a growing urban economy, such as Dallas, this method may overstate the life of a job, because we count only the net employment figures in each month. If there was significant job turnover *within* a single month, we have not accounted for it.

In comparison, consider the situation in Pittsburgh. Here a meagre 4% of the new jobs created during the study period survived the remainder of the decade. In fact, the median survival time of a new job in Pittsburgh was only 8 months. Additionally, while it is still true that the majority of jobs lost were lost within the space of two or three months, there are recurrent times of risk for an employee in Pittsburgh. These are at 9 months, 21 months, 32 months, 45 months, 63 months, 78 months, and so on. These can be read from the nonzero observations in the "Proportion terminating" column.

If these results are translated into the terms of personal job risk ("What are the chances that I shall lose my job?"), there are obvious and striking differences between the two local economies. Personal job risk is best assessed in the "Hazard rate" column. This column tells us the probability that a job which is "i" months old will be lost. In Dallas, the hazard rate is effectively zero after a year. In other words, if a worker can manage to hold on to a job for a year in Dallas, s/he will probably keep it as long as wished. And, in fact, the risk of losing it in the first year is small anyway. The situation is quite different in Pittsburgh. If a person was able to hold a job for year, there are still significant points of risk down the road. For example, at 45 months (almost 4 years) there is an 11% chance of losing a job; at 63 months there is a 17% chance of job loss; and, at 114 months an 11% chance.

Of course, the greatest trauma in Pittsburgh is surviving the first year.

Table 6.1 Life-table of jobs created in Dallas: total urban employment, January 1972–December 1982.

Interval start time	Number entering this interval	Number withdrawn during interval	Number exposed to risk	Number of terminal events	Pro-portion termin-ating	Prop-ortion surviving	Cumulative proportion surviving at end	Prob-ability density	Hazard rate
0	831 700	0	831 700	0	0.0000	1.0000	1.0000	0.0000	0.0000
1	831 700	2 200	830 600	105 600	0.1271	0.8729	0.8279	0.1271	0.1358
2	723 900	0	723 900	32 900	0.0454	0.9546	0.8332	0.0397	0.0465
3	691 000	0	691 000	8 300	0.0120	0.9880	0.8232	0.0100	0.0121
4	682 700	8 000	678 700	25 200	0.0371	0.9629	0.7926	0.0306	0.0378
5	649 500	1 700	648 650	10 900	0.0168	0.9832	0.7793	0.0133	0.0169
6	636 900	0	636 900	5 100	0.0080	0.9920	0.7731	0.0062	0.0080
7	631 800	0	631 800	7 000	0.0111	0.9889	0.7645	0.0086	0.0111
8	624 800	0	624 800	1 600	0.0026	0.9974	0.7625	0.0020	0.0026
9	623 200	7 500	619 450	6 900	0.0111	0.9889	0.7540	0.0085	0.0112
10	608 800	8 600	604 500	8 000	0.0132	0.9868	0.7441	0.0100	0.0133
11	592 200	8 200	588 100	1 200	0.0020	0.9980	0.7425	0.0015	0.0020
12	582 800	0	582 800	1 600	0.0027	0.9973	0.7405	0.0020	0.0027
13	581 200	0	581 200	0	0.0000	1.0000	0.7405	0.0000	0.0000
14	581 200	0	581 200	0	0.0000	1.0000	0.7405	0.0000	0.0000
15	581 200	0	581 200	0	0.0000	1.0000	0.7405	0.0000	0.0000
16	581 200	0	581 200	0	0.0000	1.0000	0.7405	0.0000	0.0000
17	581 200	0	581 200	0	0.0000	1.0000	0.7405	0.0000	0.0000
18	581 200	0	581 200	0	0.0000	1.0000	0.7405	0.0000	0.0000
19	581 200	100	581 150	0	0.0000	1.0000	0.7405	0.0000	0.0000
20	581 100	4 500	578 850	0	0.0000	1.0000	0.7405	0.0000	0.0000
21	576 600	13 300	569 950	0	0.0000	1.0000	0.7405	0.0000	0.0000
22	563 300	13 500	556 550	0	0.0000	1.0000	0.7405	0.0000	0.0000
23	549 800	6 100	546 750	0	0.0000	1.0000	0.7405	0.0000	0.0000
24	543 700	0	543 700	0	0.0000	1.0000	0.7405	0.0000	0.0000
25	543 700	1 700	542 850	0	0.0000	1.0000	0.7405	0.0000	0.0000
26	542 000	5 100	539 450	0	0.0000	1.0000	0.7405	0.0000	0.0000
27	536 900	1 200	536 300	0	0.0000	1.0000	0.7405	0.0000	0.0000
28	535 700	13 700	528 850	0	0.0000	1.0000	0.7405	0.0000	0.0000
29	522 000	1 400	521 300	0	0.0000	1.0000	0.7405	0.0000	0.0000
30	520 600	0	520 600	0	0.0000	1.0000	0.7405	0.0000	0.0000
31	520 600	0	520 600	0	0.0000	1.0000	0.7405	0.0000	0.0000
32	520 600	4 400	518 400	0	0.0000	1.0000	0.7405	0.0000	0.0000
33	516 200	5 700	513 350	0	0.0000	1.0000	0.7405	0.0000	0.0000
34	510 500	16 300	502 350	0	0.0000	1.0000	0.7405	0.0000	0.0000
35	494 200	3 600	492 400	0	0.0000	1.0000	0.7405	0.0000	0.0000
36	490 600	2 200	489 500	0	0.0000	1.0000	0.7405	0.0000	0.0000
39	488 400	34 200	471 300	0	0.0000	1.0000	0.7405	0.0000	0.0000
42	454 200	15 500	446 450	0	0.0000	1.0000	0.7405	0.0000	0.0000
45	438 700	43 100	417 150	0	0.0000	1.0000	0.7405	0.0000	0.0000
48	395 600	0	395 600	0	0.0000	1.0000	0.7405	0.0000	0.0000
51	395 600	27 000	382 100	0	0.0000	1.0000	0.7405	0.0000	0.0000
54	368 600	26 400	355 400	0	0.0000	1.0000	0.7405	0.0000	0.0000
57	342 200	49 600	317 400	0	0.0000	1.0000	0.7405	0.0000	0.0000
60	292 600	1 700	291 750	0	0.0000	1.0000	0.7405	0.0000	0.0000
63	290 900	17 800	282 000	0	0.0000	1.0000	0.7405	0.0000	0.0000
66	273 100	23 500	261 350	0	0.0000	1.0000	0.7405	0.0000	0.0000
69	249 600	40 200	229 500	0	0.0000	1.0000	0.7405	0.0000	0.0000
72	209 400	0	209 400	0	0.0000	1.0000	0.7405	0.0000	0.0000
75	209 400	8 800	205 000	0	0.0000	1.0000	0.7405	0.0000	0.0000
78	200 600	8 800	196 200	0	0.0000	1.0000	0.7405	0.0000	0.0000
81	191 800	29 300	177 150	0	0.0000	1.0000	0.7405	0.0000	0.0000
84	162 500	1 100	161 950	0	0.0000	1.0000	0.7405	0.0000	0.0000
87	161 400	21 700	150 550	0	0.0000	1.0000	0.7405	0.0000	0.0000
90	139 700	600	139 400	0	0.0000	1.0000	0.7405	0.0000	0.0000
93	139 100	6 200	136 000	0	0.0000	1.0000	0.7405	0.0000	0.0000
96	132 900	0	132 900	0	0.0000	1.0000	0.7405	0.0000	0.0000
99	132 900	0	132 900	0	0.0000	1.0000	0.7405	0.0000	0.0000
102	132 900	0	132 900	0	0.0000	1.0000	0.7405	0.0000	0.0000
105	132 900	2 400	131 700	0	0.0000	1.0000	0.7405	0.0000	0.0000
108	130 500	0	130 500	0	0.0000	1.0000	0.7405	0.0000	0.0000
111	130 500	8 800	126 100	0	0.0000	1.0000	0.7405	0.0000	0.0000
114	121 700	20 500	111 450	0	0.0000	1.0000	0.7405	0.0000	0.0000
117	101 200	35 100	83 650	0	0.0000	1.0000	0.7405	0.0000	0.0000
120	66 100	0	66 100	0	0.0000	1.0000	0.7405	0.0000	0.0000
123	66 100	21 300	55 450	0	0.0000	1.0000	0.7405	0.0000	0.0000
126	44 800	14 200	37 700	0	0.0000	1.0000	0.7405	0.0000	0.0000
129	30 600	30 600	15 300	0	0.0000	1.0000	0.7405	0.0000	0.0000

Table 6.2 Life-table of jobs created in Pittsburgh: total urban employment, January 1972–December 1982.

Interval start time	Number entering this interval	Number withdrawn during interval	Number exposed to risk	Number of terminal events	Proportion terminating	Proportion surviving	Cumulative proportion surviving at end	Probability density	Hazard rate
0	474500	0	474500	0	0.0000	1.0000	1.0000	0.0000	0.0000
1	474500	0	474500	93100	0.1962	0.8038	0.8038	0.1962	0.2175
2	381400	0	381400	41400	0.1085	0.8915	0.7165	0.0872	0.1148
3	340000	0	340000	40500	0.1191	0.8809	0.6312	0.0854	0.1267
4	299500	0	299500	35400	0.1182	0.8818	0.5566	0.0746	0.1256
5	264100	0	264100	6600	0.0250	0.9750	0.5427	0.0139	0.0253
6	257500	0	257500	7100	0.0276	0.9724	0.5277	0.0150	0.0280
7	250400	0	250400	22200	0.0887	0.9113	0.4809	0.0468	0.0928
8	228200	0	228200	34300	0.1503	0.8497	0.4086	0.0723	0.1625
9	193900	0	193900	48300	0.2491	0.7509	0.3068	0.1018	0.2845
10	145600	0	145600	28200	0.1937	0.8063	0.2474	0.0594	0.2144
11	117400	0	117400	4700	0.0400	0.9600	0.2375	0.0099	0.0409
12	112700	0	112700	6100	0.0541	0.9459	0.2247	0.0129	0.0556
13	106600	0	106600	0	0.0000	1.0000	0.2247	0.0000	0.0000
14	106600	0	106600	0	0.0000	1.0000	0.2247	0.0000	0.0000
15	106600	0	106600	0	0.0000	1.0000	0.2247	0.0000	0.0000
16	106600	0	106600	0	0.0000	1.0000	0.2247	0.0000	0.0000
17	106600	0	106600	0	0.0000	1.0000	0.2247	0.0000	0.0000
18	106600	0	106600	0	0.0000	1.0000	0.2247	0.0000	0.0000
19	106600	0	106600	0	0.0000	1.0000	0.2247	0.0000	0.0000
20	106600	0	106600	0	0.0000	1.0000	0.2247	0.0000	0.0000
21	106600	0	106600	900	0.0084	0.9916	0.2228	0.0019	0.0085
22	105700	0	105700	11500	0.1088	0.8912	0.1985	0.0242	0.1151
23	94200	0	94200	0	0.0000	1.0000	0.1985	0.0000	0.0000
24	94200	0	94200	0	0.0000	1.0000	0.1985	0.0000	0.0000
25	94200	0	94200	0	0.0000	1.0000	0.1985	0.0000	0.0000
26	94200	0	94200	0	0.0000	1.0000	0.1985	0.0000	0.0000
27	94200	0	94200	0	0.0000	1.0000	0.1985	0.0000	0.0000
28	94200	0	94200	0	0.0000	1.0000	0.1985	0.0000	0.0000
29	94200	0	94200	0	0.0000	1.0000	0.1985	0.0000	0.0000
30	94200	0	94200	0	0.0000	1.0000	0.1985	0.0000	0.0000
31	94200	0	94200	0	0.0000	1.0000	0.1985	0.0000	0.0000
32	94200	0	94200	900	0.0096	0.9904	0.1966	0.0019	0.0096
33	93300	0	93300	7500	0.0804	0.9196	0.1808	0.0158	0.0838
34	85800	0	85800	2400	0.0280	0.9720	0.1758	0.0051	0.0284
35	83400	0	83400	0	0.0000	1.0000	0.1758	0.0000	0.0000
36	83400	0	83400	0	0.0000	1.0000	0.1758	0.0000	0.0000
39	83400	0	83400	0	0.0000	1.0000	0.1758	0.0000	0.0000
42	83400	0	83400	0	0.0000	1.0000	0.1758	0.0000	0.0000
45	83400	0	83400	23800	0.2854	0.7146	0.1256	0.0167	0.1110
48	59600	0	59600	0	0.0000	1.0000	0.1256	0.0000	0.0000
51	59600	0	59600	2000	0.0336	0.9664	0.1214	0.0014	0.0114
54	57600	0	57600	0	0.0000	1.0000	0.1214	0.0000	0.0000
57	57600	0	57600	0	0.0000	1.0000	0.1214	0.0000	0.0000
60	57600	0	57600	0	0.0000	1.0000	0.1214	0.0000	0.0000
63	57600	0	57600	23700	0.4115	0.5885	0.0714	0.0166	0.1727
66	33900	0	33900	0	0.0000	1.0000	0.0714	0.0000	0.0000
69	33900	0	33900	0	0.0000	1.0000	0.0714	0.0000	0.0000
72	33900	0	33900	0	0.0000	1.0000	0.0714	0.0000	0.0000
75	33900	0	33900	0	0.0000	1.0000	0.0714	0.0000	0.0000
78	33900	0	33900	400	0.0118	0.9882	0.0706	0.0003	0.0040
81	33500	0	33500	0	0.0000	1.0000	0.0706	0.0000	0.0000
84	33500	0	33500	0	0.0000	1.0000	0.0706	0.0000	0.0000
87	33500	0	33500	0	0.0000	1.0000	0.0706	0.0000	0.0000
90	33500	0	33500	0	0.0000	1.0000	0.0706	0.0000	0.0000
93	33500	0	33500	0	0.0000	1.0000	0.0706	0.0000	0.0000
96	33500	0	33500	0	0.0000	1.0000	0.0706	0.0000	0.0000
99	33500	0	33500	600	0.0179	0.9821	0.0693	0.0004	0.0060
102	32900	0	32900	4000	0.1216	0.8784	0.0609	0.0028	0.0431
105	28900	0	28900	0	0.0000	1.0000	0.0609	0.0000	0.0000
108	28900	0	28900	0	0.0000	1.0000	0.0609	0.0000	0.0000
111	28900	0	28900	0	0.0000	1.0000	0.0609	0.0000	0.0000
114	28900	0	28900	8500	0.2941	0.7059	0.0430	0.0060	0.1149
117	20400	0	20400	3100	0.1520	0.8480	0.0365	0.0022	0.0548
120	17300	0	17300	0	0.0000	1.0000	0.0365	0.0000	0.0000
123	17300	0	17300	0	0.0000	1.0000	0.0365	0.0000	0.0000
126	17300	1200	16700	1400	0.0838	0.9162	0.0334	0.0010	0.0292
129	14700	14700	7350	0	0.0000	1.0000	0.0334	0.0000	0.0000

There is a 22% chance of job loss within a month, 11% within two and 13% within three months. But the greatest period of risk appears after about nine months of employment when the risk of job loss is fully 28%. For the two months on either side of this point the risk varies from 16% to 21%. This is a dramatically different situation from Dallas. In Pittsburgh most (97%) "new jobs" do not last out the decade, and, instead of the risk of job loss being small and all concentrated within the space of two or three months, it is large and spread over an extended period of time.

Analysis was also done to describe how in Dallas and Pittsburgh the risk of job loss varies over time. A variety of phases of recent economic history in the USA were considered: the period January 1972 to November 1973 (boom); November 1973 to March 1975 (bust); the period March 1975 to January 1980 (boom); and the period January 1980 to December 1982 (bust). It was found that in Dallas in periods of boom the hazard rate was absolutely negligible – and probably attributable to voluntary job switching (Whiteman 1985). All the risk of job loss in Dallas was evidenced in periods of bust where employment suddenly becomes much more volatile, and the first year of employment is quite "Pittsburgh-like" in profile. This was less true of the early 1980s in Dallas where recent recessions have had little impact. In Pittsburgh the patterns of boom and bust were again quite different from those in Dallas. Only one period in Pittsburgh, January 1972 to November 1973, showed the characteristics of job risk which can be associated with local growth – all the risk concentrated into the first year of employment and the levels of risk much reduced.

This result was still very different from the scenario in Dallas for the same period, where the risk of job loss was effectively zero. The subsequent three economic periods in Pittsburgh bore the now recognizable marks of continual recession. While it was true that in the recession of November 1973 to March 1975 there were significant risks of job loss in the first three months of employment (14% to 17%), the greater risks appeared later in the first year (8 months: 45% risk). The same basic pattern was true of the "recovery" (so-called) in Pittsburgh from March 1975 to January 1980 and also of the recession of January 1980 to December 1982.

A quick way of summarizing these patterns is to compare the median life of a job (survival time) in the two cities over each of the periods of boom and bust in the national business cycle. In Pittsburgh, the median life of a "new job" over the whole period was 7.6 months (Table 6.3). For the boom period January 1972 to November 1973, this increased to 11.7 months, but in the subsequent three periods this was dramatically reduced. The early 1980s were particularly severe in Pittsburgh. This was in contrast to Dallas where the median life of a "new job" over the whole period was 129 months (Table 6.3). For the boom period January 1972 to

Table 6.3 Median life of a 'new job' in Dallas and Pittsburgh by period of the business cycle (figures in months).

Episode	Dallas–Fort Worth SMSA	Pittsburgh SMSA
Jan. 1972–Nov. 1973 (boom)	129.0	11.7
Nov. 1973–Mar. 1975 (bust)	6.5	6.7
Mar. 1975–Jan. 1980 (boom)	93.0	8.6
Jan. 1980–Dec. 1982 (bust)	35.0	2.9
whole study period Jan. 1972–Dec. 1982	129.0	7.6

November 1973 this was unaltered. There was a significant contraction during the recession November 1973 to March 1975 (down to 6.5 months). But this was short lived. Thereafter the median life of a "new job" increased to the maximum possible estimate – i.e. at least until the end of our study period. Taking a job in Pittsburgh was a far riskier proposition than taking one in Dallas over this period.

A second way to summarize the two situations is to note how many jobs created in a particular business-cycle period survived to the end of that period. These figures are presented in Table 6.4, and reveal a picture very consistent with the interpretation of Table 6.3 regarding median job lives. The alternate contraction and expansion of the proportions of "new jobs" surviving in Dallas, coupled with very high proportions which did survive, suggest a healthy buoyant economy. In Pittsburgh, on the other hand, fewer and fewer new jobs survived as each successive economic episode came and went.

Such is the profile of economic risk in the two cities when viewed from the perspective of total urban employment. We also considered how the profile of local economic risk varied from sector to sector by examining the individual industrial divisions (Whiteman 1985). The hazard rates of job loss for each of the major industrial divisions in both cities, Dallas and Pittsburgh are shown in Table 6.5. Recall that the hazard rate expresses a

Table 6.4 Proportion of 'new jobs' created during business-cycle period which survive to end of period (figures in percentages).

Episode	Dallas–Fort Worth SMSA (%)	Pittsburgh SMSA (%)
Jan. 1972–Nov. 1973 (boom)	74	51
Nov. 1973–Mar. 1975 (bust)	45	20
Mar. 1975–Jan. 1980 (boom)	79	9
Jan. 1980–Dec. 1982 (bust)	68	1
whole study period Jan. 1972–Dec. 1982	74	4

Table 6.5 Hazard rates for job loss in Dallas–Fort Worth SMSA (D) and Pittsburgh SMSA (P) by major industrial division.

Interval (months)	Mining		Construction		Manufacturing		Transportation		Wholesale and retail		FIRE		Services	
	D	P	D	P	D	P	D	P	D	P	D	P	D	P
1	7.6	11.1	11.0	2.8	11.7	25.1	17.8	27.9	4.2	8.0	2.8	—	2.8	7.4
2	2.4	7.3	7.9	4.8	7.0	10.9	3.3	23.6	2.9	30.2	4.8	—	4.8	8.4
3	1.6	5.2	10.2	4.9	2.7	21.7	3.7	18.9	4.8	10.5	3.4	19.9	3.4	10.1
4	0.8	5.5	6.5	8.3	2.1	20.6	2.8	22.9	3.5	4.6	2.0	12.1	2.0	8.9
5	0.4	2.9	4.3	9.4	1.3	11.3	1.3	3.7	1.6	4.5	0.7	8.7	0.7	1.2
6	—	4.8	9.6	15.8	0.7	23.2	5.6	7.8	1.2	1.7	1.1	4.2	1.0	0.3
7	—	—	16.6	22.6	2.2	13.3	2.0	9.5	2.3	14.9	0.6	3.5	0.5	3.8
8	—	4.4	5.3	31.9	0.8	9.3	1.7	6.9	0.2	16.8	1.5	6.5	1.4	3.0
9	—	3.2	6.3	50.1	0.4	8.8	—	1.2	0.6	24.3	0.8	1.1	0.7	4.1
10	—	2.0	9.8	57.2	0.9	6.2	2.4	12.8	—	22.2	0.3	—	0.2	0.5
11	—	0.7	4.3	17.6	1.5	5.4	4.9	—	0.2	9.7	—	—	—	0.3
12	—	4.1	—	—	1.3	10.5	2.6	2.8	—	—	—	—	—	—
15	—	18.5	—	—	0.1	—	—	1.4	—	—	—	—	—	—
18	—	16.2	3.3	—	2.0	5.9	0.7	2.9	—	—	—	1.1	—	—
21	—	—	2.3	22.6	1.3	23.7	1.4	13.1	0.2	2.5	—	—	—	—
24	—	—	3.3	—	1.1	6.1	1.1	—	—	—	—	—	—	—
27	—	1.3	—	—	1.9	—	—	2.1	—	—	—	1.1	—	—
30	—	9.5	5.9	—	0.5	—	—	2.1	—	—	—	—	—	—
33	—	—	—	—	0.4	1.6	0.4	10.3	—	1.9	—	1.2	—	—
36	—	53.8	—	54.6	0.3	12.3	—	9.9	—	—	—	—	—	—
39	—	—	—	—	1.1	—	—	16.2	—	—	—	—	—	—
42	—	—	—	—	0.5	—	—	—	—	0.5	—	—	—	—
45	—	—	—	—	—	—	—	—	—	—	—	—	—	—
48	—	26.7	—	—	—	—	—	—	—	—	—	—	—	—

Note: values not shown are equal to zero.

measure of personal job risk by answering the question, "What is the probability of my job being lost (either through my being fired or by my quitting it), given that I have held the job for "*i*" months?"

Immediately obvious from Table 6.5 is the fact that employment risk in Pittsburgh was far greater and far more extended over time than in Dallas, across every industrial sector. This empirical observation is nothing more than a reflection on local growth and decline, since growth will (by definition) compensate any short-run losses with long-run gains – decline will not. We should therefore expect a growing city to present its workers with a very specific profile of economic risk – one in which the greatest risks are confronted in the first few months of employment. For a declining city, on the other hand, we might imagine a number of profiles. Decline might involve a smooth spectrum of risk for the worker or a more episodic one in which there are specific times of increased hazard (job risk). Each of these profiles would be highly suggestive of different processes of decline.

A smooth and even spectrum of job risk could *not* be produced by a temporal process of decline which contained repeated and severe bouts of job loss at approximately constant intervals. Such an episodic process would by definition concentrate all the risk of job loss at very specific frequencies, corresponding to the intervals of depression. A temporal profile like this could reflect either a process which was basically cyclical in nature or a process which reflected a sequence of regular crises. To distinguish between the two it would be necessary to provide a theoretical rationale for the kind of spectrum to be expected at other frequencies. For example, a proposition of the new "catastrophe" theories of urban and regional decline (see Casetti 1981a) is that smooth periods of employment are followed by periods of rapid and severe decline. Catastrophe theory would therefore predict that there is only a small degree of job risk at small intervals of one or two months. The major burden of risk would be concentrated at much longer intervals. The same need not be true of a temporal process which was basically cyclical in nature, and which could easily be overlain with significant amounts of short-term risk (reflecting high levels of short-run fluctuation in the series). A smooth and even spectrum of job risk is therefore seen to be a special and ideal case corresponding to a specific level of random variation (white noise) in the employment series. It is a spectrum signifying a temporal structure without any particular peak of job risk at any one employment term over another.

Actually, none of the estimated hazard rates resemble such a smooth function. And every industry group presents its workers with riskier times than others, although these may vary from one city to another. For example, all the risk in Dallas' mining sector was concentrated in the first month of employment. Thereafter it was negligible. This is not surprising given the meteoric employment growth which Dallas has experienced. And the level of risk is small (only 8%), which is mirrored in the fact that 88% of "new jobs" in Dallas' mining sector survived the decade and the median life of a "new job" was 10 years (see Tables 6.6 and 6.7 respectively). In contrast, Pittsburgh's mining sector displayed employment risk concentrated in the first month, and its job risk was more extended and later on in the employment term. This is reflected in the fact that in Pittsburgh's mining sector only 1% of "new jobs" survived the decade and the average life of a "new job" was only 15.5 months.

But when we consider the construction industry, the picture is somewhat different. In Dallas there were higher short-term risks than for construction workers in Pittsburgh, but job risk in Pittsburgh was the more severe at later points in the employment term (see Table 6.5). In both cases, only a few "new jobs" survived the decade; 29% in Dallas, only 2% in Pittsburgh (Table 6.6). And in both cities the average life of a new job was only 8 months (Table 6.7). Although job risk in Dallas' manufacturing sector was extended (Table 6.5), the long-term levels were low and the biggest risk of job loss came in the first month of employment (12%). The same was not true of Pittsburgh's manufacturing sector where the levels of extended risk remained high – for example, 24% at 21 months (Table 6.5). The initial risks of job loss were also much higher in Pittsburgh than in Dallas, running between 11% and 25% for the first 4 months. In fact, the difference between the manufacturing sectors of the two cities could hardly be greater. In Dallas, 52% of "new jobs" survived the decade; in Pittsburgh the same percentage was zero (Table 6.6). Or again, in Dallas a new manufacturing job lasted more than 10 years; in Pittsburgh, the same kind of job lasted only 4 months on average (Table 6.7).

These statistics reflect the fact that Pittsburgh's manufacturing sector was in decline, whereas Dallas' manufacturing sector was still growing. An almost identical situation characterizes employment risk in the transportation and public utilities sectors of the two cities (see again Tables 6.5–7). However, the situation in these cities' wholesale and retail trade sectors was different. Here, the risk of job loss was overwhelmingly concentrated in the first year of employment. In Dallas, the risks were small (4% or so) and were concentrated in the first four months of employment. In Pittsburgh, they were much larger (often ranging from 10% to 30%), and extended throughout the first year of employment (Table 6.5). Again, the dramatic difference between the two city economies was emphasized by the fact that in Dallas 81% of the "new jobs" survived the decade, while in Pittsburgh only 21% did (Table 6.6). In Dallas, the median life of a "new job" was 10 years; in Pittsburgh just 8 months (Table 6.7).

In both cities, the two sectors which grew the most over the sample period were the finance, insurance, and real estate (FIRE) sector and the

Table 6.6 Proportion of 'new jobs' created in Dallas (D) and Pittsburgh (P) during business-cycle period which survive to end of period by city and industry.

Period	Mining		Construction		Manufacturing		Transportation		Wholesale and retail		FIRE		Services	
	D	P	D	P	D	P	D	P	D	P	D	P	D	P
Jan. 1972–Nov. 1973 (boom)	71	33	2	5	33	5	60	12	94	19	93	51	93	50
Nov. 1973–Mar. 1975 (bust)	80	15	8	2	9	0	11	23	40	11	44	78	46	85
Mar. 1975–Jan. 1980 (boom)	93	39	50	2	82	7	72	1	88	31	84	51	84	65
Jan. 1980–Dec. 1982 (bust)	86	31	17	2	7	8	37	0	73	9	88	21	88	52
Entire study period Jan. 1972–Dec. 1982	88	1	29	2	52	0	57	1	81	21	84	61	84	62

Table 6.7 Median life of 'new job' in Dallas (D) and Pittsburgh (P) by period of the business cycle and by major industrial division.

Period	Mining		Construction		Manufacturing		Transportation		Wholesale and retail		FIRE		Services	
	D	P	D	P	D	P	D	P	D	P	D	P	D	P
Jan. 1972–Nov. 1973 (boom)	120.0	3.3	9.4	7.3	22.5	8.4	129.0	3.0	129.0	7.2	129.0	129.0	129.0	129.0
Nov. 1973–Mar. 1975 (bust)	108.0	13.0	4.1	7.4	3.4	3.7	2.5	3.5	6.2	3.3	8.8	67.0	8.7	105.0
Mar. 1975–Jan. 1980 (boom)	93.0	16.3	31.9	8.4	93.0	3.8	81.0	4.8	81.0	8.4	93.0	81.0	93.0	93.0
Jan. 1980–Dec. 1982 (bust)	36.0	12.8	4.9	7.9	10.0	3.7	11.7	3.4	36.0	7.3	36.0	24.0	36.0	34.0
Entire study period Jan. 1972–Dec. 1982	120.0	15.5	8.6	8.0	129.0	4.3	129.0	3.9	129.0	7.7	129.0	69.0	129.0	129.0

services sector. Both sectors displayed continual growth trends with some adjustment for the influence of the business cycle. Here again the risks of job loss were all concentrated in the first year of employment. But in comparison with other industrial divisions, the levels of risk were small, and the difference between the two cities was much diminished. As usual, the employment risks in Pittsburgh were both higher and more extended than in Dallas. Again, as usual, fewer "new jobs" survived in Pittsburgh than in Dallas – 61% in Pittsburgh as against 84% in Dallas (Table 6.6). However, the median life of a "new job" was much the same.

When we considered a life-tables analysis on the individual episodes of the business cycle the same basic distinctions in the economic behavior of the two cities were observed. That is to say, job risk in Pittsburgh tended to be higher and more extended over time, while in Dallas risk was lower and immediate. The effect of the business cycle was as follows: in times of boom, job risk is lower and more concentrated in the first few months of employment. Job lives lengthened and more "new jobs" survived the period. In periods of bust the opposite happened. Job risk increased and became more extended over time. The median life of a "new job" became *much* shorter, and many fewer "new jobs" survived the period.

The effects of the business cycle vary from place to place. They are most pronounced in Pittsburgh and less so in Dallas. Each city has an anomalous period. In Pittsburgh the "boom" of March 1975 to January 1980 was hardly experienced at all – a fact which is even more striking in sectors like mining and manufacturing and less so in FIRE and services. Job risks remained high and extended, and job lives short. Few "new jobs" survived. In Dallas, on the other hand, the bust of January 1980 to December 1982 was hardly felt at all. Job risks remained low and were concentrated in the first few months of employment. Most "new jobs" survived, and their median life was long.

Conclusions

This method of risk analysis generates what might be termed a spectrum of job risk facing the individual worker in a specific industry in a particular city (this is the hazard function). The hazard rate describes when quitting or firing is likely during an employment term. In situations of decline this statistic highlights very specific points of danger for the worker. These functions may take on a variety of forms, and in this chapter we have only worked out a small portion of their possible meanings. For example, we have deduced that an even, smooth hazard function is generated by an employment series which is essentially random (white noise). We have concluded that discrete (not continuous) periods of extended risk could be characteristic of either a cyclical pattern or a series of regular catastrophies.

We also know that a decision between the two might be made on the basis of the pattern of shorter frequencies.

We have seen that a growth trend tends to reduce the risk of job loss (obviously), but also tends to compress it into the first few months of the employment term. Decline, on the other hand, increases job risk (again obviously), but also presents the worker with a more extended period of risk. An interesting experiment would be to run the analysis on de-trended series, because we could see more clearly whether the pattern of employment change and the risk which it brings is significantly different between growth decline, and whether we can distinguish between *types* of growth and decline. Only with this more detailed analysis could we attempt more definitive answers to the questions surrounding the dynamic of urban growth and decline, questions concerning "circular and cumulative causation" and "catastrophe" theory.

In general, however, our results have proved to be quite within the realm of expectation, providing pictures of economic risk which, once seen, have a ring of truth about them. However, because of the generality of our method, they hide a wealth of detail. One implicit assumption which must be considered is the fact that all the estimates of employment which we make must be taken as applying to all production workers as a whole. This is rather crude, especially in the light of much recent research into internal labor markets which shows that the risk is not evenly distributed within the overall body of workers. Instead, economic risk is seen to be divided unequally between privileged or secure positions ("primary") and underprivileged or insecure ones ("secondary"). We cannot catch these effects, since we are unable to disaggregate our data by type of worker. We cannot distinguish labor-market segments. Because of this, the estimates of job risk which we have provided may severely underestimate the risks to some (the "secondary" segment), while overestimating the risks to others (the "primary" segment). However, once it is known how economic risk is distributed between classes of workers and how this broadly varies across sectors and places, then our estimates can be much improved.

PART III

Regional wages and prices

In this section of the book, we examine the movements of local wages and prices. In the neoclassical account of regional economic performance, prices (including wages as prices; see Ch. 5) play a central role in the spatial allocation of resources and the subsequent stability of the aggregate economy. The whole landscape is ordered according to transient price differentials in the production and consumption of goods and services. It is thus very important to examine movements of prices (both real and nominal) with a high level of temporal and spatial detail. Our interest is in the empirical patterns of local prices, and whether the identified patterns correspond in any way to the theoretical propositions of neoclassical theory. Upon empirical investigation, we find that local price behavior cannot be reasonably accounted for within the parameters of a strict neoclassical model. It is argued that notions from adjustment theory (such as contract and the distribution of uncertainty) form a much firmer basis for empirical description of the performance of the space economy. In Chapter 7, we examine the geography of consumer price volatility and inflation. In Chapter 8, we examine the components of urban consumer price inflation. And finally, in Chapter 9, we examine the relationships between price and wage inflation.

In Chapter 7, the focus is on how price changes are played out over time and space. We are not so much interested in price levels *per se*, but rather in forming an account of when and where price changes occur, and how. Identified profiles of local prices, which are records of how local economic changes actually occur, are juxtaposed with theoretical inferences regarding likely profiles of local prices. Our empirical findings are significant. There has been much more temporal variation than geographical variation in inflation since 1950. Indeed, it could be concluded that, in general, local price changes are fairly well approximated by national price changes. At one level, these findings would seem to support those neoclassical theorists of regional economies who treat local economies as simply members of a fully price-integrated spatial economic system. However, it was also found that an *accurate* forecast of a region's prices required knowledge of the patterns of local price series.

The actual temporal process of local price adjustment also proved to be an interesting phenomenon. The more sophisticated, and recent, neoclassical versions of price adjustment theory (e.g. the rational expectations school) would argue price changes to be both volatile and transitory over space and time. Equilibrium should be reached without hesitation, hindered perhaps only by government policy. On the other hand, there are those who argue that prices are fixed by the institution of contract which renders price changes smooth and recursive over time. It is the former school that emphasizes the crucial allocative role of the price mechanism, whereas the latter school suggests the existence of quantity rather than price adjustment in economic changes. Our evidence suggests that prices do not respond in the instantaneous way suggested by the newest and most narrow of neoclassical economic theory. Instead, prices at both the national and local levels adjust quite slowly, being recursively linked to previous price levels. This kind of price rigidity in the time-series of urban prices studied in this book is, we argue, indicative of a contract model of price formation.

Concluding that local price movements are fairly approximated by national price movements does not mean that local prices mirror national prices from one time to the next. When the components of local prices are studied a more complex story emerges. In Chapter 8, we concentrate on the local effects of price shocks in the three major components of the aggregate price index: food, energy and housing. It is shown that in terms of these components economic events are often temporally discontinuous, and so largely unanticipated. Additionally, a distinction is discernible between the sources of local price inflation; specifically, a distinction between exogenous 'import' price shocks and endogenous, demand induced, commodity price inflation. These distinctions are borne out in our episodic analysis of local inflation over time.

We find that distinct episodes can be discerned in the pattern of national price inflation, and that each component (food, energy, housing) can make a qualitatively different contribution to local price adjustment. It is readily apparent that exogenous price shocks need not be spatially homogeneous in their effects on local price inflation. This is especially significant in the energy sector. And yet we still would conclude that there is little evidence of temporally consistent and significant local inflation effects in the United States. Local component effects are never strong enough to shift local price movements systematically from the overall path of national prices.

Finally, in Chapter 9, we examine the dynamic relationships of price inflation to regional wage increases. Here the focus is on money wages as the actual medium of negotiation between labor and capital, with respect to expected price levels. Real wages are introduced as a target variable in our analysis, representing the desired balance between expected price increases and obtainable wage increases. In this chapter, we pose and test alternative hypotheses about wage adjustment within the structure of regional economies. Since it was shown earlier (Chs 4 & 5) that changes in local wages seem unrelated to local labor demand effects, it is important at this juncture to demonstrate an analytical and empirical link between local prices and wages.

Two issues are of central importance in our analysis. First, there is the issue of price expectations. Unlike rational expectation theories of the economy which reformulate all price volatility so that it becomes antici-pated (and therefore endogenous), we are at pains to deal with price volatility as genuine uncertainty. Testable empirical formulations concerning price volatility and inflation, and the *degree* to which it may be anticipated in the movement of regional wages, are developed as a prelude for empirical inquiry. The second issue of importance in our analysis of the relationships of price inflation to the progress of regional money wages is the actual institution by which anticipation of price changes is achieved. This issue reintroduces our central notion of contract as the institutional mechanism which sets a specific distribution of economic uncertainty between labor and capital.

Given our assumption that production is largely financed out of retained earnings, and given that labor costs are both an integral cost of production and the major component of all costs, a zero-sum distributional game is set up concerning who should bear the brunt of revenue fluctuations, and where such costs could be allocated in space. Specific aspects of this distribution of uncertainty are set by institutional mechanisms such as wage indexation and the length of the contract. An argument is made that these mechanisms have particular spatial configurations, thereby differentially affecting regional real incomes. Central to this adjustment formulation is the proposition that regional wages follow local prices and not vice versa. These empirical findings deny the conventional wisdom that wage increases push inflation – empirically, just the reverse appears to be true.

It is also shown that temporal and regional variations in real wages are likely to be derived from local variations in local money wage indexation to national price inflation. Indexation is by no means automatic, and is less common in the south than in the north. There are also sectoral variations in wage indexation. Finally, we show how indexation is at the heart of the dispute between labor and capital concerning the distribution of economic uncertainty. Full indexation may assure the worker of a steady real income but, to the extent that price changes are unforeseen, may involve significant, unexpected costs to the firm and thereby threaten the continuity of production.

7 Does inflation
vary between cities?

Introduction

The 1970s were characterized by a steady worsening of economic conditions, increasing unemployment and inflation – a combination thought to be implausible by some experts only 10 years ago (see for example Hudson 1982). Baily (1982), amongst others, has suggested that economic theory and policy are in disarray, and that there is no convincing theory which can explain current economic conditions. Given the obvious importance of these issues, it is surprising that few researchers have considered the geographical dimensions of inflation. Donald Jones (1976), in a review of the issues concerning the 'geography of inflation', made a similar observation, noting that knowledge of the monetary system is of crucial importance if we are to understand the structure and performance of urban economies. His subsequent historical and contemporary research on regional monetary crises and wage inflation has indicated the potential richness of this topic, as well as the possible contributions that monetarism could make in understanding the spatial dimensions of the monetary system (Jones 1981, 1983).

Even so, there have been few studies of geographical monetary processes and certainly some confusion over the actual geography of inflation (for an extended analysis see Harvey 1982). Genberg (1977) found no significant within- and between-country variations in inflation. Based on a 10-year period (the 1960s) he concluded that inflation did not vary between countries any more than it did between US cities. Since it is commonly assumed that the USA is a spatially price-integrated economy, Genberg (1977) suggested in fact that there is a world price level. Lawrence (1979) disputed that claim by arguing that Genberg's statistical tests failed to distinguish between the temporal and spatial effects of variations in inflation. In reconsidering the evidence, Lawrence concluded that inflation varies considerably between countries, more so than between US cities. Even his analysis can be faulted however, principally because no direct test is made of the correlation between US national and city inflation data, and because there is no direct test of the relative contributions of time and space to variations in inflation between cities. The evidence remains ambiguous and largely anecdotal, even though most researchers assume spatial price integration within the USA.

One explanation for this assumption could be theoretical. Assuming a common currency and commodity trade between regions, neoclassical theory presumes an integrated market and, ultimately, spatial price equilibrium. Essentially, spatial integration means that the "prices of goods, financial assets, and factors of production are equalized across boundaries" (Whitman 1979: xxi). That is, differences in prices between regions should be only a function of transportation costs. Hence, assuming a standard transportation cost structure, price inflation should be a purely national phenomenon. On theoretical grounds, however, Sheppard and Curry (1982) have argued that spatial price equilibrium is implausible. Spatial market segmentation, information costs and the heterogeneity of location itself should effectively conspire to sustain variation in local inflation. Thus there is a weaker hypothesis that deserves recognition: spatial price interdependence, where local prices are sensitive to the patterns and fluctuations of other regions' prices but do not map exactly, one-to-one, onto national prices.

This chapter is concerned with the relative merits of the spatial price integration and interdependence hypotheses. Quarterly time-series of local price inflation are compared to national price series over the period 1950–80. Using Box and Jenkins (1976) autoregressive integrated moving average (ARIMA) models, some 16 US urban price series are analyzed in order to establish their degrees of similarity and patterns over time. At the same time, we are also concerned with more general issues, specifically the costs of inflation, its changing volatility over time and space, and competing explanations of inflation. We seek to establish in the next section the importance of analyzing the variance in inflation over time and between places. Then we deal more directly with the adjustment properties of prices, focusing upon rational expectations (Lucas 1981) and Keynesian fix-price formulations (Morishima 1976). By doing so, we establish a rationale for empirical analysis.

Costs of inflation

In a decentralized market economy, prices are the principal signals or sources of information regarding the best uses of resources (Morishima 1977). Assuming for the moment conditions of pure competition, neoclassical theory predicts that prices will reflect the relative scarcity of goods and services. To that extent, prices allocate resources, and are the principal means of transacting and exchanging among private decision makers. Prices are also relative in the sense that competing demands on resources are valued in terms of their opportunity costs. Neoclassical theory supposes that prices sustain exchange, and assuming the veracity of price signals, exchange will occur to the point where no person can be made better off and no other person made worse off. However, under conditions of less than pure competition, equilibrium may not result in full employment. That is, transactions may stabilize prices at a point where some resources are not fully utilized. Even so, prices should still reflect the *relative* patterns of demand and supply as well as the opportunity costs of alternative resource allocations.

For such a system to function efficiently, a number of conditions must be met, including spatial price synchronization, veracity and neutrality. Market economies are characterized by decentralization in production and exchange. Firms produce specialized commodities as direct consumption goods and as inputs for other firms. In doing so, firms buy from others, and sell to others – in sum a massive system of linked buyers and sellers. The price of any one good reflects a whole sequence of pricing and allocative decisions made by producers of component parts and consumers of those parts and of the final good. Prices are made not only with respect to competing uses of any one good, but also with respect to the whole system of production and exchange. In such a system, the prices of all goods are interrelated and cannot be isolated from one another. For such a geographically and functionally decentralized system to work, prices must be synchronized so that the whole structure of production and exchange adapts to changes in relative prices. In this context price synchronization is a necessary condition for the reproduction of the economy as a whole.

Without a market coordinator or auctioneer, there are good reasons for expecting inertia in price adjustments and thus, more generally, geographical discontinuities in price inflation. Simply, the complexity of interdependence in production and exchange could create lags in price adjustments, if not distinct differences in the actual extent of adjustment itself. Price synchronization will then inversely depend upon the interdependence between producers, or the number of separate pricing decisions that make up the total price of any good. Where trade and exchange take time, the existence of different trading schedules should also contribute to discontinuities in price inflation. Similarly, to the extent that trade and production has a distinct geographical configuration, there may exist space–time lags in local price adjustment. In the abstract, these lags in price adjustment could be thought of as costs of price inflation, or the additional costs of transacting.

There are additional problems with inflation, mostly concerned with unanticipated changes. Imagine, for example, that the prices which firms take for their goods in the market begin to rise. What kind of response might we see? One answer could be that as prices rise, firms increase output believing that observed price increases are indicative of increases in real demand. As output increases, this will stimulate price changes and output responses throughout the economy as the initial impulse is transmitted through the linkage system. According to conventional neoclassical price theory, the end result should be stable prices and a reallocation of resources. But it is just as plausible that unanticipated price changes are purely monetary as opposed to real phenomena (Sims 1980). If firms are unaware of the causes of price changes they could mistake price increases or decreases as real changes in demand where in fact they may be only transitory monetary effects.

Mistakes in recognition can lead to overproduction, as in the example noted above, or in other instances (if price increases do in fact reflect demand but are believed to be simply nominal shifts) underproduction. For firms, the effects of such recognition problems will be felt in profits, wages, and output. For the economy as a whole, mistaken recognition of the meaning of price changes could result in a systematic misallocation of resources plus greater volatility in real output and employment. Once price signals lose their veracity then the whole system of resource allocation is threatened.

A second problem with unanticipated inflation could be termed the coordination problem. If, as we have suggested above, prices become unreliable as indicators of *real* as opposed to transitory *nominal* effects, then decentralized market decision making becomes a very real danger to the economic systems' reproduction. That is, the complexity and atomistic nature of market decisions, so dependent upon the veracity of prices, may become totally unwieldy, confused by many different expectations concerning prices and their meaning. In these circumstances a coordinating agent will be needed to ensure stability. But in a highly decentralized system there could be lags of adjustment, errors in response, and a great deal of uncertainty with respect to the perceived behavior of the coordinating agent (what Grossman and Stiglitz (1980) termed the costs of heterogeneous information). Stability would be transitory and economic crisis a continual threat. The costs of unanticipated inflation, in this context, are the costs of coordination, both in terms of the existence of the institution itself and the effects of its actions.

So far we have discussed the costs of inflation in terms of a quite conventional neoclassical flex-price model of resource allocation. The only modification introduced was uncertainty with respect to the meaning of prices. Even here, it was assumed that prices allocate resources albeit, at times, inefficiently. In situations where prices are not the sole allocation devices, and where prices are sticky in the short-run, understanding the exact costs of inflation is more problematic. Fix-price allocation models depend upon the flow of quantities produced and sold to provide the signals to firms regarding market conditions of demand and supply. If it is assumed that firms set their prices to cover the costs of production plus an increment for profits, unanticipated price changes would be less important than changes in firms' inventories. As price increases diffuse through the economic system, firms add on price increases without necessarily changing their production schedules.

Even so, there can be considerable distributional effects associated with unanticipated price inflation. For those firms unable to adjust their prices in response to unanticipated increases in prices, their relative wellbeing would be adversely affected. If, for example, labor contracts for a wage over a given period of time, labor must attempt to estimate the likely pattern of price inflation and bargain for a wage which would accommodate the most likely possibility. The risk is, of course, that labor may underestimate inflation, leading to a decline in real wages over the length of the contract. One option in these circumstances is to bargain for automatic cost-of-living adjustments (assuming some form of labor monopoly), thereby insulating workers from any unanticipated shifts in real income. This does not mean that the costs of inflation are in any way reduced, rather that the burden of uncertainty is shifted from labor to employers through the medium of contracts (Phelps 1979).

To summarize, the costs of price inflation are most significant when dealing with unanticipated inflation. In a flex-price world, unanticipated inflation may drastically affect the veracity of prices, leading to misallocations of resources, poor market coordination, and perhaps even economic crisis. The greater the volatility of prices in these circumstances, the more difficult it may be to approximate the likely pattern of real demand as opposed to transitory monetary effects. In geographically and sectorally decentralized economies, unanticipated price inflation may cause both *lags* in adjustment and differential rates of adjustment. Not only would spatial price equilibrium be problematic, but spatial price integration would actually collapse. Spatial price interdependence would then be the more likely result, although the actual dimensions of interdependence are not *a priori* predictable. Of course, in a fix-price world, unanticipated price inflation may be of less significance *vis-à-vis* the spatial allocation of resources and the overall coordination of the economy. Even so, unanticipated price inflation can still have important distributional effects (Fischer 1981).

Properties of price adjustment

Whether or not inflation is best represented as a spatially integrated as opposed to an interdependent process will be considered by comparing local inflation to national inflation. The extent of price volatility was noted to be an important aspect of the costs of inflation, particularly for flex-price models of resource allocation (Taylor 1981). We also need to consider the adjustment properties of inflation. If a flex-price system of market exchange is assumed, then the following scenario would seem plausible. Since prices are the indicators of supply and demand, as real economic activity changes, prices will similarly change so as to clear the market. If we assume that all inflation is fully anticipated, then price changes would instantaneously allocate resources efficiently. In such a system, prices would be stable in the short run and in the long run. Aggregate price stability in the short run would be the product of the length or sequence of decentralized price adjustments necessary completely to shift resource allocations over time and space. General equilibrium (GEM) theorists assume that price adjustments would be instantaneous, or if not instantaneous, then with few lags.

Rational expectations (REX) theorists argue for a similar result, although with a number of modifications to the conventional GEM formulation. First, it is assumed that prices are determined in a perfectly competitive environment and, like GEM theorists, REX theorists also assume complete flexibility in prices. Secondly, it is assumed that people use all the information available in a completely efficient manner. The rational expectations approach implies that decision makers understand how the economic system functions, *and* how known possibilities will affect their wellbeing through the price adjustment system. In this manner, resources are allocated rationally in accordance with the arrangement of the economic system. Thus prices would hardly vary, remaining both stable and predictable over the short and long-runs. Thirdly, it is also argued by REX theorists that price fluctuations in the economy must be the result of unexpected shocks or disturbances. If these shocks are isolated to particular sectors or regions, there may be quite large real-resource adjustments in response to price changes. And, to the extent that the economy is interdependent, such shocks should spread quickly throughout the whole economy, with the minimum of lags and differentiation in effects.

The consequences or costs of such unanticipated monetary shocks for real economic activity were considered in the previous section and do not bear repeating here. To summarize, the behavior of prices in the REX (modified GEM) world could be expressed as follows:

$$P^n_{t+1} = P^e_{t+1} + \theta_1 a_{t+1} \quad \text{where} \quad 0 < \theta < 1 \qquad (7.1)$$

and where P^n_{t+1} is the price of a bundle of commodities at time $t + 1$, over a set of regions n, P^e_{t+1} is the expected price of the same bundle of goods, based on the price of that bundle in the previous period (t), and $\theta_1 a_{t+1}$ is a random disturbance term with a weight θ_1 on a_{t+1}. It is conceivable that previous disturbances (say at time t) could have a residual effect on P^e_{t+1}, particularly if there are lags in price adjustment and resource allocation due to the frictions of space. Those readers familiar with Box and Jenkins (1976) time-series models (see Bennett 1979 for a review) will immediately recognize that the $\theta_1 a_{t+1}$ term is a moving average process, while P^e_{t+1} may be functionally estimated as an autoregressive process.

The implications of the rational expectations formulation for understanding the temporal properties of price inflation are far-reaching. First, if the sole determinant of unanticipated price fluctuations is $\theta_1 a_{t+1}$, then price inflation could be quite volatile, subject to sharp and unpredictable shifts. Secondly, to the extent that the price system is efficient with no impediments to adjustment, price disturbances will be quickly (if not instantaneously) integrated into the overall economic system. Thirdly, if there are impediments to adjustment (such as heterogeneous information), then these shocks will be distributed over time and space, according to the underlying structure of linkages in the economic system. The crucial assumption of this model is that sources of unanticipated shifts in prices are *exogenous* to the economy. Many REX theorists also argue that the principal source of such shocks is government manipulation of the money supply. Consequently, government-induced shocks at the national level will determine not only national price inflation, but also local price adjustment.

This conceptualization suggests a further REX price formulation:

$$P^i_{t+1} = P^e_{t+1} + \theta^i a^n_{t+1}, \quad \text{where} \quad 0 < \theta < 1 \tag{7.2}$$

and where P^i_{t+1} is the price level for a bundle of goods in region i, time $t + 1$, P^e_{t+1} is the national expected price for that bundle of goods at time $t + 1$, and $\theta^i a^n_{t+1}$ is the national expected price for that bundle of goods at time $t + 1$, and $\theta^i a^n_{t+1}$ is the national disturbance term weighted by a local factor θ^i. If there were complete spatial price integration all θ^i would equalize. However, spatial lags in adjustment would show up as differential temporal adjustments to national shocks, plus variable rates of adjustment (θ^i) itself. More generally, if spatial price integration is in fact a characteristic of the urban system then all exogenous shocks could be represented as the national series simply because their origin is not important.

To say that the rational expectations hypothesis has been received with a great deal of controversy would be an understatement. Empirical estimation problems abound, with many critics noting the severe problems of defining expected or anticipated prices as opposed to unanticipated prices (Buiter 1980). Also, more than one critic has noted that the empirical form of REX is actually hard to distinguish from more conventional Keynesian formulations (Pesaran 1982). It is not the purpose of this chapter to test formally the REX formulation in the spatial context, or for that matter to re-specify in some better manner the REX model itself. Rather, we have focused on rational expectations because it provides us with a specific hypothesis regarding the underlying temporal adjustment properties of inflation.

There have been a number of attempts to reformulate conventional Keynesian notions regarding the adjustment properties of inflation. And these attempts, summarily termed fix-price contract models (FPC), provide an alternative conceptualization of inflation as well as the likely patterns of price adjustment. Fix-price contract models assume *quantity* adjustment in the short run, not price adjustment. Given a price, firms are assumed to ration output in response to changing demand. According to Gordon (1981), the advantages of fixed price contracts for firms are twofold. First, fixed prices reduce the uncertainty of price volatility over the short run. By agreeing to supply goods at a certain price from t to $t + 1$, the firm is able to estimate revenue, assuming a reliable estimate of likely quantities sold. Production is then more stable and less likely to be affected by unanticipated inflation. Notice that there are risks with fixing prices, notably the prospect of underestimating increases in the prices for finishing goods. Even so, this risk must be related to the advantages of knowing input costs from one period to the next. Secondly, fixed prices also minimize the costs of adjustment to each shock. This may be of marginal importance to some firms, especially those privileged to have a guaranteed demand. On the other hand, for firms dealing with large numbers of commodities and with variable consumer preferences (like supermarkets), adjustment costs may be a considerable burden.

Although FPC prices will be more stable and less responsive to disturbances than predicted REX prices, exactly how stable FPC prices are remains unknown. Overall price stability will depend on the synchronization of contracts and the existence of space–time lags in contract synchronization. If all contracts are assumed to be revised at time t, and to run for a period t to $t + 1$, price series would be characterized by steps in prices at specific dates. To the extent that lags in adjustment exist over space, steps in prices should be similarly sequenced over time and space. If, on the other hand, contracts are written and revised over time such that there is no specific revision date, then prices would change continually over time.

Prices would then have a long "memory," with respect both to past patterns and to more recent changes in the price level. To summarize:

$$P^i_{t+1} = \phi_2 P^n_t + \phi_2 P^n_t + \theta^i a_{t+1} \quad \text{where} \quad 0 < \phi < 1, 0 < \theta < 1 \quad (7.3)$$

and where the price at time $t + 1$ in region i is a function of past prices in the region (i) and nation (n) distributed over time, and a stochastic or random shock, also distributed over time. Like REX models, the FPC price adjustment system could be conceptualized as an autoregressive (AR) process coupled with a moving average (MA) process. This latter

(MA) component may be, however, of limited importance, because contracts are designed expressly to circumvent their effects. Consequently, the major determinant of price adjustment may be previous national and local prices. The implications of such a formulation for predicting the patterns of urban inflation are twofold. First, instead of rapid shifts in inflation we should expect price adjustment to be smoother and more gradual than predicted by REX theory. Secondly, we should not expect to see prices fully synchronized over space and time. Significant lags should be apparent, and in consequence, spatial price interdependence is likely to be the rule.

We have, then, two basic and competing empirical propositions regarding the temporal properties of price adjustment. Rational expectations theorists predict rapid and sudden shifts in prices with few lags over space or time. Fixed price contract models predict slower and more stable adjustments, based primarily on past patterns, not so much on random disturbances. As well, fixed price models imply significant lags in adjustment.

Empirical methodology

Data on price inflation for US cities are, unfortunately, quite scarce. The Bureau of Labor Statistics of the US Department of Labor has collected price data on a quarterly basis for a small sample of cities since World War II. For consistency's sake, the price data analyzed here were collected for some 16 cities over the period 1950–80, 31 years and 124 data points in total. Cities represented in this sample were on average larger, older and more stable in terms of their growth patterns over the period (Clark 1982b). The sample was dominated by northeastern and midwestern cities (including Baltimore, Chicago and Pittsburgh, for example), with a small number of western cities. Unfortunately, inconsistencies in the temporal frame of data collection precluded the inclusion of southwestern cities such as Houston and Phoenix. Even for those cities included in the sample, there are differences in the quarterly time-series that make direct comparisons difficult. The data for three cities (including Portland, for example) were based on a January–April–July–October quarterly sequence, nine cities were based on a February–May–August–November quarterly sequence, and four cities were based on a March–June–September–December quarterly sequence. Fortunately, national price data were available for all three temporal sequences.

Measurement of price inflation is actually a product of transforming the consumer price index (CPI) to rates of change. This procedure is well known and is described in detail by the Bureau of Labor Statistics (1982a). More important to recognize is the meaning of the index itself.

The CPI measures changes in the market price of a fixed bundle of goods and services. Items included in this bundle are food and beverages, housing, fuels, household furnishings, apparel, transportation, medical care, entertainment and the like. Some items are given more weight than others, particularly housing, transportation and food, in that order. A consequence of weighting items is that rapid price changes in lowly weighted items (such as entertainment) may have little effect on the overall CPI compared to smaller price changes in more highly weighted items (such as housing). Wahl (1982) provides an extensive discussion of this issue and noted over the year 1978–9 that while most items in the CPI increased by 10%, the fuel category increased 56% and the housing finance category nearly 24%. Even though the bundle of goods and weights may be fixed over time, in our case centered upon 1972 (CPI = 100), there may be significant shifts in the contribution of different items to overall inflation.

Empirical analysis of urban inflation patterns was conducted in two stages. The first stage documented and analyzed the spatial and temporal volatility of inflation. Previously, it was noted that price volatility implies significant allocative and distributional costs. Exactly what kinds of costs are important in this context depends of course on the significance of prices in allocating resources. Empirically, however, we must also measure volatility itself and its relationship to the overall inflation rate. To that end, the price series were divided into three periods of time: the 1950s, 1960s and 1970s. Following a number of recent studies, particularly Blanchard (1981), average city inflation rates for each decade were correlated with their variance in inflation. An analysis of variance was then conducted to discriminate between the contribution of time and space to variations in overall inflation.

The second stage of analysis involved filtering each city price series through national univariate time-series models and then testing for the existence of significant residual patterns. Existence of significant residual autocorrelation effects was taken to indicate the inadequacy of the spatial price integration hypothesis. Forecasting models for local price inflation were also developed, with their *form* being used to indicate whether or not spatial price interdependence exists. Returning to our previous discussion of the time-series properties of inflation, the *form* of the local and national price models was also used to indicate the relative smoothness or discontinuity in the price adjustment process. To summarize, the empirical analysis will consider the following questions: (a) Is the average rate of inflation correlated with the variance of inflation? (b) Does the strength of this relationship vary over time? (c) What are the relative contributions of time and space to overall variations in price inflation? (d) Does the national pattern of inflation fairly represent local inflation? (e) Is local price inflation best characterized as an autoregressive or a moving average process?

Urban inflation patterns

Average quarterly inflation rates increased in almost all cities over the three decades, 1950–60, 1960–70, and 1970–80 (Table 7.1). The only exceptions were Chicago and Pittsburgh, both of which exhibited a slight decline in average quarterly inflation rates from the 1950s to the 1960s. Not surprisingly, average inflation rates were more similar between the 1950s and 1960s than between those two decades and the final, 1970s decade. And, again not surprisingly, cities in the first two decades had significantly smaller quarterly rates of inflation than the same cities in the final decade. Generally, urban inflation paralleled national inflation, leaving aside for the moment the exact relationship.

Those cities with the highest average quarterly inflation rates in the 1950s did not necessarily retain their rank over subsequent decades. For example, San Francisco, the city with the highest average inflation during the 1950s, was ranked equal fifth in the 1960s and sixth in the 1970s. Washington, DC, which ranked sixteenth in the 1950s, ranked equal second during the 1960s and was ranked thirteenth in the 1970s. Local economic growth is obviously reflected in the changing rankings of these cities, as is the economic stability of cities such as Cleveland reflected in the stability of its ranking in terms of average quarterly inflation over this period of time.

Table 7.1 Correlations between mean and standard deviations of city inflation rates.

Time/City	1950–60 Mean	1950–60 Standard deviation	1960–70 Mean	1960–70 Standard deviation	1970–80 Mean	1970–80 Standard deviation
Baltimore	0.59	1.10	0.65	0.71	1.91	1.33
Boston	0.56	1.12	0.72	0.78	1.75	1.16
Chicago	0.61	1.40	0.58	0.49	1.81	0.92
Cincinnati	0.53	1.01	0.60	0.70	1.97	1.01
Cleveland	0.58	0.97	0.66	0.72	1.85	1.06
Detroit	0.53	0.84	0.69	0.85	1.86	1.10
Los Angeles	0.61	0.96	0.61	0.93	1.91	1.34
Milwaukee	0.57	0.92	0.60	0.73	1.88	1.05
New York	0.55	1.21	0.73	0.56	1.70	0.67
Philadelphia	0.58	1.69	0.68	0.56	1.76	0.89
Pittsburgh	0.59	0.90	0.57	0.87	1.83	1.14
Portland	0.58	0.95	0.60	0.75	2.01	0.96
San Francisco	0.66	1.26	0.68	0.56	1.90	1.29
Seattle	0.59	1.02	0.63	0.68	1.92	1.16
St. Louis	0.57	1.10	0.66	0.68	1.88	1.10
Washington, DC	0.47	1.11	0.72	0.59	1.80	0.79
correlation	0.21		−0.30		0.46	

There does appear to be more variation in the standard deviation of urban price inflation during the 1950s and 1970s than in average urban inflation rates. For instance, during the 1950s the standard deviation of city inflation rates varied between a maximum of 1.69 (Philadelphia) and a minimum of 0.84 (Detroit) compared to the 1960s (maximum of 0.93 for Los Angeles and minimum of 0.49 for Chicago). Although differences exist between cities in the variance of their inflation rates, it is difficult to provide a systematic explanation of such variations. Since all cities in the sample are relatively large, it is hard to discern any size effects, such as maximum variance being associated with small cities or vice versa. Also, there is little evidence of significant regional effects. For example, there are noticeable differences between New York, Baltimore, Philadelphia and Pittsburgh in their standard deviations of price inflation over all three decades. Finally, there is only a weak correlation between the average rate of inflation and the standard deviation of inflation. Table 7.1 indicates that the observed correlations were 0.21, −0.30 and 0.46 for the 1950s, 1960s and 1970s respectively.

Thus, the answer to the first question noted in the previous section is a qualified "No." Not only is the relationship very weak in the first two decades, there is also a mixture of signs implying that in the 1950s there is a weak positive association, and in the 1960s a weak negative association. The answer is qualified because it is apparent that the relationship strengthens over time as the average rate of inflation increases for all cities. Thus we are able to answer the second research question in the affirmative. This finding implies that with the higher rates of inflation of the 1970s, the variance of inflation increased across urban areas. Put differently, volatility of inflation is in part linked to the average rate of inflation and a certain threshold level of inflation (perhaps 10% per year). For those who assume flex-price models of resource allocation, this evidence is cause for concern. Volatility may create errors in allocation, inefficiencies in adjustment, and consequently costs in resource use.

The relative contributions of location (city) and economic situation (time) to the variance in inflation are summarized in Table 7.2. Without

Table 7.2 Analysis of variance: temporal and spatial effects on the variation of inflation, 1950–60, 1960–70, 1970–80.

Source of variation	Sum of squares	Mean square	F Statistic	Significance of F
time	1.75	0.87	19.84	yes
city	0.23	0.01	0.36	no
explained	1.98	0.11	2.65	
residual	1.32	0.04		
total	3.30	0.07		

doubt, the largest and most significant component in the variance of inflation rates for the cities under study is time. Essentially, national macroeconomic events significantly contribute to the variation in urban price inflation. The contribution of space to total variations is very small and insignificant. There is little significant inter-urban variation when compared to the variation over time in overall inflation rates. Thus the answer to the third research question is: more significant variation occurs in *time*, not space! This result is clear evidence for spatial price integration. After all, if there were significant spatial variations in price inflation, as well as temporal variations, then we would have had to conclude that the spatial structure of the economy contributes to national inflation as much as separate economic events. Lack of a significant spatial factor is an important result, indicating that however important local variations in inflation are to individual consumers, this may not be a significant issue for national macroeconomic planners.

Predicting local inflation

Even so, we would suggest that this evidence is not conclusive. We still cannot tell whether or not knowing the national price model is enough to predict local inflation. To do so requires, as a first step, estimating the national price inflation model. Using Box and Jenkins (1976) ARIMA techniques, the relevant models are detailed in Table 7.3. Three models were necessary because of the different quarterly time sequences in the urban price data. At the national level, there seem to be few differences in choosing different quarterly sequences of data. The major difference between models 1, 2 and 3 is in the first model's ARI (3) structure.

Table 7.3 Univariate time-series models of national price inflation.

Quarter sequence	Model form	Mean square error	Estimated form	K–S test
(1)J/A/J/O	ARI(3,1)	0.16×10^{-5}	$(1 + 0.55B + 0.43B^2 + 0.18B^3) Z_t = a_t$ -6.28 -4.46 -2.01	no
(2)F/M/A/N	ARI(2,1)	0.16×10^{-5}	$(1 + 0.55B + 0.39B^2) Z_t = a_t$ -6.65 -4.63	no
(3)M/J/S/D	ARI(2,1)	0.15×10^{-5}	$(1 + 0.55B + 0.34B^2) Z_t = a_t$ -6.50 -3.92	no

Notes
(a) *t*-values for each parameter are immediately below; all are significant at the 95% level.
(b) $Z_t = (1 - B)Z_t = (1 - B)[(CPI_t - CPI_{t-1})/CPI_{t-1}]$.
(c) J/A/J/O refers to January/April/July/October; F/M/A/N refers to February/May/August/November; M/J/S/D refers to March/June/September/December.
(d) "no" for the K–S test indicates no significant deviation of the residuals from white noise.

Instead of including two previous observations of the national inflation rate in forecasting Z_t (the case in models 2 and 3), the first model also includes a third lag term. The size of the parameters on the first and second lag terms are very similar, if not identical, between these models. Thus, in effect, there are only marginal differences between the models. In estimating these models each series had to be log-transformed and differenced so as to achieve stationarity (for a detailed discussion of these issues see Solo 1982).

Immediately apparent from these models is the implied smoothness in price adjustment from one time period to the next. The *form* of these models is autoregressive, not moving average, and consequently more consistent with fix-price contract models of price adjustment than with the rational expectations hypothesis. This is consistent with other macroeconomists who have argued that prices adjust slowly and in relation to previous price levels (Gordon 1981). Stochastic shocks are then much less important than past values of inflation in the short run. Of course, it may be true that monetary shocks are implied in previous values of inflation. However, there is no evidence that current or lagged shocks are directly linked to current price inflation.

Using these three models to filter local inflation time-series, the evidence presented in Table 7.4 provides support for both the spatial price integration *and* interdependence hypotheses. Nine of the 16 cities' price

Table 7.4   City inflation series filtered using national inflation models.

National model	City	t-Value, r_j acf	Model form residuals	K–S test
(3)	Baltimore	−2.68*	MA(1)	yes
(1)	Boston	−3.09*	AR(1)	yes
(2)	Chicago	−2.83+	MA(1)	yes
(3)	Cincinnati	−1.76	—	no
(2)	Cleveland	−2.19*	MA(3)	yes
(2)	Detroit	−1.90	—	no
(2)	Los Angeles	−2.60+	AR(1)	yes
(2)	Milwaukee	−1.92	—	no
(2)	New York	−0.94	—	no
(2)	Philadelphia	−1.54	—	no
(1)	Pittsburgh	−1.76	—	yes
(1)	Portland	−1.60	—	no
(3)	San Francisco	−0.90	—	no
(2)	Seattle	−2.20*	MA(3)	yes
(3)	St. Louis	−2.47*	MA(1)	yes
(2)	Washington, DC	−2.79+	AR(1)	yes

Notes

(a) r_j refers to the highest value, regardless of lag, in the autocorrelation function of the resulting residual series.

(b) "no" for the K–S test indicates no significant deviation of the residuals from white noise, "yes" indicates the opposite.

(c) + indicates significance at 95% level; * indicates significance at 99% level.

(d) acf – autocorrelation function.

series, filtered by their relevant national models, had significant nonrandom residuals. In most instances a model form could be identified for those residuals, implying that the national model is inadequate in those instances. Cities included in this group were Chicago, Los Angeles, Seattle and St. Louis. There was no clear association between these cities in their rates of economic growth or regional identity, or for that matter population size. Similarly, those cities (seven in total) that could be approximated by their respective national models without systematic error ranged in terms of regional identity, size, and economic growth.

It is nevertheless tempting to suggest that the inclusion of Los Angeles and Washington, DC, in the former group is evidence of some underlying growth pattern. However, the inclusion of San Francisco and Portland in the latter group makes such a hypothesis difficult to sustain. The answer to the fourth question: does the national pattern of inflation fairly represent local inflation? is consequently yes and no. The evidence tends to support both spatial price integration and interdependence depending on the city concerned.

Just because there may be no systematic residual deviation in some cities does not necessarily mean that the national model is the best predictor of local inflation. Clark (1984a) reports the results of modeling local inflation by means of transfer functions (Tiao *et al.* 1981); that is, assuming local inflation to be both a function of national and local components. In all instances, local inflation was better predicted by including local and national data. To that extent, spatial price interdependence is the strongest conclusion that can be made given the results. All estimated parameters reported in Clark (1984a) were significant at the 95% level, and K–S tests for residual patterns found no significant residual autocorrelation. Although spatial price interdependence is clearly the best representation of inflation amongst US cities, we should not exaggerate its importance. The results of filtering local inflation through the national model suggest that national prices may be a fair approximation for many larger cities, if not the *best* predictor of local inflation.

With respect to the autocorrelation form of the forecasting equations, ten were autoregressive processes of similar orders to the national price inflation models. That is, time lags extend over some two or three previous quarters, implying a relatively smooth quarterly price adjustment sequence. Given the similarities of the form and order of these processes with the national models noted above (Table 7.3), similar conclusions hold. In essence price adjustment is a "sticky" rather than a volatile and discontinuous process. This is quite consistent with fix-price contract theories of adjustment, implying quantity rationing in the short run. Without belaboring the point, REX models seem inappropriate. As in previous results, those cities characterized as ARI processes were from all regions and size categories, indicating no obvious geographical groups in adjustment patterns. Also noticeable were similarities in the parameter sizes on current and past lagged local and national quarterly observations.

Not all cities were characterized by simple autoregressive processes. Six of the 16 combined autoregressive structures with moving average components (ARIMA). In these instances (including Los Angeles, New York and Philadelphia), local price adjustment was not only related to current and previous local and national price patterns, but also to local current and lagged (one-period) stochastic shocks. Although in all instances, these shocks were not the most important components in determining local price adjustments, they nevertheless represent disturbances that may shift local inflation away from the national patterns. The cities in this group were very large, even given that the sample of cities was biased towards the largest of US SMSAs. The only exception was perhaps Portland, which is clearly not in the same class as cities such as New York, Los Angeles and Philadelphia. Despite evidence of a significant stochastic element to some cities' price series, price adjustment is best characterized in terms of fix-price contract models. Rational expectations theory assumes that the stochastic component is the principal determinant of price inflation, something not plausible here. Also REX theorists assume disturbances to be exogenous, yet for the six cities noted to have moving average components, disturbances are local, national, or even international in scope.

Conclusions

There are differences between US cities in terms of price inflation. Average quarterly rates vary, and so do the standard deviations of local inflation. Yet we must be careful not to overestimate the significance of these differences. Over time, many of the observed differences are the result of macroeconomic changes rather than spatial factors. Essentially, there is more temporal variation than spatial variation in inflation. This conclusion is given greater force by the finding that in a number of cities, local prices are fairly approximated by national prices. In this sense, spatial price integration seems a plausible assumption. It was also found, however, that in some cities there were systematic differences between national and local price series, implying that there may be significant risks if national prices are assumed to represent local prices. There were no apparent relationships between city size, regional location, or rate of economic growth of those cities fairly predicted by national trends. Forecasting local inflation does require both local and national price data. In this sense, local price adjustment is perhaps best described as a strongly interdependent process.

The actual process of price adjustment, local and national, is also of importance. Rational expectations (REX) theorists argue price adjustment to be volatile and discontinuous, a moving average process in the jargon of Box and Jenkins (1976) time-series philosophy. On the other hand, fix-price contract (FPC) theorists argue that prices adjust more slowly and in relation to previous observations. The former school emphasizes the importance of prices in allocating resources, the latter school emphasizes quantity adjustment. In the flex-price world of REX, unanticipated inflation may create *real* misallocations of resources and disruptions to economic activity. In the fix-price world of FPC, unanticipated inflation may be of less immediate importance, the crucial issue being distribution (who bears the costs of uncertainty). The evidence presented in this chapter tends to support the FPC school. Prices adjust quite slowly at the national and local levels, with past quarterly observations being most important.

8   *Components of local inflation*

Introduction

In the previous chapter, we argued that US city inflation rates hardly vary
significantly from national inflation rates. Various empirical tests were
used to establish this thesis. An analysis of variance was used to evaluate
the relative contributions of time (the three decades since 1950) and space
(a sample of 16 US cities) to variations in city inflation rates. As well,
autocorrelation time-series models of national price inflation were used to
filter local series so as to establish whether or not significant local effects
(residual periodicities) could be observed in each city's inflation series.
These and other tests indicated that most, if not all, of the post-1950
variation in city inflation rates seems to have been a product of time, not
space. That is, for many urban areas national price inflation seems fairly to
approximate local inflation, even though the popular press seems to
suggest distinct local inflation effects. Thus, in terms of inflation, the US
economy should be best characterized as a tightly interdependent system
of national and local prices.

This conclusion, however, was based on a relatively small sample of
large US SMSAs, using aggregate quarterly city price data for the period
1950 to 1980. A number of critics of this approach have suggested that
there may be, nevertheless, significant local inflation effects despite the
time-series evidence. Two related objections have been made. First, it is
possible that aggregate city price series mask inter-city differences in
energy, food and housing inflation rates. Since these three components
have been of major national significance, there does not seem to be any
reason why they should not vary in importance between cities. Local
inflation in one component may cancel out or compensate inflation in
another component so that, in aggregate, local inflation "appears" like
national inflation.

A second objection is that the time-series evidence masks local responses
to sudden unanticipated price shocks. It is possible that significant local
short-run deviations from national inflation patterns are lost because of the
temporal averaging effects of using decade-based data (as in the analysis of
variance) and the quarterly time-series model of the period 1950 to 1980.
The issue here is one which concerns the appropriateness of longer-term

time-series analysis as opposed to event-specific analysis. Since price shocks have been largely a function of unanticipated changes in specific components like energy prices, we may have to be cognizant of local composition effects and local event sensitivities before we can decide whether or not inflation varies between cities.

The aim of this chapter is to reconsider the evidence for urban price inflation variations, focusing upon the issues of the composition of local inflation and short-run discontinuities. At the outset, however, we should acknowledge that it is impossible to discern the existence (or nonexistence) of local substitution effects which may be the result of local inflation in one or more components of local consumption. All we can do is look closely at the specific episodes, the rates of local inflation, and spatial variations in food, energy, and housing price inflation. Market basket substitution effects, whether at the local or national levels, are virtually impossible to discern (Wahl 1982), even though there may exist "poor people's" baskets, "retired people's" baskets, and perhaps "southern" baskets. The next section reviews the theoretical and empirical evidence for short-run discontinuities, and the following sections deal in turn with national and local inflation. The chapter concludes with a reconciliation of the various arguments and data concerning local inflation.

The shocks hypothesis

There are a number of ways of classifying the many theories of inflation (Hudson 1982). For instance, a most obvious dichotomy is to classify inflation according to market pressures. On the demand side, inflation might be analyzed as the consequence of consumers wishing to buy more of a limited stock of goods despite higher and higher prices. Thus, for example, a sure sign of economic recovery is when producers begin bidding up the prices of inputs as they expand production beyond that which was anticipated by the suppliers of input commodities. This kind of inflation is surely the simplest, and is associated with the postwar Keynesian stabilization policies which assumed that the single most important source of price instability was consumer demand. Policies which would dampen demand, like credit-rationing, high interest rates, increased taxes, even higher levels of employment were all conceived in an environment which was assumed to be price competitive or at least price conscious. At the limit, prices in this conceptualization were assumed to represent true market conditions, thereby being the signals for private and public response (Okun 1981). Assuming a market of known extent and capacity, demand inflation is very much a neoclassical model of inflation.

On the other side of the market, supply factors can also affect inflation. Instead of demand being measured against supply, suppliers could introduce, exogenously, their own pricing schedules (Bruno & Sachs 1982). For example, the OPEC energy price shocks of 1973–4 and 1979 were instances of administered price increases that had less to do with demand (at least in the short run) and more to do with the objectives of oil suppliers. Here, of course, one objective was to maximize revenue given demand. Similarly, monopoly pricing and restricted price competition would have the same effect: autonomous price rises given an existing level of demand. On the supply side, inflation results because the cardinal rule of neoclassical economics is broken. That is, competition is circumvented, whether because of the nature of the good (there were no short-run substitutes for oil) or because of the nature of the institutional structure of the market. This kind of analysis is as relevant for industrial commodities as for raw unprocessed commodities. The crucial insight is, of course, that market prices may be ambiguous in these situations – perhaps reflecting "real" shortfalls in supply, but perhaps also reflecting pricing practices.

One of the more important subtleties of an analysis of inflation via a simple comparison of demand and supply has to do with the spatial *origins* of price pressures. In excess demand circumstances, it could be reasonably suggested that the cause of inflation is endogenous, that is, derived internally. With a highly integrated national commodity market, inflation could be controlled, attacking the forces of demand like real incomes, credit availability, expectations, and so on. By "endogenous" we mean that the causes of inflation are internally integrated with the functioning of the economy. In contrast, supply-side inflation may not be endogenous. Price increases can be imposed on the market by institutions, governments, and private individuals regardless of the internal mechanics of the market. Thus, supply-side price increases may be termed exogenous, in that they are derived from the external environment. Of course, not all supply-side price increases need be exogenous; a situation in which demand and supply simultaneously and respectively increased and decreased due to differing market expectations would give rise to endogenously determined price inflation.

Classifying inflation as endogenous depends very much on the geographical scale of analysis. For instance, it is easy enough to agree that OPEC-induced energy price increases are exogenous to the US economy and all its geographical regions. But it is also plausible that increased electricity charges which result from local (state) level demand conditions which then spill over to adjoining regions will be both endogenous and exogenous. Obviously local demand pressures would be classified as endogenous, but the spill-over of price increases into other regions would have to be classified as exogenous. In the former case it is the local conditions driving local prices. In the latter case, local conditions are irrelevant: electricity price increases are imported and exogenously determined and will "appear" as supply-side increases. The implication is that the larger the geographical scale of production and consumption, the more likely price inflation will appear as endogenous. On the other hand, the more an economic system is geographically segmented, the more likely endogenous events will appear as exogenous, and the more likely the economy will be judged interdependent rather than integrated (Whitman 1979).

The shocks model of inflation is based on these kinds of distinctions. Most generally, the shocks argument goes as follows (see, for instance, Blinder 1979). First, it is assumed that there is an underlying rate of inflation, endogenously determined by the existing balance between demand and supply. In any given market, this rate of inflation will obviously depend on what is produced and consumed locally. An economy which does not produce for local consumption could hardly have a local inflation rate. At the US regional or even SMSA scale it is entirely possible that some commodities may be in limited supply, especially those that have a high locational fixity, like housing. However, we must be careful not to overemphasize this possibility, as very few commodities have such fixity in the USA, especially as the distance component of market prices for many goods is very small. At the international level, locational fixity is more important for a wider range of consumer and production goods, although rapidly declining locational fixity over the past decade has severely shaken even the most traditional US industries such as autos, steel, chemicals, electricals, and machinery.

Given an underlying (or *core*) rate of local inflation (Eckstein 1981), the second part to the shocks argument is that a significant portion of local inflation is exogenously determined. Since exogeneity implies autonomous behavior of outside economic agents, such price increases will appear as "shocks" because they are not internally determined or generated through an integrated set of factor commodity markets. For inflation to be imported, there must be some measure of interdependence, whether through trade or currency exchange (Cassese & Lothian 1982). At the regional or city levels, interdependence is virtually guaranteed by the use of a common currency. Similarly, through commodity imports, external prices are rapidly factored into local production and consumption. Indeed, even in the housing industry, there are good reasons for expecting some measure of interregional price conformity, as materials for new houses are imported into almost all areas and interest rates on home mortgages are practically universal in the USA.

But price shocks are defined by more than their location of origin. What makes a price shock a shock is the fact that it is relatively unanticipated (Rotemberg 1982). Compared to endogenously determined price inflation, imported price shocks are less predictable and less easy to handle by conventional contracts. By this we mean that local demand conditions are more known to local market participants. Not only are current conditions well known, but so too are past conditions and expectations of likely future conditions. There are established information channels and recognized market leaders who set the datum points for the behavior of other market participants (cf. Rosenberg & Weisskopf 1981). This is not to suggest that local conditions are completely known nor completely stable. Rather, points of discretion and likely behavior in response are relatively well known at least for their boundary conditions – the limits on individual behavior. In this context, inflation may not be a surprise; inflation may be reasonably anticipated. In contrast, not only are exogenous shocks unanticipated because of inadequate knowledge, but local responses are likely to be more varied and less predictable because they disturb customary behavior (Piore 1981).

Consequently, price shocks are short-run phenomena, and appear as sudden unanticipated events. Notice, however, that price shocks need not be immediately integrated into local price levels. Contracts to deliver commodities at certain fixed prices in the future are designed explicitly to deal with such unanticipated events. Contracts in these circumstances attempt to forestall changing circumstances, distribute the costs of unanticipated events and, at the same time, ensure continuity in exchange relationships. Thus, we can have both short-run price shocks or events and temporal rigidity in local prices. In this respect, the model of price rigidity summarily termed the fix-price contract model (FPC) (see Clark 1984a) is entirely consistent with the shocks hypothesis. Indeed, the FPC model depends on the existence of shocks; without shocks there would be no need for contracts. Inflation in these conditions would be reasonably anticipated, integrated into current and future prices and, as a consequence, radically reduced in importance as an economic problem (Hahn 1982).

At this level of abstraction, it could be argued that the shocks hypothesis is not so much a criticism of time-series analysis of local inflation so much as an embellishment of the principal thesis advanced in the previous essay. Even so, the shocks hypothesis does indicate that a different methodology could be employed to analyze urban inflation. In particular, it is apparent that an episodic analysis may be warranted, based on the principal price shocks of the past 30 years (but see also Blinder and Newton (1981) on government policy). For urban areas, these shocks would include energy prices, housing prices, and food prices, to name the three major contributors to post-1950 price instability (Blinder 1982). Whether or not these price shocks have had significant differential urban impacts remains a moot point, since there has been little research on this issue apart from the observation made above that urban price inflation is hardly significantly different from national inflation.

A priori, we can hypothesize differential urban impacts in these types of price shocks (see Sheppard and Curry (1982) for a more detailed analysis). Given that the Bureau of Labor Statistics (BLS) measures the CPI based on a standard basket of commodities across localities, we doubt that there would be significant urban differences in impacts of food and energy shocks. In both instances, virtually all urban areas generally import their food and energy requirements. The only exceptions are likely to be found in energy-rich regions such as Texas where local prices may dominate. Generally, however, international oil companies sell imported gasoline at very similar prices (certainly rates of increase) across the nation in company-owned retail outlets. Similarly, food production and retailing are highly spatially integrated businesses dominated by corporate buying and selling practices. It is difficult to imagine that the BLS's food and energy components would not be priced or at least inflated at similar rates across the USA, even though food "shocks" are more national than international. One might expect, however, some local endogenously induced inflation effects in the housing sector. The locational fixity of the housing industry makes it virtually unique in this regard, even though home-building materials are generally imported.

National versus local inflation patterns

For the period 1950 to 1980, the CPI data used to measure local and national inflation were derived from unpublished sources at the Bureau of Labor Statistics. Generally, the CPI "measures the average change in prices of goods and services purchased by consumers for day-to-day living" (BLS 1980: 321). The market basket of commodities upon which the CPI is based was the same across locations and over the time period studied in this book. Thus, what we have is a relative measure of the changing cost of living in 26 locations across the USA. Notice that the CPI measures relative changes in prices against a standard base year of 1967 = 100. Thus, while we can establish whether or not one area has higher or lower inflation relative to all other areas and the nation, the CPI cannot indicate the existence or otherwise of absolute differences in the cost of living between places (BLS 1982a). Here the CPI index used was for all urban consumers, based on the January 1978 BLS market basket. The BLS collects price data on some 85 cities, suburbs, and towns and weighs their 1970 populations to arrive at a national CPI measure.

The sample of cities included for analysis cover all major regions of the USA. Of course, these cities are relatively large but, even so, they capture many economic circumstances including economic collapse (Buffalo, New York) and explosive growth (Dallas, Texas). The sample is larger than in the previous chapter because we were able to use yearly data rather than the more restricted and synchronized quarterly aggregate urban price data. Since the object of this chapter is to look for variations in the components of local inflation, it was thought best to sacrifice some of the detail of the quarterly data for the wider spatial breadth of the yearly data.

To begin, we wish to indicate the extent to which national and urban aggregate price inflation indices are closely related, even temporally synchronized. For instance, using the previous quarterly data it can be shown graphically that all US cities follow national price inflation patterns very closely. For a sample of US cities, Figure 8.1 demonstrates this phenomenon for the period 1950 to 1980. On each graph the diagonal line extending out from the origin is at 45 degrees to the axes. Any deviation of the CPI away from that line would indicate a shift away from equal national and urban price indices. A shift above would indicate that, for the period under review, the national CPI was higher than the local CPI, thus reflecting a difference in inflation rates. Conversely, a shift below the 45 degree line would indicate the opposite. Obviously, this graphical exposition is a qualitative measure of the existence and extent of temporal variations between local and national inflation.

Figure 8.1 provides some evidence that there are distinct, albeit marginal, short-run differences in local and national CPIs. Taking Chicago as an example, both local and national CPIs begin around 70.0 in 1950 ($1967 = 100.0$), and then rise in a closely synchronized fashion through to the early 1970s. So closely do national and local CPIs track one another that there is hardly a single quarterly step off the 45 degree line. The only exception is to be found in the mid-1950s when Chicago's CPI was slightly higher than the nation's. A similar pattern can be observed for Detroit during this period and, interestingly enough, both cities are midwestern. Generally, however, there was no interruption in the sequencing of national and local CPI's over this period (1950–70) for Philadelphia, Los Angeles, Seattle and Washington, DC, cities located in very different regions of the country and experiencing markedly different rates of growth over this period of time (Clark 1982b). In terms of aggregate price indices it could be reasonably argued that national and local inflation were equivalent for this sample of cities, indeed for the whole nation.

But beyond 1970, a different picture of national and local inflation emerges from Figure 8.1. For a start, it is apparent that the pace of inflation quickly increases, leading to rapid shifts in national and local CPIs. Indeed, while local and national CPIs barely increased more than 40.0 points from 1950 to 1970, they increased at least another 150.0 points over the next ten years. More importantly, instead of local and national prices tracking one another in a tight step-by-step fashion, it is apparent that there were marginal differences in local and national inflation over the period 1970 to 1980. Clearly, these differences were marginal and not significant when compared to temporal variations over this period based on the analysis of variance test reported in the previous chapter. Even so, their increased variability deserves recognition. For instance, in Seattle, local inflation fell marginally behind national inflation through to about 1977. This was also

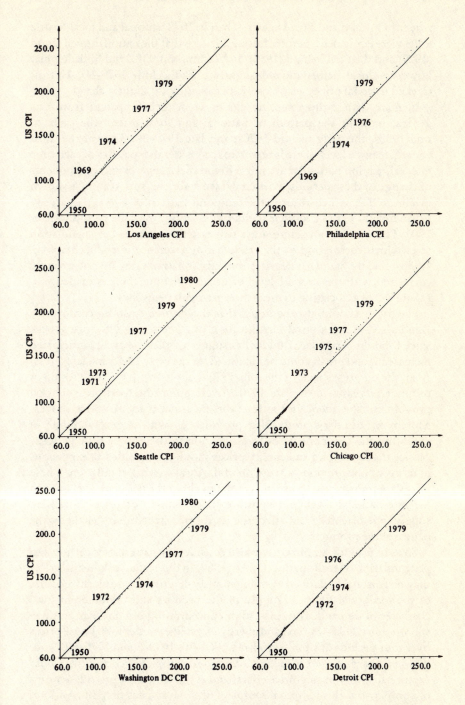

Figure 8.1 Urban price inflation versus national price inflation, 1950–80.

true for Chicago and Los Angeles. Then in 1978 national and local Seattle CPIs were equivalent, before shifting again so that the nation moved ahead (1979) and then fell behind (1980). In Washington, DC, and Philadelphia, however, local prices moved slightly ahead. Until 1979–80, Detroit tracked national prices very closely, before moving slightly ahead.

In many cities, three specific phases seem to be apparent from this general view of the pattern of national and local prices: the early to mid-1950s, the early to mid-1970s, and late 1979–80. Thus at the most aggregate price level, there is reason to reconsider the specifics of each time interval, paying particular attention to the special events and components of change of these periods. Further evidence for this supposition is shown in Figure 8.2, which records the temporal pattern of average quarterly urban inflation rates and their standard deviations over the period 1950 to 1980. There are obvious shifts and changes in the average of urban inflation rates which correspond to the crude dating sequence introduced above. And, while the standard deviations of city inflation rates are not strongly correlated with the average level of urban inflation, there is evidence in Figure 8.2 of association in these three particular episodes.

Finally, it should also be noted that these three episodes conform to Blinder's (1982) temporal identification of three major US price shocks since 1950. In particular, Blinder has suggested that a sharp unanticipated increase in food prices could be identified for the early 1950s and late 1970s. Also, the oil price shock of the mid-1970s coupled with a second round of oil price increases in the late 1970s (overlapping the food price shocks) provide initial evidence for at least three distinct phases of price shocks. Moreover, Blinder's study also provides us with a general guide in exploring the components of local inflation in these three time periods. Notice that both food and energy prices should be classified as exogenous in terms of our previous discussion of the local sources of inflation. These prices are transmitted to urban areas from either the national level or even the international level. Furthermore, both sources of price shocks are supply-side oriented, and affect the local price structure by virtue of the nature of the products.

So as to provide a contrast, we also consider the pattern of local housing price inflation over the period 1950 to 1980. In this instance, housing prices may be reasonably defined as endogenously determined primarily because of the locational fixity of supply of the product and the inherent local character of demand. But, instead of concentrating our analysis on three specific episodes as for food and energy, we will consider local house prices over four periods of time – 1950–60, 1960–70, 1970–5 and 1975–80. Since it is very hard *a priori* to define a temporal sampling scheme that could capture all local housing price effects and at the same time provide a means of comparison, this temporal sample will serve as a datum point for local house prices in general.

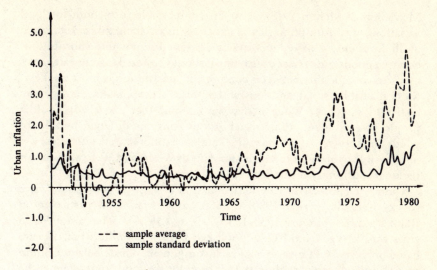

Figure 8.2 Average quarterly urban inflation, 1950–80.

Components of local inflation

Strictly speaking, food, energy, and housing have quite specific definitions in the Bureau of Labor Statistics CPI survey. *Food* is a very general category referring to the price of food whether bought at a retail establishment and consumed at home or purchased at a restaurant. *Energy* is actually a more general term for the BLS CPI category called fuel and other utilities. This category includes utility rates (electricity, water, etc.), gas, oil, coal, and gasoline. It can be interpreted as consumers' energy prices since oil price shocks have had significant impacts on the prices of close substitutes like gas, coal and electricity. Notice that the energy component may include international, national, and even regional fuel-related commodities bought at the local level. *Housing*, the final component to be considered, is the BLS category of shelter. This category is basically the measured prices of providing a "roof-over-head," whether rented or owned, new or old. It is not the most general housing category, but rather refers to the direct costs of providing family shelter.

These three components have considerable importance in the BLS market basket. All told, these components account for 48.6% of the total basket and individually account for the following proportions: shelter (21.3%), food (18.9%), fuel and other utilities (8.3%). By using these three components we are able to account for the major sources of CPI variations over the 1950 to 1980 period. Notice, of course, that we are unable to measure prices directly, but instead we use a standard index (cf.

McMahon & Melton 1978). Also, it is impossible to account for local variations in consumption (if any exist) because a standard basket is used in all locations. Finally, we cannot account for possible substitutions between goods and services, although it should be noted that the categories used are so wide that between-component substitution is most unlikely. More plausible are substitutions within the subcomponents that make up each CPI category. While it may be possible that poor people, older people, and different ethnic/racial groups consume different bundles of goods and services, and as a result experience different inflation rates, it is not possible to account for such segments as we are unable to account for regional consumption patterns.

Table 8.1 summarizes the local inflation effects of food-related price shocks over the period 1950 to 1980, concentrating in particular on Blinder's three episodes: 1950–1, 1972–5, and 1977–9. The sample of 26 cities was derived from BLS unpublished statistics and the actual data are based on yearly CPI measures of each component. The left-hand column of each episode refers to the city CPI level for the food component at the start of the episode. The right-hand column then indicates the percentage increase (or rate of inflation) in the food component during each particular episode. The US city average is the whole BLS CPI food component estimate for the 85 survey locations. This arrangement of data is replicated in Tables 8.2 (energy) and 8.3 (housing), although the actual dates of the episodes change in accordance with Blinder's (1982) scheme. Finally it should be noted that each pair of columns are summarily described using sample averages, standard deviations, coefficient of variations, and correlation coefficients.

In the first episode, food prices increased in the sample of cities by an average of 11.3%, closely matching the US average of 11.2%. The lowest increase was in Boston (9.8%) and the highest in Atlanta (13.4%). There were no obvious regional effects and no correlation between the starting CPI level and the rate of increase over the episode. What is interesting is that the sample standard deviation of food inflation is significantly lower than the standard deviation measure for the starting CPI level. However, it is also apparent that their respective coefficients of variations were reversed in order of size, suggesting that there was more variation in local response to the price shock than in the initial level of city-based CPI levels. This was also true for the two other episodes. More interesting was the fact that in the 1972–5 food price shock, local variation in response actually declined (as measured by the coefficient of variation) even though the price shock was at least three times larger (42.6% as against 11.3%). Also noticeable in this second episode was the markedly similar sample average city inflation rate (42.6%) as compared to the national rate (43.6%).

The third food price shock was about half as large as the preceding food price shock and about double the first. Compared to the previous episodes,

Table 8.1 Rates of change in city CPIs: food.

City	1950–1 Start CPI	1950–1 Increase (%)	1972–5 Start CPI	1972–5 Increase (%)	1977–9 Start CPI	1977–9 Increase (%)
Anchorage			113.1	48.2	189.8	19.7
Atlanta	75.5	13.4	124.4	46.1	186.4	21.3
Baltimore	73.4	10.7	124.7	42.9	199.9	19.9
Boston	72.2	9.8	123.7	41.6	190.9	20.4
Buffalo			123.3	40.8	189.2	19.8
Chicago	76.2	11.2	123.9	41.3	191.0	23.9
Cincinnati	75.5	10.6	124.5	42.5	197.8	23.6
Cleveland	78.9	11.1	123.3	42.4	196.1	20.5
Dallas			123.0	40.6	191.3	23.2
Denver			118.8	44.2	190.8	20.6
Detroit	76.4	12.6	122.9	39.6	184.4	22.8
Honolulu			123.3	43.3	193.0	24.2
Houston	76.3	10.7	125.0	44.9	198.8	24.9
Kansas City	75.1	11.9	123.6	43.8	193.0	23.9
Los Angeles	72.0	12.9	120.4	41.3	185.8	23.5
Milwaukee	78.1	10.2	120.6	42.5	189.0	24.2
Minneapolis	76.4	11.9	124.4	42.0	196.7	34.6
New York	73.7	10.7	128.6	39.6	195.4	19.0
Philadelphia	73.7	11.3	124.4	44.4	198.4	20.8
Pittsburgh	76.1	10.8	122.8	44.4	193.6	20.5
Portland	74.6	12.6	118.0	42.7	188.8	23.7
San Diego			123.3	40.8	190.5	23.9
San Francisco	72.6	10.9	121.4	41.0	187.4	24.4
Seattle	74.1	10.7	120.7	40.5	187.9	19.9
St. Louis	72.3	11.8	122.5	42.3	192.8	21.7
Washington, DC	73.0	10.7	125.8	43.6	199.7	25.0
US city average	77.6	11.2	121.6	43.6	190.2	22.3
sample average	74.8	11.3	122.7	42.6	192.6	22.7
sample SD	1.9	0.9	2.9	2.0	4.4	3.1
sample CV	0.03	0.08	0.02	0.04	0.02	0.13
correlation	−0.004		−0.380		+0.109	
r_s	+0.047		+0.064		+0.088	

there was more local variation in response although, on the average, the sample rate of increase was almost exactly the same as the US city average. It would be very hard to argue in these cases that there are distinct differences between the sample of cities and the nation in terms of their responses to food price shocks. Granted, there are a range of responses, and even a few dramatic differences. For instance in Anchorage, Alaska during the second episode, the local food price increase was 48.2% as compared to the sample average of 42.6% and the national average of 43.6%. Also, during the third episode, local food prices rose 34.6% in Minneapolis, Minnesota as compared to the sample average of 22.7% and the national average of 22.3%. One looks in vain, however, for consistent spatial temporal patterns in these responses. These instances are exceptions to the rule. Given that food is a major component of local CPIs, dramatic increases in food prices in Anchorage, for example, should be enough to shift (if only marginally) local prices off and to the right of the 45 degree line (as in Fig. 8.1). However, it is easy to see why most cities trace out the national CPI given the close conformity in local responses to food price shocks.

When we compare local responses to food price shocks (Table 8.1) with local responses to energy price shocks (Table 8.2), it becomes quickly apparent that the latter responses are more variable than the former. For the two energy price shocks (1972–5 and 1978–9), the coefficients of variation of local response are significantly larger (0.2 and 0.3) than was the case for the local responses to food price shocks (0.08, 0.04, and 0.13). Although the average 1972–5 local energy price shock was lower than the 1972–5 price shock (35.2% against 42.6%), the range of local response to the energy price shock was greater. For instance, Boston and New York City recorded 53.5% and 50.1% increases respectively in energy prices, while Kansas City recorded a 23.2% increase in energy prices. What is also obvious is that there are distinct geographical patterns in these responses. It appears that larger eastern and midwestern cities recorded the largest energy price increases while southern and southwestern cities recorded the lowest energy price increases. There are some exceptions to this generalization. For instance, Pittsburgh energy prices rose at about the same rate as San Diego energy prices, with both being lower than the sample and national average energy price increases during this episode. Even so, it seems a fair characterization.

But in the episode 1978–9, this geographical pattern of high and low energy price responses observed in the previous episode does not seem relevant. While a number of larger eastern cities did record quite dramatic increases in energy prices (for example, Boston's energy prices increased 48.5% as against the sample average of 27.9%), some southern and western cities also recorded above average rates of energy price increases. For instance, energy prices rose 35.6% in Houston and 33.4% in Los Angeles. Although Dallas again recorded quite a low energy price increase (15.2%), consistent with the previous episode (23.4%), Cincinnati also recorded quite a low price increase (15.5%), inconsistent with the previous episode (40.4%). The larger coefficient of variation on local responses in this second episode confirms an overall impression that while there may be distinct differences between some cities and the nation in terms of their responses to energy price shocks, it is difficult to predict which cities will be above and which will be below the national average. Since energy prices are quite a small component of the overall CPI, a city clearly has to record a very large response to an energy price shock, compared to the nation,

Table 8.2 Rates of change in city CPIs: energy.

City	1972–5		1977–9	
	Start CPI	Increase (%)	Start CPI	Increase (%)
Anchorage	110.1	35.2	172.3	14.0
Atlanta	125.2	28.1	212.0	17.4
Baltimore	117.4	38.3	223.6	22.4
Boston	117.3	53.5	214.0	48.5
Buffalo	140.1	48.1	266.3	29.3
Chicago	115.4	30.8	188.8	30.3
Cincinnati	121.7	40.4	249.1	15.5
Cleveland	121.5	31.5	224.8	24.0
Dallas	116.5	23.4	207.3	15.2
Denver	112.6	25.1	190.7	32.2
Detroit	114.4	38.5	224.4	27.8
Honolulu	110.4	42.2	201.0	20.9
Houston	116.2	37.4	225.5	35.6
Kansas City	119.7	23.2	202.8	23.6
Los Angeles	123.9	26.5	173.0	33.4
Milwaukee	123.4	34.4	217.0	34.3
Minneapolis	122.9	31.9	228.4	15.7
New York	124.2	50.1	232.8	34.4
Philadelphia	117.5	41.7	207.5	40.2
Pittsburgh	119.7	32.1	210.2	19.0
Portland			226.1	41.0
San Diego	113.8	30.2	170.2	35.8
San Francisco	121.3	28.1	204.9	38.6
Seattle	114.4	36.5	187.8	40.2
St. Louis	118.0	34.9	208.2	15.2
Washington, DC	118.2	37.7	213.1	22.2
US city average	120.1	39.7	216.0	28.7
sample average	119.0	35.2	210.8	27.9
sample SD	6.1	7.9	22.4	9.8
sample CV	0.05	0.2	0.1	0.3
correlation	+0.194		−0.097	
r_s	−0.010		−0.027	

before there would be an appreciable effect on a city's overall CPI compared to the nation's. Perhaps Boston's 53.5% and 48.5% energy price increases over these two episodes would be enough to shift Boston's overall CPI away from the nation. To do so, however, would require all other major components of the local CPI to be very close to the national CPI. In 1972–5 and 1977–9 food prices in Boston actually increased less than the national average, so that some of the effects of large local energy price increases would have been lost. On the other hand, during the same episodes Dallas' food prices also rose less than the average, and this coupled with dramatically lower energy price increases could result in a lower local inflation rate.

Notice what is more important here: the timing and geographical impact of different types of price shocks. There may not be enough consistency or overlap in the right direction between price shocks for there to be systematic differences in local inflation rates. Indeed, the evidence noted in the previous chapter for aggregate data, and now at the individual component level, suggests that there has not been enough consistency in the effects of different price shocks to make a significant difference between the overall inflation rates in many cities and the national inflation rate. One other related observation has to do with the variable capacities of cities to absorb exogenous energy price shocks. Notable in this regard are cities like Dallas, Atlanta, Kansas City, and St. Louis, all of which had lower than average responses to OPEC oil price shocks. One explanation of their lower than average responses may be related to their use of particular southwestern oil and gas reserves which were bound by long-term pricing contracts pegged at below world energy price standards during the 1972–9 period. Only since Congress has moved to deregulate southwestern gas prices (post-1980) have cities like Dallas had their energy prices change to the levels of other eastern and midwestern cities.

So far, we have concentrated on two major sources of exogenous price shocks: food and energy. Another major source of local price inflation is the housing sector. But in this regard housing prices are more likely to be an endogenous source of local inflation, although the financing and building of new homes will be affected by national costs. Here, we consider the total shelter component on the BLS CPI market basket, not just new construction costs. Table 8.3 summarizes the patterns of local housing price inflation of the period 1953–80. (The beginning date of 1953 was made necessary because of data availability.) As expected, there is quite a range in local housing price inflation, although it would not be true to say that the local variation in housing price inflation was so much larger than local variations in energy price inflation. For housing price inflation, the sample cities' coefficients of variation ranged from 0.4 to 0.2, while for energy price inflation the sample cities' coefficients of variation ranged from 0.2 to 0.3. Notice as well that in all four periods, the sample cities' average housing price inflation rates were very close to the national average.

Taking the first two episodes to begin with, it is apparent that there were wide variations in local housing inflation during 1953 to 1960 and 1960 to 1970. For instance, Boston recorded the highest rate of housing price inflation in 1953 to 1960 of 30.5%, more than double the average city sample housing inflation rate (14.0%), while Washington, DC, recorded the lowest housing inflation rate of 3.9% – less than one-third the sample average. In the second episode the range of local variation was much narrower with, for example, San Francisco having the highest housing price inflation rate of 54.7% as compared to the sample average of 40.6%.

The lowest city housing price inflation rate during this episode was Cincinnati's 31.2%. Geographically, during the first episode the largest housing price increases were recorded by larger eastern, midwestern, and western cities. However, in the second episode it is more difficult to establish this pattern although some eastern, midwestern, and in particular western cities again recorded above average rates of housing price inflation. Given that there were no other price shocks during this period, it is the housing price inflation component which would have contributed to any inter-city variations in overall price inflation.

From Figures 8.1 and 8.2 it is apparent that it is difficult to identify significant local variations in overall price inflation during these two episodes. Perhaps the only exception might be Chicago during the mid-50s. What is interesting in both periods is that, unlike all other components, the rate of housing price inflation is significantly (but inversely) related to the beginning local housing CPI level. That is, areas with relatively low housing CPIs experienced the most rapid increases in housing prices over these two periods. Notice, however, that this relationship was not as significant during the subsequent episode 1971–5, and was insignificant during the last episode 1975–80, although the inverse sign was maintained in both cases.

During 1970–5, it was the midwestern cities of Chicago (64.5%), Milwaukee (59.0%) and St. Louis (69.6%) which recorded the largest rates of housing price increases as against a sample city average of 38.8%. Californian cities experienced about average housing price increases and the larger eastern cities experienced slightly above average housing price increases. This third episode exhibited a rate of housing price increase about equal to that of the previous episode, even though the time horizon was only half as long (5 years as against 10 years). Again, the geography of rapid price increases changed dramatically, as was the case in the previous analysis of food and energy price shocks.

When we compare the third episode to the last, yet another picture emerges. For a start, the rate of housing price inflation is much larger (almost double), and this is reflected in the highest local rates of house price inflation. For instance, San Diego recorded the highest rate of increase, 100.0%, followed by Dallas (90.7%), Denver (89.6%), Seattle (88.0%), Cleveland (82.7%) and Houston (82.6%). Again, midwestern cities like Detroit, Cleveland, and Cincinnati experienced above average increases in their housing prices. However, in this episode the larger eastern cities such as New York and Philadelphia experienced less than average housing increases. This episode clearly expressed the importance of the southwest as the strongest economic growth region in the USA, and indicated that there may indeed be quite distinct geographical patterns of housing price inflation. This result was, of course, entirely expected.

Table 8.3 Rates of change in city CPIs: housing.

City	1953–60 Start CPI	1953–60 Increase (%)	1960–70 Start CPI	1960–70 Increase (%)	1970–5 Start CPI	1970–5 Increase (%)	1975–80 Start CPI	1975–80 Increase (%)
Anchorage					119.2	17.5	140.1	50.5
Atlanta	81.2	10.9	90.1	42.5	128.4	34.0	172.1	55.7
Baltimore	77.6	16.1	90.1	35.4	122.0	53.2	186.9	62.0
Boston	65.2	30.5	85.1	46.3	124.5	32.9	165.5	47.5
Buffalo					121.5	33.7	162.5	43.3
Chicago	74.4	22.0	90.8	33.1	120.9	64.5	198.9	39.1
Cincinnati	82.4	11.6	92.0	31.2	120.7	40.3	169.3	73.9
Cleveland	80.4	15.4	92.8	33.0	123.4	29.0	159.2	82.7
Dallas					127.7	27.6	162.9	90.7
Denver	82.7	6.3	87.9	51.5	136.2	37.6	187.4	89.6
Detroit					133.2	27.8	170.3	81.9
Honolulu					120.7	23.0	148.5	48.2
Houston	87.5	5.6	92.4	37.4	127.0	40.9	179.0	82.6
Kansas City	81.3	11.0	90.3	34.7	121.6	34.9	164.0	77.2

City								
Los Angeles	71.7	14.6	82.2	47.0	120.8	39.2	168.1	75.4
Milwaukee	83.6	10.0	92.0	40.0	120.5	59.0	191.6	52.2
Minneapolis	76.2	11.9	85.3	49.7	127.7	37.2	175.2	69.9
New York	72.9	19.5	87.1	41.3	123.1	40.7	173.2	38.6
Philadelphia	78.7	12.1	88.2	42.4	125.6	43.9	180.7	43.7
Pittsburgh	80.9	14.1	92.3	33.7	123.4	37.4	169.6	79.7
Portland								
San Diego	67.6	21.9	82.4	54.7	132.1	41.5	186.9	100.0
San Francisco	71.8	17.0	84.0	48.4	127.5	33.5	170.2	64.7
Seattle	80.0	11.7	89.4	31.9	124.7	36.2	170.0	88.0
St. Louis					117.9	69.6	199.9	44.8
Washington, DC	84.1	3.9	87.4	37.2	119.9	34.9	169.7	66.7
US city average	76.5	14.8	87.8	40.7	123.6	38.8	169.7	66.7
sample average	77.9	14.0	88.5	40.6	124.4	38.8	172.5	65.7
sample SD	5.9	6.4	3.4	7.3	4.6	12.0	14.2	18.6
sample CV	0.07	0.4	0.03	0.2	0.03	0.3	0.08	0.3
correlation	−0.866		−0.810		−0.260		−0.042	
r_s	−0.907		−0.746		−0.157		−0.073	

But can these patterns of local housing price inflation be linked to aggregate shifts in local inflation compared to national inflation? Perhaps. Take, for example, Philadelphia in Figure 8.1. During the period 1970–5, it was apparent that Philadelphia's overall price level increased more than the nation's. In terms of food, energy and housing, Philadelphia's prices grew faster than the national average in all three components. During the food and energy price shocks of 1972–5, Philadelphia's price indices increased 44.4% and 41.7% respectively with the latter rate of increase being quite above the national average. We could conclude that there was enough overlap in the effects of these price shocks to push Philadelphia's inflation rate marginally higher than the national average. On the other hand, for Detroit (Figure 8.1) the main cause for the apparent shift in local inflation during the late 1970s must have been housing prices, since local energy and food price increases were about average.

Conclusions

In the previous chapter, we argued that local US inflation is hardly significantly different from national inflation. To sustain our argument we used aggregate local CPI data in a variety of time-series tests of the relative contributions of *time* and *space* to variations in local inflation. In this chapter, we have been more detailed in our analysis, concentrating on the local effects of price shocks in three major components of the BLS CPI market basket: food, energy, and housing. This analysis was premised on a couple of methodological propositions: first, that economic events are actually discontinuous and often unanticipated; secondly, that a distinction should be made between the sources of local price inflation, specifically a distinction between exogenous imported price shocks and endogenous, demand-induced, commodity price inflation. These two propositions implied the need for an episodic analysis of local inflation, focusing in particular on the three major components of the BLS market basket.

The results reported here suggest that both propositions are consistent with the post-1950 local experience of inflation. Each episode and each component had a distinct contribution to the pattern of price inflation. And it was also apparent that exogenous price shocks were more spatially homogeneous in their effects on local price inflation than endogenously induced local price inflation in the housing sector. This does not mean that there were no local variations in the effects of food and energy shocks. There were some differences, and there were a couple of instances in the energy case where cities seemed to experience quite marked differences in price inflation. However, it was also apparent that there were no obvious and stable geographical patterns in these variations, especially when compared to the housing sector. In this respect, we would contend that there are no local variations in food price inflation, only minor local differences in energy price inflation, and some significant local differences in housing price inflation. This hierarchy of local inflation effects is consistent with our prior expectations.

Whether or not these separate component effects translate into significant aggregate differences between local and national inflation remains problematical. There is no evidence of temporal consistency in the spatial impacts of exogenous price shocks. Thus, to shift local inflation significantly away from national inflation requires a certain serendipity of circumstances; circumstances which are unlikely to be repeated on any consistent basis. When this conclusion is coupled with shifting geographical patterns of housing price inflation, it is obvious why we would conclude over the 1950–80 period that local inflation hardly varies from national inflation. The fact of the matter is that whatever the separate local effects of specific price shocks, national and local prices are closely synchronized and coordinated. Thus there is little evidence of temporally consistent and significant local inflation effects in the United States.

9 *Regional wage indexation*

Introduction

Most regional economic models are based on levels and real balances. For example, firms' employment decisions are thought to be a function of local relative wages (relative to the wage levels of other places) discounted by local price levels and labor productivity. Such models are based on comparative statics and reduce decision variables to their "real" values, supposedly untainted by monetary effects. This modeling strategy is appropriate if the spatial economic system is at equilibrium. At equilibrium, we do not need to know how the economic system gets from one point to another, or how economic agents are going to respond to changes in the economic environment. These issues are irrelevant in a world which is stable, certain, and complete. But, of course, this picture is hardly an accurate characterization of reality.

In a world characterized by disequilibrium, nationally and locally, different issues arise (Benassy 1982). It becomes very important to understand how the economic system adapts and adjusts. Levels are not as important as changes, and money balances are now very important, rivaling real balances in terms of their effects on output and employment. Not only are money variables decision variables, in a world of uncertainty they are also the approximate variables for the underlying economic structure. As Tobin (1980) and others have noted, unanticipated changes in price variables can have significant real effects on economic activity. Once the comfortable world of certainty and equilibrium is left behind, the crucial issues concern the temporal relationships between variables. Walrasian instantaneous simultaneous adjustment and real balance models must be replaced with models which can deal with temporal discontinuities in price variables.

In this chapter we analyze the temporal relationships between regional money wage and price inflation. In a real balance equilibrium world such relationships, if they existed at all, would be of little interest. Real wages would be directly considered. In reality, however, money wages are a crucial behavioral variable, being a proximate measure of labors' income and firms' costs. Prices are also vital, but are not so obviously endogenous decision variables. Price inflation can hardly be directly manipulated, only responded to in some manner. Real wages result from money-wage contracts which attempt to approximate future price changes (amongst other variables). The extent to which money wages fully anticipate price changes will then determine the local pattern of real wages. Implied here are a couple of hypotheses: money wages are endogenous and prices exogenous, their interrelationships may be characterized by significant temporal lags, any identified relationship will probably be less than unit elastic. This chapter aims at developing a theoretical understanding of why these propositions are true, while at the same time introducing empirical evidence in support of these hypotheses.

Not only are the relationships between wages and prices crucial for understanding patterns of local real wages, but regional variations in such relationships imply a spatial heterogeneity of economic experience which may threaten aggregate reproduction of the entire macroeconomic system. A further issue to be considered, then, is the spatially decentralized character of money-wage adjustment to price fluctuations. We analyze the relative contribution of industry and regional affiliation in describing variations in wage–price adjustment. Generally, we use a relational theory of labor contracts to help understand regional patterns in wage–price indexation.

Wage bargaining and indexation

At the outset, we assume that money-wage bargains are made by workers and employers at the beginning of the work period for a specific duration of time. Such contracts are made in money terms for at least two reasons. First, as we argued before, money wages are the immediate endogenous decision variables. Money wages are the proximate instrumental levers that aim at a target real wage. The target wage is the expected money wage discounted by expected prices. At one level, money wages may be reasonably predicted by virtue of contractual agreements regarding seniority, productivity and the like (assuming employment; see Baily 1977). However, at another level, expected prices are exogenous to any firm and its workers. Price inflation must be responded to and forecast, but hardly directly controlled. In an economy characterized by uncertainty and time–space heterogeneity, money is vital because it represents a means of sustaining interdependent and decentralized decisions, storing wealth, and spreading risks (Radner 1982). Thus the second reason bargains are made in money terms is that the medium itself is desirable for its own properties: money matters (Rowthorn 1980: Ch. 6).

Equally important for our purposes is the assumption that wage bargains are made at the beginning of the work period. This assumption can be justified on at least two grounds. First, even though wage contracts remove (for the firm) the possibility of making serendipitous extra profits if the market wage for labor were to fall suddenly and unexpectedly, contracts aim at ensuring a certain level of profits at the end of the work period. Since production and subsequent sale of commodities is actually comprised of a set of interdependent, serially autocorrelated actions and events, the costs of disruption implied in repeated bargaining and renegotiation may loom larger than each single action. The temporal sequence or flow of production must be sustained if revenue and a profit are to be derived. Thus there are quite clear imperatives faced by the firm temporally to stabilize labor negotiation, even if this means that during the contract period, lower wage opportunities are foregone.

So far our discussion has assumed a flex-price market for labor. However, realistically speaking, this assumption is difficult to sustain. As Keynes (1936) and many others have observed, money wages are "sticky"; rarely do wages fall, although the pace of wage inflation may slow. Thus it may be more important to stabilize wages over the short run, primarily on the "up-side" of the market. Wage contracts can then ensure predictable wage costs per employee over the life of the contract, a crucial issue if firms promise to sell their products at a guaranteed future price per unit produced. Of course, it is also plausible that continuously changing product prices involve costs as well, both in terms of the confusion engendered in the market and the actual costs of changing announced prices (Iwai 1981). Gordon (1980b) has observed that commodity prices are similarly very sticky, due in part, no doubt, to the existence of such transaction costs.

A second reason for assuming that wage bargains are made before production commences implicitly involves understanding the process of financing production itself. We assume that production plans are paid out of past sales. Rather than labor supplying its services on credit, we assume that it is paid regularly throughout the production sequence. Thus knowledge of the projected money-wage bill is crucial for any firm planning production, because labor cost must be covered and the wage fund replenished so that the whole production sequence can begin again. The size of this receipts fund depends on the relative shortness of the production sequence relative to the wage payment cycle. Furthermore, the length of the contract and the money-wage bargain would also affect the funds that firms would have to commit to a production sequence before beginning production. In this respect, both the length of contract and the money wage are endogenous to the economic system and depend on the bargains struck between workers and employers. Notice, of course, that such production funds are also necessary for adapting to unanticipated changes in the external environment. Money itself is a necessary asset for production.

These assumptions are the basis for our conception of the dynamics of money-wage contracts. Obviously, a crucial issue is specification of the length of the contract itself. As we noted above, this depends, in part, on the temporal sequence of production. With shorter and shorter production sequences, employment contracts could also be shorter, at the limit coinciding with workers' payment cycles. Where capital rigidities exist, such as in steel mills, foundries and the like, there may be little opportunity to narrow contract periods (from the firms' perspective). On the other hand, to the extent that production is divisible and capable of segmentation, contracts could likewise be temporally, perhaps even spatially, segmented. We will discuss this issue in more detail in the next section. For present purposes, however, it should be acknowledged that the length of contract does depend, in part, on the arrangement of production.

Other variables enter the picture. For instance, workers may bargain to reduce the length of the contract in the expectation that future labor demand conditions will favor them more than current conditions. Similarly, firms could bargain to lengthen the contract period following the same logic – if future labor demand conditions look bleak (i.e. high demand), then firms may attempt to internalize their labor markets by tying their workers to lengthy contractual relationships. The limit on such bargaining is reached where the benefits of complying with the contract are outweighed by opportunities outside the contract. Notice that in pricing such limits, firms and workers have to ensure that the costs of breaking a transaction are fully acknowledged and factored into the equation.

This issue of the length of a contract is important for a number of reasons. In terms of money-wage adjustment to price inflation, two implications deserve explicit acknowledgement. First, longer contracts may dampen wage volatility. By agreeing to a certain wage over a specified period of time, workers essentially give up their claims for money wages to be immediately adjusted to unanticipated changes in inflation. Of course, contracts may have all kinds of adjustment clauses. However, these clauses depend on knowledge of likely events for their specification. Completely unanticipated changes cannot be written into contracts, and thus wages may be less volatile than prices simply because the contract removes the possibility of immediate response. Thus we should not be surprised to find significantly less wage volatility compared to prices over the length of any contract. A second implication is that there also should exist significant lags in the adjustment of money wages to unanticipated price changes. The length of such lags would of course depend on the length of contracts, their internal design with respect to possible *ex post* revision, and the temporal sequencing of production itself.

Having noted the issue of contract length, the more basic question is setting future money wages. As the proximate and instrumental variable of real wages, money wages are assumed in this chapter to be set according to predicted future prices (see Taylor 1980). But there are a couple of problems here. The most obvious problem is forecasting future prices, an exercise that must build on past experience and expectations of likely future patterns. However, a more subtle problem is that of setting the degree of indexation, that is, the extent to which the money-wage contract will match forecast prices. There is no necessity that money wages should completely cover changing prices. Real wages could then fall or rise over the length of the contract, and even after the contract is terminated, subsequent catch-up adjustments also need not cover past price increases. Both issues have their own nuances.

The process of forecasting future prices, thereby establishing a benchmark for negotiation over the money-wage contract, is necessarily complex. It involves at least the following three steps. First, based on past patterns and an assumption of complete knowledge of the past, if not of the exact process whereby the identified patterns were generated, price changes can be projected into the future. Secondly, given a complete time-series of past observations, likely possible scenarios could be constructed and rules formulated to indicate likely responses in terms of money-wage contract provisions. For example, based on past experience, the predicted average inflation rate may be 5.0% per annum although it is possible that for a short period of time the inflation rate may be 12.0% p.a. One possible rule may be to increase money wages by an extra 5.0% for each quarter that inflation is over 10.0%. The third step could be to identify events or contingencies whereby the contract clauses do not apply. For example, if inflation accelerates to 25.0% p.a., the contract itself may be voided.

In all this discussion of possible wage setting rules, we have assumed a quite conventional notion of uncertainty and rationally constrained expectations of future price patterns. Alternatively, we could have argued that economic agents construct their forecasts based on complete knowledge of the economic process and the behavior of contingent variables, real and money. Such a rational expectations formulation would, at one stroke, remove problems of uncertainty and the allocation of risk. After all, rational expectations would make a direct determination of the rate of price inflation and the rate of money-wage inflation necessary exactly to match such inflation.

However, we reject this approach on two grounds. First, like Buiter (1980), we cannot conceive that economic agents know all the information needed to have such rational expectations. Not only is information incomplete, it is itself a strategic variable between various economic groups including labor and employers. We do not believe that cooperative knowledge sharing is a plausible assumption. There are substantial costs in acquiring information, and even greater costs in constructing the "models" necessary to systematize such information. Sharing of all the facts seems implausible in a capitalist economy. Secondly, nominal unanticipated random disturbances may shift the economy from its prefigured path to such an extent that the parameters describing the system may also change. This is possible because in a sequence economy, unanticipated shocks would have to be contended with, and decisions would have to be made regarding the likely permanence or impermanence of such shocks *before* all relevant information becomes available. Although contracts can help by postponing decisions, contracts may not be able to cover the time frame of stochastic events such as OPEC oil price increases (Tobin 1980).

Our notion of prediction depends on a time-series extrapolation model modified by a variety of rules which would accommodate identified significant possibilities (see Jacobs & Jones 1980). Of course, this does not settle the issue of indexation – the extent to which money wages should cover all anticipated increases in prices (Gray 1978). For labor the issue is obvious: maintenance of their real wages depends on complete indexation, whether during the life of the contract or immediately after it lapses through some kind of catch-up clause. But for employers, indexation is an obvious added cost to doing business, especially important if they operate within fix-price market regimes. Full indexation by firms could translate into rapid and unanticipated increases in the costs of doing business without any means of passing on such costs in the form of higher prices. Such costs could put a firm out of business before the sale of their commodities commences.

Wage bargaining in this context is an antagonist bilateral process. For any one firm, wage indexation is both a cost and an undesirable risk, a contract clause which shifts the burden of risk away from labor. The temporal pattern of real wages is then a highly charged political issue, one that depends on firms' and workers' joint decisions concerning the indexation of money wages in relation to forecast price inflation. In this sense, real wages are only approximated, and are derivative, not directly manipulated. For the local economy, the temporal pattern of real wages is a very important issue. Real wages drive effective demand. Thus, what may be good for any one firm – no wage indexation and long-time lags in adjusting wages to prices – may threaten the wellbeing of the local economy. So not only do we have to consider the temporal patterns of wage adjustment to prices and the relative strengths of such adaptations, we need also to consider the spatial heterogeneity in real wages. Much of our empirical analysis is concerned with the first two issues; in the next section we briefly consider the last issue as well.

Regional wage–price dynamics

So far the discussion has centered upon the temporal dynamics of wage bargaining and indexation. We need also to be explicit about our notions of spatial wage–price adjustment. In particular, two issues need to be addressed: the possible spatial variations in price inflation as well as price expectations, and the possible spatial variations in local wage indexation to local price inflation. From this discussion we turn to establishing a set of hypotheses which will guide our empirical analysis.

It was observed in the two previous chapters that there are only marginal differences between US cities in their temporal patterns of price inflation. Tests for spatial variations in price inflation have indicated that such variations are largely insignificant when compared to temporal variations in inflation. Of course it might be the case that regional capital markets are imperfect and, as a result, there may be differential access to money capital in different regions. Yet even if we were to accept this argument, it need not translate into variations in price inflation. On the demand side, if we were to assume perfectly competitive commodity markets, then it is plausible that local variations in price inflation could exist. However, to sustain this argument we need to assume that prices are flexible, are set according to demand and, ultimately, that the whole production system itself is decentralized (like labor markets). Of course, it may be true that there are price *level* differences between areas of the USA. Even so, for workers and firms bargaining over future money-wage adjustments, their respective real wages will depend on indexation with respect to price inflation. Indeed, for both parties, their relative real wages will depend on matching price changes. Otherwise, the spatial relative price level would itself change.

Nationally, Gordon (1981) has noted that commodity prices are not as flexible as implied by neoclassical price theory. Whether for reasons of transaction costs, market signaling, or other, the fact is that commodity prices adapt only very slowly to demand: quantity rationing is more normal (Tobin 1980). If this is true nationally, then there is good reason to expect similar patterns at the local level. Indeed, we have argued above that national and local time-series models of price inflation are very similar – both in terms of their form (autoregressive time-series models of orders 2 or 3) and in terms of their parameter estimates. Similarly, it was also shown that the identified time-series are dominated by weighted past observations and adapt only slowly to changing exogenous forces.

We would also suggest that commodity production itself is a more centralized national, and even international, system than is often assumed (cf. Jones 1983). Distance costs are now such a small portion of production costs that the spatial balkanization of production is very rare. Even if there are local production plants, this does not necessarily indicate any comparative advantage *vis-à-vis* access to the local commodity market. Moreover, if we also assume that commodity prices adjust only very slowly to demand, then many commodities are rarely priced using the simple cost-competitive rules of neoclassical economics. Rather, average (or what Okun 1981 termed "standard") pricing prevails which typically depends on mark-up and cost-plus formulae.

So if price inflation is virtually the same throughout the national space economy, what remains to vary? Obviously, the only other possibility is spatial variation in money-wage indexation. In this context, it is more difficult to propose definite rules. We expect that there would be both sectoral *and* spatial variations in money-wage adjustment. In terms of the former, if it is true that commodity pricing is largely a sector-related phenomenon, based on a cost-plus mark-up system of price setting, then differences in money-wage adjustment to price inflation are likely to reflect sectoral variations in mark-up policies.

Elsewhere it has been observed that money wage inflation over the 1970s was largely industry contingent (Ch. 4). That is, the rate of increase in average per employee money wages was more homogeneous with respect to industry affiliation than geographical affiliation. Even so, there are empirical and theoretical reasons to doubt the generality of this finding. For instance, the sample of cities used was quite small (two northern and two southern cities per industry) and consequently may not have adequately captured the geographical diversity of money-wage inflation. Also, it should be remembered that no direct test was made of the contribution of geography and industry affiliation to variations in local money-wage inflation. This does not mean that we wish to deny the previous results. Rather, the issue is one of generality.

More theoretically, there are a couple of reasons for expecting some geographical (as well as industrial) diversity in money-wage adjustment. First, if commodity markets are largely national, then regardless of location, firms in any given industry will operate under a relatively fixed price–cost regime. The price structure will, accordingly, reflect the cost structure of the "average" firm or market leader. Assuming cost-plus mark-up behavior, the wage structure of the industry will consequently tend to reflect longer-term consumer demand elasticities, capital intensity, productivity and the like. In these circumstances, extra profits can only be made by producing at lower costs, within a relatively stable (and given) industrial price regime. There are a number of options for any firm attempting to improve its profitability. Given our particular interest in the geographical stratification of wage adjustment, one relevant strategy would be for firms to segment and decentralize their production plans according to *existing* variations in local labor market adjustment.

Notice that this scenario depends on a quite distinct institutional arrangement of spatial labor markets. Unlike commodity markets, labor markets are assumed to be spatially heterogeneous with respect to social custom, contract structures, and perhaps even price. Their heterogeneity is then an opportunity for firms to make extra profits. This does not necessarily mean that local wage *levels* are different by industry or commodity produced. Indeed, as we mentioned above, industry-specific production techniques and capital intensities may encourage spatial homogeneity with respect to the average costs of production. The point is that production is a time-dependent sequence of action which depends much more on adjustment to anticipated and unanticipated shocks than on levels. Thus, geographical heterogeneity in money-wage indexation practices will appear as extra profit opportunities for firms which operate at a more extended spatial scale. Spatial labor market heterogeneity is not an accident. It has been consciously fostered by both national and state governments over the past 200 years (Stone 1981). The only limits on this system are formal contracts, negotiated by industry-wide unions. Even here, such union contracts may serve only to push extra profit-seeking firms overseas.

A second, and related, reason for expecting some geographical variations in money-wage indexation depends on the internal arrangement of firms *vis-à-vis* their production capabilities. It has been noted elsewhere that functional specialization also implies a quite specific division of labor (Clark 1981a). Moreover, some tasks may require very long temporal sequences before a commodity becomes available for sale. The most obvious example has to do with product development and research. For these tasks, long money-wage cycles may be required before a product is sold. In contrast to more standardized production sequences, longer contracts may be required for specialized workers. At the same time, longer contracts may also require strong wage indexation clauses. Otherwise, workers would be induced to break their contractual obligations to take advantage of other offers. In these circumstances, firms are quite vulnerable in any bilateral bargaining situation, not only because of the specificity of their labor requirements, but also because of their extended temporal production sequences. Implied, moreover, is an assumption that in these situations firms bear much of the burden of uncertainty and cost regarding future price inflation.

In response, firms may attempt to shift the burden of uncertainty from one group of workers to another by limiting indexation agreements with production workers. To be effective, however, such a strategy would have to deny the relevance of contractual agreements with their skilled workers. This is entirely possible if negotiation takes place in different local labor markets. "Customary practices" are essentially spatially balkanized by such a strategy, and geographical variations in wage indexation are "created" through a combination of firms' internal production agreements and the institutional arrangement of local labor markets (Whiteman 1985). Thus, theoretically, within-industry geographical differences in money-wage indexation are entirely plausible and, indeed, should be expected.

Generally, our empirical and theoretical discussion leaves us with a set of hypotheses which will form the basis of subsequent empirical analysis.

The most general hypotheses are, first, that price inflation will be more volatile than wage inflation, largely because price inflation has a significant (unanticipated) stochastic component which is outside the direct control of workers and firms; and, secondly, that wage inflation will tend to lag behind price inflation by at least a year because of the inertial properties of contracts (see also Gertler 1982). It is further contended that price inflation causes local wage inflation, a product of the particular institutional (or structural) arrangement of American commodity and labor markets. More specifically, a further hypothesis can be recognized which is directly related to the spatial dynamics of inflation. That is, thirdly, that there should be distinct geographical and industrial differences in wage adjustment to price inflation, the exact differences being a product of the underlying arrangement of production.

Regional wage and price inflation

Wage and price data were collected from the US Departments of Commerce and Labor for some 74 state and industry combinations. The states analyzed covered all the major geographical divisions of the United States, although the northwest was not as well represented. For instance, states such as Maine and Massachusetts were included, as were Texas and California. Four industries were analyzed: textiles (SIC 22), apparel (SIC 23), fabricated metals (SIC 34), and electrical and electronic equipment (SIC 36). The first two industries tend to be nonunionized, undercapitalized, and nationally declining in terms of their employment. There are, of course, north–south differences in these two industries according to these three descriptive dimensions. For example, the south has shown significant employment and capital growth in these two sectors over the period 1954 to 1976. Fabricated metals has been more concentrated in the midwest and is linked of course to the transportation industry. It is characterized by very high capital–labor ratios and stable employment. On the other hand, electrical and electronic equipment has undergone a fundamental transformation during the last 15 years and remains largely nonunionized. The time interval was chosen so as to be consistent with our larger project, and covers a major portion of the postwar recovery and the onset of economic stagnation in the 1970s.

As state-level consumer price data is largely unavailable, larger city price series were used to approximate their state or adjacent state series. The wage data, on the other hand, are state and industry specific and are derived from the Census and Annual Surveys of Manufacturers. The wage series include all employee compensation for the calendar year analyzed. Thus, the wage data should be interpreted as annual, nominal wages for employ-

ees for the sector and industry under study. Since many wage contracts –
formal and informal – are published yearly and are revised in accordance
with yearly inflation rates, the time interval of the data studied here
represents actual labor market practice. Thus, any degrees of freedom lost
because of the aggregated temporal sampling scale (yearly as opposed to
quarterly or even monthly) should be compensated for by a more inter-
pretable temporal adjustment sequence. Consumer price and nominal
wage time-series data are serially autocorrelated. In was necessary, then,
to attempt to account for autocorrelation, thereby improving the
efficiency of our attempts to analyze the impacts and relationships between
these variables. Accordingly, the money-wage and price data were converted to rates of change so that inflation rates were derived as indicated by
Equations 9.1 and 9.2. That is:

$$\dot{P}_t^i = \frac{P_t^i - P_{t-1}^i}{P_{t-1}^i} \times 100 \tag{9.1}$$

$$\dot{W}_t^{ij} = \frac{W_t^{ij} - W_{t-1}^{ij}}{W_{t-1}^{ij}} \times 100 \tag{9.2}$$

where P_t^i is the consumer price index at time t in the city representing state
i, and W_t^{ij} the nominal average wage per employee at time t in state i,
industry j. The resulting transformed wage and price inflation time-series
were then analyzed for their stationarity and autocorrelation structures.

To help understand the spatial and temporal patterns of inflation, Figure
9.1 illustrates, for a sample set of states and industries, the variety of
time-series profiles of local wage and price inflation. Each observation is a
pair of price ($\dot{P}$) and wage ($\dot{W}$) inflation rates for a given time (t), state (i)
and industry (j). The dotted 45 degree diagonal line extending from the
origin allows us to see which years had real-wage declines (where price
inflation was greater than wage inflation – below the 45 degree line) and
which years recorded real-wage gains (where wage inflation was greater
than price inflation – above the 45 degree line). Given our *a priori*
expectation of significant north–south, industry–industry variations, the
states included in Figure 9.1 illustrate the diversity of local real-wage
variations.

For example, real wages declined during 1967–8 and 1973–4 in almost all
states for the four industries. The only exceptions to this were in the
electronics industry for Arkansas in 1968 and, more generally, in the
fabricated metals industry (SIC 34), although in Figure 9.1 our sample
does not represent the more general pattern. Beyond the similarities in

---

Figure 9.1 Wage–price dynamics by industry and state, 1954–76. (Figures in
parentheses are SIC nos.)

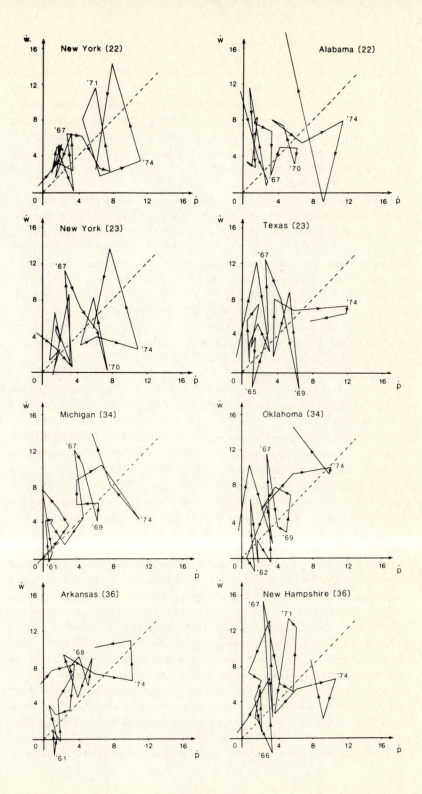

1967 and 1973, the four industries displayed some individual trends. In textiles (SIC 22), after bad years (when many states experienced declining real wages) in 1956 and 1957, real wages then grew through to 1968. After 1968, however, textiles experienced bad years in five of the next eight years. Textiles was the most volatile industry in terms of the number of "consistent" years among price–wage profiles, measured most simply by the number of years where 75% of the states had the same sign (positive or negative) on real wages.

The apparel industry (SIC 23) had a number of good years through to 1968. After that date, however, the industry suffered bad years every year except 1971 across almost the whole nation. Fabricated metals, on the other hand, suffered bad years in 1968, 1969, 1972, and 1973. Unlike textiles and apparel, however, this industry bounced back in 1974 and 1975 to record stable real wages (see Oklahoma). Electronics was the only industry consistently to suffer bad years in the early to mid-1960s, although there were distinct geographical variations in this pattern.

In just about all states and industries (including the sample), price inflation showed more volatility over the time period 1954 to 1976. For example, NY22 (New York textiles) in Figure 9.1 indicates a wide range of price inflation, beginning in 1954 with negative inflation. This should not be a surprise. On the other hand, wages were more variable. For instance, wages in some states or industries either became less volatile (as in OK34, NH36), stayed about the same (TX23), or became less volatile in the 1960s but fluctuated wildly in the 1970s (NY22, 23, AL22, AR36). There were observed to be distinct industry variations. Again, industries displayed individual characteristics, with textiles and apparel being more volatile than fabricated metals and electronics. Textiles, for instance, either became more volatile in the 1960s and 1970s or displayed the "down–up" trend. Apparel, for the most part, became more volatile. Fabricated metals and electronics showed less volatility over this period. In particular, electronics was the most stable.

Three temporal episodes were identified, each with its own wage–price characteristics. The late 1950s and early 1960s mostly exhibited wage–wage adjustments with very slight price adjustments. Wage changes tended to stabilize after a rash of sharp wage fluctuations. In contrast to this, the early 1970s exhibited a marked price shock in 1973–4 (sometimes a 1972 shock also), followed by wage–price adjustments in 1974 and 1975. From 1964 to 1971, however, the picture was rather ambiguous. In the majority of cases (depending somewhat on the industry), wage changes seemed to lead to price changes; however, wage–price adjustments were also evident. In addition, in some cases there was no clear wage or price shock, but rather there were wage–price adjustments followed by wage–price adjustments (see OK34 in Figure 9.1). Because of these differences, a clear adjustment pattern was not always evident and it was difficult to generalize. Because of the variety and descriptive nature of these observations, we systematically analyzed the statistical relationships between local wage and price inflation.

Causality between regional wages and prices

The first step in analyzing the local structure of wage and price inflation was to use cross-correlation function analysis so as to identify temporal lead and lag relationships between $\dot{P}_t^i$ and $\dot{W}_t^{ij}$. This analysis enabled us to make an initial approximation of which variable determined the other, as well as establishing more generally the timing sequences of these variables. The results of this analysis are summarized in Clark and Tabuchi (1984). When the lag on the maximum (cross-correlation) r-value is positive, this indicates that $\dot{P}_t^i$ leads; and when the lag is negative, $\dot{W}_t^{ij}$ leads. Since most of the signs on the identified lags were positive, it is plausible that price inflation leads wage inflation and, perhaps more strongly, consumer price inflation determines current local, industry-specific wage inflation. It was also established that in most cases only one lag was significant and the pattern of cross-correlations typically symmetrical.

Geographically and sectorally, the results exhibited few obvious patterns. Only in the northeastern region could there be some doubt about the strength of the relationship between regional price and wage inflation. Of the ten industry–state combinations, ranging in order from Maine textiles (ME22) through to Connecticut electronics (CT36), only five were significant at the 0.05 level. No clear industry pattern could be established for the nonsignificant group, although it might be suggested that non-significance was more apparent in the less urbanized states of Maine, New Hampshire, and Rhode Island. In many other regional groupings, cross-correlations between wage and price inflation were strong and consistent. The only other exceptions were found in the southern and southwestern groups, from AL22 through to TX23. Indeed, only five industry–state combinations were significant out of a combined southern and southwestern industry–state total of eleven. This result is intriguing and suggests that a geographical pattern may exist in terms of wage–price adjustment.

A second major finding was that the time lag between the two variables was typically one or two years. This significantly reduced the complexity of subsequent bivariate time-series modeling and encouraged us tentatively to accept the second hypothesis. This direct evaluation of the significance of different time lags contrasts with the *a priori* "blind" approach of Koyck-type distributed lag models. The following system of equations was considered to be sufficient to describe the temporal auto- and cross-relationships between $\dot{P}_t^i$ and $\dot{W}_t^{ij}$:

$$\dot{P}^i_t = a_{11}\,\dot{P}^i_{t-1} + a_{12}\,\dot{W}^{ij}_{t-1} + b_1 + \varepsilon_{it}$$
$$\dot{W}^{ij}_t = a_{21}\,\dot{P}^i_{t-1} + a_{22}\,\dot{W}^{ij}_{t-1} + b_2 + \varepsilon_{it}$$

$$(9.3)$$

where the a's and b's were parameters to be estimated and the ε's were the stochastic error terms. Notice that the lag variables on the right-hand sides of the equations presume a causality sequence in time, consistent with Granger's (1982) theory of unambiguous causality. To be viable, this model must depend on a temporal sampling interval which is fine enough to capture the "true" timing sequences. And it is possible that there are fractional (of a year) sequences. However, institutionally there are good reasons to be confident with the yearly sampling interval as there is also good preliminary evidence to support such a supposition.

Equation 9.3 and its related parameters were estimated using the "seemingly unrelated regression" technique (Maddala 1977). Those parameters were simultaneously estimated for each state and industry combination. Note that unlike single equation estimation, simultaneous estimation is able to reduce cross-correlation between error terms of the two equations. The parameter estimates, their t-values, and the derived Durbin–Watson statistics (indicating first order autoregressive serial autocorrelation) are reported in Clark and Tabuchi (1984). The actual estimation procedure was based on a nonlinear maximum likelihood method described in Solo (1982). The simultaneous model coupled with the MLE helps in circumventing problems of linear single equation models which cannot deal with spiral forms of wage and price interdependence (Fig. 9.1). As noted by Gersovitz (1980), such spirals may lead to severe specification problems.

From these results it was found that most Durbin–Watson statistics were between 1.43 and 2.57, implying little evidence of first-order autoregressive serial autocorrelation in the residuals at the 0.05 level. Thus we had some confidence that the modeling strategy was able to deal with the inherent temporal structure of the data. More importantly, clear patterns in the significance of the parameter estimates were also found. Generally, the parameters a_{11} and a_{21} were significant, while a_{12} and a_{22} were insignificant. In fact, of the 74 states and industries, 100% of a_{11} estimates, 68% of a_{21} estimates, 8% of a_{12} estimates, and 18% of a_{22} estimates were found to be significant at the 0.05 level. Put more directly, the significance of a_{11} suggests that $\dot{P}^i_t$ is autoregressive (AR(1)) and is a function of $\dot{P}^i_{t-1}$ but not of $\dot{W}^{ij}_{t-1}$. The significance of a_{21}, on the other hand, would suggest that $\dot{W}^{ij}_t$ is a function of $\dot{P}^i_{t-1}$. That is, last year's inflation rate determines this year's price inflation rate and wage inflation rate. Thus we could argue that wage inflation $\dot{W}^{ij}_t$ is endogenous and is caused, at least in part, by the previous consumer price inflation. The year-to-year sequencing in wages and prices also indicates that these variables are dominated by the past and are in this sense relatively "sticky." The lack of wage effects on prices is also an important result. Local prices are exogenous.

Of course, this result is consistent with our previous discussion concerning the relative importance of geographical price variation compared to temporal price variation. Local price inflation is very closely related to national price inflation; indeed, the former is a function (if not an exact echo) of the latter. The nationally determined inflation rate can be inferred to be a crucial exogenous factor in determining nominal wage inflation in the various states and industries studied in this paper. Basically, the spatial economy is highly integrated and interdependent at least when it comes to monetary effects.

There were, however, some differences in the parameter estimates. So as to investigate the possible existence of regional and industry differences in the responsiveness of $\dot{W}_t^{ij}$ to changes in $\dot{P}_{t-1}^i$, the magnitude of each coefficient estimate of a_{21} was analyzed. The coefficient estimate a_{21} can be defined in the following terms:

$$a_{21} = \frac{\dot{W}_t^{ij}}{\dot{P}_{t-1}^i} = \frac{(\dot{W}_t^{ij}/\dot{W}_{t-1}^{ij})}{(\dot{P}_{t-1}^i/\dot{P}_{t-2}^i)} \tag{9.4}$$

This estimate definition is somewhat different from the normal cross-elasticity definition (Gandolfo 1971):

$$\eta = \frac{\dot{W}_t^{ij}/\dot{W}_{t-1}^{ij}}{\dot{P}_t^i/\dot{P}_{t-1}^i} \tag{9.5}$$

An analysis of variance (ANOVA) was used to discriminate differences in a_{21} by industry and region, the parameter estimate being defined as the dependent variable. The first nonmetric independent variable was geographical region, classified as northeast, northcentral, south and west. The second nonmetric independent variable was industry (SIC), including textiles, apparel, fabricated metals, and electrical and electronic equipment. The geographical variable is necessarily crude. The four-region classification enables a two-way ANOVA, and should be thought of as a means of summarizing the results as much as testing hypotheses.

It was found that both regional and industrial variations were significant at the 0.05 level (the latter at the 0.01 level) in explaining variations in wage adjustment to price inflation (Table 9.1). That is, the impact of (national) price inflation on (local) money-wage inflation differs amongst regions as well as amongst industries. Specifically, the mean value of the price impact on wages (average value of a_{21} estimates) is large in the west (0.93) and small in the south (0.53), while it is large in fabricated metals (0.79) and small in the apparel industry (0.43). Although a two-way interaction between region and industry was also included in the ANOVA test, it was far from significant at 0.05 level. Essentially we can conclude that there exist two independent sources of variation in wage adjustment: geographical region and industry type.

Table 9.1 Analysis of variance: Contributions of region and industry to real wage variation.

Source of variation	Sum of squares	DF	Mean square	F statistic	Significance of F
main effects	2.064	6	0.344	4.410	0.001
region	0.880	3	0.293	3.762	0.015
industry	0.967	3	0.322	4.135	0.010
two-way interactions					
region–industry	0.859	8	0.107	1.377	0.226
explained	2.923	14	0.209	2.677	0.004
residual	4.602	59	0.078		
total	7.524	73	0.103		

These results are consistent and have some similarities with the results of our earlier study of local wage inflation. In studying the rate (monthly) of money-wage increase over the period 1972 to 1980 for four US industries and twelve cities, it was found that industry affiliation was a very important variable in describing money-wage patterns. Less important was geographical region, although the sample was really too small to indicate whether or not it was a significant descriptive variable. In the study reported here, the sample of places (states) is larger, although the temporal frame is quite different both in terms of sampling interval (yearly) and period (1954–76). In terms of the hypotheses established in the preceding section, the results provide support for their veracity, albeit at an aggregate level. Those industries facing the strongest market pressures, like apparel and textiles, exhibit the smallest rate of money-wage indexation. Consistent with our previous argument, these industries place most of the burden of risk concerning the changing rate of price inflation on workers. On the other hand, fabricated metals and electronics exhibit higher rates of wage indexation, and accordingly share more equally the burden of price uncertainty.

Geographically similar observations could be made. The social contract between southern workers and employers seems to externalize the real wage. That is, instead of making real-wage parity and its continuity an internal aspect of contracts (as seems the case in northern and western states), southern contracts place much of the burden of price uncertainty on individual workers. This observation is consistent with many other studies which have emphasized the different social relations that dominate southern labor markets. Right-to-work laws, anti-union policies and a much reduced public involvement in terms of private labor contracts all suggest an externalized and privatized conception of labor market uncertainty. In this regard the institutional design of local labor markets has a large role to play in "creating" private outcomes. The maintenance of workers' real wages in the south seems far more problematic than in the north and west. Indeed, the much lower response of money wages to prices year-to-year in the south implies more stable but lower real wages. this may well translate into lower commodity demand and even higher volatility in local employment.

Conclusions

This chapter was concerned with the regional dynamics of wage and price inflation over the postwar period. We argued at the outset that understanding wage and price dynamics, not so much levels, is the crucial analytical task for economic theorists. The reasons for this methodological argument are twofold. First, in a world of change, of history and experience, uncertainty is a major attribute of the spatial economic system. Furthermore, disequilibrium best characterizes the economic environment. Thus how firms and workers adapt to change should be a crucial concern. It is this process of adjustment that dominates our world. A second, and related, argument is that the processes of disequilibrium imply a monetary economy. Comparative statistics based on real balances cannot approach the complexities faced by economic agents who must adjust to changing fortunes through monetary aggregates. In this context, money balances are crucial, as is the distribution of the costs of uncertainty between contractual partners. Real income, for example, should be thought of as being derived out of bilateral negotiations with respect to money wages and prices.

One important conclusion derived from our analysis is that wages follow prices. That is, at the state and industry level, wages adjust to prices lagged by about one year. This result is somewhat counter to Bator's (1981) argument, where he suggested that wages push prices. In fact, it seems that money-wage changes are endogenous and it is prices that are exogenous. Granted, it is possible that, at the most aggregate level, the process works in reverse. However, it should also be recognized that the institutional structure of the labor market virtually ensures prices which cause local wages. Basically, wage indexation is a local phenomenon. For any single bargaining unit, prices will appear exogenous. For an economy explicitly designed according to such a decentralized logic, it is difficult to take Bator's argument seriously. Even if he was right (and this has not been empirically substantiated), wage bargaining takes place on a much more local level. On the other hand, commodity pricing appears as a more national, even international, process. The differences between product and labor markets include their actual institutional and spatial arrangements (cf. Medoff 1983).

Temporal and regional variations in real wages derive from local variations in money-wage indexation to national price inflation. Indexation is by no means automatic. Indeed, for the south, indexation is relatively limited when compared to the north. Similarly, there are industry variations in money-wage indexation, as for example between apparel (low indexation) and fabricated metals (high indexation). The existence of these types of variations should not come as a surprise. Unanticipated price inflation may entail significant costs for firms that provide full indexation, costs that could threaten the continuity of the production process. Similarly, for workers, incomplete indexation could significantly reduce their real incomes. Essentially the problem for firms is that production sequences depend on establishing wage contracts prior to the sale of commodities. Revenues are anticipated as are wage costs. Full indexation may lead to wage escalation beyond that of prices. Firms may then be forced to reduce profit margins, or even to go out of business. In this context indexation is a very real point of contention in any labor contract. North–south variations in wage indexation illustrate a more general argument: the social-*cum*-spatial relations of production are crucial for understanding regional economic patterns.

In the past many researchers have emphasized the contribution of industry mix to regional differences in economic performance (Martin 1981). Here, our results suggest that this type of argument is inadequate by itself. There appear to be very real spatial effects that go beyond industry mix. In fact, there are significant real wage differences between places due to differing rates of money-wage indexation. Although price inflation hardly varies from place to place, wage indexation does (holding industry constant). Thus we need to look more closely at local labor market practices and their institutional structures (as in contracts and rules of bargaining before a complete picture can be drawn of local dynamics.

PART IV

Interregional labor migration

PART IV   *Interregional labor migration*

Part IV of this book deals with the dynamics and logic of interregional labor migration. The mobility of labor is a key variable in the adjustment of regional economies to varying economic fortunes. The movement of labor from one region to another in search of employment and higher wages is thought to act as one of the essential equilibrating mechanisms in the evolution of the regional structure of an economy. There are, of course, other theories of regional growth which focus on, and try to explain, the processes of growing inequality among regions.

Central to the dispute between the two schools of thought regarding the dynamics of regional growth are the different theoretical suppositions about the patterns and determinants of labor migration. The "competitive market" school (the first of the two theories) supposes that labor is constantly seeking to maximize its welfare, and will therefore move to exploit economic opportunity wherever located. Theorists, whether Keynesian or marxian, who suppose that accumulating regional inequality best characterizes the economic landscape, argue the reverse: that is, with respect to the mobility of capital, labor is relatively immobile and dependent upon capital for defining the landscape of options. These opposing suppositions concerning labor mobility are central pieces in generating the regional configuration of production predicted by each model. In this part, we examine the spatial and temporal dynamics of interregional migration. Our adjustment perspective is used to reveal more precise information regarding the patterns and processes of migration, and to suggest which growth mechanisms are at work in US regions.

In Chapter 10, the temporal and spatial structure of labor migration is analyzed, using yearly state-based data. These data are very unusual in that they provide the basis for analyzing the temporal adjustment patterns of interregional migration. Our empirical investigation focuses on gross flows in migration. The reason for this is that the volumes of in- and outmigration for individual states are both significant. Net migration is merely a small residual between two otherwise very much larger flows. This means that any unidirectional explanation of migration – for example, that people should move from point A to point B because of higher wage levels – will be likely to miss the fact that almost as many people are moving in the opposite direction. By using the Box–Jenkins time-series methodology, we avoid the need to "specify" the temporal structure of migration in advance of empirical examination. Instead, it becomes the very thing which is investigated.

The empirical analysis of the dynamics of labor migration is largely descriptive. However, our findings point toward some radical conclusions. First, interregional labor migration is much more volatile over time than is commonly supposed. Additionally, the patterns of in- and outmigration from individual states are highly synchronized in time. This contradicts the basic suppositions of conventional models of labor migration which assume that the temporal processes of in- and outmigration are fundamentally different. Secondly, it is also found that in the fastest and slowest growing (declining) states, the process of labor migration is non-recursive – present levels are rarely linked to past levels in a systematic way. This empirical evidence specifically runs against the markovian assumptions of most cohort-based models of migration. Finally, it is concluded that levels of net migration are essentially generated by a quite volatile process of job generation and job switching. Even in declining areas, levels of labor in-migration can be relatively high (relative to outmigration). What determines the path of regional decline is the lack of sufficient jobs to retain outgoing workers.

In Chapter 11, we examine the causal relationships between regional capital formation and labor migration. There are two schools of thought on this issue, for which there has been very little empirical investigation to date. One school emphasizes the efficiency of regional economies as integrated systems of prices and markets. The inference drawn from such a theory is that capital and labor are ceaselessly adjusting to changing external circumstances, but that the processes of capital formation and interregional labor migration are not systematically linked one to another in a prolonged internal dynamic. The second ("capital logic") school of thought emphasizes the primacy of capital investment in the logic of regional development. The inference from this body of theory is that labor migration lags behind developments in capital formation in a systematic and recursive way.

We employ time-series based causality tests to analyze the evidence for and against the various causal propositions. Our empirical findings on these issues are somewhat ambivalent. While we have assembled what is probably the most complete empirical evidence on the subject, there are still significant technical difficulties in establishing causality in the time domain, especially in complex interdependent processes such as regional growth. However, we do provide certain key empirical findings. First, it appears that in the "lead" instances of regional restructuring (i.e. the fast growing or declining states) the "capital logic" school of thought dominates. This is an important finding, since it specifically denies the logic of the competitive market theory for the crucial instances of adjustment in the spatial system; at least in the short run. For those cases of moderate regional growth or stagnation, no unidirectional and determinate causal relationships could be established between regional capital formation and labor migration.

Secondly, it is also shown that there is no determinable difference between the patterns of in- and outmigration in their relation to the temporal patterns of regional capital formation. This is surprising, since it has long been assumed that in- and outmigration have fundamentally different effects on the path of regional capital formation. Notice that this chapter introduces for the first time a regional capital data set which is temporally consistent with the overall structure of our study. While more is made of this data in the next part of the book, it is important to acknowledge that our study of the space–time dynamics of migration and capital formation depend on the structure of both sets of data. And it is just as important to note that our study represents the first attempt to integrate in an empirical sense both processes.

In the final chapter of this part on labor migration (Ch. 12), we take a more qualitative look at the process of labor migration itself. The issues here have to do with the costs and uncertainties of migration, formalized through the notion of transaction costs. Conventional models of regional growth assume that these issues are minor impediments to the workings of an otherwise efficient spatial labour market system. We identify three types of transaction costs: (a) those associated with the *means* of labor exchange; (2) those associated with the *organization* of a market, such as the regional exchange of labor; and (3) those associated with the problem of uncertainty. Each of these problems is widely agreed to prevent the efficient spatial allocation of labor.

In examining the arguments of a recent Michigan court case (*Hackett* v. *Foodmaker, Inc.*), which involved the migration of a person across the USA for a promised job, we focus on the allocation of the costs of uncertainty between the contracting partners. The issue confronting the courts was that as labor often undertakes significant risks and commitments in moving for employment, and given the promise of a contract, is the employer bound to respect his promise? The case is interesting to us since it brings to the fore all the issues of contract and uncertainty which are taken for granted in neoclassical analysis. We use the case to show how the idealized version of labor exchange in neoclassical models (idealized in that both parties are implicitly assumed to anticipate all contingencies) cannot be substantiated in practice. We then show how the uncertainty surrounding labor migration is not merely an extrinsic factor to be minimized by theoretical assumptions, but lies at the very core of labor mobility. In this respect, the allocation of uncertainty is at the heart of any system of regional labor markets.

10 Dynamics of inter-state labor migration

Introduction

Accurate prediction of the patterns and structure of inter-state labor migration has become more important than ever. Not only are government grants and entitlements allocated on the basis of current population levels, but planned public sector investments also depend upon forecasts of population (Rives 1981). Similarly, private location decisions have a strong *expectational* component, especially investment decisions taken with respect to likely market conditions. Forecasts, whether accurate or not, have a self-fulfilling dimension: if an area is designated as a future growth area and public sector investments are targeted accordingly, private investment often follows (Alonso 1973). Also, precipitous declines in the national birth rate have given migration a relatively more important role in determining overall inter-state variations in population growth and decline. The need for dependable and accurate forecasts of migration has become more acute (National Academy of Sciences 1982).

Yet, for variety of reasons, traditional methods of forecasting regional migration have come under increasing scrutiny. As court challenges to the 1980 Census of Population demonstrated, there are instances of incorrect estimates of current population, let alone the forecasts made from such data. Researchers such as Jackson *et al.* (1981) claimed that Census forecasts of inter-state growth and decline have often been wrong. Growing areas which were predicted by the Census to slow their growth rate maintained their growth, and areas predicted to grow did not. Of course, hindsight is far more accurate than forecasts, and it is easy to find fault in the Census. Academics have, with rare exception, also been poor judges of likely spatial growth patterns (see the comments by Zelinsky 1977).

With the recognition of these empirical realities and the urgent need for more effective forecasting methods, greater attention has centered upon the demographics and economics of inter-state migration. Rogers (1979), for example, extended the simple cohort-demographic accounting model to the multiregional context and, in doing so, has focused attention on notions such as the stability, spatial distribution, and trajectory of regional growth and decline. The spatial and temporal dynamics of migration are given explicit recognition in Rogers' analyses, characteristics virtually ignored in Lowry's (1966) model which dominates much of the geographical and economics literature on migration. Associated with this type of macro-demographic research has been a critical reassessment of the usefulness or otherwise of analytical categories such as net migration. Alonso (1980) put the issue succinctly when he noted that "net migration is, of course, a statistical abstraction; the real behavior consists of immigration and emigration." Essentially there is no such person as a "net migrant," and gross flows of migration must be considered separately even if they respond to similar determinants. Unfortunately, conventional migration forecasting models have shown little appreciation of these analytical and theoretical questions.

This chapter deals with the temporal dynamics of gross inter-state migration over the period 1958 to 1975. It is argued that a better understanding of the macro-demographic temporal patterns and structure of gross migration is a prerequisite for better theory and forecasting. The subsequent sections review current perceptions of the stability properties of gross migration, model migration gross flows and rates (adjusted non-moving employment) using Box and Jenkins (1976) time-series techniques, and compare the timing patterns of in- and outmigration via cross-correlation analysis. In addition, the likely forecast errors involved in using gross migration rates and net migration, rather than gross flows, are investigated. Analysis is conducted on five groups of US states using yearly labor force migration estimates derived from the Continuous Work History Sample (CWHS) of the Social Security Administration and the Bureau of Economic Analysis (1976). Each group includes three states and each group represents different growth patterns in employment over the 1958 to 1975 period: rapid and continual growth; average and then accelerated growth; average continual growth; average and then decelerated growth; and finally, low overall growth. Growth of US employment over this period is the basis for comparison.

Adjustment properties of labor migration

The Borts and Stein (1964) model of regional growth and income convergence depends on interregional migration to allocate labor efficiently according to the spatial pattern of demand and supply. Quite simply, labor should migrate from low- to high-wage areas. And, with added labor supply in high-wage areas, wages should fall at the same time as restricted labor supply in low-wage areas increases wages. The result should be wage equalization, and presumably labor migration should decline. This neo-classical model implies a quite specific directional component; migration should go from low-wage to high-wage regions, a prediction that goes to the very heart of the model. Either net migration is the analytical variable or it is assumed that one gross flow dominates the other such that wage equalization is the result (Greenwood 1975). There are two key issues here that could compromise the neoclassical model. First, questions could be raised concerning the empirical significance of gross flows as opposed to net flows. Secondly, the theoretical structure of the neoclassical growth model seems incapable of directly dealing with the dynamics of inter-regional migration. Essentially, migration is conceived in terms of comparative statics, not dynamics.

It is commonplace to recognize that the Lowry (1966) model summarizes empirically the principal elements of neoclassical theory. Origins and destinations are directly paired and the volume and direction of migration between pairs is related to differences in relative wages and unemployment. This model is asymmetrical in that labor is assumed to flow from one area to another; regional economic growth and decline has its analogue in the spatial pattern of net migration. The "pull" effect of economic opportunities is a well known empirical regularity; however, less recognized in this context are the realities of gross migration. In the first place, net migration is typically a very small statistical residual of the difference between much larger gross flows. High immigration is associated with high outmigration, and in general the volumes of gross migration, whatever their magnitudes, are strongly and positively correlated (see Gleave and Cordey-Hayes 1977 for a demonstration for Great Britain). While high migration to high-wage areas is predicted by the neoclassical model, high outmigration from such areas is not. On net, the differences between gross flows may be positive, as predicted, but at the same time quite small.

The implication from the preceding discussion is that gross flows can be effectively modeled separately rather than paired. For example, it has been shown that outmigration is related to local (origin) prosperity (wages, employment, and unemployment) relative to national indicators, whether a region is growing or declining (Clark & Ballard 1980). As an area declines (grows) relative to the nation, the volume of outmigration increases (decreases). Conversely it can also be shown that in-migration to an area is related to local opportunities weighted by national indicators (Ballard & Clark 1981). The primary issue here is separating out questions of the determinants of migration from questions of the resultant spatial "efficient" allocation of labor *vis-à-vis* the pattern of relative wages and employment. Basically, migrants do not necessarily come from and go to the "correct" regions as predicted by neoclassical theory. However, this does not mean that gross flows are unrelated to local opportunities. The point is that once the gross flows of labor migration are modeled separately, the net results of gross migration for the landscape of spatial equilibrium are more problematic: flows may be interrelated in terms of local determinants, but not neoclassically "efficient" in allocating labor over space.

Other, more theoretical issues must also be recognized if we are to understand the adjustment dynamics of labor migration. Pasinetti (1981) argued in an analogous situation that trade, despite its flow connotation, is actually a static concept. The question for trade theorists is the best allocation of resources given existing factor endowments. End-points are compared by comparative statics, and not by the modeling of the process of temporal adjustment. Of course, commodity exchange is required, but is analyzed *not* in terms of its own dynamics, rather in terms of its effectiveness in allocating resources judged at a particular time. Labor migration in this context is similarly a static concept. The pairing between origins and destinations is no accident in the Lowry (1966) model, because the issue is allocative efficiency from one time to the next. Again, the research question is not the dynamics of adjustment, but rather, how efficient labor migration is in responding to the map of economic opportunities. It is no wonder that net migration is preferred to gross migration in neoclassical theory. Net migration fits the comparative statics framework; the adjustment properties of gross migration do not.

It might be protested that our argument is surely only one of emphasis. Why cannot the Lowry model be interpreted as an adjustment model? After all, its log-linear structure is often used to run experiments on the migration effects of marginal changes in the independent variables. Obviously, it is possible to evaluate what impact a one-unit change in wages would have on the allocation of labor. However, these types of experiments are only conducted in logical time, and are not given any temporal sequence of adjustment (Hicks 1979). Is adjustment slow or fast? Are gross flows synchronized in time? And does labor adjustment have specific trajectories? These are all questions that cannot be answered by the Lowry model. Time only enters this model in an *ad hoc* manner. Since the data source for migration is often the Bureau of the Census, comparative statistics are given a five-year time frame, regardless of the underlying temporal structure of adjustment. As well, because cohort-specific migration propensities are often invoked to explain outmigration, there is a tendency to treat outmigration as a long-run generational phenomenon, without regard to its dynamic properties (Pittenger 1976). The issue is then more than one of emphasis; it concerns the key assumptions of the analytical paradigm.

Here, by way of contrast, the focus is reserved for analyzing the temporal dynamics of gross migration. However, having said that, it is immediately apparent that there has been very little research on the topic. There is very little in the way of hypotheses that could give structure to

empirical analysis structure. Of the few studies on the adjustment properties of gross migration, only Alonso (1980) has attempted to relate the
time-paths of in- and outmigration. He suggested that in-migrants have a
high propensity to outmigrate again, although this declines with length of
residence. Presumably a rapidly growing area with high in-migration will
have high outmigration. The question here which remains unresolved is:
does outmigration lag behind in-migration or is it closely synchronized in
time? Implicit in Alonso's argument is a dichotomy between fast-growing
and slow-growing areas. The former type of area is presumably dominated
by high rates of migration, the second type of area is likely to have much
less volatility in migration as the proportion of recent arrivals diminish(es)
relative to total retained immigration. Less volatility implies different
temporal structures in gross flows: we should be able to distinguish
between areas and their gross migration flows in terms of their underlying
temporal qualities.

Alonso's argument is not unlike that of others who have argued, at
least in effect, that outmigration from economically depressed areas
occurs at a constant rate. Lowry (1966) came to that conclusion after
finding that origin characteristics were unimportant in "pushing" migration. His reponse to this finding was to invoke cohort-specific rates of
outmigration related to the migration propensities of the population.
Less apparent from this discussion is the expected temporal structure of
in-migration to slow growth areas. Neoclassical theory assumes it to be
negligible compared to outmigration, which is not in fact the case.
Presumably, following Alonso's logic, in-migration would not be volatile, and perhaps might even be dominated by long-run return migration of those who left earlier in their lives. In any event, if outmigration
is relatively stable, then by implication the rate of in-migration must be
small relative to those retained in-migrants. What of the degree of
temporal synchronization between in- and outmigration, to and from
slow growth areas? One would expect little synchronization if outmigration is constant and related to the local age structure, and if in-migration
has more to do with return migration.

Demographic accounting models of gross migration are essentially
markovian (see for example Irwin 1977 and Pollard 1973). Previous
population levels coupled with age-specific migration propensities determine future in- and outmigration. In their crudest form, cohort models use
net migration as a residual applied to future time periods. More sophisticated models apply age-specific outmigration rates and use in-migration as
the balance. Some models even work on the basis of a total accounting of
all flows prior to summation of the population and migration estimates.
Total gross migration in these accounting models is derived for each
population cohort and is then weighted implicitly by the age-structure of
the area. For example, an area dominated by younger adults will have very

different gross migration estimates than an area of the same size dominated by middle-aged adults. The time frame of migration will then depend on the data used, and inherently upon the projection intervals. Typically most cohort models are based on Census data, and it is no surprise that migration is similarly analyzed by these conventional notions. As with Lowry's approach, time in cohort models is relative, not historical, and migration forecasting takes on the character of the time frame of analysis, not its underlying structure.

Econometric models of migration typically deal with net migration; few model gross migration, although this is changing (see Milne *et al.* 1980). One example of a gross migration model is Treyz (1980), in which gross migration from one state to another was related to variables such as relative wages and previous employment levels. Although untested, Treyz pointed out that his methodology could be extended to the time domain using the CWHS file. A model in which origins and destinations are not paired was developed by Clark and Ballard (1980). Change in the volume of gross migration was related to local characteristics linked to national indicators. Variables often used to determine migration, such as wages and employment, were included, along with other variables such as labor turnover. The adjustment of gross in- and outmigration to these types of variables over time was analyzed on a yearly basis. However, the temporal character of adjustment was given an *a priori* structure through the use of a set of five-year Koyck distributed lags. Use of this lag structure is warranted if the adjustment characteristics of labor migration, and the independent variables, are autoregressive and spaced or distributed geometrically over five years.

A major conclusion of the models of gross in- and outmigration developed by Clark and Ballard (1980) was that both gross flows are adaptive to short-run fluctuations in economic activity. It can be reasonably assumed from those results that labor force migration is a short-run phenomenon, like most other regional economic processes. This further implies that as the economy moves through a sequence of economic events, the pattern of inter-state migration will similarly vary. Moreover, with significant temporal fluctuations, observed at less than the census interval of five years, it is also apparent that a great deal of volatility in migration over time goes unrecorded by cohort-type models. Presumably, average propensities to migrate remain the same for different age cohorts over the long run, but in the short run migration decisions may be postponed or even accelerated. As Vining (1981) noted, the exclusive concern of economists with issues of *stability* and spatial allocative *efficiency* has led many to ignore widespread discontinuities in the interregional migration process. Unfortunately, the problem is not only related to questions of conceptualizing the process; forecasting techniques also suffer if the process of migration is misspecified.

Dynamic statistical models

Granger and Newbold (1977) described in detail the technical, empirical problems of misspecifying the underlying time-series structure of economic processes. For example, if two independent random walk (moving average) time-series are regressed against one another, high but spurious R^2 can result. As the authors noted, there is a good risk of this happening since many economic processes are best modeled as moving average processes. That is,

$$Z_t = a_t - a_{t-1} \tag{10.1}$$

where Z_t is a direct observation of the process Z_n and a_t and a_{t-1} are random shocks. What are thought to be empirically verified relationships may be completely spurious. Tests of serial autocorrelation like the Durbin–Watson statistic only deal with one type, particularly first-order autoregressive serial autocorrelation. One further consequence of misspecification is that forecasts would be seriously compromised. A spurious relationship is hardly likely to forecast accurately, except perhaps by accident. Also, misspecification can mean that the confidence intervals around any forecast may be quite different from the true intervals. Hence even a close but inaccurate specification is likely to be useless.

Thus we have two problems associated with understanding the dynamics of gross labor migration. The first is theoretical; basically a question of stepping out of the straitjacket of conventional neoclassical models that assume stability where in fact there may be significant temporal discontinuities. The second problem is empirical and is linked to the initial time-series specification of the process of migration. Markovian models of interregional population dynamics – the standard fare of economists and demographers – are essentially autoregressive. That is,

$$Z_t = Z_{t-1} + a_t \tag{10.2}$$

Whatever the drawbacks of these models concerning stability and equilibrium versus adjustment and change, as important in terms of forecasting is the simple assumption that gross migration is an autoregressive process. If incorrect, such an assumption implies very poor prediction. The only justification that comes to mind is if forecasting is oriented toward long-run issues such as the age structure of a region 20 years hence. However, even in that case doubts arise, especially as Alonso (1980) has suggested that the fertility patterns of interregional migrants are the prime determinants of differences in short-run and long-run regional growth patterns. The key question is then: what are the underlying dynamic (time-series) structures of gross migration?

Our approach to this question is to model gross migration flows using the stochastic time-series techniques made popular by Box and Jenkins (1976). There are many reviews of these techniques and some applications to regional economic phenomena (see Bennett 1979). Rather than repeat these extensive reviews, the modeling methodology and conceptual basis of autoregressive integrated moving average (ARIMA) will only be briefly discussed. Assume for any state that in-migration over time can be represented as a set of discrete observations such that Z_t is the current observation and Z_{t-1}, Z_{t-2}, Z_{t-3}, and so on, are previous observations. Because most economic processes are nonstationary, having no natural mean or constant variance, it may be necessary to difference the series so that

$$\nabla Z_t = Z_t - Z_{t-1} = (1 - B)Z_t \qquad (10.3)$$

where ∇ is defined as the backward difference operator and B is the backward shift operator. In this case differencing of the series can be summarized simply as $d = 1$. Differencing has its analogue in economic theory when *adjustment* is the object of inquiry. That is, instead of dealing with the determinants of levels, we deal with the determinants of changes or the pattern of adjustment to changes in the independent variables.

An autoregressive process is simply one that can be expressed as being a function of previous values of the process plus a random shock. For example, let any $\bar{Z} = Z_t - \mu$ where μ is the mean about which the process varies, then

$$\bar{Z}_t = \phi_1 \bar{Z}_{t-1} + \phi_2 \bar{Z}_{t-2} + \phi_3 \bar{Z}_{t-3} + \cdots + \phi_p \bar{Z}_{t-p} + a_t \qquad (10.4)$$

where $\phi_1 \cdots \phi_p$ are the parameters of an autoregressive process of order p and a_t is a random shock at time t. Typically, demographic forecasting models are autoregressive (AR) models of order $p = 1$ (using census data implies 5–10 year intervals). That is

$$\bar{Z}_t = \phi_1 \bar{Z}_{t-1} + a_t \qquad (10.5)$$

In more general terms an AR process of order p can be represented by

$$\phi(B) = 1 - \phi_1 B - \phi_2 B^2 - \cdots - \phi_p B^p \qquad (10.6)$$

or

$$\phi(B)\bar{Z}_t = a_t \qquad (10.7)$$

Basically, an AR process depends on previous observations of the dependent variable weighted by a linear set of parameters plus a random shock. For example, the population at time t is a function of previous population estimates plus a random element not accounted for endogenously in the system.

Moving average (MA) processes, on the other hand, express $\bar{Z}_t$ as being dependent upon a finite number (q) of previous and current random shocks, a.

That is,

$$\bar{Z}_t = a_t - \theta_1 a_{t-1} - \theta_2 a_{t-2} - \cdots - \theta_q a_{t-q} \qquad (10.8)$$

In time-series forecasting this does not mean that the weights (1, θ_1, θ_2, etc.) need total to unity or be positive. More generally,

$$\theta(B) = 1 - \theta_1 B - \theta_2 B^2 - \cdots \theta_q B^q \qquad (10.9)$$

and

$$\bar{Z}_t = \theta(B) a_t \qquad (10.10)$$

A moving average process of order $q = 1$ would then be written as

$$\bar{Z}_t = a_t - \theta_1 a_{t-1} = (1 - \theta_1 B) a_t \qquad (10.11)$$

Imagine what such a process would imply about gross migration. Essentially, the volume or change in the volume of in-migration, to take one example, would simply depend on the current random shock and some weighted portion of the previous shock. Instead of depending on the past volume of in-migration, as in autoregressive models, random disturbances would generate each successive year's in-migration to a given state. As indicated above, such a model would go against virtually all conventional assumptions regarding the time-path of labor force migration, not being dependent on long-run or previous patterns of migration.

Demographic forecasting models presume to be able to specify fully the determinants of population change by accounting for births, deaths, and migration. Such models are autoregressive and assume a_t to be negligible. But as Chow (1975) and others have noted, few economic processes are completely deterministic; most are stochastic. That is, either variables are omitted because they are unknown, or a random element, generated exogenously, may affect the dependent variable. Thus, when the dynamic path of adjustment is considered, what is actually being discussed is an underlying stochastic process, be it AR, MA or some combination ARIMA. It may be convenient to treat population systems as complete deterministic accounts if only static description is involved; however, once the time domain is introduced one should reasonably expect that population systems are stochastic, not wholly deterministic.

Box and Jenkins (1976) have a three-step procedure of time-series modeling. First, the type of process (AR, MA, etc.) and its order are identified using the autocorrelation and partial autocorrelation functions. At this point, these functions are checked for indications of nonstationarity and if necessary differencing is used to induce stationarity. Having a preliminary identification, the parameters are estimated using Marquardt's (1963) algorithm and the maximum likelihood function. The third stage is diagnostic checking: testing the residuals from the fitted series for underlying nonrandom patterns. A given series might well be fitted by a set of possible ARIMA models. There are two key ways of discriminating between alternative models: parsimony with respect to the number of parameters required to represent the series adequately; and accuracy, indicated by the mean square of the error terms. Thus, while it is quite possible to fit a series with low- and high-order AR or MA processes, once parsimony and accuracy are invoked, the choice between models is quite straightforward. Essentially, the aim of time-series modeling is to estimate the underlying temporal process as accurately and parsimoniously (in terms of the number of parameters) as possible, a goal not dissimilar to that of maximizing R^2 in regression for forecasting.

The data used to analyze the dynamics of inter-state gross migration were made available through the Continuous Work History Sample (CWHS) (Bureau of Economic Analysis 1976). These data were collected on a yearly basis from 1958 to 1975, and represent employed workers between the ages of 25 and 64 who migrated between states over a time span of one year. Excluded are unemployed workers, the young, and the old. Since it is well known that migration is very selective with respect to occupation, this data file deals with a quite specific portion of the total work force and those who migrated in any one year. This selectivity is precisely that implied by most regional economic models of migration. Also implied in the data are job switches within firms or corporations which involve inter-state relocation. Consequently the data measure the conventional turnover conception of labor migration and the less familiar but, according to McKay and Whitelaw (1978), often as important, intrafirm job relocations. There is virtually no evidence available to indicate whether or not this latter type of migration is important in the United States.

A set of US states was selected for analysis of their dynamic gross migration structures (Table 10.1). These 15 states were arranged into five different groups according to their growth of employment over the 1958 to 1975 period (Bureau of Labor Statistics 1977). Using national growth rates as reference points, the first group can be characterized as a *maxigrowth* group. Basically all three states grew very fast over both the

Table 10.1 Employment growth by state and the USA, 1958–75.

State	Growth rates (percent)	
	1958–66	1967–75
Arizona	151.6	162.5
Florida	145.6	150.3
Virginia	132.9	131.9
New Mexico	123.1	133.8
Texas	127.0	135.7
Wyoming	110.8	147.3
Delaware	129.3	114.8
Iowa	124.6	118.7
Kentucky	126.4	124.7
Connecticut	124.4	107.9
Indiana	130.3	108.6
Michigan	129.8	107.7
Illinois	119.5	105.5
New York	111.3	(99.0)
Pennsylvania	111.3	106.0
United States	124.5	116.9

1958–66 and the 1967–75 periods. The second group had average initial growth rates and then took off (described here as the *accelerated growth* group). The third group grew in both periods at much the same rate as the nation and is summarized as being the *average growth* group. In contrast to the second group, the fourth can be summarized as the *decelerated growth* group. And, in contrast to the first group, the last group grew very slowly or even declined, and is referred to (relative to the nation) as the *maxi-decline* group. Consistency and similarity in growth patterns were the primary criteria for the inclusion of any state in a particular group. Not surprisingly, the southwest of the USA is represented in the first two groups while the northeast of the USA is represented in the last two groups.

Time-series structure of gross migration

So as to illustrate the variety of time-series patterns in gross migration, five states were selected to demonstrate the patterns of in- and outmigration (Fig. 10.1). Vertically, each graph was scaled by logarithms and represents the yearly rates of change in gross migration. Notice that no attempt was

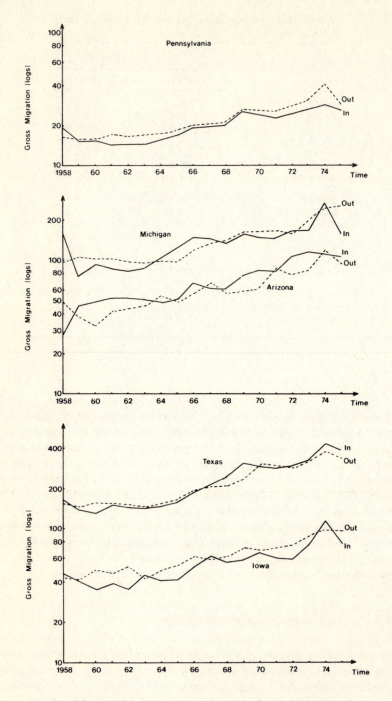

Figure 10.1 State gross migration flows, 1958–75.

made to standardize each flow by total state employment or population. Gross migration rates were modeled separately, and compared against the results of modeling raw gross flows. Arizona in particular experienced significant fluctuations in both gross flows over the period 1957 to 1975. This is perhaps not unexpected, since Arizona is a representative of maxi and accelerated economic growth. Note, however, that it was only in the latter half of the period (the acceleration stage) that in-migration to Texas overtook outmigration. The pairs of gross flows for each of these five states were, however, quite similar to one another, in terms of volumes at least. Only in Arizona were there marked divergencies between in- and outmigration although total volumes were generally close. Even in Pennsylvania, a state characterized by marked relative decline, only small differences exist between in- and outmigration. What we can demonstrate is a strong association (correlation) between gross migrations over time, something noted cross-sectionally by Gleave and Cordey-Hayes (1977).

The results of modeling each raw gross flow for each state are summarized in Clark (1982a). Taking in-migration first, 9 of the 15 states modeled had identified AR time-series processes, 5 had MA processes, and 1 was mixed, ARMA. Of the states requiring differencing to induce stationarity, most were either growing or declining states, indicating the existence of an important trend component. In addition, four of the five states with MA(1) in-migration time-series processes were shared equally between two groups of states: maxi growth and maxi decline. In-migration to Wyoming, an accelerated growth state, was identified as the other MA process, while in-migration to Florida, a maxi-growth state, was identified as a mixed ARMA process. Implied in a MA(1) process is that the current observation can be best (parsimoniously and accurately) expressed as a function of current and immediately prior random shocks. This would seem to imply that in-migration to this type of state is a quite volatile dynamic process, more vulnerable to exogenous and rapid shocks than to previous patterns of in-migration. In contrast, average and decelerating growth states are better approximated by first-order AR processes. Implied in these cases, which constitute the majority of the in-migration series modeled, is that in-migration is a function of previous changes in in-migration plus a random shock. Thus it is no accident that cohort or similar markovian demographic accounting models perform so poorly when attempting to predict the future of rapidly growing or declining areas; at least one side of gross migration process is often misspecified.

From these results it was clear also that outmigration for some states can be best modeled by first-order MA processes. However, fewer states were in this category, notably Texas and Wyoming (accelerated growth states) and Indiana (decelerated growth). The risks of misspecifying outmigration processes are obviously much lower, as most states were best modeled using first-order AR or mixed ARMA processes. This was true for maxi-growth and declining states as well as average growth states. Notice, however, that knowing the order and process of in-migration for any given state was not sufficient to guess the order and process of out-migration from that state. Only three states had the same time-series process for both in- and outmigration. Further, there was no clear pattern with respect to economic growth or decline. The mixture of ARIMA processes has greater implications than simply differences in forecasting technique. If in- and outmigration are different time-series processes, or only of a different order, net migration (the difference between in- and outmigration) is not an ARIMA-type process and has incredibly complex characteristics. The simplicity of modeling each gross flow is not reflected in net migration, and because of the mixture of processes implied above, net migration cannot be an MA or markovian process. Thus a second source of predictive error, again misspecification, can be identified for cohort models that use net migration. The order, process, and even parameter values would have to be exactly the same for an ARIMA-type model to be derived from net migration.

For the most part, the estimated parameters of the in-migration models were statistically significant, the exceptions being found in the states of Virginia, Texas, Wyoming, and New York. All except Texas were identified as MA processes. In effect, because the parameter on previous values of in-migration to Texas was insignificantly different from zero, any current value of in-migration was only significantly dependent upon the current random shock. Again, this is a source of volatility in any estimate of in-migration, even though previous values of in-migration do marginally lower the forecast errors. Large and significant in-migration AR parameters were found in both growing and declining states. The lowest parameters were found in the average growth group of states, indicating again that in-migration in those states is less volatile than for growing or declining areas – a result that should not come as a surprise! Some parameter estimates for outmigration time-series processes were found to be not significantly different from zero. This was true for Florida, Virginia, Texas, and Wyoming (accelerated or maxi-growth states), although there was a mixture of AR and MA processes involved. The implication was that the current random shocks have an important role in determining the current rates of outmigration. Given the conventional assumptions of the long-run stability of outmigration, especially with regard to declining regions, these results indicate that forecasting models prefaced on such an assumption are likely to be fundamentally compromised.

Having considered migration in terms of gross flows, an obviously related issue is to analyze the results obtained by modeling gross migration standardized by the level of employment for each time period – gross migration rates. Patterns of gross migration rates for the five states initially selected to indicate volatility in the raw gross flows are shown in Figure 10.2. As expected, in-migration and outmigration rates are very close for any given state. Similarly, it is apparent that there are only marginal differences between the pairs of gross migration in terms of their rates at any point in time. The scales of volatility are, however, much reduced for each state and it is obvious how important migration is for a maxi-growth state, such as Arizona, compared to a maxi-decline state, such as Pennsylvania. Essentially, migration is a major component of employment change in Arizona, much less so for Iowa and Pennsylvania. Since many cohort models use migration rates as opposed to raw flows, the identified time-series processes are of crucial importance in evaluating their potential effectiveness as forecasting tools.

As in the previous modeling exercise, we deal primarily with the summary results *vis-à-vis* type of process and its order (Clark 1982a). When compared to the previous results, we were immediately struck by the basic differences in identified time-series processes and orders for both gross flows. Of the 15 in-migration rate time-series, all but two were MA processes: Kentucky's in-migration rate time-series was an ARI(1,1), while Pennsylvania's in-migration rate was an ARMA(1,1) process. Previously, most states' in-migration series were AR processes. Furthermore, a number of in-migration rate time-series were MA processes of order 2, more complex than the simpler MA(1). These more complex functions were concentrated in two employment growth groups: accelerating and decelerating growth states. On the other side, most outmigration rate time-series were also MA processes of either order 1 or 2. In this case 6 of the 15 series were either AR or mixed ARMA processes. Incredible as it seems, by standardizing in- and outmigration at each time period by current employment, most gross migration time-series changed from AR to MA processes. Note again that only Connecticut had the same process and order for both in- and outmigration.

It is obvious that the problems noted with the raw gross flows regarding misspecification of the time-series apply with much greater force if gross migration rates are used. In fact, given these results, it is highly probable that most markovian gross migration models are misspecified. Following Granger and Newbold (1977), the use of gross migration rates in markovian formats will inevitably lead to poor forecasts. A more subtle problem is also involved. Compared to the raw gross flow estimates, gross migration rates models are inherently less accurate and prone to greater errors. Basically, the errors of two time-series are compounded when modeling gross migration rates, a serious problem identified by Alonso (1968) some time ago when combining variables to form other variables.

Differences in the accuracy of raw flow models versus rates models were found for all states. The source of larger errors in the rates models was

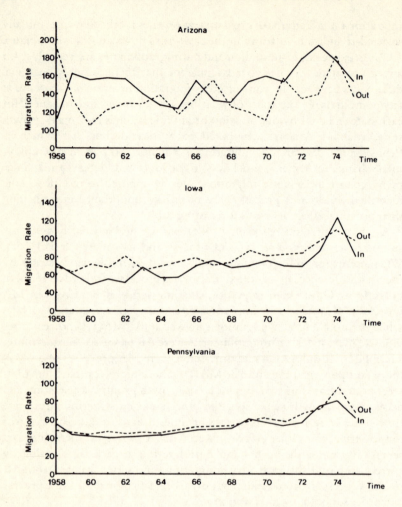

Figure 10.2   State gross migration rates, 1958–75.

obviously the combination of two different variables. Less obvious was the impact on the identified type of time-series process. When using rates rather than gross flows for prediction purposes in markovian models, we run a serious risk of misspecifying the process and thus generating very unreliable forecasts. If, by luck, the time-series is in fact an AR process, by using rates we generate the potential for greater errors in forecasting. Finally, if net migration is used, not only are the error structures incredibly complex and unrelated to the family of ARIMA models, but misspecification is likely to be endemic. Simplicity is the key to modeling migration over time.

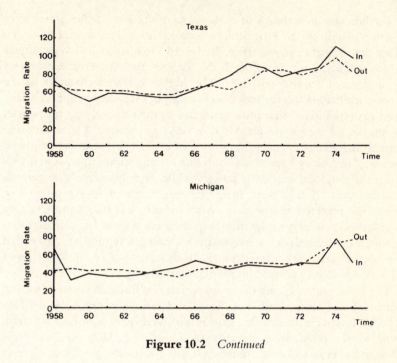

Figure 10.2 *Continued*

Relationships between gross flows

So far discussion has centered on the particular time-series structures for each gross flow and state. Graphically, it was observed that in- and outmigration appear correlated, both in terms of the volume of gross migration and their rates of change. As well, it was noted that Alonso (1980), among others, has contended that in-migration can lead to outmigration; that is, in-migration over time causes outmigration. The primary question here is then: are in- and outmigration temporally related? We emphasize the phrase *temporally related* because it is very difficult to demonstrate causality in this context. The basic problem is that both gross migration flows are related to the same set of exogenous variables: wages, employment, and investment, for example. Consequently their error structures are intercorrelated, not independent as required when testing for causality in the time domain. While issues such as lead/lag structures and correlation between gross flows at particular points can be investigated, according to Granger and Newbold (1977), any argument concerning causality would simply be spurious. In this section we focus upon the cross-correlation functions of gross migration for each state; in the next chapter we consider causality more directly.

To illustrate the patterns of cross-correlation, three sample states were selected to indicate the relationships between in- and outmigration over a given set of leads and lags (Fig. 10.3). All three states had very similar cross-correlation functions, with the highest cross-correlation estimates being centred around zero lags. The highly centered character of the cross-correlations and the lack of other significant spikes might well have been expected given that most estimates of their underlying time-series properties were quite simple AR(1) or MA(1) processes. Yet, at the same time, these results are surprising, at least in the context of conventional theory. The Lowry hypothesis holds that in-migration responds to differential shifts in local economic activity while outmigration is a longer-run phenomenon. If this were true, one might expect to see quite long leads/lags reflected in the data. Also, Alonso's (1980) argument that in-migration *causes* outmigration implies some type of lag structure, but again the evidence does not necessarily support his hypothesis. After all, if the highest cross-autocorrelation is at lag zero, then both gross flows adjust coincidently in time, although separately.

The results of analyzing the cross-correlation function between in- and outmigration, using both raw flows and rates, are reported in Clark (1982a). Based on the raw flows the results were quite uniform, with high cross autocorrelations in virtually all states. Only Delaware and New Mexico had cross-correlations below 0.800. Moreover, in all but two cases the highest correlation was centered around the zero lag. Florida's highest correlation was centered on one year, indicating that in-migration may lag outmigration, while for Delaware the results implied that in-migration may lead outmigration by one year. Consistent with the previous results of modeling gross migration rates as opposed to the raw flows, the cross-correlation results for the former series were more variable. In particular, it is apparent that cross-correlations were higher for declining states and were lowest for growing states. In fact, one would hesitate in the cases of Arizona, New Mexico, Florida, and Wyoming to suggest that the estimates of cross-correlation are statistically significant. Given the relatively limited length of time-series, the ten-year lag for New Mexico, coupled with low cross-correlation, is quite difficult to interpret. Again, the errors involved in combining variables such as the estimates of in-migration and total employment for any given year must have a large role to play in radically altering the cross-correlational time-series structures between in and outmigration.

Conclusions

This chapter was primarily descriptive and empirical, being concerned with the temporal dynamics of gross migration. Rather than focusing

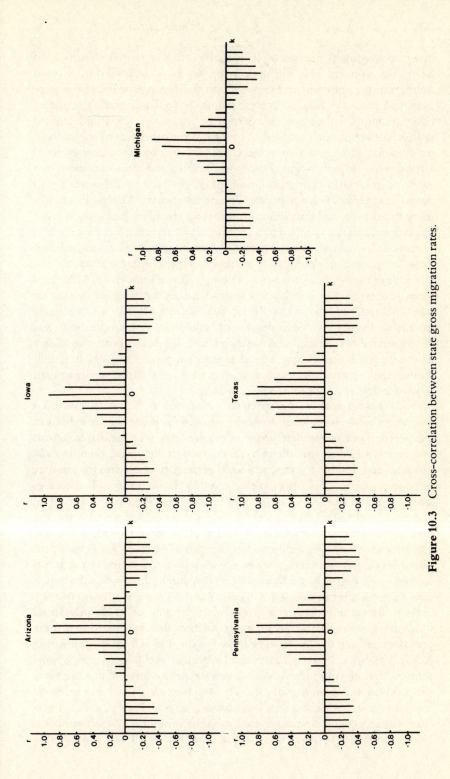

Figure 10.3 Cross-correlation between state gross migration rates.

upon conventional questions such as the efficient spatial allocation of labor, our concern was the underlying temporal structure of in- and outmigration. Different techniques from those commonly used in geographical studies of migration were employed to demonstrate the underlying temporal adjustment properties of migration. Box and Jenkins (1976) ARIMA models enabled us to look at the other side of migration – its dynamic as opposed to static character. In doing so, conventional assumptions of cohort-type models were tested and found wanting. For example, the markovian assumptions of cohort-type models were found not to be appropriate for many rapidly growing states. Misspecification is more than likely, and thus significant forecast errors are inevitable if gross migration flows are assumed to be AR processes where in fact they are MA processes. It was also noticed that the common practice of standardizing gross migration by population or employment often transforms the underlying time-series processes, creating, almost uniformly, MA time-series processes. The conclusions from these results can only be that by standardizing the raw gross flows, we run major risks of unreliable forecasts. Finally, a high degree of temporal synchronization was demonstrated between in- and out-migration. Typically both gross flows have very similar paths of temporal adjustment and are highly correlated, if not causally related. Labor migration is far more volatile over time than most researchers have previously recognized.

From these results we can speculate on the role of US inter-state labor migration vis-à-vis regional economic growth and decline. It is hard to escape the conclusion that gross migration has very similar dynamic properties in Texas and Pennsylvania, two archetypical economically growing and declining states, although in the former case migration may be more volatile. This suggests that the CWHS migration file measures labor turnover; that is, job switching. It is well known that job switching is highest among younger workers, and this is consistent with the age profiles of employed migrants. It is also well known that job switching typically involves promotion and higher pay (Bartel 1979). Thus, at the micro-level, job switching carries obvious rewards, whether the job is located in a growing or declining state. How might this explain the higher rates of gross migration in growing areas and net in- and outmigration?

First, let us deal with the question of the rate of gross migration. Growing areas are characterized by high labor turnover; quitting is more prevalent and can be shown to be linked to the rate of local wage inflation (Clark 1981b). Turnover is associated with the level of economic opportunities, and in growing areas labor turnover is a means of gaining rapid job promotion and higher salaries. Thus, to the extent that labor turnover involves relocation across state boundaries, the actual rate of gross migration will reflect this particular kind of labor mobility. Elsewhere, it has been observed that inter-state migration in the south and southwest is highest among rapid growth states, indirect evidence for our hypothesis (Clark 1982b). Why then the differences in net migration between growing and declining areas? We would contend that there are simply not enough job opportunities in the slow-growth states. Voluntary turnover is significantly less in these types of states. Job switching that involves out-migration can of course occur with relative ease. However, job switching that involves in-migration is less likely because of the more limited set of destination opportunities. Also, declining industries in low-growth states do not provide the same number of middle-level jobs that are needed to attract younger workers. Consequently, younger workers are lost to the region (through turnover) and not completely replaced.

11 *Migration and capital*

Introduction

Policy intervention to stimulate regional economic development depends on a thorough understanding of the roles of labor and capital in the growth process. Although most regional growth models owe their origin to macroeconomic models, the issue is made more complex because of the interdependent nature of regional economic systems. Interregional wage relativities, spatial variations in the quality and quantity of labor, and the adaptability of labor to the economic geography of demand are important variables on the labor side of the development process for radical (Walker & Storper 1981) and orthodox (Wheaton 1979) theorists alike. On the capital side, issues such as the availability, cost and adaptability of local capital also figure prominently. Local economic development potential must then be considered in the context of how labor and capital intersect in the development process.

The pioneering work of Greenwood (1981) and Muth (1971) indicate that the 1970s was a decade of sustained empirical research on the interrelationships between labor and capital, and especially the interactions between labor migration and regional growth as measured by employment and population. Using econometric models that are often quite complex, researchers have sought to answer questions such as: which comes first, economic growth or population in-migration? Are there distinct lags in the growth process (or vice versa)? Does outmigration contribute to economic decline at the origin? And does economic decline precede outmigration? Moreover, a number of academics have sought to determine the lines of causality between growth and migration although, early on, Muth (1971) conceived of the issue as a "chicken-or-egg" problem, implying that causality on one side or the other is logically uninteresting and difficult to sustain empirically. A consequence of this type of reasoning has been the proliferation of models which simultaneously determine migration *and* regional economic growth.

For some the results have been satisfactory, and yet in the abstract realm of regional growth theories, whether radical or orthodox, many still seek distinct lines of causality between labor migration and regional growth. One way of resolving this apparent gap between empirical results and theoretical expectations is to question whether or not the empirical models have been adequate to the task. There are reasons for questioning the accuracy of many empirical models of migration and regional growth. Obtaining adequate data on migration and economic growth has been a continuing problem. Census estimates of migration are crude in that they lump together employed, unemployed, and those not in the work force. Similarly, indicators of economic growth have rarely, if ever, measured investment directly, relying instead on proxies such as employment and population. Not only have adequate data been a problem but perhaps more critical has been the lack of time-series data which could directly illuminate the dynamic interrelationships between capital growth and labor migration. Comparative statics can only imply dynamics; yet empirical models have been essentially compromised by the data and their temporal (or should we say, static) character. Another important issue is the continuing use of net migration rather than gross flows (see the previous chapter on the problem of using net migration). Generally speaking, however, the point is quite simply that empirical models have been rarely equal to the task, something noted by Casetti (1981a), amongst others.

In this chapter we wish to reconsider the dynamic relationships between migration and regional growth. So as to provide a structured analytical framework for this task a sketch is required of the contending theories of labor and capital mobility. In the interest of clarity and for the purpose of generating a set of empirical propositions, we wish to concentrate on two schools of thought which are mutually exclusive: the capital-logic and competitive market schools. These theories are analyzed using two sets of data and times-series techniques which are more suitable for economic adjustment analysis than conventional, regression-based models. Yearly estimates of inter-state labor migration were made available by the Bureau of Economic Analysis (BEA) from its Continuous Work History Sample (CWHS), and yearly estimates of capital stocks at the state level for manufacturing industries were made available by the Federal Reserve Bank of Boston. Analysis was conducted over the period 1958 to 1975 using Box and Jenkins (1976) univariate and multivariate techniques as well as Granger and Newbold (1977) tests of causality.

The capital-logic school

The capital-logic school focuses on the social relations of production and especially strategies of domination and exploitation used by firms to control labor. Firms are assumed to be more mobile than labor, if not in terms of the physical stock of production, then at least in terms of their financial assets. The case studies of the New England economy by Bluestone and Harrison (1982) have gone some way to confirming this proposition. Because of the interdependent nature of production, firms need labor and labor needs firms if both are to survive. The central problem for labor is its dependence, its lack of ownership of the means of production, and its reliance on firms for jobs. Firms *own* the jobs, have the power of hiring and firing, and ultimately the right of initiating and terminating employment. Power in the employment relation is unevenly distributed unless labor can constrain the actions of firms through tactics such as unionization and the use of state apparatuses like courts to prohibit runaway plants. To the extent that capital is not dependent on a limited geographical set of locations for resources and markets, firms will locate so as to avoid entrapment by labor and thereby maximize exploitation.

Given these assumptions, a series of scenarios can be identified so as to represent the interrelationships between labor migration and capital growth. First, imagine that a firm has the choice of a wide number of locations for production (as, for example, an electronics firm may have when assembling transistor radios; see Clark 1981a). Walker (1978) suggested that such a firm will locate so as to exploit an immobile and vulnerable labor force. Two sets of variables will dominate the choice of location: the degree of local worker organization and labor costs. Meyer *et al.* (1980), not noted for their radical opinions, similarly argued that these two variables are crucial locational criteria. To manage, organize, and control this workforce, a technocratic class loyal to the firm and not the location is required. In addition, uniquely skilled workers may be needed. In this context, employment is initiated by the firm using local labor and outside workers. Thus we would expect empirically that there would be an observable lag between capital growth and in-migration. Also, this scenario suggests that as labor begins to exert power over the firm, relocation of capital will occur, initiating outmigration of its technocratic elite. Again, change in the capital stock (in this instance decline) initiates migration but, of course, only for a narrow portion of all employees.

A similar argument has been made by Massey (1978a) in her study of capital restructuring, relocation, and the economic crisis of Great Britain. Her evidence, and that of Bluestone and Harrison (1982) for New England, suggested that restructuring has a fundamental spatial component. Relocation enables firms to leave behind old forms of organization (technocratic and social) and out-moded capital stock. The consequences of relocation are a decline of local employment and selective outmigration of certain primary workers. Often coupled with this process is a second sequence of events: selective centralization and decentralization of, respectively, corporate control functions and production facilities. To the extent that corporate control functions require a technocratic elite, then capital growth and labor migration are likely to be closely related with small temporal lags in adjustment. However, decentralized production may require few outside workers, implying that capital investment may not be related at all to labor migration. By decentralizing production, firms may be able to invade existing and vulnerable local labor markets and thus maintain exploitation. Again, capital retains the initiative and, more technically (empirically), such a role provides the underlying rationale for assuming labor migration to be dependent on capital growth.

A third scenario has been suggested by Markusen (1978a), who emphasized how labor reserves can be manipulated in mediating the power of labor. For firms that are geographically bound by reason of resources or markets, a way of maintaining control over wages and the conditions of work is to import labor to the region. In contrast to the scenarios suggested above, the type of labor imported may be unskilled. Individual firms may arrange to import this type of labor although it is clearly possible for the state to encourage labor migration through policies such as guest-worker visas. This latter approach has been quite popular in western Europe, but less so in the United States, although it could be argued that the massive, and largely uncontained, volume of illegal immigration is a tacit "reserve army" policy. Clearly labor migration in this context is dependent on demand and the level of investment. However, it is also possible that among larger multilocational firms there will be firm-initiated labor migration that is unrelated to demand. McKay and Whitelaw (1977) have suggested that maintenance of discipline among the technocratic elite may involve firms frequently moving their staffs so as to enforce their dependence and allegiance to the firm. In this case there may be no clear relationship between labor migration and capital growth.

The capital-logic school maintains that firms have the ultimate power of initiative with respect to labor migration. This does not necessarily mean that labor is forced to migrate. The structure of American legal rights is at least nominally universal – free will is a fundamental underlying principle. Yet, to the extent that labor is dependent on capital for jobs and choice in employment between firms is limited, labor migration is structured by forces outside its direct control. Generally, these organizing assumptions provide us with a strong *a priori* argument for the direction of causality. Capital growth initiates labor migration.

The scenarios described above maintain this central proposition whether or not capital is assumed to be mobile or immobile. In some instances, of course, labor migration may be temporally coincident with capital growth, especially if specialized labor is actually imported to build the capital stock. It is also plausible that once initiated, labor migration to a particular region will continue over time as new investments are made and economic growth sustained. Labor migration in this manner may appear to any one employer as autonomous, but in aggregate be linked to the overall level of capital growth. Thus, labor migration may be coincident with growth, especially if the region is large and its economic base diverse. In other instances, for example where outside labor is used to break the power of local labor, there may be quite long lags between labor migration and the initial phase of capital growth. Similarly, with the decline of capital (through relocation or restructuring), outmigration may be coincident or lag over a longer period.

The competitive market school

The neoclassical theory of factor mobility and regional growth is well known, so it is hardly necessary to review extensively its intricacies. However, at the minimum, its principal assumptions regarding the relationship between labor mobility and capital growth need to be explicitly noted to facilitate empirical analysis and comparison with the capital-logic school. We have chosen to characterize the neoclassical model, and its variants derived from international trade theory, as the competitive market school for two reasons. First, since it is assumed that workers and firms pursue goals of utility and income maximization within the structure of market opportunities, it is obvious that how labor and capital function and intersect with each other will determine the empirical relationship between migration and capital growth. Secondly, because it is the market that provides rewards, this approach is quintessentially one of applying the rules of supply and demand to labor and capital as if they were solely exchange commodities. The market conceptualization is used by neoclassical theory to provide order to the exchange process.

Very simply, labor is assumed to migrate in response to geographical variations in wages, climate, and job opportunities. These types of variables are assumed to figure prominently in individuals' utility functions. Moreover, it is assumed that it is the individual that initiates migration. These economic variables are crucial for the individuals concerned and the broader regional economic system alike. By migrating to a high-wage area, the individual benefits *and* labor is allocated more efficiently with regard to the spatial configuration of the demand and supply of labor. Consequently, as labor migrates to high-wage areas, the supply of labor is increased at the destination and decreased at the origin, so that over time, following a sequence of such moves, wages will be equalized among all regions of the spatial economic system. For the labor market, migration has two virtues: it rewards individuals in the sense that their welfare increases, and it efficiently allocates labor between areas so that factor price equalization is achieved. Because it is assumed that labor migrates in response to economic opportunities, to the extent that capital growth spurs higher wages, labor migration will *follow* capital.

From the perspective of capital, it is apparent that the spatial configuration of labor costs will structure capital mobility. Following Romans (1965) and others, capital is presumed to migrate from high-wage to low-wage areas. Holding the location of labor constant, the result will be an increase in labor demand in low-wage areas and decline in labor demand in high-wage areas. Consequently, wage equalization should occur between the regions of the economy. Assuming perfect information of all wages and prices, free capital and labor mobility, and rational optimizing behavior, capital and labor adjustment (migration) should occur simultaneously. This is the basis for assertions by members of the competitive market school that economic and demographic variables are mutually interdependent in the regional growth process. Muth's (1971) chicken-or-egg problem (what comes first, labor migration or capital growth?) is a question of partial equilibrium analysis; that is, designating the point or stage in the interdependent process to begin analysis. Following this logic, an obvious solution (and one promoted by Greenwood 1981) is to model the system as a simultaneous process. The problems of designating causality (the chicken-or-egg problem) are circumvented, and thus the assumptions of non-contingent individual optimizing behavior can be maintained.

Unfortunately for the competitive market school, reality intrudes on this ideal world in quite savage ways. Imagine that labor is not as *fast* as capital in adapting (migrating) to opportunities such as higher relative wages (which is surely a realistic hypothesis), then the result would be that labor migration would lag behind capital growth. Labor might in-migrate to a once high-wage region not knowing that the reason for high wages (previously strong capital growth) had since moved. To specify correctly an empirical model of the simultaneous relationship between migration and capital, such a possibility (leads and lags) would have to be taken into account. However, because the competitive market school has no *a priori* expectation of whether or not labor lags behind capital, extensive empirical analysis would have to be undertaken, prior to modeling simultaneously these two markets, to specify correctly the adjustment characteristics. But what if lags were found? Could their existence be explained? The most obvious response would be that the initial assumptions were not met. Information about competing opportunities is not complete nor uniformly available. Most empirical models deal with this problem in a pragmatic manner and, depending on the situation, leads and lags are introduced to improve the models' predictive performance. Causality in this context (that is, migration causing capital growth or vice versa) is an *ad hoc* response to reality, rather than a theoretical proposition.

Our argument is not so much criticism of the underlying principles of competitive market equilibrium as a recognition that the predictive quality of the model, *vis-à-vis* temporal relationships between labor migration and capital growth, is quite poor. Traditionally, trade theorists suppose that market price equalization across regions will force each region to produce goods for which they have a comparative advantage. The Heckscher–

Ohlin theory of trade (Ohlin 1933) can be modified in accordance with the reality of factor mobility. In fact, authors like Horiba and Kirkpatrick (1981) have sought to demonstrate the relevance of this theory, albeit modified by Leontief (1956). Even so, these modifications still do not enable us to formulate distinct *a priori* propositions regarding labor migration and capital growth in the time domain.

The issue is then more than empirical; it involves us in understanding the *nature* of adjustment assumed in the competitive market model of regional growth. Put simply, the model assumes that labor and capital adjust to the landscape of opportunities in a logical sequence; it is inherently unable to consider directly questions of temporal adjustment. The implied Walrasian recontracting process is ahistorical and describes a system that "moves" from one equilibrium to another. The parameters that describe the system remain the same; the problem is simply deriving the optimal spatial allocation of resources. Inherent in this approach is an unstated assumption that the temporal lead–lag issue is only one of mechanical coordination. For instance, back to our imagined case of labor adapting more slowly than capital, not only is there a lag between capital growth and labor migration, but the actual economic system changes its basic character in response, so that labor and capital are both out of sequence and face markedly different current and historical conditions. As Iwai (1981) has recently demonstrated, short-run disequilibrium can cumulate over *time* into the long run wherein real events and actions, their locations in time and space, determine outcomes (see also Ch. 3).

There is no reason to believe that distinct lines of causality between capital growth and labor migration do not exist. But unfortunately the competitive market school cannot provide concrete expectations based on theory. Perhaps the only exception to this characterization is Kaldor's (1970) model of regional imbalanced growth. By invoking scale economies and labor productivity related to the level of output, Kaldor (1970) argued that initial advantages of capital richness can offset higher relative wages, leading to further in-migration and further investment. In this instance the direction of causality depends on the phase of growth that one chooses to model. It is not immediately clear what determines the initial advantage (was it capital investment in response to demand initiated by labor inflow?), but it is obvious that once set up, capital growth induces further investment. It is not surprising that this model can suggest a distinct causal structure between migration and capital, for like Iwai's (1981) analysis, it is bound by real events and their locations.

What, then, should we expect to see in any empirical analysis of the temporal characteristics of migration and capital? The capital-logic school clearly suggests that capital has the advantage of initiation – of ownership of jobs. Thus, to the extent that labor is required outside the local labor market, whether the technocratic elite or the reserve army of the unemployed, capital growth should lead migration. Presumably the lags should be shorter when technocratic labor is involved. It is also plausible that once initiated, migration and capital growth may become a simultaneous process, especially if the region is large and economically diverse. At the same time it is also clear that the capital-logic school predicts that a certain portion of labor will migrate regardless of demand, primarily for discipline-related purposes. If all the assumptions of the competitive school are met, then presumably there would be no leads or lags between labor migration and capital growth – the markets of labor and capital would operate and intersect simultaneously. Otherwise, no concrete expectations can be noted other than those implied in previous empirical observations, for example, that labor is less mobile than capital.

Modeling regional growth and decline

So as to establish temporal patterns between migration and capital, cross-correlation functions were computed between capital growth and in- and outmigration as a preliminary step in identifying lead–lag relationships. Based on the sample of 15 states for the period 1958 to 1975 introduced in the previous chapter, the use of cross-correlation functions was primarily descriptive. Although cross-spectral methods could be used here, the length of the time-series of capital and gross migration were insufficient for the prudent application of this technique. Depending on the actual character of the autocorrelation and partial autocorrelation functions, these series may have to be differenced in order to achieve stationarity. The second stage of analysis involved fitting bivariate autoregressive (AR) models to determine, in an exploratory manner, whether or not the relationships between capital growth and migration for any state could be adequately modeled using successive combinations of lagged values of each to predict current values of either variable under consideration. The underlying time-series structure of each pair of variables was identified from a range of autoregressive (AR), moving average (MA), and ARMA formulations. More complex MA and ARMA formulations required the use of transfer functions. From these results, the third stage was to estimate the transfer function models for those bivariate relationships not adequately represented by an autoregressive or bivariate scheme.

Tests of causality were employed in both stages two and three of the analysis to help identify the directions and patterns of the relationships between capital growth and migration for each state (see Clark & Gertler 1983 for more details). These types of tests have become more popular in recent years as a way of indicating and verifying theoretically derived relationships, particularly in economics (see Sims 1977, Caines et al. 1981,

Granger & Newbold 1977). They have been suggested as useful diagnostic tools for constructing econometric forecasting models (Pierce 1977), although at this time their applications in regional econometric modeling have been limited (for one example see Green & Albrecht 1979; and the comments by L'Esperance 1979a).

Granger and Newbold (1977) suggested two basic conditions for the assignation of causality. First, the future cannot cause the past; strictly speaking, only the past can cause the present and future. Secondly, it is impossible to identify causality between two deterministic processes; causality is only sensibly applied to two or more stochastic processes. From this definition it is clear that causality in this context takes on a rather restricted meaning. Its application may not necessarily uncover the "true" causality, if such can ever be found at all. Nevertheless, this method has the advantage of providing a testable definition and, in common with the overall philosophy of recent time-series approaches, it systematically induces the researcher to test alternative hypotheses which might potentially challenge the legitimacy of suspected or observed causal relationships. Notice, though, that causality need not be unequivocal even in the limited sense noted above unless and until the converse of the originally derived relationship is also tested and disproved. For the issue posed in the preceding section – what is the true direction of causality between capital and migration? – these tests for causality are more powerful than a simple regression model; no *a priori* assumption is needed regarding the direction of causality.

Finally, a set of more general methodological issues need to be recognized before discussing data and results. The study of Clark and Gertler (1983) employed a time-series framework for three reasons. First, time-series frameworks naturally lend themselves to the analysis of dynamics. As such, no assumption is made of a stable equilibrium process (which underlies static cross-sectional models); rather, emphasis is on the short-run adjustments which accumulate into the long-run. Secondly, time-series philosophy based on Box and Jenkins (1976), obviates the need for an *a priori* (and arbitrary) specification of the importance of lagged values of the independent variables, characteristic of more traditional econometric distributed-lag methodologies. Given that the competitive market school cannot provide any theroetical clues as to the precise nature of such lags, this is surely a virtue. Thirdly, the Box and Jenkins (1976) approach allowed us to account for autocorrelation among the error terms of more complex varieties than is possible by using standard econometric techniques. Granger (1977) and Pierce (1977) have noted that inadequate attention to the autocorrelation structure of errors can lead to an acceptance of spurious relationships.

Our study hinged on the availability of reliable data on inter-state labor movements and changes in the capital stock of each state. Using the

Continuous Work History Sample (CWHS) of the Social Security Administration and the Bureau of Economic Analysis, yearly estimates of inter-state gross in- and outmigration were collected for the period 1958 to 1975. The CWHS data file provides longitudinal micro-level migration estimates based on individual work histories (this data file is described in the previous chapter). Data on capital stocks at the regional level are not routinely collected and must be inferred or estimated from estimates of gross investment. For our study, yearly data on state capital growth were made available by the Federal Reserve Bank of Boston. This data set is unique both for its annual time-series nature and its level of spatial disaggregation. The capital stock estimates were based on new capital expenditure data for plant and equipment reported in the Census and Annual Survey of Manufactures. To account for the age of existing capital stock it was necessary to consider past investments dating back to 1921 for equipment and 1904 for plant. Industry-specific rates of technological depreciation (incorporating physical decay, declining productivity, and technological obsolescence) were obtained from the Bureau of Labor Statistics and were applied separately to plant and equipment series for each industry so as to derive annual capital stock estimates for each state. (For an extended treatment of the steps in constructing these data, the reader is referred to the seminal studies by Browne *et al*. 1980, Gertler 1983 and Part V of this book).

Cross-correlation analysis of migration and capital

The first step of analysis was to estimate the temporal pattern of cross-correlation between capital formation and gross migration. It was clear that when cross-correlated with capital growth, both in- and outmigration had very similar cross-correlation functions (Table 11.1). For each pair of functions there was a similar symmetry on either side of the peak cross-correlation value. For Arizona, as an example, the peak cross-correlation value between capital growth and in- or outmigration occurred at plus one lag. That is, both gross migration flows lag capital by one year. This symmetry was repeated for all states included in the analysis. Only rarely were there differences between the pairs of cross-correlation functions in terms of their peak values or lags. The most obvious examples were for the states of Illinois and New York. In both states, in-migration lagged capital growth by two years and outmigration lagged capital growth by six years. But it is also clear that these results were the exception, not the rule (Clark & Gertler 1983).

Five of the six states that had strong growth records over the period 1958 to 1975 (Arizona, Florida, Virginia, New Mexico, and Texas) had quite marked peaks in their estimated cross-correlations at zero, plus one, or plus two lags for both gross migration flows. When we considered

Table 11.1 Cross-correlation functions between capital growth and in- and outmigration.

State	Capital and in-migration maximum		Capital and outmigration maximum	
	CCF	Lag b	CCF	Lag b
Arizona	0.84	+1	0.87	+1
Florida	0.86	0	0.88	0
Virginia	0.71	+1	0.75	+2
New Mexico	0.71	+1	0.76	0
Texas	0.78	0	0.71	0
Wyoming	0.26*	+10	0.29*	+10
Delaware	0.51	+9	0.60	+8
Iowa	0.87	0	0.87	0
Kentucky	0.64	+2	0.67	+2
Connecticut	0.61	+8	0.55	+8
Indiana	0.50*	+5	0.60	+6
Michigan	0.79	+1	0.62	+2
Illinois	0.47*	+2	0.53*	+6
New York	0.59	+2	0.60	+6
Pennsylvania	0.55	+7	0.57	+7

* Not significantly different from zero at the 95% confidence level.

slow-growth or declining states such as New York and Pennsylvania, it was readily apparent that the cross-correlation estimates were smaller and the results more mixed. The only exception to this generalization was at the upper end of the growth scale: Wyoming had no significant cross-correlations, and a plus-ten years lag between capital growth and each gross migration flow had to be viewed with skepticism. Elsewhere it has been noted that in- and outmigration to and from Wyoming over this period is best described (temporally) as random noise. Perhaps this was also evident in the results of cross-correlation. Moreover, in the previous chapter it was also shown that in- and outmigration for all states, except Wyoming, is highly correlated and clusters around zero lags, especially for higher growth states. Thus it should not come as a surprise that there was a great deal of symmetry in the pairs of cross-correlation functions reported here.

However, in relation to the standard literature on inter-state migration, a number of surprising contrasts deserve mention. First, supposed differences between in- and outmigration in their responsiveness to economic variables must be questioned. Both gross flows were temporally interrelated with capital growth for growing *and* declining states. We cannot assume, as Lowry (1966) would have it, that outmigration is unrelated to economic change. Moreover, the symmetry between in- and outmigration in this context has gone largely unrecognized in the literature. Obviously we cannot conclusively deduce from these cross-correlation functions either the direction or even the strength of causality, but at the same time there is enough evidence to proceed further.

Secondly, these results provide weak evidence for the question of whether or not migration and capital act simultaneously in time with respect to one another. The strongest claim of the competitive market school is simultaneity, and should be reflected in zero lags between capital and migration. Yet this was hardly the case for the majority of states analyzed here. Only in a few cases, notably strongly growing states, were there zero lags between migration and capital. Most states ranged between one and two year lags. As we noted previously, writers in the tradition of the competitive school such as Greenwood (1981) are clearly aware of this issue. Nevertheless, the evidence is systematic enough to suggest that lags (nonsimultaneity) are the rule, not the exception.

Capital, in-migration, and causality

What could not be directly ascertained from cross-correlation functions were the directions and strengths of relationships between variables. To accomplish this task, capital growth and in-migration were modeled in a time-series framework, concentrating on establishing causality and the estimates of structural parameters. The first step in this process was to model their joint error structures so as to provide a preliminary guide to the underlying time-series properties. An incorrect assumption of the process or its order can, as noted above, lead to spurious and misleading conclusions *vis-à-vis* causality and the significance of parameter estimates. Many states had autoregressive (AR) processes of low orders, indicating two key implications. First, the histories (or previous values) of each variable, capital formation and migration, are obviously important *in conjunction with one another* in determining current and future levels of capital growth and migration. As Granger and Newbold (1975) have noted, this need not be the case as many economic processes can be best characterized as stochastic random walk time-series processes.

Secondly, the relatively low orders of the underlying time-series suggested that time lags are limited between capital and in-migration, a proposition entirely consistent with the cross-correlation function results. But the implications of this observation are more important than the simple question of consistency. In essence, the fact that most time-series were autoregressive of order one or two indicated that the distributed lag between capital growth and in-migration may be only of one or two years.

Some writers have suggested that the distributed lags are in the order of five, or even ten years. Thus these results are of crucial significance because they enable a *direct* evaluation to be made of previous studies' assumptions regarding the nature of lags. Obviously these results are a product of the data: its time-series as opposed to cross-sectional character. However, these results are direct, not simply inferred.

The results of causality tests between capital growth and in-migration are shown in Clark and Gertler (1983). Generally, it was found that for Arizona, Virginia, and New Mexico the evidence suggests that in-migration at time *t* is a function of previous years' capital growth (Table 11.2). As suggested by the capital-logic school, capital growth determined migration. Within this group the exceptions were Florida and Texas. In the former case the result is not unexpected; previous in-migration of even employed individuals (not retirees) determined capital growth, a result consistent with the particular history of economic growth in Florida. A simple characterization of the differences between Arizona and Florida might be that, in the first case, autonomous investment determined migration while, in the second case, demand initiated investment. For Texas, however, the process is simultaneous and jointly determined with no apparent time lags. In this instance in-migration and capital growth

Table 11.2   Causality: capital and in-migration.

State	Functional form
Arizona	$IM_t = f(K_t')$*
Florida	$K_t = f(IM_t)$
Virginia	$IM_t = f(K_t')$
New Mexico	$IM_t = f(K_t')$
Texas	$IM_t = f(K_t)$ and $K_t = f(IM_t)$†
Wyoming	—
Delaware	$IM_t = f(K_t')$ and $K_t = f(IM_t')$
Iowa	$IM_t = f(K_t)$ and $K_t = f(IM_t)$
Kentucky	—
Connecticut	$IM_t = f(K_t')$ and $K_t = f(IM_t')$
Indiana	$IM_t = f(K_t')$ and $K_t = f(IM_t')$
Michigan	$IM_t = f(K_t')$
Illinois	$IM_t = f(K_t')$ and $K_t = f(IM_t')$
New York	$IM_t = f(K_t')$
Pennsylvania	$IM_t = f(K_t')$ and $K_t = f(IM_t')$

* K_t' indicates that the determining variable is lagged over time.

† Combination indicates that capital and in-migration are determined simultaneously.

were mutually interdependent *and* (most importantly) behave coinciden-
tally in time. Given that the data were yearly, there may be, of course,
within-year time lags. Even so, this result tends to provide the strongest
support for the case made by the competitive market school.

Of the remaining average and declining growth states, only Iowa had a
similar causal framework to that of Texas. All other states were characterized by time lags in their adjustment to changes in in-migration and
capital growth. Like Texas however, many slower-growth states had
simultaneous processes: in-migration causes capital growth as capital
growth causes in-migration. The autoregressive nature of this process is
evident in the time lags associated with both capital and migration. Again,
however, this evidence tends to support the competitive market school
rather than the capital-logic school because of the implied multidirectional
simultaneous temporal structure of economic change. The exceptions to
this were Michigan and New York, where lagged capital growth caused
in-migration. Perhaps one consolation for the capital-logic school is that
where it really matters (strong-growth states), capital determines in-
migration. Florida is an exception, but is easily explained. On the other
hand, the competitive market school is surely compromised by its inability
to predict correctly the patterns of causality among these types of states.
The growth process and its relationship to in-migration are obviously
simpler and more direct than it would contend, but the middle order – of
average growth or decline – is much more complex.

Capital, outmigration, and causality

As in the previous section, the first step in establishing the directions and
strengths of causality between capital growth and outmigration for each
state was to model their joint error structures. Clark and Gertler (1983)
report the results of this analysis, indicating that all processes were
identified as autoregressive (AR) of very low orders. When we considered
capital and in-migration, most states were found to have AR(1) structures,
but a few also had more complex ARMA structures. In this instance it is
clear that the past histories of each variable interact in determining present
and future levels of capital growth and outmigration. Also consistent with
the previous results is the fact that the time lags implicit in an AR(1) process
were small, indicating that the interaction between capital growth and
outmigration is quite dynamic. This is an important implication once we
remember that many authors, including Lowry (1966), have assumed
outmigration to be unaffected by short-run economic variables, being a
product of very long-run changes in state-level age composition. Again,
in relation to the previous results, Wyoming proved resistant to ready
identification.

Table 11.3   Causality: capital and outmigration.

State	Functional form
Arizona	$EM_t = f(K'_t)$ and $K_t = f(EM'_t)$
Florida	$EM_t = f(K'_t)$ and $K_t = f(EM'_t)$
Virginia	$EM_t = f(K'_t)$
New Mexico	$EM_t = f(K'_t)$ and $K_t = f(EM_t)$
Texas	—
Wyoming	—
Delaware	$EM_t = f(K_t)$ and $K_t = f(EM_t)$
Iowa	$EM_t = f(K_t)$ and $K_t = f(EM_t)$
Kentucky	$EM_t = f(K'_t)$
Connecticut	$EM_t = f(K_t)$ and $K_t = f(EM_t)$
Indiana	$IM_t = f(K_t)$ and $K_t = f(EM'_t)$
Michigan	$EM_t = f(K'_t)$
Illinois	$K_t = f(EM'_t)$
New York	$EM_t = f(K'_t)$
Pennsylvania	$K_t = f(EM_t)$

The results of testing for causality between capital growth and out-migration can be easily related to the previous results. It was immediately apparent that states with simple unidirectional relationships switched from the fast-growth (as in capital and in-migration) to the very slow-growth instances (Table 11.3). Those states were, moreover, split evenly between those that were found to have capital growth causing outmigration (Michigan and New York) and those that were found to have outmigration causing capital growth (Illinois and Pennsylvania). When we looked for other examples of unidirectionality, only two other states were found – Kentucky and Virginia. In these two states capital growth caused outmigration. For the capital-logic school, these results are of some significance. Capital obviously plays a significant determining role *vis-à-vis* outmigration. Yet in two instances the converse was true. How can this be explained? One possibility is that outmigration causes a change in capital investment due to a shift in demand. It is plausible, for example, that as the population of a state declines due to autonomous outmigration, capital investment declines in response. Of course this explanation begs the question of what causes outmigration from depressed areas.

No functional or causal relationships were found for Texas and Wyoming, which should not be surprising at least in the latter case. With reference to the remaining state it was clear that simultaneity is a strong characteristic for fast- and medium-growth states. In some cases, capital growth and outmigration are interdependent and coincident in time; in other instances there are time lags involved. There are no clear patterns with regard to the rate of growth of the states concerned. It should be noted that very-fast-growth and average-growth states were found to have causal relationships with no evidence of lags. Again, this is evidence of temporal adjustment that is much faster than commonly supposed in the literature. An assumption of five- or even ten-year distributed lags clearly would be hard to sustain in the face of this evidence. For the competitive market school, of course, the simultaneity of capital growth and outmigration for 7 of the 15 states must be counted as evidence for their propositions regarding adjustment. At the same time, the evidence is hardly cause for rejoicing; unidirectional causality dominated the slow-growth states and tends to support the capital-logic school's notion of capital determinacy.

Conclusions

In this chapter we were concerned with the relationships between capital growth and labor migration for 15 US states over the period 1958 to 1975. The capital-logic school argues that capital determines migration primarily because of rights of ownership and the power of initiation. In some instances, where a floating technocratic cadre of workers is involved, the time lags between capital growth and migration are presumed to be quite small. In other instances, perhaps where the reserve army of the unemployed is concerned, the time lags may be quite large. On the other hand, the competitive market school argues that migration and capital growth are initiated separately but in reaction to similar macroeconomic variables. The result for the competitive market school should be an intersecting and interdependent set of labor and capital markets that, in the absence of market imperfections, should behave coincidently in time. In such a system, migration causes capital that causes migration; it is a simultaneous process. Lags can only be identified in an *ad hoc* manner. The goal of this chapter was to establish the lines of causality, of determinacy between these variables in the context of two contending schools of thought.

The results of analysis provided two general conclusions. First, the temporal dynamics of the relationships between capital growth and in-migration and capital growth and outmigration are quite similar, at least in terms of their patterns of adjustment, underlying temporal processes (typically autoregressive), and relatively short time lags. This conclusion directly contradicts those authors, including Lowry (1966), who maintain that in- and outmigration react to different determinants over different time scales. Secondly, neither the capital-logic nor the competitive market school completely dominate the other in terms of their predictive (empirical) abilities *vis-à-vis* causality. It is clear that in some instances, notably fast-growing states for in-migration and slow-growing states for outmigration, the capital-logic school can provide a convincing theoretical and empirical exposition of the determining role of capital. In these instances, and some other exceptions, capital formation determines migration. Of course, for those interested in theory, policy, and forecasting this result is of major importance, especially since the capital-logic school is so adept at explaining and predicting the *crucial* (or difficult) cases: economic growth and decline. By itself this conclusion has a great deal of force since it is those instances where economic events rapidly shift and change that provide the major challenge to theoretical and empirical analysis. Thus the empirical case for the capital-logic is quite strong. But also important is the consistency of the initial assumptions regarding the determining influence of capital. The competitive market school is extremely weak at this level, and must be viewed with a great deal of caution regarding the reliability of its predictions regarding causality and timing. Yet it is also true that middle-order growth states are best modeled via a simultaneous framework. Causality, in the sense employed here, cannot always be uniquely determined.

12 *Labor migration and uncertainty*

Introduction

Growth and decline characterize the American economy. On one hand, a set of high-technology industries have grown rapidly over the past decade, stimulating the economic fortunes of certain regions (northeast and southwest) and cities (such as the Route 128 area of Boston). On the other hand, employment in traditional heavy manufacturing industries, such as steel, has drastically declined, severely depressing the midwest and mid-Atlantic regions, and many inner cities. Geographical mismatches between the demand and supply of labor are argued by policy makers and academics alike to contribute to higher overall national unemployment and rigidities of wage adjustment to aggregate labor demand patterns (see, for example, Rogerson & MacKinnon 1981, Gordon 1981). In the search to find a plausible explanation of current national economic difficulties (a crisis of reality *and* theory; see Baily 1982), the poor geographical coordination of the demand and supply of labor has become an important public policy issue.

Supporters of the geographical mismatch hypothesis have not been the only ones to promote more efficient spatial labor market coordination and allocation. Two Presidential reports, one initiated but subsequently disavowed by President Carter, *Urban America in the eighties* (President's Commission on the Agenda for the Eighties 1980), the other written by the US Department of Housing and Urban Development (1982) for President Reagan, the *President's national urban policy report*, loudly proclaimed the virtues of greater geographical mobility. It was asserted that greater labor and capital geographical mobility would bring about a renaissance of national economic strength. It was also asserted that the market system is the best allocator of resources (see, for example, US Department of Housing and Urban Development 1982: Ch. 2). Conservative theorists suppose that existing "spatial misallocations of resources" (a euphemism for massive unemployment in the midwest and relative economic growth in the southwest) will disappear if only the market is allowed to operate free from government "interference" (McKenzie 1981).

At the most general level theorists from a wide variety of ideological perspectives agree that the geographical labor market system is not particularly efficient.

Sources of spatial labor market inefficiency vary by perspective. Liberal theorists suggest that in reality there are significant transaction costs in labor markets because people may not be completely rational and because they lack complete information. Market signals, such as prices and quantities, can be misinterpreted and the signals themselves are subject to random, unanticipated shocks or distortions. Where second- and third-best solutions dominate, and where there are any number of possible market outcomes, uncertainty abounds. Workers may then invest in the wrong human capital, and as local industries close, workers are often unaware of other options. Searching for a job takes time and money with no certainty as to the likely outcome. Thus, spatial labor market adjustment is thought to be slow and cumbersome, characterized by many false leads and imperfect solutions (Clark & Whiteman 1983).

Complicating this picture further is a fundamental principle, often noted in the job-search literature, that information itself has a price. Information is a scarce resource and is, in consequence, a commodity in demand. As information about job opportunities, conditions of employment, and so on is unevenly distributed and allocated in space, the whole spatial allocation system is likely to be inefficient. Uncertainty in this *realist* vision of modern labor markets is an unavoidable characteristic of an environment in which people must nevertheless act and make decisions. For many liberal theorists, it is the less than perfect nature of reality which is the principal source of transaction costs. The policy issue is not one of minimizing government intervention – the conservative argument; rather, it is one of improving the operation of the market system by providing scarce information (Rogerson & MacKinnon 1982).

Two propositions are advanced in this chapter. First, it is argued that labor markets must necessarily operate under conditions of uncertainty. The rules of exchange can never be exhaustive of all possible contingencies. Procedural rules of exchange are designed to deal with a specific class of issues and can only accommodate known or anticipated events. This is not solely a characteristic of *capitalist* labor markets. To the extent that all markets are procedural, rule-oriented systems, then all markets share this characteristic. A review of procedurally based, spatial labor market policies is followed by an analysis of the underlying principles that give US local labor markets their particular form. These principles are liberal conceptions of individual autonomy and decentralized decision making. They ignore the social structure of existing patterns of resources, being premised on universal ideals of discrete exchange.

Having argued that transaction costs are inevitable given the nature of market form, our second proposition is that these costs are sustained and manipulated by employers and employees through their employment relationships. The character of unilateral power and specific bilateral contingencies structures uncertainty and the distribution of its costs. While the existence of labor market uncertainty itself is not simply a function of capitalist social relations, its distribution and allocation are. These propositions are then used to interpret a recent case in Michigan concerning interregional labor migration and job tenure which has gone unnoticed in regional analysis. It is argued that adjudication of contending arguments for the distribution of transaction costs inevitably has to take into account the underlying pattern of economic power. Consequently, spatial labor market policies which provide information are inevitably compromised by the very principles that structure labor market form *and* are largely irrelevant once questions of distribution are introduced.

Transaction costs and policy

The rules and procedures that structure conventional economic models of labor market form are well known and are essentially utilitarian liberalism. Individuals are assumed to be utility maximizers, to be choice oriented, and are thought to decide voluntarily their own actions. As well, exchange is assumed to take place between equals. These rules do not allow for coercion, domination, or unequal control over the structure of opportunities. Utilitarian theory, and its economic representative neoclassical theory, rarely invoke standards, except by way of implication. For example, "fair" compensation is considered only as a by-product of individual utility-maximizing behavior. If the rules are followed, then every individual will be paid his/her marginal product which is implied to be the "just" way of determining compensation. That is, workers are paid what they are "worth," a by-product of the marginal productivity rule. Standards such as "good" behavior do not apply and may even be thought to be inefficient if utility maximization is not followed. The neoclassical rules of labor market exchange are procedural and formalistic rather than substantively oriented.

Given this particular intellectual definition of labor market form, how it should function in an idealized world is then quite obvious. If all individuals are utility maximizers, exchange should only take place if both parties gain more than they would compared to if they were not to transact. At the limit, pareto equilibrium should be attained wherein no person would contract and exchange without making another worse off (Hall 1980). It is also apparent that labor market exchange would be discrete in that the cost–benefit calculus for any one transaction is assumed to be serially independent of previous agreements or relationships. A further implication is that if a better opportunity appears, then any previous contract would be voided. Walrasian re-contracting is assumed to exist without transaction costs.

What is described here is a "spot-market" for labor, little different from the most conventional commodity exchange or auction. Demand and supply are mandated as the means of social exchange. There is, embodied in this model, an important (albeit limited) role for government. In the interests of facilitating voluntary exchange and transaction, employees and employers are given the right to withdraw their labor and job offers at any time. Conventionally, this is known as the "employment-at-will" doctrine. In addition, contracts are guaranteed, although not necessarily enforced. By that we mean that if two parties enter into a contract to exchange at a certain date, plans are expected to be met. If one party withdraws, invoking "employment-at-will," damages may be assessed. Expectational contracts are those which set the conditions and circumstances for action in the future, although action may not necessarily be undertaken before reaching those conditions (Atiyah 1981). It is argued that without guaranteed rules of exchange, transactors would become risk averse and parochial, reducing market efficiency, economic growth and social wealth (Kennedy & Michelman 1980).

Assuming a perfect exchange process is, of course, hardly an adequate description of real labor markets. Nevertheless, the model is used as a datum point by many liberal theorists as a means of comparison between reality and its idealized form. Assuming rational, goal–oriented maximizing behavior, the crucial problem of reality for liberal theorists is the existence of transaction costs. These costs are generally a product of uncertainty and lack of complete information; they also interfere with the efficient operation of the rules of exchange.

According to Coase (1960) and Dahlman (1979), there are three kinds of transaction costs: those that are a function of the means of exchange (Type I); those that are a function of the organization of exchange (Type II); and those that are a function of uncertainty (Type III). Type I transaction costs result from the existence of inefficiences in exchange. For example, transportation between buyers and sellers might be neither cheap nor quick. Innovations such as electronic mail could speed transactions (although it may not actually cheapen them) compared to normal surface mail. The dispersed nature or organization of exchange may also figure in the costs of transactions (Type II) even though trade may be costless. An appropriate policy in this regard may be to centralize exchange, spatially and sectorally. Type III transaction costs, those that are a function of uncertainty, can be broken down into three interrelated elements. There are costs that result from discovering who it is that one wishes to exchange with and then informing them of the terms (search and information costs). There are costs inherent in conducting negotiations and initiating contracts (bargaining and decision costs). And there are costs in ensuring compliance (policing and enforcement costs). Generally, all these Type III costs occur whatever the methods of exchange and organization of production. Public policy, according to the terms of the neoclassical model, should be primarily concerned with the procedural efficiency of transactions, thus minimizing the impact of these three types of costs. To the extent that public policy can improve transactional efficiency, then the social costs of exchange would decline.

In terms of interregional migration, the best example of an American policy consistent with these notions of transaction costs and uncertainty was the Jobs Search Relocation Assistance Project (JSRA). This pilot project involved 8 southern states and included 40 local employment service offices. Although the experiences of previous mobility projects were used to help develop JSRA, there were two significant departures from the program design of its predecessors. First, previous relocation assistance projects were in response to the problems of economically depressed areas such as the Appalachians. Such policies targeted mobility assistance to depressed areas and to permanently laid-off workers. In contrast, JSRA was designed to deal with no specific labor market problem of local unemployment or underemployment. The program contractor for JSRA described the purpose of JSRA as assisting all those workers who are "in the wrong place at the right time" (Clark 1983c). Thus, the major goal was not interregional equity but inter-market allocative efficiency. JSRA offered job search information, job search grants and relocation grants.

The Department of Labor's Job Search Relocation Assistance experiment followed closely Canadian mobility policy which is administered by Employment and Immigration Canada (EIC). The guiding principles behind this system are twofold. The underlying principle is choice oriented: participants choose whether or not to relocate. Local manpower centers are reluctant to encourage clients to consider outside listings and will only provide that information upon request. Of course, in depressed regions, many unemployed have had to look elsewhere for jobs, and EIC has played an important role in helping these individuals once the decision has been made to relocate (even if temporarily). Like the United States, relocation expenses incurred by individuals can be claimed on federal taxes. Thus, the Canadian government facilitates relocation decisions directly and indirectly, at a level of commitment unknown in the USA.

The second organizing principle of this system is distinctly Coasian in that it seeks to improve the efficiency of labor market transactions. By improving the match between employees and employers, the market is made more responsive to geographical frictions. The key objective function of the system is to minimize the transaction costs of a spatially dispersed and heterogeneous national labor market. For example, the costs of the means of exchange (Type I) have been minimized through the use of computer technology. Secondly, the costs of the organization of exchange (Type II) are also important aspects of Canadian policy. Mining towns that are very isolated, away from centers of industry and trade, have been integrated into the national labor market network through listing of inter-labor market job vacancies and the use of relocation grants. Plant closings have also been considered an integral responsibility of this system, with cooperative tripartite agreements between companies, unions, and the government facilitating the transition from unemployment (in one area) to employment (in another area).

But most importantly the costs of uncertainty in labor market transactions (Type III in the Coasian model) have been directly tackled. Search and informational costs have been minimized – the job bank finds workers and employers and transmits the terms of employment. The costs of negotiation and contracting have also been lessened – the job bank allows comparisons between job offers and terms and conditions, and interview grants speed face-to-face contracting – and, through screening, manpower centers seek to reduce potential problems of employee compliance (like absenteeism). The key issue for the Canadian government is the procedural efficiency of the labor market system. For employers and employees, this matching process is able to deal with a number of different types of labor market transactions: where employers and employees are indifferent with respect to their identities so that it is a simple price (quantity nonspecific) transaction; where employers may require specific skills related either to their industry or to particular modes of operation (mixed transactions); and where there may be unique skill or personal requirements between employers and employees, either in production teams or in research and development.

Empirically, it is plain that transaction costs are endemic to modern labor markets. But their existence is more than a "simple" problem of reality. Other issues intrude, particularly the underlying principles that structure labor market form. Although it is sometimes thought that there is a choice between using rules and procedures in defining labor market form as against standards, substantive outcomes are necessarily implied in the specification of rules (Kennedy 1976). The existence of these types of rules does not (and cannot) mean precise outcomes in terms of actions or responses. Rules cannot cover all events and actions; their specification depends on known possibilities and the goals they serve (Dworkin 1972). Where "new" events appear, discretion is required to allocate the appropriate rule. A rule may be required for the choice of rules. Yet "new" events can threaten even that rule. This interaction between reality and underlying principles provides a fundamental structure to the existence of uncertainty. The most immediate questions are: what are these principles? How do they structure outcomes?

Decentralized labor markets and transaction costs

In this section, the substantive principles of American decentralized labor markets are described. In this discussion we assume a nationally integrated market for goods and services. This assumption corresponds to reality in a superficial sense, in that firms generally sell commodities in markets much larger in extent than the areas from which they draw their labor requirements (Clark 1983c). In this section we do not directly consider the social relations of capitalism, but rather the related but simpler issue of procedural uncertainty. Following the previous section, procedural uncertainty is defined as that uncertainty which is a function of the technical organization or rules of labor market exchange. In this discussion we again assume goal-oriented rationality, profit maximization by firms and wage or income maximization by workers.

Stone (1981) suggested that American labor market decentralization is a product of an underlying pluralist vision of labor and management relations. For any given firm the workers and managers must negotiate the terms of contracts on the assumption that each market transaction should only involve those directly affected. Hence, this pluralist model depends upon the rationale of consent and a more general conception of the workplace as being representative of democratic decision making. Even the largest of firms and unions (the automobile industry, for example) are forced to negotiate and ratify contracts at the firm and plant level. Clearly there are spillovers between contracts within the same industry. Nevertheless, the *form* of the labor market, its rules and procedures, have implicit normative goals of decentralization and local self-determination that structures local outcomes.

Decentralization has a number of quite specific implications for bargaining. First, even though a firm may control a national commodity market and may have many plants scattered around the country producing that product, decentralized labor relations require that workers and management negotiate over wages, conditions, benefits, and so on, at the local level. Of course, in highly unionized industries, both firms and workers only pay "lip-service" to this concept. Industry agreements often determine the local agendas and consequently local negotiations may well be inconsequential. Yet even here there are many instances where union solidarity and management agreement have collapsed at the local level. A good recent example was the 1981 strike by Canadian (Windsor) Chrysler workers over contract conditions agreed to and ratified by their American counterparts. Strikes, wage reductions, and lock-outs have been significant catalysts in this context.

Secondly, because firms operate in a wider geographical context than workers, the former may have less stake in maintaining local production facilities and harmonious labor relations. After all, a national commodity market can be served from many different locations. Firms have no "home" in America apart from that which is the result of their history. Government policy has consciously sought to integrate the national market, ensuring open trade, not geographical balkanization. Workers, on the other hand, are situated within a very different, institutionally defined, spatial labor market system; the ideology of decentralization does not legitimate geographical referencing and the actual practice of labor relations is parochial.

In a competitive environment, firms do not have complete information regarding the future demand for their output. If product segmentation is not the complete solution, another option may be to ration production in accordance with the short side of the market. This option would contrast with that of trying to meet every fluctuation in demand. Rationing may reduce the costs of attempting to shift and change production schedules in response to short-term market conditions. However, such a strategy may mean that profit opportunities are lost when demand rises above the average production rate, and inventories may build if demand suddenly collapses. Another way of rationing output is for firms to write longer-term contracts with major consumers. Such contracts would avoid having to respond to short-term fluctuations and would stabilize, in the short run, output and prices. This strategy is one of avoiding uncertainty, not actually reducing uncertainty.

Uncertainty with respect to production levels inevitably spills over into firms' labor requirements. As firms attempt to vary labor inputs through overtime, employment, and wage variables, workers also have to predict the demand for their particular services. But workers, unlike firms, rarely operate on the scale of a national labor market. Procedurally based decentralized employment relations, coupled with limited skill differentiation amongst workers, sustains a highly localized labor exchange process. Workers are then limited in terms of their "normal" action space to a specific geographical network of job offers and employment opportunities. Since, procedurally, wages are determined locally and firms' labor requirements are drawn largely from specific localities, workers inevitably lack complete information regarding the overall pattern of demand for their labor.

Workers' uncertainty exists not only with regard to firms' likely labor requirements in the future; workers are also uncertain with regard to the pattern of contemporaneous labor demand in other areas of the country. Unions, which might have been integrating "reference" institutions, have hardy been effective in organizing American workers, let alone spatially integrating, in an informational sense, the labor market. Uncertainty in this sense is a *procedural* aspect of institutionally defined decentralized labor markets.

One extreme example of how formal rules structure the functions of local labor markets in the United States is to be seen in the construction industry. Although one of the more unionized and competitive industries, the construction labor market is fundamentally spatially dispersed. Its particular form is based upon a set of laws enacted through 1929 to 1931 by the US Congress, specifically the Davis–Bacon Act. That Act prohibited the importation of cheaper (lower-wage) labor to work on federally funded construction projects in specific localities. Procedurally, this Act depends on two basic rules: (a) workers are to be paid the local prevailing wage for their particular occupation and skill, and (b) local labor market conditions are to determine local contracts between firms and workers concerning local working conditions. The consequence of these rules and procedures is a national construction industry functionally dominated by spatially fragmented labor markets. It has remained relatively untouched by firm conglomeration and consolidation, and the ever-present threats posed by nonlocal and nonunion labor and firms to the integrity of local bargaining (Clark 1983c).

The very organizing principles of American labor markets *create* the prospects for significant transaction costs (in Coase's terms, Type II transaction costs). By structuring labor relations according to principles of decentralized autonomy, inter-labor market referencing is denied a place in the overall functioning of labor markets. Thus Type II transaction costs are built into the very fabric of local labor markets. Also, Type III transaction costs are inevitable. Information on outside job offers is difficult to find, and it is difficult to initiate bargaining and contracting in other labor markets as conditions vary across regions. And, with the emphasis on local decision making, it is hard to sustain inter-labor market contract compliance. The very structure of the spatial labor market system logically denies the virtues of JSRA-type labor market policies, because these policies directly confront the underlying principles of local labor market structure.

Even within specific local labor markets there remains a great deal of ambiguity and uncertainty. The rules themselves are not seamless, they cannot cover all eventualities. With reference to the rules that structure American construction labor markets, it is relatively easy to imagine exceptions. For instance, assume that a firm contracts to build a nuclear power station in an area where none has been previously built. Specific categories of skills may be required that do not readily fit existing local job types. One option would be to attempt to find the closest local category, another might be to invent a new category and apply outside standards which would then become the "local" standards. The first option would require adjudication of a technical nature, although there is no guarantee that there would be an unambiguous technical solution. A continuing issue of litigation and investigation by the US Department of Labor (the enforcer of the Act) has been the appropriate classification of workers.

Employers often attempt to downgrade skill requirements of particular jobs so as to avoid the prevailing wages of higher classified local workers. Custom and local history play an important part in defining the appropriateness of job classifications, and yet it is easy to see that such "rules" may be inadequate in the face of a changing economic environment. But, without such rules, adjudication would be a nightmare.

The second option would be no less problematic. Invoking outside standards would directly contravene the second rule – that local conditions determine local contracts. Exceptions could be made, and qualifications inserted to the effect that the second rule should be *generally* held, if not always held. There may be no other choice if there is no obvious technical solution and if employers and employees cannot agree on the appropriate local reference point. Yet exceptions themselves require rules, as exceptions require definition. And there may be difficulty in narrowing the definition of exceptions. At this level, transaction costs (Type II) and uncertainty (Type III) are procedural issues; they are a function of the rules and their application. For an analyst schooled in conventional neoclassical theory, the implication of the above might be that the rules are inadequate because of inadequate information. Better information in the beginning, according to this claim, would reduce subsequent ambiguities. However, with more information, more rules would be required.

Although this objection is quite simple, it is nevertheless quite powerful because it raises a second issue implicit in this whole discussion – the actual object of rules. With a myriad of events and rules there would still be questions of appropriateness. Adjudication would still be necessary to sort out their applicability. To do so effectively would require a higher order principle or an ordering of the desirability of different substantive outcomes. In either case, the court or whoever has responsibility would have to decide which rule best serves the substantive intent of the whole market system. This means considering not only the procedures of labor market exchange but also their underlying substantive principles. Construction labor markets are clearly more organized than most local labor markets. And the principle of local bargaining integrity may not be relevant in other instances. Different substantive assumptions would imply different rules and different uncertainties – information itself would vary in terms of its utility. Generally, transaction costs cannot be avoided; they are a necessary product of procedurally based, rule-oriented definitions of American spatial labor markets. The most important question in this regard is: how are the costs of uncertainty distributed?

Substantive bases of labor exchange

In order to answer this question adequately we are required to deal with a quite specific context: capitalism, a particular social system, and

American labor practices. Inevitably, any understanding of spatial labor market relations is based upon a quite specific theory of society. We do not presume that our analysis will be appropriate for all countries. Of course, this position contrasts starkly with the conventional approach of spatial labor market theorists. For example, those who write on migration often assume decentralized decision making in a choice-oriented framework, implicitly reflecting the dominant ideology of American society. Utilitarianism in economic and geographical theory is as much a product of the cultural milieu as it is an objective and conscious choice of academic theorists. However, once the theory is fleshed out, theorists claim universality, a generality that is thought to be not context specific.

Theories begin with observed conditions, and then negate them in the drive to a general explanation. Since we deal specifically with American capitalism, focusing upon its labor exchange characteristics and the propositions necessary for understanding how it functions, our analysis will obviously be quite specific.

Previously we were concerned with the technical or procedural aspects of labor market exchange, transactional costs, and uncertainty. Although it is conventionally thought that capitalism *is* the market system, market systems can exist in noncapitalist settings (Dworkin 1981). As markets are rule-oriented procedures of labor exchange, they fundamentally depend on the initial specifications of rights and the entitlements of those who function in the market. For instance, we could imagine a socialist labor market wherein equality of property ownership was the initial and continual attribute of the system. Conversely, in a world of inequality, labor has to offer its productive power for sale. Without choice, there can only be coercion, and without choice, exploitation is a basic characteristic of any labor market system. Substantive decisions as to who bears transaction costs must recognize the reality of social structure. In this manner, liberal formalism, so characteristic of neoclassical labor market theories, becomes largely irrelevant.

Capitalism can be described by four "first-order" conditions (Clark & Dear 1984). First, property rights are protected and enforced by the state. Secondly, there is no right to equal ownership of property, but rather a protected, universal right to buy and sell property if able to do so. Thirdly, firms own *what* is produced and have the right to decide *how* goods are produced and sold. Fourthly, firms own the jobs; they hire workers to produce at specified wages (in this sense they "lease" jobs to workers). Firms also have the unilateral right to "hire and fire" at will, the "employment-at-will" doctrine.

In recent years this doctrine has come under challenge from a variety of quarters (see MacNeil 1980). Some writers have suggested that the many legal exceptions to the rule, for reasons of public policy, have severely restricted its meaning. Yet it remains, as Atiyah (1979) has noted, the principal formal model that orders employment relations.

These first-order conditions are, as Calabresi and Melamed (1972) noted, the essential entitlements and obligations of society's citizens. In this context, our argument has some elements in common with Hart's (1961). For instance, first-order conditions could be thought of as being equivalent to Hart's primary rules; procedures in their technical sense (the rules of exchange) could be considered equivalent to his secondary rules. However, unlike Hart, we believe that first-order conditions derive from social relations which can be quite coercive, or at least based on underlying power relations.

These conditions are social structures and are also unilateral rights wherein no person can force another to give up their entitlements unless they consent to do so. For example, as personified agents in American law, firms have the unilateral right to produce whatever they want, with whatever technology they decide appropriate, and with workers hired for that particular task. Of course, unilateral rights may not be absolute; the state may enact, for example, equal opportunity laws. Yet, even in this instance, property rights themselves are generally protected.

The first two conditions are crucial descriptors of capitalism; the latter two conditions derive from the structure of property rights. Notice that the state is intimately involved in the definition of society. Only through the specification of entitlements and their enforcement does capitalism itself exist. In this respect, capitalism, like any other mode of production, is as much a political system as a purely economic arrangement of production. This proposition depends on a relatively autonomous state and, in the lexicon of marxist theory, integrates the "base" and "superstructure" categories of conventional theories of the state into one category.

While these four propositions define the necessary conditions of capitalism, they are hardly sufficient as a complete analysis of employment relations. One further crucial assumption needs to be made: labor is the source of surplus value (Harvey 1982). Defenses of this proposition are either technical or moral. That is, in the first instance labor is considered to be unique as the sole *active* agent that can mold materials into products and machinery. It may well be true that some machines can produce commodities with little direct labor; nevertheless, in the final analysis the source of productive activity is assumed to be labor. Technically, labor must produce more than its subsistence wage (its biologically necessary output) if machinery is to be built and if economic growth is to outstrip population growth. Because of firms' property rights, any surplus generated belongs to capitalists, not to workers. Exploitation is legitimated by the state's definition and enforcement of property rights and is a consequence of employers' control of the production process – ultimately the labor process itself (Morishima & Catephores 1978).

Objections to this technical argument usually claim that capital itself can contribute to surplus value. However, two counter-arguments can be made to this position. First, there is the very real problem of measuring capital as a category distinct from labor. An external *numéraire* is required which could adequately measure *both* labor and capital. Prices are unsatisfactory because they are relative measures of value, usually conceived in terms of opportunities foregone and the like. Without scarcity, prices would have little meaning, but surely the problem of value would remain (Coleman 1980). Measurement in terms of commodities or other precious goods runs a further risk of commodity fetishism – that is, of reducing individuals to mechanical or commodity equivalents. One does not need to invoke naturalistic doctrine of the uniqueness of man to realize that commodity values are hardly adequate for the task. Moreover, there is an implied moral argument about the hierarchy of individuals *vis-à-vis* the instruments of survival. In this respect, the labor value theory is a moral argument as much as a technical proposition. It is hard to take seriously the idea that a person may be worth a certain number of objects. Such reductionism would place greater *value* on objects than people, even though the creation of objects is only possible through the direct activity of individuals.

This brief excursion into marxian theory provides us with some basic context-specific principles for understanding capitalist employment relations. In particular, we must recognize that at the heart of capitalist social relations is the notion of interdependence. Firms need workers for their fundamental contribution to the creation of surplus value. Workers need capitalists because of their ownership of the means of production. Interdependence is a social category created through the initial specification of property rights *and* the socially productive activity of labor. Notice as well that interdependence is a necessarily tense power relationship. The unilateral power of capitalists' property rights must be accommodated with the fact that workers are the source of surplus value. As a result, in bilateral negotiations with labor, capitalists may have to hold their unilateral power in abeyance. This does not mean that unilateral power is irrelevant. Rather, given initial conditions of ownership, capitalists may be forced to minimize exercise of their total power. It is not automatically true that firms have overwhelming power in employment relationships.

A second major implication to be drawn from our discussion of the social relations of capitalism is that labor market exchange – between employers and employees – cannot be neutral. As a procedure, it depends upon an initial specification of rights and privileges. Whatever the claims of universality in the abstract, regarding free choice and the like, once capitalism is introduced, the issue of choice depends upon the structure or distribution of social resources. Our argument breaks with conventional neoclassical notions on at least two fundamental points. First, beginning and ending conditions are crucial for interpreting the consequences of labor market procedures. This proposition contrasts with conventional neoclassical texts which deny distributive issues except perhaps in terms of compensation. Secondly, our argument is contextual in that, instead of assuming that workers behave solely with respect to their own objectives, workers are assumed to act in relation to the existing social structure. The distinction is one of individualism versus social determinism. In the former instance, individuals operate rationally to the extent allowed by events and opportunities. In the latter instance, individual action is socially conceived so that their behavior is not rational-but-constrained, but rather rational-in-place. The distinction is important because it emphasizes the underlying social design of institutions such as markets and the consequent behavior of workers.

A third implication to be drawn from this discussion concerns the legitimacy of notions such as freedom of contract. If, as we have suggested, firms have unilateral powers of ownership and control, bilateral negotiations between employers and employees must reflect these underlying patterns. Freedom of contract must be judged in relation to existing opportunities, and the terms of disputes over employment contracts must then reflect relative powers. Instead of conceiving of contracts in simple procedural terms, substantive issues must be introduced to allocate transaction costs and uncertainty.

Social relations of uncertainty

So as to understand the significance of the previous discussion of market procedures and capitalist social relations, in this section we review and interpret a recent Michigan judicial decision, *Hackett* v. *Foodmaker, Inc.*, 69 Mich. App. 59 (1976) as reported in 245 N. W. 2d series 140 Mich. In doing so we are concerned with the social relations of local labor markets in the context of a case which, on its surface, appears to be a simple case of breach-of-contract. In the language of our previous discussion of transaction costs, breach-of-contract would be identified as a Type III transaction cost – that uncertainty which results from unexpected actions and creates costs in ensuring compliance with the terms of the previously agreed contract. As we shall see, however, one party argued that in fact the relevant rule was "employment-at-will." Any uncertainty resulting from employment termination would, according to this argument, appear as Type II transaction costs – those costs which are a function of the underlying structures or rules of market exchange. Although the Michigan Appeals Court used language related to the former, Type III transaction costs (breach-of-contract), their argument went very much further, implicating the substantive structure of labor market power.

The details of the case were as follows. In early 1971 a Mr. Hackett was living in San Diego and was a photographer with the US Navy. Just prior to his discharge from the Service, Mr. Hackett was working at a Foodmaker, Inc. restaurant (Jack-in-the-Box) through a Navy-sponsored transition program. Sometime during March or April he was interviewed for a job as manager of a Jack-in-the-Box restaurant to be located in Ypsilanti, Michigan. According to the Foodmaker Inc. personnel manager at the time, Mr. Hackett was promised the job, conditional upon his relocation to the Detroit area. The Michigan Court of Appeals established that a contract was in fact entered into by Mr. Hackett and Foodmaker Inc. to that effect. While no formal contract was signed, the verbal promise of the personnel manager of employment as the Ypsilanti manager was taken by the Court to indicate the *bona fida* existence of a contract.

Based upon this promise of employment, Hackett obtained an early release from the Navy and moved his family from San Diego to Detroit in June 1971. Upon arrival in Detroit, however, Hackett was told that the restaurant was not open. Although Foodmaker Inc. did employ him, it was only as a relief manager at a salary significantly less than previously agreed upon. By October 1971 the Ypsilanti restaurant was officially opened, but Foodmaker employed another manager thought to be more qualified. (During that period Hackett was apparently also involved in an antitrust suit against Foodmaker Inc. – it seems qualifications for being manager included being loyal to the firm.) Hackett remained as a relief manager until early 1972 where upon he left the company and sued Foodmaker Inc. for breach of contract.

The Lower Court decided in favor of Hackett and compensated him for the lost earnings he would have received as the Ypsilanti manager, over the period of time between his arrival in Detroit and his quitting the firm. The Lower Court refused to take into account the earnings of Hackett as a relief manager in Foodmaker's other restaurants as part of his compensation (albeit reduced). The Lower and Appeals Courts both held that the contract had been totally repudiated by the defendant. The Courts also held that Hackett's performance as relief manager could not be used either as a qualifications test or as employment *in lieu* of the original position. The Lower Court jury awarded Hackett $8995.00 for Foodmaker's breach of contract. This liability was assessed in accordance with Michigan's Master and Servant Act wherein liability is measured in terms of "his [Hackett's] inability to ever commence performance of the contract" (p. 140). In this context, the transaction costs and uncertainty initially borne by the employee were reallocated by the Courts to the employer.

On appeal, Foodmaker Inc. argued that the contract had been for an indefinite period of time, terminable at the discretion of either party to the contract. Put crudely, the defendant claimed that its failure to employ Hackett in the position initially agreed upon amounted to a quite legitimate "at-will" termination of his employment with the company. The Appeals Court dismissed this claim, arguing that the plaintiff was never actually employed in the contracted position and could hardly be fired. Breach-of-contract referred in this instance to the total *repudiation* of the initial terms of the contract. Hackett's work as a relief manager was considered by the Courts as another contract, unrelated to the initial one that brought him from San Diego. At first sight, this case appears to be simply one of the company failing to live up to its promises or its side of the (bilateral) bargain. Moreover, it appears that the Court conceived the issue in quite narrow terms – an expectational, discrete contract that was not carried out.

Yet while the Appeals Court went to some length to ensure the nonapplicability of the employment-at-will rule, the logic advanced to support this notion can be reasonably questioned. Instead of respecting the ad hoc *ex post* (after migration) employment relationship between Hackett and Foodmaker, the Court focused exclusively upon the initial agreement. What might be implied by such a rationale? First, even though Hackett presumably consented to the *ex post* arrangement, the Court gave precedence to the first agreement. One argument advanced by the Court was that Hackett had no other reasonable choice, having given up whatever options he may have had in San Diego by relocating to Detroit. In fact his subsequent suit against Foodmaker and his voluntary termination from the company in January 1972 suggested that the ad hoc arrangement was his only option. Once having found another job, he initiated civil proceedings against the company. This interpretation is premised upon the existence or nonexistence of choice, the latter implying some form of coercion. In this respect the *ex post* arrangement could hardly be interpreted as Hackett's free choice *given the circumstances*.

Notice that the Court in making this judgment had to go beyond issues of voluntary exchange and directly address outcomes and choices. Hackett could not refuse work, for he had no other form of income. Even unemployment insurance (UI) would have been difficult to procure. Not only does UI discriminate against those who voluntarily leave their jobs (as Hackett would have been classified), it is not easy to establish the residence and previous work history necessary to minimize the time between application for benefits and first payment. The substantive judgments made in this interpretation depend on limited choice, a specific *a priori* distribution of resources, and some understanding of the relative distribution of power between Foodmaker and Hackett when it came to negotiating a "new" arrangement after the initial arrangement had fallen through. The Courts are rather vague on the terms of their analysis. In particular, it is difficult to establish how much weight they gave to the choices that existed after migration versus the opportunities Hackett may have given up in San Diego by migrating.

But this is not the end of the story because once we look more closely at the Court's strategic separation of the two employment arrangements (*ex ante* and *ex post*), an even more complex picture emerges. On the one hand, the separation of employment contracts is consistent with conventional neoclassical models of labor market relationships. That is, by ignoring other subsequent relationships between the employer and employee, each contract is treated as a discrete, voluntary transaction. In this instance, however, this assumption can hardly be sustained despite the Court's weak attempts to legitimate such a stand. The logic presented above demonstrates that a good argument can be made for interpreting the second contract in terms of the first (what MacNeil 1981 terms a *relational* interpretation of the labor market transactions). The employment-at-will doctrine is sustained in this instance by ignoring it, an ad hoc move employed by the Court to remove its confounding significance. Presumably if Hackett had been found to be incompetent or if Foodmaker had to close the Ypsilanti restaurant after subsequently employing him as manager, then the employment-at-will rule would have applied.

We use the word "presumably" quite deliberately because a second interpretation is also plausible. The Courts' emphasis on the breach-of-contract rule, and its careful skirting of the relevance of the employment-at-will rule, require some further explanation. Either the Courts used an external, but unstated, rule of adjudication, or for whatever reason considered the "facts" to speak for themselves. What rules would assign priority to breach-of-contract? There are two possible candidates, an *expectations rule*, wherein trustworthy labor market behavior is judged more important than the other rules of discretion in worker termination, and a *reliance rule*, wherein outcomes are judged in accordance with the resources of the parties involved. Both rules would seem to have explanatory power in this instance.

The *expectations rule* is quite familiar to neoclassical theorists, being used by many to encourage certainty and reduce Type III transaction costs (see Kennedy & Michelman 1980). If individuals are to make optimal decisions as opposed to safe but second-best decisions regarding job opportunities, they must be sure or have reasonable expectations of the veracity of employment offers. In more technical language, derived in part from our previous discussion of uncertainty, market signals must be trustworthy, as should be the behavior of market actors. If job offers can be withdrawn without notice or without due compensation for the efforts of the other party in undertaking the terms of the contract (like migration), then the whole coordination of the spatial labor market system would be threatened. The crucial issue here is not the terms of any one contractual dispute, but rather system-wide imperatives of spatial labor market efficiency. Without such a rule, uncertainty would dominate the whole system. In this respect, the expectations rule aims at sustaining the functioning of lower-order market procedures.

There are a couple of reasons to suggest that the Appeal Court considered these issues to be relevant. For instance, it is highly unlikely that the Court would have been so concerned with breach-of-contract if Hackett had resided in Detroit. Migrating across the country on the basis of a promise of employment indicates that Hackett placed a great deal of faith in the veracity of the promise. Without a reasonable expectation of employment it is inconceivable that Hackett would have relocated. Although the Court goes to some length to emphasize that such a promise was made *and* that it was the basis of Hackett's decision to relocate, the existence of a promise *per se* is not a fundamental requirement for invoking the expectations rule. For the rule to be used (Atiyah 1979: 783), it is up to the Court to decide the reasonableness of expectations, the significance of each instance of failed expectations, and the damages to be assessed. In this sense Foodmaker's failure to fulfill its promise to Hackett was a more serious issue than if Foodmaker had made the same promise to a local resident. It is not obvious that the Court considered the system-wide implications of failed promises in deciding the case.

In fact, we would argue that the Court decided the issue by invoking the reliance rule, rather than the former rule. Hackett more than expected the contract to be fulfilled, he actually relied upon it. In doing so, Hackett spent a relatively large amount of his own money in moving his family, ignored other job opportunities in the San Diego area, and placed himself in a dependent relationship with Foodmaker in Detroit, having no other options. Without doubt, the very long move undertaken by Hackett established reliance in the eyes of the Court (Murg & Scharman 1982: 359). The crucial issue here is that Hackett acted or relied upon the contract; if he had waited in San Diego for confirmation of his position but then had been rejected, only his expectations would have been denied. Reliance implies action; judging the significance of reliance requires an appreciation of the circumstances and relationships between the contracting parties.

While the expectations rule is very much a procedural issue, the reliance rule is a substantive or distributive issue. Furthermore, even the relevance of the reliance rule depends upon the circumstances. Surely it would have been easy for the Court to argue "breach-of-contract" and also take into account the earnings of Hackett in his relief position. The manager's job would have paid $225.00 per week as against the $175.00 per week Hackett earned as a relief manager. It would have been entirely consistent to award Hackett the difference while at the same time maintaining the applicability of the breach-of-contract rule. As it happened, however, the judiciary did more than simply compensate for lost earnings. Not only did the Court award Hackett six months' pay at $225.00 per week, it also awarded him some $3000.00 extra in recompense for the cost of relocation. In sum, the Court took the side of Hackett in framing a substantive interpretation of the firm's liability in repudiating the entire terms of the contract. By doing so, the court was involved in more than procedural adjudication – that which would be a function of the simple application of a rule – it chose a very specific ordering of available rules and thereby allocated costs accordingly.

Conclusions

We have come a long way from this chapter's initial point of departure. It remains true that information is limited and the whole spatial labor market system is subject to crises of coordination and allocation. And uncertainty with respect to future events and the behavior of complimentary agents is a continuing problem for parties to employment relations. Yet "solving" these informational problems is not an easy task. Uncertainty is a *procedural* attribute of the rules that govern labor exchange. Thus part of the explanation of labor market uncertainty and transaction costs has to do with rules that structure the geographical framework of exchange. Creation of more rules will not necessarily resolve the problem. It is impossible to construct rules for unknown events, and even if you could, another set of rules would be required to discriminate between them *vis-à-vis* their applicability in specific instances. To the extent that rules conflict and different rules cover similar situations, higher-order principles are required. That is, a *substantive* meaning must be given to the structure of rules – outcomes matter, as does the underlying intent of the rules themselves.

Substantive interpretations of the rules of labor market exchange transform the problem of uncertainty from being a technical matter to a question of substance that implicates the entire social structure. Choices between rules not only imply distributive outcomes but, more to the point, can only be made with respect to what outcomes are intended. Uncertainty, then, is not a neutral problem. To understand this argument American labor markets were taken as the analytical context of the chapter. Rules of labor exchange that essentially structure its geographically decentralized character were critically considered and an example based on the construction industry was used to illustrate the dilemmas of such procedural models. The social relations of capitalism were then introduced to give a substantive interpretation to the meaning of market exchange. In this sense, liberal images of procedural equality and a choice-oriented democracy were replaced with images of inequality and coercion – the real world.

These issues were then explored with reference to a judicial case from

Michigan where a worker won damages from a firm that had completely repudiated its prior contract. This case concerned a worker who had migrated from California on the promise of a job in Michigan. A couple of rules could have been applied by the Courts to decide the case. They chose to apply a rule favoring the worker over the firm. Possible reasons and rationales were then advanced to understand the Courts' actions. These rationales were shown to be premised upon specific substantive arguments regarding the structure of opportunities and relative powers.

Our argument that transaction costs can only be marginally reduced, not eliminated, given existing procedural frameworks and the social relations of exchange should not be construed as implying that there is no role for public policy. On the contrary, the structure of labor market outcomes depends on the political will of workers to force changes to the substantive interpretation of market rules and who should bear the costs of transactions. For example, by passing plant-closing legislation, governments could force employers to provide more job security and readjustment assistance and thus greater certainty in workers' labor market prospects. Of course this would mean denying conventional employment-at-will doctrines and designing rules to restructure capitalist employment relations. But this would not be so exceptional, despite the normative implications of discrete-exchange neoclassical models of the spatial labor market. Alternative rules exist that promote longer-term and more dependable employment relationships. One example is the reliance rule. It is not a matter of the choice between more or less labor market uncertainty (although it is plausible that procedures could be improved), but rather the distribution of the transaction costs inherent in any capitalist, decentralized labor market system.

PART V

Regional capital dynamics

PART V *Regional capital dynamics*

We conclude the book by examining that economic entity which we have hitherto only considered obliquely – namely, capital. At various previous points in this work, we theorized about the dynamic interrelationships between capital and labor at the regional scale. We have also subjected some of these conjectures to empirical inquiry in Chapters 3, 5, and 11. Our concern now is to address explicitly some essential questions about investment and capital and to reconsider its relation to labor in a regional context. We proceed from an appraisal of regional capital theory, such as it exists, to an exploration of the forces influencing differential rates of regional capital accumulation. We conclude by analyzing the impacts of regional investment and rates of technological change on the income fortunes of local labor.

In Chapter 13, the theory of regional capital accumulation is found to be in a state of neglect and disrepair. In fact, we find the bulk of regional capital theory to abide in a handful of largely untested truisms concerning the perfection of capital markets, the mobility and availability of capital, and the relationship between regional savings and investment. We examine each of these truisms systematically, in the context of findings at the national level concerning the determinants of capital formation. Three major concepts emerge from our review of the national theory and empirical findings; the notion of an accelerator relationship underlying investment behavior, the proposition that past profits and changes in profits are the driving force in such a relationship, and the idea that the existing stock of productive capacity exerts a negative influence on net investment in the short run.

Another major strand of contemporary capital theory is also woven into our analysis at this stage, namely, the controversies surrounding the meaning and measurement of capital as an aggregate entity in economic theory. These debates have tremendous relevance for the research program of this study, for they highlight the shaky conceptions upon which the notion of an aggregate measure of capital must ultimately be based. An equally important caveat which is gleaned from these debates concerns the necessity of distinguishing in theory between movement through time and the comparison of unrelated equilibria with time suspended. It is in this regard that much of the recent theory and empirical research in the fields of geography, regional development and the related spatial sciences, from both traditional and radical perspectives, are found to offer valuable insights into the process of investment and technological change which have escaped the consideration of theorists working aspatially at the national level.

In Chapter 14 we address the task of describing the spatial and temporal dimensions of change evident in American capital accumulation over the period 1954 to 1976. Focusing on total manufacturing plus four two–digit SIC sectors (two durable, two nondurable) at the state level, we first describe the percentage growth in each state–industry over the entire period as well as for three subperiods (1954–60, 1961–9, and 1970–6). We then determine the extent to which these various local growth rates have changed the spatial distribution of productive capacity within each industry. Next, to assess the volatility or predictability inherent in the experience of each industry in a given place, we employ a univariate time-series analysis using Box–Jenkins methods to characterize each local capital series as predictable (autoregressive), unpredictable (moving average) or some mixed process, without reference to other variables. Through this combination of descriptive techniques we are able to assemble a picture of regional growth and decline which offers some interesting highlights. We observe that the same industry often "behaves" very differently in different locales, and that its behavior even in a given locale also changes over time. For example, the same industries exhibit distinctly different temporal structures in areas where they are growing and declining. Similarly, we are able to discern some important qualitative differences between the experiences of relative and absolute decline. The evidence underscores the importance of exogenous or random endogenous shocks in determining the time-path of capital formation in regional economies, a finding which undermines the conception of smooth and steady growth or decline associated with a simple cumulative causation scenario. This scenario, and the more recent conception of regional growth or decline histories as catastrophes, are further undermined by a longer-run analysis of regional investment stability which concludes this chapter.

In Chapter 15, we explore some dynamic explanatory models of regional capital accumulation and its impact on the welfare of regional labor forces. While mindful of the considerable spatial interdependencies within production systems between both contiguous and noncontiguous spatial units, our approach is to model these links implicitly, by examining the impact of past profits generated in local production (but arguably at least partially determined by extra-regional demand) on subsequent local capital investment. This analysis employs an intra-regional accelerator based on past profit levels, changes in profit, and the pre-existing capital stock, in the tradition of Kalecki (1943) and Klein (1950). The success of this formulation underscores the importance of retained savings from past production in financing future investment, thus confirming propositions put forward by Kalecki and others. It also suggests that profits are a key behavioral variable in the investment decision of the entrepreneur. Nevertheless, strengths of relationships vary considerably from state to state and industry to industry, and some state–industries cannot be adequately explained in the terms described above. These latter cases suggest the importance of modeling some local investment processes as a function of external events, as well as lending some implicit support to the Keynesian notion that the "animal spirits" of entrepreneurs drive the will to invest. Notably, the impact of the pre-existing local capital stock is frequently found to be significant and almost always exerts a negative influence on the further accumulation of local capital in the short run. This result emphasizes the volatility of the investment process even in rapidly growing regions, and it offers us a potentially richer vehicle by which to understand the difference between growing and declining regional economies than do recent attempts to impose a catastrophe paradigm on regional dynamics.

From this point, we develop our model further by explicitly introducing information about the regional cost and productivity of labor into the analysis. We examine the impact of wage rates, productivity and profitability on capital accumulation rates, finding that lagged profit rates do encourage greater capital growth, while wage rates (with productivity held constant) exert a negative influence on net investment in some states and industries, although this effect is far from universal. The results of the analysis are more consistent when we choose to model state technological change (capital intensity) as a function of the same variables. We find a negative relationship with past changes in the profit rate, a positive link to past wage-rate change, and a positive impact from past productivity change.

Our final aim in this chapter is to integrate the processes of regional growth, distribution and technological change. For this purpose we choose to model the intra-state distribution of production incomes as a consequence of the rate of accumulation and changes in capital intensity. Our results indicate that, *ceteris paribus,* a higher growth rate or increase in capital intensity induces a shift in the income distribution in favor of capital, although the effect is more consistent in the case of capital intensity. These findings lend considerable credence to the idea that the distribution of income, even at the regional level, is largely determined by the growth rate of capital and degree of mechanization in production.

The above findings suggest a number of interesting implications for public policy concerned with rekindling growth in declining regions. First, the apparent importance of retained earnings in financing further capital formation suggests that, at least for the industries and regions examined here, the public capital markets may be of less importance as a source of finance for economic development than some might have imagined.

At the same time, for small and young firms whose capacity to generate the required funds internally is limited, and for whom Kalecki's "principle of increasing risk" arising from investment of profits is particularly onerous, the public capital markets, both local and national, may be the only source available. Nevertheless, as Kalecki (1971) points out, and as we observe in Chapter 13, one of the prerequisites to gaining access to capital in the public markets is the prior ownership of sufficient capital (often measured as a firm's debt-to-equity ratio). Furthermore, there exist all of the impediments, of both public and private origin, which effectively prevent many small and young firms from gaining any access to the public capital markets. Therefore, *if* one accepts the recent evidence concerning the beneficial impact of small businesses on local job and innovation generation, then the evidence garnered in this section would support the usefulness of public venture capital funds and the various capital "market-perfecting" devices which seek to pool and spread the risk associated with such firms as well as reducing the flotation costs of raising public capital. However, it needs to be said that the quality of employment experiences associated with such firms leaves much to be desired in terms of working conditions, stability of employment tenure, prevalence of basic employee benefits, and overall pay-scales. These issues must first be addressed before definitive policy decisions can be made.

Given the traditional and continuing attention devoted to the wage rate as an instrumental policy variable, our findings here concerning its impact on regional growth rates and technological change bear some relevance to this aspect of the current discourse on development strategies. In more than two-thirds of our state–industry cases there was no significant negative relationship between the cost of labor and subsequent rates of capital formation. While this relationship did materialize in 24 state–industries, significant positive relationships were also found in 6 other cases. Furthermore, there is substantial evidence that this negative effect is mainly operating at the highest end of the wage scale, since it was most prevalent in fabricated metals and electrical equipment, the two highest-wage industries in our sample. These findings pose serious questions for those who favor the use of wage subsidies or reduced minimum wages as a panacea for regional unemployment problems. At the same time they underscore the importance of other forms of intervention in the labor market, such as effectively targeted occupational training programs and job search assistance.

13 *Regional capital theory*

Introduction

Like most economic phenomena, capital is unevenly distributed across the regional landscape. Yet the precise nature of its distribution, the manner in which that distribution changes, and the forces behind such changes are subject to great debate. Little has been resolved, due to the lack of pertinent data on capital stocks and flows (both temporal and spatial) for the regions of most developed countries. Despite this relative state of ignorance, we have come to rely on a number of truisms about capital's role and behavior in regional development. These truisms are based more on theory and informal observation than on systematic empirical observation. While these truisms are often faithfully reproduced in introductory texts on regional economics (see O'Sullivan 1981, Heilbrun 1981, Smith 1971), they also form the basis of more sophisticated works in this area, including Romans (1965) and Borts (1971).

The most prominent of these truisms can be summarized as five canons.

(a) Investment capital is perfectly mobile in space, hence equally available anywhere within a given developed country.
(b) Geographic differentials in the cost of capital are nonexistent or insignificant, only reflecting minimal transportation costs to the location in question.
(c) Regional rates of investment bear little relationship to regional rates of saving.
(d) Capital is allocated by its price (interest rate) and flows to the highest available return.
(e) Physical or "fixed" capital is virtually immobile in space, once installed, and exerts a positive inertial force on subsequent capital flows.

In this chapter, we examine the theoretical arguments and (when available) empirical justification behind these five canonical assertions as they have emerged in the literature. Having developed a rigorous conceptual background, we turn to the empirical analysis of regional capital dynamics in later chapters.

252

The local capital market

It is commonly accepted that the capital markets of most developed countries have been successfully integrated into a unified national system. In the United States, this "reality" is believed to have been the consequence of the establishment of a fully national Federal Reserve system, progress in communications technology which has enhanced nationwide access to all major public capital markets, and the birth of secondary markets at the national level for mortgages (FNMA and GNMA) in order to improve the availability of financing for housing (Hoover 1948, Litvak & Daniels 1979). As a result of this integration, it is believed that investment capital is equally available everywhere and its price is more or less invariant over space. The major work usually cited in support is that of Straszheim (1971), who conducted a brief empirical study of interest rates for various types of capital across the USA. While mindful of the scanty available data on which his analysis was based, he nevertheless asserted in his conclusions: "as a good first approximation, the assumption of perfect capital markets employed in modeling long-run regional growth is probably reasonable" (p. 239).

Of course, prior to the functional geographic integration of the United States, differentials in both the cost and availability of financial capital were known to exist and played an important role in shaping the historical geography of growth in the USA (see Lloyd & Dicken 1972). Davis (1966) documented the existence of many local, non-integrated markets for capital in the late 19th century, in which differences in interest rates between New York City and the West Coast were as great as 10%. Davis also suggested that the growth of the textile industry in the south was inhibited and retarded by the concentration of investment capital in the northeast.

Even as late as the 1920s and 1930s, considerable geographic variation in interest rates was still evident. In assembling his evidence in support of a central place hierarchy in the United States, Lösch (1954) gathered data from 20 financial centers for the period 1919 to 1930, and computed the average interest rates on six major types of bank credit. He observed an increasing trend in interest rates as one traveled away from New York City, punctuated by "troughs" at particular regional centers (presumably of inferior order to New York) and "peaks" for the more remote centers (such as El Paso, Texas, and Helena, Montana). Lösch concluded that, despite the attractive force of high western interest rates, New York capital found it difficult to overcome the physical distance and lack of knowledge concerning investment conditions in the more remote locations.

There can be little doubt that information technology and the institutional innovations referred to earlier have greatly enhanced the ability of capital to flow within large, developed countries such as the United States, reducing supplies where investment capital has accumulated to levels higher than can be locally absorbed, and meeting demand in locations which have a relatively low supply in the immediate area. As Hoover noted in 1948, "regional and local differences in interest rates have been notably diminished in the United States by the Federal Reserve banking system and the national systems of insurance of bank deposits and real-estates mortgages" (p. 256). Furthermore, a number of studies of regional flows of money capital during the 1950s lent additional credence to the idea of a fully integrated national market for capital (Bowsher *et al*. 1957, Emmer 1957). More recently, some have contended that the multi-regional market for investment capital is still far from perfect, suggesting that the national integration of capital markets has occurred only in a very limited sense. Citing evidence from Carr (1960) and Meyer (1967), L'Esperance (1981: 6) concluded, "it is clear that there are regional differences in interest rates." The explanations advanced for this situation take three basic forms.

The first argument asserts that increasing concentration in the American investment banking and brokerage industry has reversed much of the technological and institutional progress of the past 50 years. For example, a study by the National Association of Securities Dealers (NASD) in 1979 documented several significant trends in the industry. It noted the declining numbers of securities businesses nationally since 1970 due to declining numbers of private investors, the poor performance of the stock market, increasing lack of confidence in the economy, and a fall in personal savings rates, all of which have made the smaller investment dealers exceedingly vulnerable to acquisition and consolidation (dealer membership on the New York Stock Exchange has declined by 13.3% between 1970 and 1979, and participation in the over-the-counter market has fallen by 37.1%). This decline has had direct spatial implications as well. The number of locations from which securities dealers operate has declined from 11 460 to 9140 (a 20.2% decline), and most of this contraction has occurred in the more remote parts of the country. Many of these "regional" brokerage businesses had previously specialized in the investment opportunities of their immediate area, making their research findings available to investors in the national public markets. Those regional houses which were acquired by national firms have since directed much less attention to local investment opportunities. According to NASD (p. 28):

> Recent acquisitions of regional brokers by national firms with offices located in major financial centers brought about a significant change in the types of stocks recommended by the offices of what were once independent firms. With a national audience, national firms usually spend their research dollars on issues with a national following. Thus much of the sponsorship of smaller issues has been lost.

These same trends have been noted by others, including Hayes (1979), Osborne (1980), and the study by Hayes *et al.* (1983). Similarly, Meyer (1967) found that regional interest rate differentials can be explained in part by bank size and local concentration in the banking market.

A second argument against perfection of capital markets centers on firm size. Beginning in 1937, Kalecki observed the difficulty which small firms had in expanding, due to a lack of access to capital and the risk involved in investing all of their own savings in themselves.

> Many economists assume . . . a state of business democracy where anybody endowed with entrepreneural ability can obtain capital for starting a business venture. This picture of the activities of the "pure" entrepreneur is, to put it mildly, unrealistic. The most important requisite for becoming an entrepreneur is the *ownership* of capital. (1937: 109)

Kalecki maintained that larger firms are likely to experience easier access to capital for two reasons: first, a greater capacity for internal financing from retained earnings; and, second, greater collateral and perceived security in capital markets which make external financing more readily available at favorable terms.

This theme has been reiterated more recently by others, including Chinitz (1961), Thompson (1965), Estall (1972), Sullivan (1978), Light and White (1979), Litvak and Daniels (1979), Meyer *et al.* (1980), Vaughan (1980a), and L'Esperance (1981a). These writers contended that the market for capital may indeed be fully national for the largest of firms, but for many smaller firms this is simply not the case. The major reasons advanced were risk aversion and discrimination on the part of conservative lenders, high transaction costs associated with entering the public capital markets which are proportionately more prohibitive for smaller firms seeking smaller amounts of capital, and the high costs of informing investors nationwide about the characteristics and soundness of small, relatively unknown investments.

In fact, Estall (1972) suggested that interest rates alone do not adequately describe the range in availability of investment capital across space. He asserted that "the growth or expansion of enterprise in different locations is affected by market differences in the availability of capital" (p. 195). Implicit in this is an idea of crucial importance: that the *price* of investment capital is not the sole means by which it is allocated. This contention was given empirical support in a study by Cebula and Zaharoff (1974) which examined the sensitivity of US interregional capital flows to interest rate differentials over the period 1950 to 1971. The authors concluded that "in almost all of the cases, financial capital flows were shown to be insensitive to interest rate differentials" (p. 92). While the authors tentatively attributed this outcome to systematic differences in risk associated with the investment prospects of particular regions, others would contend that there is an uncoupling of risk, return and the interest demanded by potential investors. Litvak and Daniels (1979) argued that the result is credit rationing, and suggested that this was related to the peculiar moral basis surrounding the setting of interest rates. They observed that interest rates beyond a certain level, even if they are justified by the probable risk and return of a given investment, are considered to be immoral by many of the financial community. In this vein, Estall (1972) concluded that "capital is not equally available at all locations, given identical risks and opportunities" (p. 198).

Thus a third dimension of imperfection or failure in national capital markets is recognized. This is the phenomenon of discrimination or rationing against entire regions, usually of a more remote or under-developed character, regardless of the potential for profit which existing or potential ventures in such regions might offer (Hirschman 1958, Friedmann 1966, Alonso 1968, Richardson 1973, L'Esperance 1979b). To cite just one of these authors, Hirschman (1958: 184–5) argued:

> Investors spend a long time mopping up all the opportunities around some "growth pole" and neglect those that may have arisen or could be made to arise elsewhere. What appears to happen is that *the external economies due to the poles, though real, are consistently over-estimated by the economic operators.*

From the above discussion it appears that financial capital may range less widely than some have suggested, and in response to factors other than the workings of the price mechanism. A corollary is that the economies of particular regions, at least with respect to capital flows, may not be quite as "open" as usually assumed. Since it was this presumed openness which led some writers to conclude that savings and investment in a regional context do not bear the same relationship to each other as they do at the national level (Vietorisz 1967, Hartman & Seckler 1967, Richardson 1973, Miller 1979), it may be necessary to re-examine this general proposition. Certainly, if retained earnings are as important a source of investment capital as Kalecki (1937) suggested, then regional savings rates will be likely to have a positive effect on regional investment, though the extent of this correspondence is not easy to quantify. Perhaps a first approxi-mation would base the relative importance of regional savings rates (versus national sources of capital) on the relative size-distributions of firms in each region.

It is essential to point out at this juncture, however, that for certain classes of firms or investors, the range of potential mobility is almost boundless by virtue of the reality of the basic freedom of mobility which is conferred on producers by the right of property underlying capitalist society and production. This potential mobility may be further enhanced by multilocational organizational structures (themselves evidence of past capital mobility). For such firms, intra-firm reinvestment of retained earnings may occur through the interregional transfer of capital. Hence, the distinction between actual, realized mobility and latent or potential mobility becomes a key one.

The holy grail of regional convergence

If financial capital is not allocated solely on the basis of its price, and if its mobility is imperfect, it is difficult to conceive of capital as "flowing to the highest available return." Of course, this idea is itself derived from a neoclassical conception of multiregional growth which incorporates the first four canons mentioned above into a unified, consistent theory. In this framework, capital is assumed to be perfectly mobile (implying perfect knowledge of demand by would-be consumers), so that it may flow to those firms/sectors/regions which offer the highest price and away from those offering the lowest price. Through the continual adjustment of supply to locational demands (an adjustment which is assumed to be instantaneous or close to it), the price of capital attains interregional equality (see Chapter 11). Furthermore, this equality is maintained by the constant and effortless movement of capital, to ensure interregional price equilibrium. In short, "the capital market is analogous to the wheat market" (Romans 1965: 7).

In the full-blown version of this theory, labor is also assumed to migrate toward areas of high demand (high wage) and away from low-demand (low-wage) regions. Capital and labor are assumed to be perfectly interchangeable in the production process, so that an entrepreneur can adjust the level of either in favor of prevailing relative prices of each and the contribution which an additional unit of each factor will make to the firm's revenue (marginal revenue product). In an interregional context, the theory dictates that capital should flow to low-wage areas (having standardized for differences in labor productivity) and capital–labor ratios should be highest in high-wage areas (as entrepreneurs replace expensive labor with capital). In the face of imperfect factor mobility, production technologies and the interregional trade of commodities interact to achieve factor price equalization.

Obviously, in light of the preceding discussion, many of the assumptions and mechanisms on which the model is based may not actually hold true, or may be operating at approximations to this theory (on this the reader is referred to the debate between Richardson 1973 and Borts 1971). Nevertheless, the neoclassical paradigm has been the dominant one in empirical work to date on interregional capital flows. This is, no doubt, due partly to the simplicity of the formulation and the seductively simple prediction of equilibrium (and equalization of incomes) as the outcome.

The work of Borts (1960, Borts & Stein 1964, Borts 1971) stands out in this respect. His work was based on estimates of the income accruing to capital in 48 states, derived from early estimates of state income by the Department of Commerce and NBER. Taking changes over three intervals (1919–29, 1929–48, and 1948–53), Borts and Stein (1964) measured the growth of capital, expecting it to grow fastest in low-wage states. In fact, this occurred only in one period (1929–48), casting some doubt on this aspect of the simple model they had chosen to test (in part because their capital figures included the housing and service sector, rather than just manufacturing alone).

Romans (1965) also employed a neoclassical model, and was interested in gauging the effect of interregional capital flows on state and regional growth rates. After generating state estimates of income and product accounts from sources similar to those used by Borts, Romans used net regional exports on current account or net "foreign" investment as a measure of capital out- and in-flows respectively. He hypothesized that regional growth rates are a direct function of net importation of capital from other regions, and that capital flows should create a convergence of state income differentials as high-income states "export" capital to low-income states. In fact, he did find considerable correspondence between predicted and actual rates of capital growth (1953–7) and found strong evidence for convergence of per capita income between 1929 and 1959. However, his results have since been criticized by Richardson (1973) on the basis of his data construction, which assumed an even rate of technological progress in all regions and rates of employment growth equal to rates of growth in the labor force.

In 1971, Olsen constructed a model of state capital growth (again, based on an estimated income approach) which expressed capital growth as a function of per capita income, the rate of return to capital, and income potential. Based on personal income data constructed by Easterlin for 1880, 1900, 1919–21, and 1949–51, Olsen's test produced somewhat surprising results, as the parameters on rate of return and income potential were both negative and insignificant.

The first significant test of the neoclassical theory based on estimates of regional capital stocks was by Persky and Klein (1975). In their cross-sectional analysis of capital growth in ten regions for the period 1965 to 1969, they found some evidence for faster capital growth in low-wage regions. However, in a later study Persky (1978) found the rather contradictory result of high capital–labor ratios in low-wage areas, a conclusion consistent with our model (see Ch. 3), but inconsistent with the neoclassical model. Other studies employing direct capital stock estimates include Mera (1969, 1975), who computed regional rates of return to both private and public capital using different forms of production functions based on the unusually complete Japanese data, and Horiba and Kirkpatrick (1981), who used data on the book-value of fixed assets reported in the 1963 Annual Survey of Manufactures to evaluate the role of interregional trade in reallocating factor inputs.

Engle (1974) approached the issue from a somewhat different perspective. He formulated an investment model based on the *a priori* assumption of interregional disequilibrium. He reasoned that under such conditions, rates of return on a given type of investment can be expected to vary across space. Hence, if one presumes mobile and omniscient capital, then investment in a given region ought to be determined by "the opportunity cost of investing elsewhere" (p. 368). To test this proposition, Engle estimated the following function for four Massachusetts industry groups over the period 1954 to 1971 using OIS time-series regressions:

$$I^M = a + b_1 \frac{r^M}{r^*} + b_2 I^{US} \tag{13.1}$$

where I^M and I^{US} were investment in a particular industry in Massachusetts (M) and the USA; r^M was the marginal value product of capital in the given industry in Massachusetts) and r^* was the rate of return elsewhere (either the national average or the maximum value in another state). Engle estimated r^M and r^* by deriving an approximate measure of the average value product of capital based on the difference between regional value-added and the total wage bill (divided by the capital stock). He employed book values of fixed capital derived from the 1957 and 1964 Census of Manufactures and generated by the perpetual inventory method to cover his study period.

His results, employing a three-year distributed lag of r^M/r^* based on a simple moving average, were positive for all four industry groups. Nevertheless, these results should be treated with caution for several reasons. First, his approach was "top-down" in the sense that he actually modeled regional deviations from national investment movements. The inclusion of the I^{US} term on the right-hand side of equation probably inflates the r^2 values of the fitted equations, as Johnston (1979) has pointed out on other occasions. In large regions, regional investment will be highly collinear with national investment. Secondly, Engle paid insufficient attention to possible higher-order autocorrelation in the residuals from his model, employing only the obligatory Durbin–Watson statistic. Pierce (1977) and Granger and Newbold (1977) have demonstrated how such procedures might lend spurious support to theoretically derived relationships between stochastic variables. Thirdly, Engle criticized earlier formulations of regional investment functions for mimicking nationally derived constructions, yet committed a similar error himself when deciding on the form of distributed lag to employ for his relative rate of return measure. Fourthly, Engle appeared to use gross investment as his dependent variable, yet neglected to introduce depreciation or replacement investment into the analysis. Hence, it is impossible to determine actual net additions to the capital stock of the region in question (on the importance of this, see Varaiya & Wiseman 1978, 1981). Finally, Engle's study employed a somewhat arbitrary book-value measure of capital stock which reflected all of the vagaries of taxation accounting.

Before going further, let us briefly summarize our argument. In discussion above we analyzed the first four canons concerning capital in regional development and found substantial debate surrounding each one. There is considerable evidence that the geographic availability of capital is imperfect and may actually have worsened since 1970. Furthermore, small and new firms may be at a particular disadvantage in gaining access to investment capital. While interregional differentials of the cost of capital may have declined with the integration of the national economy, it is doubtful that interest rates are a true reflection of capital availability or, for that matter, mobility. To the extent that small firms are important in a region's economy, local sources of capital may be an important determinant of regional investment rates. While interest rates undoubtedly play a role in allocating capital in the marketplace and between regions, there may be occasions where the price mechanism is completely suspended in relation to both particular regions and size classes of firms. In this sense, the supply or availability of capital, rather than its price *per se*, is the more important determinant of investment. Empirical tests of the neoclassical model of interregional growth have produced mixed and contradictory results, based largely on cross-sectional static or comparative static analyses. Sources of capital data are either income-based or derived from estimates of the value of productive capital stock.

Role of fixed capital

In all of the preceding discussion we have assumed, either implicitly or explicitly, that capital is a fluid factor of production capable of flowing – albeit imperfectly – from one use to another as the spatial pattern of demand changes. Such a conception is normally thought to be relatively accurate when describing the dynamics of financial or investment capital. However, as far as regional development is concerned, this spatial picture of the investment process is somewhat incomplete and inaccurate, for considerable rigidity is introduced into the system by the "fixed" or physical manifestation which investment assumes. Although investors are free to roam the landscape in search of worthy or promising opportunities for their capital while it is still in its money form, once capital has been committed and transformed into a productive state, it becomes relatively immobile, due to the high costs of transporting it in this form (usually referred to as industrial inertia).

Moreover, it has been suggested by some that this rigidity has important space–time dimensions as well, producing a dynamic investment process of a "sequential and interdependent" nature in which the past location of fixed capital constrains any subsequent decisions to allocate investment capital in space. This conception of regional growth as a "deviation-amplifying" or positive-feedback spatial process is at the core of the cumulative causation models proposed by Myrdal (1957), Hirschman (1958), Pred (1966, 1973, 1980), Kaldor (1970) and others. This model is based on forces operating both within the individual firm and between firms. The former include the tendency to replace worn-out capital *in situ*; the greater possibility for small increments to capital stock through expansions and improvements; and the prospect of internal increasing returns to scale. In this last "effect" are two further possibilities. The first is external increasing returns and agglomeration economies. This concept, as formulated by Kaldor (1970), relies upon Verdoorn's Law (Verdoorn 1949, 1956) that productivity is an increasing function of the rate of growth of output. The second is the influence of previously installed public or social overhead capital on subsequent private investment decisions (Richardson 1973).

Thus, not only is much of total capital relatively immobile in space, but there is evidence that the dynamic process of investment itself may contain its own spatial inertia. In fact, Richardson pointed to this fixed and self-reinforcing nature of investment as a major source of spatial imperfection in the capital market, and as bearing the prime responsibility for interregional disequilibria.

Recently, Varaiya and Wiseman (1981) have attempted to study the spatial distribution of fixed capital stock and its implications for regional growth trends. After estimating the average age of manufacturing capital stock for 77 SMSAs over the period 1954 to 1976, they observed that, while all areas have aged, this process has occurred more rapidly in the northeast and northcentral regions of the USA.

Hence, although there is still considerable investment occurring in the northeast, perhaps due to replacement of worn-out stock or the other inertial effects identified earlier, this investment is of an insufficient magnitude to maintain positive growth in manufacturing employment in the SMSAs of the region. The authors concluded that much of the new investment in the northeast is of a qualitatively different, labor-saving variety, thus implying that fewer new jobs are created for every new dollar of capital invested.

Overall, the findings of this study suggested that a simple cumulative causation model of regional investment might be inappropiate given the events of recent years. The areas of traditional dominance seem to be incapable of maintaining and increasing their capital stock in the manner suggested by the theory. Recently a number of alternative theories have been offered as explanations for such trends. Casetti (1981b) suggested that if the marginal product of capital in a particular region (MPRC) is low while regional output is still small, then, in accordance with Kaldor (1970) and Verdoorn's Law, capital's marginal product will rise in step with the region's growth in output over time, inducing further new investment. However, at a certain point, the productivity of capital will begin to fall as diseconomies of scale set in. Thus investment and output will experience relative and absolute declines, producing catastrophic shifts in the geography of production (see also the discussion contained in Casetti 1982 and Vining 1982).

Although Casetti cast his propositions in the language of catastrophe theory, using a simulation approach to show how slow changes in the marginal product of capital can induce a drastic reversal of growth trends, his arguments were surprisingly reminiscent of the well-known debates over "optimal urban size" in the 1960s. As with those earlier theories, one suspects that Casetti's propositions are also "somewhere between intuition and poetry" and lack a strong a priori theoretical basis (Alonso 1971: 78). Clearly, this debate has been hampered by an inability to address these issues directly in an empirical study which assumes a dynamic and historical perspective.

Other more process-oriented theories have been advanced which also view the inertial impact of pre-existing capital stock as relatively minimal. In recent years a number of authors have emphasized the considerable freedom of entrepreneurs to shift the location of their capital with little difficulty or regard for the consequences of their actions (Holland 1976, Markusen 1978b, Walker 1978, Bluestone & Harrison 1980, 1982, Walker & Storper 1981). This concern for "capital mobility" has surfaced in response to perceived decline of the northeast and midwest relative to the "sunbelt" states, and the much publicized shutdowns and relocations of individual plants. While some of these authors fail to specify the precise nature of the process whereby capital manifests its mobility, it is unlikely that they referred only to actual plant shutdown or relocations. Rather, the process which is suggested or implied is one in which investment and disinvestment are much more unobtrusive – where firms might slowly disinvest in one plant by failing fully to replace old, worn-out or obsolete capital, and instead choose to divert their depreciation allowances and additional investment capital to other presumably more profitable locations (Bluestone & Harrison 1980, 1982). It has also been suggested that the actions of the state have either purposely or unwittingly abetted this mobility through policies such as investment tax credits which favor investment in new locations rather than expansions or replacement at existing sites (Vaughan 1980b).

This conception of the investment process suggests the image of an entrepreneur who is continually surveying business conditions over the economic landscape and regularly adjusting the stock of productive capital in accordance with perceived or anticipated major changes in demand or other facets of the local business climate. Shorter-run fluctuations in demand would presumably be accommodated by adjustments in capacity utilization (through hours worked and numbers employed) or wage levels, although we have seen that there are many reasons for the rigidity of wages relative to employment and hours adjustments (see Parts II and III of this book).

While this more radical view of the spatial investment process ironically appears to correspond in many respects to the neoclassical view of the entrepreneur's role in the interregional allocation of capital, several important differences between the two exist. First and most obviously, the members of the capital-logic school express a deep and overriding concern for the economic and social dislocation which is wrought upon those communities that are the victims of this mobile adjustment process, since they reject the proposition that only unfettered factor mobility can maximize welfare for society as a whole.

Secondly, it is unlikely that the proponents of this view would see all types of firms as being capable of acting in this manner (or even desiring to). Though it is rarely spelled out in the literature, the kind of behavior described above is most likely to be demonstrated only by large multi-locational firms. Smaller, single-site firms will not have the same freedom of action, in part due to the capital market imperfections which they face. Of course, Kalecki (1937) suggested that even the small entrepreneur is likely to divert a significant portion of retained earnings to some other "less risky" investment as an alternative to ploughing it back into new fixed capital for the firm.

Thirdly, those sympathetic to this view emphasize the large degree of freedom which entrepreneurs possess in allocating their capital spatially. Here we return again to the distinction between realized mobility, which will be considerably less than "perfect" due to the uneven distribution of investment opportunities, and potential mobility, which for some firms approaches perfection. Fourthly, and most importantly as far as modeling efforts are concerned, the interpretation of the capital investment and disinvestment process espoused by this school is strongly grounded in local and regional events taking place in actual historical time. Hence, this perspective finds little value in atemporal theoretical constructions such as equilibrium and the production function. The mobility of capital is seen to produce not some ultimate equilibrium solution, in which welfare is equalized in all regions, but rather a continuing process of spatial rearrangement of production and the attendant social dislocation which this entails.

Thus far we have said nothing about the relevance of accelerator-type models so prominent in investment modeling at the national level (Chenery 1952, Jorgenson 1971, Clark 1979) for a regional analysis of capital formation. This silence stems from the relative absence of direct attention to this model in the regional literature, presumably due to the aforementioned paucity of suitable data. Hence, even though Airov proposed a flexible accelerator model of regional investment as far back as 1963 (for a recent revival, see Allen 1982), the idea has received little further discussion except in the curiously divorced literature on regional econometric modeling (see Gertler 1984b). Nevertheless, this concept is arguably implicit in much of the literature just reviewed. For example, Verdoorn's Law could be stated symbolically as below:

$$MP_i^k = f\frac{\Delta Y_i}{Y_i} \tag{13.2}$$

where MP_i^k denotes the marginal productivity of capital in region i. If one accepts that investment (I) flows to regions offering high returns, it follows that:

$$I_i = f(MP_i^k) \tag{13.3}$$

and

$$I_i = f\frac{\Delta Y_i}{Y_i} \tag{13.4}$$

which broadly corresponds to the definition of the output accelerator employed in national models, since $\Delta Y_i/Y_i$ denotes rate of change in region i output.

Airov's own specification takes the following form (1963: 5):

$$I_{it} = \lambda_i[b_i(Y_{it-1} - Y_{it-2})] \tag{13.5}$$

where λ represents a geometrically distributed lag coefficient. Airov extended this formulation to the multiregional case in which interregional investment might be accommodated. Hence:

$$I_{iit} = \lambda_{ii}[b_{ii}(Y_{iit-1} - Y_{iit-2})] \tag{13.6}$$

$$I_{ijt} = \lambda_{ij}[b_{ij}(Y_{ijt-1} - Y_{ijt-2})] \tag{13.7}$$

where I_{ij} denotes investment in i which originated in j. Airov was unable to test his model because of a lack of data on interregional investment flows. Nor did he express any interest in (or concern for) the influence of output fluctuations in other regions or the rest of the nation on investment in the region in question. Such a relationship might be expressed as:

$$I_{it} = \lambda_i[b_i(Y_{it-1} - Y_{it-2})] + \lambda_j[b_j(Y_{jt-1} - Y_{jt-2})] \qquad (13.8)$$

where the second part of the right-hand side denotes output fluctuations in some outside region also potentially served by production in region i. Although we show only the immediate past change in output in both regions, it is quite conceivable that the influence of output fluctuations on investment could extend beyond one time period into the future.

The above speculations suggest that a simple extension of accelerator theory to the explanation of regional capital formation could be problematic. The lone test of this proposition, and a partial one at that, is by Engle (1974), who invoked a regional accelerator in his effort to model Massachusetts investment. Engle's motivation in adopting the accelerator was to supplement his neoclassical model to accommodate the behavior of those entrepreneurs "who are not mobile and whose opportunity costs are merely borrowing rates" (p. 373). His simple accelerator (a first difference on value-added) was found to be consistently insignificant across his four industry groups, although he did not introduce a capital price or supply term into his model. These findings, which are subject to all of the objections raised earlier, nevertheless cast some doubt on the appropriateness of such a simple formulation of the accelerator for regional analysis.

Guccione and Gillen (1972) also employed an accelerator mechanism to model gross investment in Canadian regions over the period 1947 to 1968, although their formulation was modified to include the real cost of capital services and a second-order autoregressive process. As an interesting contrast to Engle, both output and capital cost were national rather than regional, although they derived separate coefficients for each region to test their sensitivity to national fluctuations. They found significant variations in their regional parameters, with Ontario most closely related to national fluctuations and the Maritimes least so. In retrospect, these findings add little to our understanding of regional investment, because of the earlier identified problems associated with employing national exogenous variables to model regional change in the same variable.

Spatial perspectives on capital controversies

Economic theory pertaining to growth and the investment decisions of firms has been characterized by considerable debate and spirited disagreement dating back at least as far as Joan Robinson's seminal article in 1953.

Yet surprisingly few of the insights or implications arising out of this debate have been brought to bear upon theoretical developments in regional analysis. Our intent in this section is to review the essential elements of this debate and explore some of its consequences for a more complete theory of regional investment. The central contention of this discussion is that the location of an investment (or disinvestment) as well as its size and timing are inescapably bound up with the choice of technique, the specific types and proportions of production inputs implied by that choice, and the overall organization of the production process within the private manufacturing firm. Furthermore, it becomes essential to examine space and production technique together with a third variable – dynamic technological change over historical time. We must consider how the process of technological change over time interacts with changes in the location of investment over time. Speculations on the nature of this complex interaction are offered prior to the comments which conclude this chapter.

Over the past 50 years or so, economists have attempted to "explain" growth in aggregate output by the relative contributions of two aggregate inputs – capital and labor – plus the overall level of technological knowledge. Moreover, such analyses have largely been conducted on the basis of the neoclassical theory of the firm, in which the following conditions hold. First, the above two factors are presumed to be employed in direct proportion to the ratio of their prices; secondly, the resulting "factor proportions" can be altered if and when relative factor prices change; and thirdly, rates of payment to each factor reflect the value of the marginal contribution to output achieved by employing one additional unit of each factor in the production process. Hence, in the empirical modeling of production relationships, a commonly employed form of production function is that originally suggested by Cobb and Douglas (1928):

$$Y = e^a K^b L^c \qquad (13.9)$$

or

$$\ln Y = a + b \ln K + c \ln L \qquad (13.10)$$

where Y is output, K is capital, L is labor, a is the level of technology, b and c are elasticities of output with respect to capital and labor respectively. The coefficients b and c also reflect the relative (partial) contributions of each production input to changes in output.

Implicit in the Cobb–Douglas production function is the perfect substitutability of one factor for another (i.e. the elasticity of substitution between capital and labor equals unity), although this assumption has been relaxed by many through the use of more flexible functional forms (see

Arrow *et al.* 1961, Christensen *et al.* 1973). A further principle which underlies the neoclassical or marginal theory of production holds that the marginal productivity (*MP*) of each factor (and therefore, its reward) diminishes as it becomes more prevalent relative to the other factor in production. Hence MP_K is expected to be a negative function of the capital–labor ratio (K/L) and MP_L should be a positive function of K/L. By implication, one expects to find high capital–labor ratios when MP_L (hence the wage rate) is high, and low capital–labor ratios when MP_K (hence the rate of profit or cost of capital) is high.

The use of aggregate production functions has been surrounded by controversy at least since Joan Robinson's (1953) article in which she posed two related questions: first, what is the real meaning of the term "capital" as used by economists, and how might one measure it consistently; secondly, how valid is an analysis which attempts to fit one functional relationship to series of data representing long periods of time? On the first point, it was contended by Robinson and her followers that the popular conception of capital as an infinitely malleable commodity (referred to metaphorically as butter, jelly, putty, or meccano sets) was misleading for a number of reasons. To begin with, it grossly understated the degree of fixity in production relationships as dictated by technological exigencies, since it supported the idea that capital could be shaped and reshaped into any desired form to accommodate any new technique at no cost. Robinson's objection on this count stems from Keynes' (1936) earlier contention that capital once invested becomes "a hostage to fortune in an uncertain world" (Harcourt 1979: 924).

In response to this criticism the idea of a vintage model of capital accumulation was developed by Johansen (1959) and others who distinguished between "*ex ante* substitution possibilities" and *ex post* fixity *à la* Leontief. Nevertheless, the question of the meaning of capital was left unanswered. In Robinson's words (1974a: 38), "does a quantity of capital mean a number of dollars or a list of machine tools, railway lines and other hard objects? And which is it that has a marginal product?" Her conclusion, later reinforced by Sraffa (1960) and acknowledged by Samuelson (1966), was that a one-dimensional factor of production (as employed in aggregate production functions) made little sense, because any nonphysical measure of this good would be directly affected by the prevailing income distribution and would therefore be inconsistent over time. This offered a definitive answer to all those since the days of Ricardo, including Marx, Bohm-Bawerk, Walras, Wicksell, and Marshall, who were plagued by this measurement problem (Harcourt 1979).

The inconsistency of meaning and measurement of capital as commonly employed had direct implications for the second of Robinson's queries, since the measure of capital used in time-series estimation of production functions is affected by simultaneous changes in the distribution of income between wages and profits. However, there are more fundamental objections to this form of analysis which stem from the basic nature of the marginal approach itself. It is well known that the theoretical underpinnings of neoclassical analysis are essentially static in orientation and that its major insights are drawn from a comparison of different equilibrium positions with time held constant (Bhaduri & Robinson 1980, Pasinetti 1981, Nelson & Winter 1982). It stands to reason, therefore, that such a theory is inappropriate for the analysis of dynamic historical change. The notion of substitution, for example, is only appropriate to an instantaneous *ex ante* consideration of alternative production techniques. It breaks down when applied to the process of accumulation with actual technological change over time. In the latter case, the quality of capital and associated labor changes over time (Robinson 1974a).

Notwithstanding Robinson's argument, it is important to acknowledge the operation of some process in real time which achieves an alteration of "factor proportions" in response to trends in prices. Pasinetti (1977) made the observation that technological change through time generally involves increasing amounts of capital per worker employed, which in turn may eventually create the potential for higher wages through potential increases in labor productivity. When this occurs, it is quite plausible that new techniques will be adopted or invented "which economise the inputs that have become relatively more expensive" (p. 394), thereby further increasing the capital–labor ratio. However, the interpretation which Pasinetti gave to this description of "substitution in the real world" was distinctly non-neoclassical. All these arguments lend substantial support to Robinson's dictum that we should not attempt to draw insights concerning actual *changes* through time from a model which compares *different* steady states. As Robinson (1974b) noted, "the real source of trouble is the confusion between comparisons of equilibrium positions and the history of a process of accumulation" (p. 57).

Thus any time-series analysis of the production function in a given place or region is less meaningful than might have otherwise been supposed, because of the qualitative changes in the production process which occur as technology develops. Although some have chosen to treat this problem explicitly by conceiving of technology as a notion disembodied from productive capacity which can be entered into production functions as a simple time trend, it has been pointed out by Arrow (1962) that to do so amounts to a "confession of ignorance." Arrow contended that a more satisfactory approach would be based on "choosing the economic variable which represents 'experience' " (p. 157) and he asserted (in a fashion similar to Veblen 1908, Schumpeter 1934, Kalecki 1943, Kaldor 1961) that the correct variable is cumulative gross investment itself. Furthermore, even with constant level and type of production inputs, technological progress may occur through the improvement of procedures or "learning-by-doing," a phenomenon which effectively "blurs the notion of a production function" (Nelson & Winter 1982: 227).

In a multiregional analysis one might be tempted to circumvent the above problems by estimating production functions in cross section, based on the assumption that the state of technical knowledge is roughly the same in all regions at any given time (see, for example, Romans 1965, Mera 1969, Buck & Atkins 1976, Tooze 1976, Lande 1978, Alperovich 1980, DeBruyne & van Rompuy 1982). As the following discussion clarifies, this latter assumption is of crucial importance to the validity of such an approach. Yet the majority of literature in economics, geography, and regional science concerning the diffusion of technology through space and time indicates that the above conception may contain some basic flaws.

Regional capital theory

The process of technological change remains one of the least understood areas of economics and the related social sciences. Consequently, much of what follows in this section should be regarded as somewhat speculative. Nevertheless, geographers, economists, and other spatial scientists have devoted a significant portion of their attention in recent years to the process of technological change in the context of innovation diffusion, urban and regional development, and industrial location theory.

The most salient characteristic of a multiregional economy is the tremendous diversity which exists in the industrial histories of different areas. Hence even economists as enlightened as Pasinetti (1981), while correctly emphasizing the importance of a dynamic production theory, scarcely acknowledge the strong spatial variations in production conditions and characteristics which typify even the most developed of economies. Robinson (1975) was somewhat more conscious of the spatial dimension as is evident in the following passage:

> Two different economies are separated either in space or time. No two economies separated in space have exactly the same technology, for many accidents of geography and history enter into the choice of technique, as well as the design of "machines." The same economy at different dates has a different state of technical knowledge. Not only is every island at a different point, but every point is on a different production function. (p. 82)

While much of this is undoubtedly true in the multiregional case, two further points must also be made. First, within developed countries such as the United States, it is no longer plausible that any two regional economies can still be considered totally unrelated "islands" in the manner of Robinson's metaphor above. Secondly, having said this, it has been possible to discern some generalities about the manner in which two areas might be interrelated (as manifested in their respective production technology sets for a given shared industry) which implicate not only "accidents of geography and history" but also some recognizable underlying processes. Lande (1978) conducted a cross-sectional multiregional production function analysis of the USA and found, under conditions of profit maximization, that a Cobb–Douglas or VES function could not be substantiated. His conclusion was that different states are not producing at different points along the same production function (in accordance with the particular factor price ratios characterizing each state), but rather that each region or state (for a given industry) is characterized by different technical relationships in production.

What, then, are the processes or forces which determine or influence the technological nature of production in particular places for a given industry? One basic insight which has sprung from empirical analyses of technical change in firms distinguishes between innovation and imitation as two sources of change (see Nelson & Winter 1982). Both of these concepts have been applied in spatial theory to help explain which areas of developed countries tend to generate new industrial products and processes, and how these innovations spread over time to become adopted by "imitators" outside the innovating areas. Traditionally, it is the largest of cities in the national urban hierarchy which have been observed to be the major sources of industrial innovation, and the reasons for this are obvious. These cities provide the widest array of technically skilled labor, general and specialized support services, and other factors such as basic research institutions. These cities are also conducive to productive research and development activity, thereby acting as "incubators" for new products, processes and firms (Hoover & Vernon 1959, Leone & Struyk 1976).

Furthermore, this process of innovation has been given a specific spatio-temporal context in what has come to be known as product-cycle theory. Vernon (1966) noted that a firm's product typically passes through three phases, each of which places new demands on the nature and organization of production. In the early phase, in which a product is first being developed, scientific and engineering skills in research and development are of paramount importance. Hence production will have a high labor content and runs will be small as adjustments are continually being made to the process. In the growth phase, when the firm is attempting to carve out its market for the product, management skills are most important. Meanwhile, mass production processes will be introduced which greatly lower the labor input (thereby increasing the capital-intensity of production). In the mature phase, in which the market is more or less stable and production processes are completely routinized, the key production input is cheap, low-skilled labor. However, with equipment now standardized and highly specialized, the production process reaches perhaps its highest level of capital intensity (especially if the labor input is measured by its total cost, as opposed to physical numbers).

Thompson (1965) and Berry (1972) observed that as products progress through this cycle, the optimum environment for production is likely to be provided in different physical locations. Borrowing from traditional central place theory, they reasoned that the demands of the early stage can best be met in the highest-order centers of the hierarchy, where large amounts of highly skilled labor and a supportive environment for research are to be found. Then, as the product moves further along the cycle, its requirements become less specialized – hence more widely available – and its production may filter down to new locations in lower-order centers where labor is presumably cheaper and more readily available. This would suggest, as Hansen (1980) noted, that we should expect to find a spatial correspondence between low wages and high capital intensity (the opposite of the neoclassical prediction), thereby providing an explanation for the results obtained by Persky (1978) and ourselves which were reviewed earlier. (For further elaboration, see Rees 1979, Erickson & Leinbach 1979, Malecki 1981).

The regularity implicit in the above description – with diffusion being routed primarily from largest to next largest to smallest urban centers, and secondarily perhaps in some distance-decay fashion from each adopting center – has yet to be confirmed through extensive empirical analysis of manufacturing products and production technologies, although it has proved to be appropriate for innovations in consumption goods (Berry 1970). Many have drawn attention to further characteristics of the diffusion process which might serve to complicate spatial patterns in the production sector – notably, the increasing predominance of multi-locational organizations, which creates the possibility for such aberrations as diffusion "steered" along intra-organizational lines (Brown 1981) and nonlocal linkages (Pred 1977). It has also been suggested that recent developments in the information transfer and telecommunications fields have enabled many headquarter-type activities, including research and development, to locate in urban (even rural) centers further down the hierarchy (Pred 1977, Berry 1980, Malecki 1981).

One recent Canadian study which explicitly examines the diffusion of industrial innovations (Martin et al. 1979) finds "significant and systematic" regional lags in adoption which contribute to the marked and persistent productivity differences between Canadian regions within the particular industries studied. However, the precise spatio-temporal pattern of diffusion defies generalization: in some sectors, evidence of hierarchical diffusion is evident; in others the market structure is preeminent. These findings underscore how poorly developed is our detailed understanding of these processes in real space and time.

The descriptions offered above do, however, share an implicit assumption which can be labelled determinist. That is to say, they seek to uncover a process of technological change which contains some inner teleology all its own. Yet we are now becoming increasingly aware of the stochastic element inherent in such processes, such that the model reviewed above might be regarded as providing some explanation of the *possibility set* of production technology in a given place at a given time without revealing *actual* choices. Massey (1978b) and others have suggested that these choices are the result of a complex dialectical interplay between the private firm making such choices and the particular place or community in which production takes place. Community characteristics of particular interest to firms might include not only factor prices *per se*, but also the vulnerability of the local labor force to workplace control and bargaining in the wage determination process (Clark 1981a). Such aspects as these might be thought of as the product of past histories of particular places, so that the time–geographic dimensions of the labor market assume a position of prominence.

The implication of the above discussion is that producers can vary their production technique to match the specific conditions encountered in particular places, and that these "conditions" extend beyond the normally considered factor prices. In fact, as we saw earlier, for larger firms, local capital cost or availability will be largely irrelevant, making labor the predominant geographically varying input. There are, of course, other possibilities presented in the multiregional framework. For example, firms may decide to hold technology more or less constant and vary location instead, in the process also obtaining a new labor force perhaps more "conducive" to profitability. Or firms which face intense competition and are under pressure constantly to innovate or at least alter production technologies may find it easier to alter their fixed capital at new locations, either to escape union strictures on the redeployment of labor or simultaneously to avail themselves of a more docile and predictable labor force (Clark 1981a, Walker & Storper 1981, Harrison 1982a).

It has also been suggested that firms do not passively accept the structure of local factor prices but act to alter those prices by, for example, importing cheaper labor or, as noted above, investing in new locations (Walker & Storper 1981). Similarly, firms do not have to accept passively the "possibility set" of production techniques which they perceive to be available, but can and do create new techniques in direct response to the economic, social and political conditions they face. Hence, Gordon (1978) concluded that the trucking technology and land-intensive plant layouts which characterized suburban industrialization in this century were specifically created and adopted to enable firms to escape the increasingly combustible inner-city labor markets in favor of more bucolic settings. In the same vein, both Nelson and Winter (1982) and Buck and Atkins (1976) acknowledged a secular trend in favor of labor-saving technology which may be driven not only by response to factor prices and the pursuit of increased productivity, but also by important political characteristics of labor.

All of this suggests that the diversity of production technology within particular industries which we observe across the spatial plane is the result not only of basic technological and scientific discoveries and innovations, but also a complex social and economic process of interaction, symbolized by the employment relation or contract itself (Simon 1951, Clark 1981a, Wallace & Kalleberg 1982). This relation conditions actual technological choices and even provides inducement for the possibility set of production techniques to be stretched in new directions. From this perspective, it makes little sense to speak of a "dominant national technology," for it consists of nothing more than the accumulation in space and time of many local practices, customs, and techniques (for similar comments pertaining to the time domain and long-run fluctuations, see Kalecki 1971). Hence, the view offered here finds considerable kinship with the "bottom-up" school of regional analysis recently espoused by Ballard and Wendling (1980) and others.

Conclusions

In the early sections of this chapter we reviewed the predominant conceptions (and misconceptions) concerning the character of regional capital markets and dynamics as they currently exist in the literature. As a general observation, it was noted that the relevant theory was somewhat underdeveloped and abides primarily in truisms concerning the presumed perfection of regional capital markets and the like. This supposed perfection or integration was subjected to further scrutiny and many doubts were raised in the process. Substantial evidence exists that firms of particular size in particular locations may encounter greater difficulty in gaining access to finance capital, and that lenders unfairly valuate the risk associated with these types of investment. By the same token, internal resources remain an important source of finance capital both for small firms (which encounter difficulty in public capital markets) and large firms (which have the ability to raise funds externally but prefer the flexibility conferred by the use of internal financing sources). Hence, the presumed dissonance between regional investment and regional saving may not be as clear cut as is widely presumed.

Furthermore, if capital is not strictly allocated by its price alone, this complicates the commonly held picture of perfect integration in the regional capital markets, for it means that capital's movements are not dictated solely by price or return differentials. It also means that spatial price convergence in the cost of capital can no longer be used as an index of capital's mobility. Important insights are found in the key distinction between actual or realized capital mobility (which is doubtless far from perfect) and potential mobility (which is of considerably higher levels). In fact, the actual mobility of capital within developed countries has attracted much attention in the face of major regional restructuring of productive capacity. This mobility is not limited only to the margin of capital but also includes depreciation allowances on fixed capital. The joint potential of these two processes to alter quickly and significantly the geography of productive capacity appears to be greater than was ever imagined in the era of monotonic growth in the traditional manufacturing heartland of the developed countries. However, our understanding of the forces behind this mobility is still somewhat incomplete.

There has been relatively little attention paid to the flexible accelerator model at the regional scale, except in the specification of regional econometric models. Even here, however, there has been very little detailed consideration of which fluctuation is the relevant one (the region, the nation, a competing region) in determining capital formation for a particular region. Similarly, the impact of the pre-existing capital stock on regional investment has not been conclusively settled. The one major hypothesis advanced (of circular and cumulative causation) appears to be at odds with the Kaleckian insight at the national level, since the latter predicts a negative feedback in the short run.

We also discussed some of the qualitative dimensions of capital formation which embody much of the essence of regional development itself. This discussion was grounded in the recent critique of traditional capital theory by post-Keynesian economists, who have uncovered inconsistencies and lack of clarity in the neoclassical definition of capital and (hence) its measurement as an aggregate entity. They emphasize the importance of qualitative variations in capital and production relationships over historical time and space; they also undermine the marginalist conception of input factor substitution. Their insights were shown to be quite compatible with the body of theory emanating from both traditional and radical scholars in the field of regional development. In retrospect, this finding is not all that surprising since by its very nature the field of regional development can potentially be predisposed to an awareness of diversity, variation, and uniqueness within a context of overarching systemic interdependence.

What, then, are the most salient questions which remain unanswered or poorly understood after the review summarized above? First, we know strikingly little about even the most basic dimensions of regional capital formation in space and time. How volatile is investment in a given industry in a given place over time? How consistent is this volatility from region to region? What is the impact of previously installed capital stocks on regional capital flows? Secondly, how might the mechanism of acceleration actually operate in a multiregional framework? Are lag structures in this relationship consistent within or across industries or regions? Finally, how does capital formation interact with aspects of the labor market and other social phenomena? How does capital intensity within a particular industry vary across space and through time? How is this variation affected by wage rates and other qualitative dimensions of the labor force? To what extent do conditions in the labor market determine capital mobility and spatial investment patterns? The next two chapters develop answers to these questions by examining, in turn, the temporal character of the regional investment process and its generating mechanisms.

14 Dynamics of regional investment

The investment process in place and time

Despite the proclivity of geographers and regional scientists for long-run theories of regional development (for evidence see Gertler 1984a), it is possible to discern, often implicitly, a variety of characterizations of the investment process in time and space which emerge from the contending theories of regional growth and decline. These can be sorted into two basic conceptions of the process, which have rather different spatial and temporal forms.

One view, associated with the cumulative causation theory of regional growth (Myrdal 1957, Hirschman 1958), conceives of the spatial investment process as self-reinforcing in the manner of a positive-feedback system. This suggests, albeit implicitly, a scenario in which the spatial distribution of capital stock changes rather slowly over time and primarily in the direction of change established in earlier periods. The forces driving such a process, including the Verdoorn effect and others, were described in the preceding chapter.

The other view envisions a process in which capital is adjusted relatively quickly over time and between places, a conception which has been identified (for differing reasons) with both the "atemporal," equilibrium-based neoclassical theories of regional growth and a collection of possible structuralist explanations (see Ch. 13). The neoclassically inspired theory contends that: (a) the monotonic episode of growth attributed to the Verdoorn effect would be terminated when entrepreneurs became aware of sufficiently large production cost advantages in previously less-developed areas, which would induce them to redeploy some or all of their capital to these new locations (thereby ultimately encouraging inter-regional convergence in degree of capitalization, marginal products of factors, and factor prices); and (b) decreasing returns to production (both internal and external) might set in at some point to lower capital's "marginal product," hence the rate of new investment, in areas of earlier industrialization. Casetti's (1981a) catastrophe theory of regional change may be subsumed within this category by virtue of its emphasis on the

276

marginal productivity of capital. However, it can be distinguished from the more traditional neoclassical theories by its explicitly dynamic orientation and its interest in "one-time" events or adjustments as the key to regional change (Gertler 1986a).

The structuralist view emphasizes the political–economic environment surrounding production, in which capital mobility affords entrepreneurs the ability to seek more favorable locations. Specific motives for this shift might include the desire to seek a more docile and passive labor force or an anti-union legislative environment; an attempt to minimize local "demonstration effects" in the determination of wages and other aspects of the employment relation; and the relative facility of implementing new production technology at new locations, through unobtrusive disinvestment in older locations while reinvesting retained earnings and capital consumption allowances elsewhere. This view also conceives of the dispersal or deconcentration of production from traditional locations as a means to accommodate new organizational forms of production (offering many of the above advantages) in which the division of labor assumes a spatial dimension. Finally, spatial differentials in "factor prices" would also play a role in this explanation, but become only one of a broad array of considerations in the locational cost calculus of the firm.

From this review, it is evident that the competing conceptions of the investment process in place and time have not been formulated in a temporally detailed way. They are more reasonably considered as heuristic caricatures of the process we are seeking to describe. However, a recent review of the relevant literature within economics and econometric modeling (Gertler 1983) has revealed a conception of investment dynamics at a level of considerably greater temporal detail whose spatial dimensions have not yet been explored. The chief insight, which stems from the work of Kalecki (1943), Klein (1950) and Goodwin (1951), and has been reflected in econometric modeling since then (Jorgenson 1971, Clark 1979), contends that the "inherited" capital stock and/or recent past changes in the size of that stock will exert a negative-feedback influence on current investment levels. This effect stems from the limiting influence of capacity expansion amongst competitors in a given product sector when demand is stable, increasing more slowly than capacity, or decreasing in actual terms. In short, the previous expansion of capacity (investment) by one's competitors can render one's current investments less profitable, particularly if capacity now outstrips demand for the given product. The entrepreneur's response will be to cut back on investment spending in the next time period, until slack capacity is utilized. Conversely, an earlier period of reduced investment within the industry will stimulate the entrepreneur's decision to spend on capital if he perceives unsatisfied demand in the marketplace.

When viewed over time, this mechanism resembles the well-known investment accelerator, and can be seen to form the core of a model describing a nonlinear business cycle (Kurihara 1972). Its operation in space has been largely unexplored but would appear to suggest an important development beyond the spatial models described earlier. It would seem to imply a local investment experience characterized by unsteady, perhaps halting growth (or, as the case may be, decline), rather than one of smooth, monotonic episodes.

For the remainder of this chapter we explore the validity of the various conceptions outlined above. To do so, we choose to focus on the *form* of the investment process as realized in the time-series characteristics of capital accumulation in a variety of sectors and regions over the period 1954 to 1976. The causal relationships which may underlie this investment behavior are the subject of the following chapter. However, using certain methods of time-series analysis (Box & Jenkins 1976, Granger & Newbold 1977, Aguado 1982), we are able to draw some useful inferences about the nature of the investment process by analyzing only its realized form.

Because the data on capital stocks are available for a number of states and regions in each industry, we will be able to assess the importance of intra-sector (i.e. place-oriented) characteristics as a source of variation in net investment rates and stability, as well as being able to compare different industries generally. Industry mix has long been hailed as a key dimension in understanding how a particular locality or region will fare relative to others, or respond to national economic fluctuations. This sentiment is perhaps most colorfully expressed in Wilbur Thompson's (1965) aphorism: "tell me your industries and I'll tell you your fortune." However, a growing number of recent studies have found industry mix on its own to be an inadequate explanatory factor when examining the recent performance of different regions, whether one considers employment (Browne 1978a, Syron 1978, Strong 1983), or unemployment (Browne 1978b). For example, while Strong observed that industry mix in different regions has converged markedly since 1947, Syron (p. 32) noted that "there does not appear to be any trend toward a convergence in regional sensitivity to business cycles. If anything, regions seem to be becoming dissimilar."

Spatial and temporal dimensions

The analysis presented in this chapter is primarily based on four industries: textiles, apparel, fabricated metal products, and electrical and electronic equipment. Table 14.1 shows the number of states for which data were available in each sector, as well as providing a regional breakdown of this coverage. For further details on the origins and construction of these data, see Browne *et al.* (1980) and Gertler (1983). Of all regions, the west is least

Table 14.1 Regional coverage of capital stock data by industry.

SIC number	Industry	Number of states enumerated				
		Northeast	Northcentral	South	West	Total
22	textiles	6	1	9	0	16
23	apparel	4	2	7	1	14
34	fabricated metals	6	9	9	3	27
36	electrical/electronic	6	7	3	1	17

well represented (especially in textiles, where no western states are included). However, the major manufacturing state of this region (California) is represented in three out of four sectors examined. Selection of individual states in the construction of capital stock series at the two–digit SIC level was determined by those states for which data on new capital expenditures were available for the entire study period. This has the unfortunate effect of biasing the remaining sample of states to those which contain the oldest stocks of capital, excluding states which might have begun production in a given sector (presumably with newer technology) at some point within the study period. Consequently any conclusions which are drawn from the analysis of these series must be tempered or qualified by this realization since, for example, older capital may on average be associated with higher quantities of labor than newer capital.

Similarly, exclusion of some recent high–growth states may overstate the importance of growth occurring in those states which are included in the sample. In this vein, we should note that many of the sectors being studied have experienced significant capital exports from the USA. This internationalization of capital also acts to overstate the importance of domestic fixed investment.

The remainder of this chapter addresses itself to the following three questions. First, What are the basic spatial and temporal dimensions of change in manufacturing capital accumulation? Secondly, which of the competing characterizations of the structure of regional capital formation is most valid? How, if at all, does this validity vary by industrial sector? And thirdly, how consistent are the experiences of different areas within the same industry? How does this degree of consistency vary by industrial sector?

The first of these questions forms the subject matter for the current section, in which we analyze the growth experiences of individual states. In the next section, we address the second and third questions by carrying out a univariate time–series analysis of the 74 state–industry series represented in this study, as a way of characterizing the relative volatility of investment in each place and industry over time. Prior to the actual analysis we provide a brief review of the Box–Jenkins methodology on which it relies. Finally, we conclude this chapter by summarizing the major findings of the empirical analysis and discussing their implications for the questions raised above.

Prior to the analysis of specific industries, we shall embark on a brief digression to examine the trends evident in manufacturing as a whole (comprising 19 two-digit industries in the SIC system). Besides providing a general backdrop for the more detailed analyses which follow, this offers us a chance to scrutinize a similar data set which covers all 48 mainland states.

Growth rates of total manufacturing capital stock for the four regions and nine subregions defined by the US Census Bureau are shown in Table 14.2. Growth rates are shown for the entire period as well as for three sub-periods: 1954–60, 1961–9, and 1970–6. These dates were chosen to represent similar points in the national fluctuations of the business cycle. Hence 1954, 1961, and 1970 all represent years in which the national cycle reached a trough, while 1976 was within one year of another trough in 1975.

In analyzing Table 14.2, the first striking fact is that, on the whole, all regions show a net accumulation of capital stock. In fact, a state-level analysis (not shown here) would reveal that only in Louisiana, Wyoming, Alaska (period two), and North Dakota (period three) did capital stocks show an absolute decline, and it is perhaps significant that each of these states is dominated in economic terms by resource development which typically exhibits a "boom–bust" cycle over time (although capital directly associated with resource extraction would not be reflected in these figures). Hence, at least for total manufacturing, "decline" is manifested primarily in *relative terms* by those regions which grow more slowly than average.

Table 14.2 Percentage growth in manufacturing capital stock (based on constant 1972 dollars).

Region	1954–76	1954–60	1961–9	1970–6
Northeast	81.2	17.6	31.0	12.5
New England	107.5	21.7	39.3	15.4
Middle Atlantic	74.4	16.6	28.8	11.7
Northcentral	87.7	16.4	34.8	15.8
East northcentral	78.5	15.1	33.4	13.3
West northcentral	152.1	25.6	44.1	30.1
South	174.9	21.0	55.6	36.4
South Atlantic	194.1	30.6	57.8	32.9
East southcentral	188.0	23.9	65.4	31.3
West southcentral	149.9	10.2	47.8	43.6
West	154.6	27.9	48.8	26.4
Mountain	247.1	38.7	49.1	54.0
Pacific	139.3	26.1	48.8	21.2
USA	115.1	19.1	40.8	22.3

For the entire period considered, the south clearly dominates all other regions, with an increase of almost 175%. However, the west is not far behind, and the mountain subregion records the highest percentage growth of any individual subregion (247%). The northeast and north-central regions both lag behind the national average of 115% (at 81% and 88% respectively), although each exhibits significant internal variation. The New England subregion is some 33 percentage points ahead of the Middle Atlantic states (107.5% versus 74.4%), suggesting that the capital in the traditional manufacturing belt must be aging relative to the rest of the region and nation, since it is being renewed at a slower rate. This is corroborated in the northcentral region, in which the east northcentral states (78.5%) lag far behind the western half (152.1%). The latter of these growth rates is more typical of the south or west than the midwest.

An examination of the three subperiods also produces some interesting insights. In the earliest period (1954–60), New England capital stock is still growing faster than the national average (22% versus 19%), although the slower Middle Atlantic subregion brings down the rate for the entire northeast to just under 18%. The northcentral region performs compara-bly, though already the ascendancy of its western half is evident. In the rest of the country, it is apparent that the 1954 to 1960 period is the tail end of the west's postwar "golden age," as growth rates there are the highest in the nation (note the early growth of the mountain states). It is also evident that the south has already begun to stir, with overall growth of 21%, though the west southcentral states of Louisiana, Arkansas, Oklahoma and Texas still constitute a national backwater area (posting the slowest growth in the nation over this period).

The boom years of the 1960s herald the first period in which the south leads all other parts of the nation in terms of investment growth rate. Its growth rate of 55.6% outstrips the nation (at 40.8%) as well as the west (at 48.8%). In this period alone, the Carolinas and Mississippi manage to double their existing capital stocks, joined in the west by Arizona.

As for the northern climes, New England trails the national average by 1.5% (although Vermont and New Hampshire register fairly impressive gains), but again, the performance of the Middle Atlantic states is consider-ably below average. The northcentral region no longer shows the slowest growth (as it did in period one), and its western half continues to surge ahead, but the sluggish performance of Michigan and Ohio keep it well below the national average.

In period three, the northeast's slide (especially the Middle Atlantic) continues. The west northcentral more than doubles the growth of its eastern neighbor. The south continues its rise, though its growth is now clearly dominated by Texas and the rest of the west southcentral sub-region. Most remarkable however, is the flagging growth in the Pacific subregion, whose investment growth rate (dominated by California) drops below the national average for the first time in the study period. In contrast to this, the Mountain states emerge as the fastest growing subregion in the country.

The overall picture, then, is fairly consistent with the "frostbelt–sunbelt" typology advanced by others, but some important trends merit particular emphasis. The northeast exhibits continual decline, although New England is markedly its most buoyant subregion. The northcentral is also dichotomized, with a western half which does not rightly deserve to be grouped with the rest of the "frostbelt." The south's rise is continuous and is notable for both its very early beginnings and its balanced character (note how the dominant subregion shifts inward from the South Atlantic in period one, to the east southcentral in two, to the west southcentral – largely Texas – in three). The west is really two wests – one whose golden age may have passed, and another whose time is yet to come.

Given that the above discussion has been couched in terms of percentage growth of capital stocks, it is important to lend it some perspective by examining the extent to which the various growth rates reviewed above have altered the spatial distribution of manufacturing capital stocks during the study period. This information is provided in Table 14.3 for the four regions and nine subregions in each trough year of the national business cycle (again, excepting 1976).

This representation mutes somewhat the trends in percentage growth described earlier. For example, it is now evident that the seemingly meteoric growth of the west's Mountain states translates into an increase

Table 14.3 Capital stock percentage distribution by region and subregion.

State	1954	1961	1970	1976
Northeast	26.1	25.9	23.9	21.9
New England	5.4	5.6	5.5	5.1
Middle Atlantic	20.7	20.3	18.4	16.8
Northcentral	37.8	36.7	34.9	33.0
East northcentral	33.1	31.7	29.7	27.5
West northcentral	4.7	5.0	5.2	5.5
South	24.9	25.4	28.6	31.6
South Atlantic	10.0	11.0	12.6	13.4
East southcentral	4.7	5.0	6.0	6.4
West southcentral	10.2	9.4	10.0	11.8
West	11.1	12.0	13.0	13.1
Mountain	1.6	1.9	2.2	2.6
Pacific	9.5	10.0	10.8	10.5
USA*	100.0	100.0	100.0	100.0

* Totals may actually differ due to rounding.

in national share from 1.6% in 1954 to 2.6% in 1976. Nevertheless, the same overall pattern emerges. The northeast begins the period with 26% of total manufacturing capital and ends it with just under 22%. The south begins at 24.9% and finishes with 31.6%, surpassing the northeast in percent-share terms sometime in the mid-1960s. However, its rise is not without some volatility, particularly in the west southcentral subregion. The northcentral remains the most important manufacturing center throughout (going from 37.8% to 33.0%), although its claim to primacy by 1976 is only by virtue of the growth experienced in its western half. Since the major growth in the eastern subregion came in earlier periods, its capital stock must be aging relative to regions characterized by more recent growth. The west starts with 11.1% and climbs to 13.1%, but notably the Pacific subregion has declined from its 1970 high of 10.8% to 10.5% by 1976.

Interesting as it is, the foregoing analysis does not convey much information about any qualitative changes in production which might have occurred over this time. To provide some general notions about qualitative changes in total manufacturing over this period, we performed an analysis of state capital–labor ratios (in constant-dollar terms) for the same base years (see Gertler 1984a). This analysis revealed surprisingly low ratios in the northeast and high ratios in the south, especially in 1954. The northcentral region was higher on average than the northeast, though lower than the south, and the west was highest of all. Similarly, the overall rankings did not change in 1976. However, the northeast was the only region consistently to double in capital intensity over the study interval (with the exception of Pennsylvania), suggesting some convergence or even reversal in the long run. The emergent pattern was broadly consistent with the product–cycle model discussed by Rees (1979), Hansen (1980) and others, in that low-wage areas such as the south are characterized by relatively high capital intensities. However, the temporal trend toward increased capital intensity in the northeast may suggest that this region's dominance in research and development functions and technological innovation is declining. It may also suggest that entrepreneurs are replacing labor with capital so as to disenfranchise a chronically troublesome or militant workforce. However, without accounting for interregional differences in industry mix it is difficult to draw many solid conclusions from these data.

This problem was largely circumvented in a further analysis (see again Gertler 1984a) which focused on similar changes within each of the four individual industries, examined in a variety of different states and regions. Our examination of these four two-digit industries found more complex patterns. It was revealed that the more labor-intensive industries (textiles and apparel) had suffered the largest losses in the northeast and northcentral regions, while the more capital-intensive industries (fabricated metals and electrical and electronics equipment) continued to thrive and grow in these areas. It is this sectoral pattern which may be responsible for the observed increases in capital intensity in total manufacturing over this period. However, this may not be a purely sectoral phenomenon, as it has been noted that the remaining establishments in textiles in the north might also be becoming more capital intensive (Department of Commerce 1981).

Beyond the level of these generalities are some other interesting trends and occurrences. For example, the geography of growth in particular industries appears to be quite volatile when analyzed over three shorter subperiods. Regions that are in retrenchment and decline in one period may reverse this trend in the next. Some, such as the west, experience a halting and unsteady growth in most industries. Patterns such as these appear to be linked to technological development in products and process, although this was only hinted at in this analysis. It is also worth noting that the greatest unevenness of growth rates in capital formation appears to occur in the fastest and slowest growth industries (electrical equipment and textiles respectively).

The implications of these findings seem to echo the conclusions of Varaiya and Wiseman (1981) in their study of metropolitan capital formation. In short, the northeast and northcentral regions are still experiencing considerable capital accumulation. However, the restructuring within industries in these regions seems to be transforming production into more capital-intensive forms, with somewhat dire consequences for local employment (particularly for those with fewer skills). Such conclusions must be regarded as tentative at this stage, pending our investigation of the motivating forces behind investment and the qualitative changes accompanying regional capital accumulation presented in the next chapter.

However, we are interested in one further dimension of each state's net investment experience for a given industry – namely, the degree of volatility or stability of capital accumulation (or decumulation) in each state and industry over our 23-year period. This issue is addressed in the following section.

Volatility of regional capital accumulation

Thus far we have not addressed directly the second and third questions posed in the previous section. Specifically, how steady or volatile is the process of capital formation in a particular region for a given industry? How does this volatility vary across places within the same industry? And how does this intra-industry variability also vary as we examine a number of different industries?

To answer these questions we employ a family of models developed by Box and Jenkins (1976), which are well adapted to analyzing and characterizing the fluctuations in univariate time-series data. In addition, the characterizations of the data which are rendered by these models are capable of imparting considerable information about the nature of the underlying process or system which generated the data. The essence of the approach lies in the characterization of time-series as relatively predictable or unpredictable processes based on a number of particular model types or components which may be fitted to the time-series data. Possible models include autoregressive (AR), moving average (MA) or mixed (ARMA) forms, with or without differencing to account for nonstationarity. (These model forms were formally defined in Chapter 10.)

Interpretation of the final model is relatively straightforward in the case of the $AR(p)$ form, in which current values of (in our case) capital formation are seen as being systematically related to recent past values of capital formation, at a strength which is reflected in the size of the autoregressive parameters ϕ_1, ϕ_2, . . ., ϕ_p. Such a model may be highly suggestive of the simple cumulative-causation scenario if the ϕ's are positive and relatively large, embodying the idea that, for a number of possible reasons, growth (decline) in a particular state or sector begets further growth (decline) in the same state or sector.

The simplest expression of this is the $AR(1)$ model, which is equivalent to a Markov process. Moreover, if a number of ϕ's are indeed significant, their time profile would provide a useful characterization of the degree of continuity or stability of capital formation over successive years for a given industry in a given locale. In the same vein, the occurrence of negatively valued ϕ's would reflect regular annual fluctuations in levels of capital formation in successive periods, suggesting frequent adjustment of investment plans in the face of regularly fluctuating demand.

Interpretation of $MA(q)$ terms in a potential model is somewhat more complex since the terms a_t, a_{t-1}, a_{t-2}, . . ., a_{t-q}, and their respective ϕ's reflect the importance of current and past random disturbances or shocks, originating either within or outside the local economy, on current levels of capital formation. Given the potential importance of isolated historical events on entrepreneurs' investment behavior (included here might be changes in defense spending, actions of the Federal Reserve Board which affect the cost of capital, other national and state fiscal policy changes, various events which influence investor confidence, the recent advent of new competitors locally, or the recent departure, downswing, or failure of a principal purchaser of output from a given sector), it would not be too surprising to find significant moving average terms in some of our models. Their occurrence would appear to undermine significantly the validity of a simple cumulative causation scenario and the stability or predictability which it implies, at least in the short run, while lending some credence to the Kaleckian image of the investment process in space.

Alternatively, one might speculate that smaller regions would be more strongly influenced by seemingly random events. For example, the closure of a single plant would scarcely be felt in New York but might amount to an event of major proportions in Rhode Island (or Arkansas, to where its capital might have been diverted). Furthermore, one could speculate that those industries which are more sensitive to movements of the business cycle (the two durable-goods industries in our analysis) ought to exhibit more variable investment behavior in the short run (although arguably such behavior might display a regular cyclical character when observed over longer periods). At the very least, the presence of moving average components would seem to emphasize the importance of current and past occurrences which are not explicitly modeled in the univariate case and which are worthy of further direct investigation.

With the above in mind, a univariate analysis of the capital formation series for each industry in each state (74 series in all) was performed. The first difference of the capital stock series was employed (a) so as to highlight the role of adjustment, and (b) because of the nonstationary trends evident in state capital stocks over time. A summary of results of the analysis is presented in Table 14.4, which shows the order of model which was estimated for individual states for each of the four industries. Further detailed estimation results are provided in Gertler (1984a). As a general prefatory comment, it is worth noting that all models were of a relatively low order; in all but one case (Arkansas electrical equipment), p, d, and q are equal to 1 or 0. This is in part due to the shortness of the series, since the confidence intervals for accepting parameters as significantly different from zero become successively more stringent as the lag (k) of the prospective AR or MA term increases.

In order to lend some structure to the analysis of 74 time-series models, the results reported here were organized according to the growth characteristics of the capital stock in each state–industry combination. Organization of the results utilized a set of growth categories into which states were grouped. Note that for all industries except textiles, fast-growth states were those which grew by 200% or more between 1954 and 1976, medium-growth states grew between 100% and 200% over this period, and slow-growth states failed to double their capital stock in 23 years. For textiles, fast growth was deemed to be in excess of 150%, medium growth was from zero to 150%, and slow "growth" covered those states which suffered absolute decline over this period.

Table 14.4 presents the states thus categorized and the type of order of model which was identified and estimated for each one. Gertler (1984a) reports the same classification for the actual parameters estimated for each state–industry series. From Table 14.4 it can be seen that textiles was dominated by AR(1) models, particularly in fast- and medium-growth states. Notable exceptions include South Carolina (MA(1)) and Texas

Table 14.4 Model type and order by growth category and industry.

Growth category	Textiles	Apparel	Fabricated metals	Electrical equipment
Fast	Ark ARI(1,1,0)	NC ARIMA(1,1,1)	Geo IMA(0,1,1)	Ark AR(2)
	Geo AR(1)	Tex AR(1)	Fla ARI(1,0,0)	Ala MA(1)
	Ken AR(1)	Ken ARI(1,1,0)	Miss IMA(0,1,1)	Cal ARMA(1,1)
	NC AR(1)	Tenn AR(1)	Ala IMA(0,1,1)	Iowa ARIMA(1,1,1)
		Ala IMA(0,1,1)	Iowa IMA(0,1,1)	Mary AR(1)
		Miss AR(1)	Minn IMA(0,1,1)	Mich IMA(0,1,1)
			Okla IMA(0,1,1)	
Medium	SC MA(1)	Cal ARIMA(1,1,1)	Ken AR(1)	Ind MA(1)
	Ala AR(1)	Mo MA(1)	Tenn ARMA(1,1)	NY AR(1)
	Vir AR(1)	Penn AR(1)	Wash IMA(0,1,1)	Ohio AR(1)
	Tenn AR(1)	Mary WN	Kan AR(1)	Ill MA(1)
	Tex ARMA(1,1)		Mich ARIMA(1,1,1)	Wis AR(1)
			Ind ARMA(1,1)	NH AR(1)
			Cal AR(1)	
			Ohio IMA(0,1,1)	
			Conn AR(1)	
			Mass MA(1)	
Slow	Ohio ARIMA(1,1,1)	NJ MA(1)	Ill IMA(0,1,1)	Mo AR(1)
	NJ RW	Ill AR(1)	Mo AR(1)	RI MA(1)
	NY ARIMA(1,1,1)	NY AR(1)	NJ MA(1)	Penn AR(1)
	Penn AR(1)	Mass MA(1)	Wis AR(1)	Conn AR(1)
	Conn ARIMA(1,1,1)		Ore MA(1)	NJ AR(1)
	Mass AR(1)		NY AR(1)	
	Mne AR(1)		WVir AR(1)	
			RI MA(1)	
			Mary IMA(0,1,1)	
			Penn AR(1)	

Notes
States are listed in order of overall capital stock growth rates. RW – Random walk. WN – White noise.

(ARMA(1,1)). Furthermore, all AR parameters were positive in these two categories except for Arkansas, for which $\phi = -0.5317$. Interestingly, Arkansas also registered the fastest overall growth in textiles and was the only fast- or medium-growth state to require further differencing due to nonstationarity. The slow-growth (actual decline) states in textiles exhibit more complex structures in more than half the cases. Ohio, New York and Connecticut are all ARIMA(1,1,1) while New Jersey's series is best characterized as a random walk. Furthermore, the autoregressive terms for New York and Connecticut are negative, implying strong volatility in net investment in successive years.

The relative absence of moving average terms in the models estimated for textiles may be indicative of the mature phase in which the industry generally finds itself, and perhaps the relative isolation from short-run fluctuations of the business cycle when compared to the other industries analyzed here. Random shocks appear to be most important in the declining states, which also happen to be in the northeast or northcentral regions of the country. Hence, in contrast to areas experiencing rapid net investment in textiles (which were characterized by a relative smoothness over time), declining areas exhibit considerable instability and volatility. This may indicate that such areas (undoubtedly possessing much older capital) feel the major brunt of cyclical downturns and shocks emanating from restructuring within the industry, since their productive capacity is older and possibly less efficient. Conceivably, if northern workforces are paid higher wages on average, this may contribute further to the lack of efficiency of these plants, given that with older capital they are likely to be less productive. Alternatively, if the prevalence of union contracts enforces rigidities in wages, employment, or hours worked, then cyclical down-turns are more likely to impact capital expenditure plans negatively than if the flexibility of the labor input was greater.

The pattern evident within the textiles industry does not materialize to the same extent for the apparel industry. Most of the fast-growth states possess an AR(1) term within their model. However, North Carolina turns out to be an ARIMA(1,1,1) and Alabama is best characterized by an integrated shock model – that is, IMA(0,1,1). Similarly, Kentucky dis-plays a negative AR(1) parameter, indicating that significant volatility has accompanied its fast growth. The medium-growth states exhibit a variety of models, such as they did in textiles, although Maryland's series was found to be statistically equivalent to white noise (no apparent pattern), and California's AR parameter is negative. Unlike the textiles group, the slow-growth states in apparel all exhibit relatively simple time-series structures – two AR(1)s, and two MA(1s) – including New Jersey, New York and Massachusetts, which were also slow-growth states in textiles. This suggests the need to distinguish between absolute decline (an appa-rently complex process) and slow growth or relative decline.

One possible explanation for apparel's distinct behavior in the fast-growth states is that every state in this group exhibits growth rates which are higher than the highest growth rate achieved in textiles. Hence, they are both quantitatively and qualitatively distinct from the fast-growth group in textiles. Moreover, as earlier analysis showed (Gertler 1984a), all of these states began with very small stocks of capital at the start of this period, and would be more vulnerable to the kind of exogenous shocks discussed earlier.

The simplicity evident in the models of the slow-growth states may be in part related to the low capital-intensity of the apparel industry overall, in that changing conditions of demand will be accommodated to a far greater extent in the labor input than in adjustment to capital. However, the presence of MA(1) models in New Jersey and Massachusetts suggests that capital formation in apparel is not entirely immune to cyclical fluctuations.

The fabricated metals industry displays an interesting pattern which is again distinct from the first two industries. Its fast-growth states exhibit remarkable uniformity, in that six out of seven are integrated moving average models, that is, driven by a previous random shock. The exception – Florida – has been shown elsewhere to be consistently atypical in terms of its time-series structure, and, notably, its autoregressive parameter is negative here, suggesting considerable volatility from year to year. The middle group of states exhibits a wide variety of model structures – AR, MA, ARMA, IMA, and ARIMA – with no apparent pattern. Meanwhile, the slow-growth states again exhibit simple structures: half are AR(1) and the other half are MA(1) or IMA(0,1,1).

The preponderance of MA terms throughout this industry may attest to the fact that this industry and its constituent subsectors comprise one of the most classic capital goods industries in manufacturing over the period, only exceeded perhaps by the machine tool industries for SIC 35. Given that it sells the overwhelming proportion of its production to other manufacturers, one would indeed expect this industry to exhibit a highly volatile and irregular profile over time. The interesting aspect of our results is the prevalence of volatile unpredictability in all growth categories, but especially in the fastest growing states. An examination of data given in Gertler (1984a) revealed that all states in this latter category began the period with very small capital stocks (1% or less of the nation's total), suggesting again that small size and volatility go hand-in-hand. However, the two largest states in terms of initial shares (Illinois and Ohio) both possess MA terms in their models, perhaps reminding us again of the volatility inherent throughout this industry.

Finally we come to electrical and electronic equipment. In this industry there was a predominance of AR(1) models in the slow- and medium-growth states (not unlike the labor-intensive apparel industry), with an increasing number of MA models or terms in the latter group. The fast-growth group demonstrates more complexity, with mixed processes and MA terms prevalent. When compared to fabricated metals, however, this group is somewhat more stable on the whole. Hence, while fast-growth states in electronics exhibit some of the cyclical sensitivity of classic capital-goods industries (much of which stems from fluctuations in government demand), this effect seems to be balanced by a general buoyancy which has given this industry the fastest overall growth rate of the four industries. Even relatively unimportant states with small initial shares such as Arkansas, Maryland and New Hampshire still manage to exhibit fairly smooth growth, as evidenced by the AR structure of their capital formation.

There is little direct evidence of the technological restructuring known to be occurring in this industry over the study period, such as the transition from analog to digital technology within the telephone industry or the disappearance of the electron tube (SIC 3671). It is plausible that this factor may have been expressed as random shocks in the estimated models. If so, then one might expect to see MA terms in both the slowest- and fastest-growth states. However, the lack of such terms in the slow-growth group again suggests that expansion and the qualitative changes which accompany it generate a time-series realization which is qualitatively distinct from that of relative decline.

What then of the validity of our competing theoretical conceptions? If one equates a simple autoregressive structure (AR or ARI) having positive ϕ with a cumulative-causative process, then this scenario is evident in 34 of 74 state–industry series analyzed. These cases are most prevalent within the two labor-intensive industries (textiles and apparel) and the slower-growth states within fabricated metals and electrical equipment. However, other more complex forms (including MA models, mixed models and AR terms with negative parameters) abound. For example, in fabricated metals, a classic capital goods industry, rapid growth was exclusively characterized by such structures. Given its inability to describe successfully more than half of the cases studied, one must question the use of this conception as a general model of regional investment dynamics.

Nevertheless, one must acknowledge the possibility of short-run instability (a nonautoregressive process) coinciding with a long-run growth path which is stable overall. Presumably, investment in a given industry and state could exhibit a rough and unpredictable temporal structure without experiencing an overall reversal relative to other states' growth rates. This line of reasoning would suggest the need to distinguish between short-run and long-run cumulative causation.

Our earlier descriptive profiles of each industry suggested a number of growth-trend reversals within the cases examined. A more direct analysis of this phenomenon is provided in Table 14.5, in which capital growth rates for each state–industry are compared to the national average growth rate within the relevant industry for the same three periods studied previously. Faced with the task of defining "regional reversal" in the present context, our earlier analysis suggests the need for an indicator which compares changes in *relative* growth rates across states, since few states (with the exception of textiles producers) showed *absolute* decline in their capital stocks. Consequently, we have chosen to define "reversal" as a situation in which a state's capital growth rate is greater (less) than the national industry average during one time period, and less (greater) than the national rate in the next period. The occurrence of such a reversal (or possibly two, given that we are examining three separate time periods) would suggest that a cumulative process was not at work, and would be indicated by a change in consecutive signs in Table 14.5.

This table reveals a number of interesting findings pertaining to a variety of the rival theoretical conceptions which we have discussed earlier. To begin with, we find that at least one reversal (as defined above) has occurred in 40 of 74 cases examined. Of the remaining 34 cases, 15 exhibit nonautoregressive processes. Hence, according to our long-run definition, cumulative causality is absent in 40 cases (54%), and 15 of the remaining 34 cases fail to show cumulative causality in the short-run sense. Only 19 cases are cumulative processes in both the short- and the long-run.

One might expect the catastrophe theorist to seize upon these reversals as reflections of the functional discontinuity which is thought to underlie interregional investment dynamics. By this judgment, the catastrophe model would be supported in those 40 cases experiencing reversal. However, our assessment of this model must be tempered by three additional insights. First, 9 of the same 40 state–industries also experienced a second reversal during our study period. Secondly, in 27 of those same 40 cases, the reversals which occurred were in the opposite direction to that which one might expect based on the simple frostbelt (northeast, northcentral)–sunbelt (south, west) dichotomy whose development prompted the original formulation of the catastrophe model by Casetti (1981a). Thirdly, of the 31 state–industries which reversed only once, 21 exhibit complex time-series structures, including such large entities as South Carolina textiles, California apparel and Michigan electrical/electronic equipment.

Finally, the Kaleckian conception of a volatile, uneven and unpredictable local investment dynamic would seem to be reflected in those state–industries exhibiting the more complex time-series structures discussed earlier (again, 40 of 74 cases). It would also be consistent with a longer-run growth scenario which saw one or more reversals during the full study period, although it is important to note that Kalecki himself (1971) conceived of the "long run" as but the sum of many short-run changes which embody the behavior of entrepreneurs in an environment of uncertainty.

Table 14.5 Relative regional growth trend reversals for four industries, 1954–60, 1961–9, and 1970–6.

Textiles					Apparel					Fabricated metals					Electrical/electronic				
TR[1]	State	I[2]	II	III	TR[1]	State	I[2]	II	III	TR[1]	State	I[2]	II	III	TR[1]	State	I[2]	II	III
	Mne[3]	−	−	−	1	Mass	+	−	−	1	Mass	−	−	+*	1	NH[3]	+	−	−
	Mass[3]	−	−	−		NY[3]	−	−	−	1	RI	−	−	+*	1	RI	−	+*	+
	Conn	−	−	−	1	NJ	+	−	−	1	Conn[3]	+	+	−		Conn[3]	−	−	−
1	NY	−	−	+*	1	Penn[3]	+	+	−	1	NY[3]	−	−	+*	1	NY[3]	−	+*	+
1	NJ	−	−	+*		Ill[3]	−	−	−	1	NJ	−	−	+		NJ[3]	−	−	−
	Penn[3]	−	−	+		Mo	−	−	−		Penn[3]	−	−	−		Penn[3]	−	−	−
	Ohio	−	−	−	2	Mary	−	+	−*		Ohio	+	−*	+	1	Ohio[3]	+	+	−
2	Vir[3]	+	−*	−		NC	+	+	+	1	Mich	−	−	+	1	Mich	−	+*	+
	NC[3]	+	+	+		Ken	+	+	−*	2	Ind	+	−	+*	1	Ind	−	+*	+*
1	SC	+	+	−*	1	Tenn[3]	+	+	+	1	Ill	+	−	−	2	Ill	+	−	−
	Geo[3]	+	+	+		Ala	+	+	+	2	Wis[3]	−	+*	−	1	Wis[3]	+	−	+
2	Ken[3]	+	−*	−*		Miss[3]	+	+	+		Minn	+	+	+	1	Iowa	−	+*	−
1	Tenn[3]	+	+	−	1	Tex[3]	+	+	+		Iowa	+	+	+		Mo[3]	+	−	+
	Ala[3]	+	+	+		Cal	−	−	+		Mo[3]	−	−	−	2	Mary[3]	+	−*	−
	Ark	+	+	+						1	Kan[3]	−	+*	+	1	Ala	−	+	+
1	Tex	+	+	−*							Mary	−	−	−		Ark[3]	+	+	+

TR[1]				Cal
				+
				+
				+
1	WVir[3]	−	−	−	+
	Geo	+	+	+
	Fla	+	+	+
2	Ken[3]	−	+	+
	Tenn	+	+	−*
1	Ala	+	+	+
2	Miss	+	−*	−*
	Okla	+	+	+
1	Wash	−	−	+
	Ore	−	−	−
1	Cal[3]	+	+	−*

Notes

[1] TR denotes the number of trend reversals during the study period. Trend reversal is indicated by a change in consecutive signs.

[2] Periods are I 1954–60, II 1961–9, III 1970–6. A positive (negative) sign indicates a capital growth rate greater (less) than the national average for the industry.

[3] State capital series is autoregressive (AR or ARI) with positive parameter.

* Denotes an "unexpected" reversal, as dictated by a simple "frostbelt/sunbelt" dichotomy.

Conclusions

At the outset of this chapter we posed a number of questions relating to the form and structure of regional capital formation in space and time. Given the novelty of the data, we were interested in describing the basic dimensions of this process. More importantly, however, we were also interested in illuminating the short-run temporal structure of capital formation for a variety of industries in a variety of states. Our subsequent analysis sought to determine the validity of the smooth growth (decline) scenario envisioned by a simple cumulative-causation theory, or alternative conceptions in which (for varying reasons) one might expect capital formation to be volatile, unstable and discontinuous. We were also interested in the extent of intra-industry variability, as expressed in the different temporal structures observed for different states in the same industry. Similarly, we sought to determine whether or not some industries might be more internally homogeneous than others.

Our industry profiles and time-series analysis clearly showed that much variability exists within particular industries, as expressed in the growth experiences and time-series structure of capital formation in different states. While much of our interpretation remains tentative subject to further analysis, it was suggested that this variability might be a function of the particular past history of a given industry in a certain place. For example, the same industries exhibited rather different temporal structures in areas where they were growing and declining. Similarly, it appeared that relative decline (i.e. slow real growth) might be structurally distinct from absolute decline (negative real growth). It was also noted that areas with relatively smaller total capital stocks had a tendency to be more vulnerable to random disturbances than areas possessing larger quantities of capital, although this effect was far from systematic and was by no means universal. The overall impression gained from this analysis was that the same industry might very well "mean different things" for different places. While some of this variability might stem from the prevalence of different subsectors of a given industry in different places (i.e. a compositional effect), the extent of variability within relatively homogeneous sectors such as textiles and apparel suggest that other explanations, based perhaps on the differing age, embodied technology, and productivity of the capital stock, might be more important. Overall, one is left with the impression that the traditional "industry mix" approach to urban and regional analysis will be of little use in helping us to understand regional investment patterns over the business cycle.

The concept of cumulative causation does not appear to be a viable construct in the current endeavor, whether one attempts to define it in short- or long-run terms. Furthermore, the insights emanating from the previous section would seem to stretch the credibility of a simple catastrophe model in the current analysis. While it might serve as a useful heuristic device for helping us to appreciate the potential for rapid change within regional systems (one of the few conceptions which is explicitly couched in dynamic terms), its conception of regional investment seems overly caricaturized in the context of the short-run timescale employed in this investigation. One suspects that its reliance on a specific and lifeless "marginal productivity of regional capital" function renders the model overly mechanistic (on this matter, see Gertler 1986a). The results of our empirical analysis suggest support for a discontinuous and unpredictable regional investment process in the tradition of Kalecki. This finding is, however, subject to further empirical analysis.

We are left, then, with a view of the capital formation process which sees it as the outcome of a complex interaction between an industry in a given place and time and the particular characteristics of that place (as embodied in its present and its past history). However, our analysis thus far has been unable to probe directly into the characteristics of place which most directly impinge on the investment decisions of entrepreneurs. Nor have we corroborated either the neoclassical or structuralist view of this process as introduced earlier. These tasks await us in the following chapter.

15 *Capital, labor, and regional dynamics*

Introduction

In the preceding chapters we have argued that the location decision and the investment decision (incorporating considerations of choice of technology) ought to be viewed as inextricably linked. In doing so, the location decision acquires new significance as a key element in a "bottom-up" view of the investment process, rather than being relegated to secondary status after questions of total national investment have been decided.

It is the aim of this chapter to explore the investment decision in its spatial context, and actively to seek relationships between regional investment, technological change, and the distribution of income between profits and wages. In the next section we briefly review some of the basic determinants of investment as suggested by various theoretical perspectives, both spatial and nonspatial. We conclude this discussion with the articulation of a simple operational model of regional investment which is subjected to empirical verification in the following section. The chapter concludes with a consideration of capital's relationship to labor in regional production. Here we examine the impact of regional wage rates on investment and technological change, as well as considering the impact of growth rates and technology on the intra-regional distribution of income. Thus we come full circle by returning to the unified analysis of regional capital and labor which we began in Part I of this book.

Profits and regional growth

Investment comprises the act of allocating liquid financial resources toward the purchase of a physical asset capable of producing output when combined with labor. Over the years, different strands of economic theory have advanced a variety of explanations for the motivations which prompt investment (see Ch. 13). All approaches share the common belief that producers invest in order to make – perhaps optimize – their profit.

296

However, each conception varies as to the specific process which ultimately produces the investment in fixed capital.

A major theme in contemporary studies of investment behavior is the stimulating effect that increasing demand exerts over the decision to invest, particularly when production is at or near the technical capacity of the firm or industry in question. This relationship forms the heart of the well known accelerator concept, in which net investment is deemed to be determined by recent past changes in output (Jorgenson 1971) as mediated by some form of lagged response function (Koyck 1954). Here output is regarded as a surrogate for demand, and it has functioned well as a predictor of investment at the national level (Clark 1979). The few regional applications which do exist (largely within the sphere of regional econometric models) often rely on national rather than local accelerators to drive their investment functions. And although Airov proposed a regional adaptation of the accelerator mechanism as long ago as 1963, this model has never been fully or conclusively tested as being an accurate representation of the regional investment process.

If one regards the national investment series as a sum of many component regional series, it is quite plausible that the process of summation across space might obscure the volatility inherent in each of the individual regional series, so that adjustment and lag structures which adequately "explain" national investment may not be appropriate for the analysis of any single state or region. Furthermore, if some portion of regional demand is satisfied by imports from other regions, or if some proportion of regional production is exported to markets in other regions, then demand within a given region (hence future investment) may bear no direct relation to lagged output in that region (Nadji & Harris 1984).

Although the accelerator theory of investment is normally considered to be part of the standard Keynesian apparatus, it should be noted that this concept predates Keynes (Clark 1917) and that Keynes himself and his disciples took a somewhat different view of the investment process (Keynes 1936). They conceived of investment as being motivated by the "animal spirits" of entrepreneurs – a euphemism for the multitude of factors which interact in a complex way to shape investors' perceptions of profitability conditions in the future. While aggregate demand plays a key role in this process, its exact relationship to the formulation of expectations and investment plans by entrepreneurs is believed to be only incompletely captured by the simple notion of the output accelerator (Robinson 1962).

In addition to the accelerator and the idea of "animal spirits," a third major conception of investment within the economics literature emerges from the work of Marx. In this view, the owners of capital, faced with the choice of enjoying their wealth through consumption or reinvesting it in physical machinery, will be induced by competitive pressure to choose the latter option. By reinvesting, capitalists can implement technological innovations which may confer upon them some temporary competitive advantage. The net result is "accumulation for accumulation's sake" (Marx, quoted in Harvey 1982: 29). Furthermore, with the introduction of money, credit and a fully fledged financial system, capitalists will divert their liquid assets to those opportunities which offer the highest rate of profit. Finally, capitalists possess an underlying incentive to disenfranchise labor from the production process through capital intensification, so as to gain control of the social relations which surround production. This desire is tempered somewhat by threat of an underconsumption crisis when labor's aggregate income becomes too small to absorb the output which industry produces, as well as by other costs associated with technological change (see Harvey 1982: Ch. 4).

From the foregoing, it is apparent that all three conceptions of the investment process share a focus on expected profitability as the chief determinant of investment expenditures. It is also evident that there is very little within any of these characterizations to suggest why producers might invest in a particular location (and not others), a finding which is not surprising in light of the national orientation of these theories.

In contrast to the "top-down" conception of regional investment outlined above, a number of scholars have recently espoused a "bottom-up" approach in which the location and timing of investment (and hence output) are determined simultaneously with decisions concerning employment and overall production technology. In this view, the investment decision can only be understood in a place-specific context (Massey 1978b). Spatial variations in the rate of investment are likely to depend not only on variations in "factor prices" such as wage rates, but also on any extant qualitative differences in the labor market and employment relationships of different localities (Clark 1981a). Of key importance here are characteristics such as the quantity of available labor of particular skill levels, the degree of organization or militance amongst local workers, and the degree of bargaining power possessed by labor relative to the owners of productive capacity (Bluestone & Harrison 1982). These variables are likely to be shaped by the past histories of production, employment and social relations in each community (Scott 1982, Pred 1984).

Implicit in this "bottom-up" perspective is a strong supply-side orientation, in which local investment is primarily a function of differential production conditions from place to place. Clearly, there is an implicit assumption that the cost of transporting output to the market is either insignificant or varies too little from place to place to be of major importance in the locational cost calculus of the firm. An equally plausible presumption is that individual production establishments are increasingly integrated into large national or international multilocational organizations characterized by a spatial division of labor (Pred 1977) within which demand-side considerations are eclipsed by local labor market characteristics in the locational decision (Walker & Storper 1981).

When contrasted against the aspatial theories of investment reviewed earlier, the above perspective appears less mechanistic than the output accelerator concept, and seems to give considerable form to Keynes' somewhat amorphous "animal spirits," suggesting the kind of supply-side considerations which might shape investors' perceptions of the local climate for investment. From a modeling point of view, these considerations (and, logically, demand-side considerations as well) could be generally subsumed by local trends in profitability – recent past changes in the level or rate of local profits – as an aggregate, "bottom-line" reflection of this multitude of influences. However, this relationship has not been tested empirically.

There are at least two other supply-side factors which might have considerable influence over the pace of investment in particular locations. First, Kalecki (1937), Meyer and Kuh (1957), and others have emphasized the importance of internal liquidity (largely retained earnings) at the national scale in enabling the realization of entrepreneurs' investment plans. As Kalecki (1937: 109) himself has put it, "The most important requisite for becoming an entrepreneur is the ownership of capital." This holds true because internal funds constitute (a) a readily accessible pool of potential equity capital over which the firm has virtually autonomous control, and (b) a source of collateral and security with which to obtain external financing (both equity and debt) at more favorable terms.

The importance of finance capital in stimulating urban and regional development has received considerable attention lately in the United States and Canada and has been touted by many as a key policy instrument for generating jobs and income in declining areas (Litvak & Daniels 1979, Meyer et al. 1980, Vaughan 1980a, Mackness 1984). At the regional scale, only L'Esperance (1981b) has incorporated such considerations into an operational model of regional investment, in the form of his "internally generated funds," profits and depreciation allowances (applied to the manufacturing sector of Ohio). This conception has not been fully tested for a variety of industries and regions.

The second additional factor influencing local investment is the spatial distribution of pre-existing capital stock. Our review of the pertinent literature in Chapters 13 and 14 uncovered a fundamental lack of consensus regarding the impact of existing capital stock on current and future investment plans. Regional theories of cumulative causation, based on the works of Myrdal (1957), Hirschman (1958) and Kaldor's revival of Verdoorn (Kaldor 1970; see also Richardson 1973), postulate a positive, self-reinforcing process whereby growth in capital begets further growth in capital. Recent catastrophe models of regional capital accumulation conceive of a process of smooth short-run growth which ultimately leads to sudden, one-time shifts of investment – presumably to greener, more profitable pastures (Casetti 1981a, 1981b, Miernyk 1982). Finally, Kalecki (1943), Klein (1950), Goodwin (1951) and others have contended that, at least in the short run, the existing capital stock will exert a negative influence on current capital formation (net of depreciation) at the national level.

In contrast to the first two models, the latter theory suggests a highly dynamic, rapidly fluctuating investment process in time. Entrepreneurs respond in overly optimistic fashion to upswings in demand by (in collectivity) overinvesting in productive capacity. Hence they are induced to restrict investment spending in the next period in the hopes that eventually the demand for their output will more closely match their capacity to produce. Presumably, in periods of downswing the same process operates in reverse order. Firm owners respond to declining demand by cutting investment spending or, in extreme cases, "laying off" capital stock. However, their eagerness to do so, in isolation from other producers, may result in an excessive reduction in capacity which, in the next period, induces significant reinvestment. The existence of excess capacity prior to upturns and the possibility of temporarily underutilizing capital (and laying off labor) in downturns provides a dampening mechanism which presumably mutes the amplitude of fluctuations in the total capital stock over the business cycle.

A simple model of regional investment

The preceding discussion highlighted the role of three major factors in the determination of local rates of capital accumulation: the social and economic conditions for local production, the supply of available savings with which to finance investment expenditure, and the pre-existing stock of local or regional capital. We have already suggested that the first factor may be represented by the recent past changes in profits generated by local production. While such a measure suffers from the problem of obscuring those specific conditions or historical events which might actually transpire in particular locales to determine the profitability of local production, it nevertheless serves as a useful aggregate measure for a "first-cut" analysis of spatial investment trends.

The second factor is somewhat more problematic, given the highly developed organizational forms and financial systems which facilitate the transference of finance capital from one location to another. Nevertheless, with the importance attributed to internally generated retained earnings by the authors reviewed in the previous section, one might at least wish to test the hypothesis that local investment will increase when the past surplus generated from local production is large. To capture this effect, one might utilize the level of profit generated by local production as one representation of the supply of available finance.

The third factor, previously invested capital, would appear to be rather simply introduced into an empirical analysis of local investment. However, the determination of a value for fixed capital, expressed in some *numéraire* capable of representing a diverse range of specific capital goods, has proved to be particularly difficult for both theoretical and methodological reasons (Robinson 1979, Miller 1983). We shall return to this theme in the description of data which follows.

Based upon the above, the model of regional net investment (ΔK_t) estimated here can be simply expressed as:

$$\Delta K_t = f(\Delta P_{t-n}, P_{t-1}, K_{t-1}) \qquad (15.1)$$

where P_{t-1} denotes profit generated from immediately past regional production, K_{t-1} denotes the pre-existing regional capital stock, and n reflects the number of past time periods over which local profit trends (ΔP) might influence current investment decisions. It should be noted that the model as formulated bears a strong resemblance to Kalecki's (1943) earlier model of national investment (now adopted by most "post-Keynesian" economists), in which profit change is proposed as a more viable alternative to the traditional output accelerator. Furthermore, it is consistent with the recent suggestion by others, working in the spatial realm, that "regional investment decisions along with other production decisions are made in response to regional profit conditions" (Nadji & Harris 1984: 273).

Thus, the factors discussed earlier would lead us to expect a positive and significant relationship between net investment (ΔK) and past changes in profit (ΔP). Similarly, the finance and savings theories discussed earlier would hypothesize a strong positive relationship between current ΔK and past levels of profit (P_{t-1}), while a weak relationship might suggest either the greater importance of external (national) public capital markets as a source of financing, or the existence of intra-firm but inter-state transfers of finance capital. One would expect the latter effect to be more likely to the extent that (a) the industry in question exhibited relatively concentrated ownership patterns, accompanied by the multilocational organization of production, and (b) the region in question was relatively small (thereby increasing the possibility of such extra-regional transfers). Finally, cumulative-causation theorists, strictly interpreted, would predict a positive relationship between ΔK_t and K_{t-1}, while the Kaleckian theory of capital stock adjustment would predict a negative relationship here.

The analysis presented in this chapter utilizes the same capital series for the four different industries (fabricated metals, electrical and electronic equipment, textiles, and apparel) which were analyzed in Chapter 14. This strategy offers the advantage of minimizing the influence of spatial variations in the sectoral composition of manufacturing ("industry mix") on local investment activity, while at the same time providing sufficient intersectoral variety to illuminate potentially interesting differences between sectors. Furthermore, because separate time-series are available for a number of states within each industry, some of the diversity of regional experience, which common sense and recent theoretical formulations (Massey 1978b) suggest ought to exist, can be captured. Hence, we are freed from the necessity to estimate models in spatial cross section, a practice which would result in the derivation of an "average" relationship across all areas. Finally, because we are seeking to explore causal relationships between regional net investment and the various explanatory variables discussed above, a dynamic time-series modeling strategy is more helpful in allowing directions of causality in a temporal sense to be ascertained.

For the analysis at hand we utilize a maximum–likelihood generalized least squares (GLS) method to estimate multivariate time-series regression models for each of the 74 state–industry cases introduced in the last chapter. The method, which is due to Beach and MacKinnon (1978), offers an efficient, two–stage estimation routine for time-series regression models when the residuals resulting from the fitting of a standard OLS regression model exhibit first–order autocorrelation, as is frequently true in time-series analysis. The basic model to be estimated is:

$$\Delta K_t = b_0 + b_1 \, \Delta P_{t-n} + b_2 \, P_{t-1} + b_3 \, K_{t-1} + u_t \qquad (15.2)$$

where b_0, b_1, b_2, and b_3 are parameters to be estimated, u_t is the disturbance term which is systematically related to its past value by the autoregressive parameter ρ as in:

$$u_t = \rho u_{t-1} + \epsilon_t \qquad (15.3)$$

and ϵ_t is an independent, normally distributed random variable with zero mean and constant variance. Using the Beach and MacKinnon procedure, the model becomes:

$$\Delta K_t - \rho \Delta K_{t-1} = b_0(1 - \rho) + b_1(\Delta P_{t-n} - \rho \Delta P_{t-n-1})$$

$$+ \, b_2(P_{t-1} - \rho P_{t-2}) + b_3(K_{t-1} - \rho K_{t-2}) + \epsilon_t \qquad (15.4)$$

The dependent variable for the current analysis, regional net investment, was derived by taking the first difference of the capital stock series for a given state and industry. It thus represents the annual accretions to a region's stock of capital, net of retirements and depreciation occurring within that year. The "inherited" capital stock variable is simply a lagged value of the state–industry capital stock. Regional (state) profit for a given industry (and its past change) was estimated from the Census and Annual Survey of Manufactures using an approach employed by Alonso (1971), Engle (1974) and others, in which the total annual wage and salary bill for both production and nonproduction workers in a given state–industry is subtracted from value-added (all converted to 1972 dollars using industry-specific producer-price indices supplied by the Bureau of Labor Statistics). This estimate of profit income should be regarded as a kind of flow of funds to producers, since it is still gross of corporate taxes, depreciation and other charges such as purchased services and equipment rental. To the extent that these charges are spatially invariant as a proportion of total production costs, their inclusion will consistently though slightly over-state gross profits.

Prior to the actual estimation of the investment model for each industry in each state, a specific choice of lag for the profit change variable was required. This lag selection was achieved through a cross-correlation analysis of net investment and profit change for each of the four industries. The aim was to allow the number of lags or leads in the relationship between investment and changes in profit to be unconstrained in order to determine at which lags significant correlations occurred. This analysis was carried out in aggregate for each of the four industries by summing the relevant state series to obtain quasi-national totals (remembering that our original sample excluded a number of states in each industry due to lack of data). The results, shown in Table 15.1, indicate significant positive lags

Table 15.1 Cross-correlation functions of investment (t) and changes in profit ($t + n$).

Lag/lead (n)	Textiles (ΔP_{t+n})	Apparel (ΔP_{t+n})	Fabricated metals (ΔP_{t+n})	Electrical (ΔP_{t+n})
−7	0.146	0.091	0.034	−0.014
−6	0.071	0.137	0.060	0.130
−5	0.023	0.109	0.029	0.206
−4	0.012	0.076	0.193	0.038
−3	−0.055	0.087	−0.024	−0.108
−2	0.131	0.155	0.373	0.229
−1	0.379	0.089	0.598*	0.611*
0	0.155	−0.022	0.234	−0.002
1	−0.219	−0.125	−0.458	−0.214
2	−0.137	−0.118	−0.029	−0.174
3	−0.138	−0.189	0.062	0.048
4	−0.102	−0.180	0.078	−0.036
5	−0.050	−0.223	−0.130	−0.119
6	0.005	−0.292	−0.199	−0.123
7	−0.066	−0.132	0.030	−0.106

* Denotes significance at 0.05 level. Values given for individual lags represent strength of association (r) between net investment and profit change at each lag.

at $t - 1$ for fabricated metals and electrical and electronic products, and suggest a positive lag at $t - 1$ for textiles. Apparel does not exhibit any significant cross-correlation at any lag or lead, although this does not preclude the possibility of significant lags arising at the spatial scale of individual states.

The lag structures depicted by these cross-correlation functions represent empirical counterparts to the distributed-lag functions which are often imposed on such relationships on the grounds of *a priori* theoretical reasoning. However, as Maddala (1977) has pointed out, and as our analysis reveals, it is hazardous to assume the existence of a distributed lag where none exists. These lags, so derived, were incorporated into the models of state–industry net investment for estimation purposes, with experimentation required in the case of apparel lag choice.

Detailed results of the time-series regression analysis of each of the 74 state–industry series are presented by industry in Gertler (1986b). Information pertaining to significant variables in the entire analysis is summarized in Table 15.2. It is worth noting that the Durbin–Watson statistics reported indicate the successful removal of autoregressive autocorrelation in the residuals of 63 of the 74 estimated models. In the remaining 11 cases, the hypothesis of no autocorrelation could be neither conclusively confirmed nor denied.

In reviewing these results a number of generalities are immediately striking. First, lagged state profit levels emerge as a strong predictor of state net investment, with positive and significant coefficients in two-thirds (49) of the cases examined. This variable was particularly important in textiles and apparel, in which 81% and 77% respectively of those states analyzed showed lagged profits to be significant. It was also the most

Table 15.2 Number and percentage of states for which variables were significant.

	ΔP_{t-1}		P_{t-1}		K_{t-1}		
	+	−	+	−	+	−	R^2
textiles (16)*	11	1	13	0	1	8	12
	69%		81%			50%	75%
apparel (14)	5	0	11	0	0	6	6
	36%		79%			43%	43%
fabricated	8	1	14	0	3	15	16
metals (27)	30%		52%			56%	59%
electrical/	8	1	11	1	0	9	7
electronic (17)	47%		65%			53%	41%
total (74)	32	3	49	1	4	38	41
	43%		66%			51%	55%

* Figure in brackets denotes the number of states tested in each industry.

frequently significant explanatory variable for electrical and electronic equipment investment, with 11 out of 17 states (65%) exhibiting the hypothesized relationship.

For fabricated metals, slightly more than half of the states examined showed a positive and significant coefficient, while a number of states in the midwest, southern and western regions failed to show a significant impact of lagged profits on current investment expenditures. Hence, while the size of financial surplus generated by past local production appears to be a generally important determinant of subsequent capital accumulation, results for a number of states (notably in fabricated metals) also suggest the significance of inter-state profit flows or other external sources for the financing of local investment.

A second generalization concerns the profit change variable, whose coefficient was overwhelmingly positive as expected, but positive and significant in only 32 (or 43%) of the 74 cases. The success rate of this explanatory variable also ranged considerably, from a high of 70% in textiles to a low of 30% in fabricated metals. It generally performed well in the southern and western states (especially in the electrical and electronic sector) although this was clearly less true for the fabricated metals sector. The performance of profit change was also somewhat poorer for the northern states, and it is worth noting that Rhode Island, Michigan, Wisconsin (twice each) and New York (four times) all failed to produce significant results for this variable in every industry group for which these states were entered into the analysis.

Thirdly, and perhaps most striking of all, is the consistent significance of the "inherited" regional capital stock (K_{t-1}) in determining subsequent capital formation. This variable was significant in 42 of 74 cases, and in 38 of these 42 cases (51% overall) the sign of the coefficient was negative. Moreover, in the insignificant cases (not reported) the prevalence of the negative sign was equally as marked. It is interesting to note that three of the four positive and significant coefficients are found in southern states in fabricated metals (Florida, Alabama, and Oklahoma). Apart from these cases (plus the fourth, Pennsylvania textiles), the pre-existing state capital stock does not appear to exert the positive, self-reinforcing impact envisioned by the theories of "circular and cumulative causation," but seems to be much more in line with the Kaleckian conception of volatile short-run adjustment to capital as outlined earlier. Moreover, this holds true for cases as diverse as Maine textiles (whose capital stock actually declined by 46% over the study period), Illinois fabricated metals (whose stock grew by 98%, some 26 points below the national industry average growth), and California electrical and electronic (which grew by 556% over this period; see Chapter 14).

Finally, we note that our analysis produced adequate explanations of regional trends in capital accumulation (as indicated by a significant R^2

in 55% (41) of the 74 state–industry cases. The overall success rate varied somewhat, with textiles and fabricated metals recording rates of 75% and 59% respectively, while apparel and electrical and electronic were notably lower at 43% and 41% respectively. The relatively poor results for the apparel sector are undoubtedly related to the considerably lower importance of fixed capital in production in this labor-intensive industry. This would go some way toward explaining the irrelevance, for example, of K_{t-1} in 8 of the 14 states examined in this sector, since most adjustment of production inputs in the face of fluctuating costs or prices would occur through changes to the labor input. However, the same cannot be said of the electrical and electronic industry, which is considerably more capital intensive. Overall, past changes in profits appear to have exerted the positive influence on capital formation which was hypothesized in the earlier theoretical discussion, although their influence was seen to vary considerably from sector to sector. While these results could have been stronger, they were somewhat encouraging, considering that more complex forms of interregional interaction were not directly explored. The R^2 values obtained in this study (even in the significant cases alone) were for the most part lower than those usually attained for similar relationships at the national scale (Clark 1979). This result suggests that the regional units being studied here are less self-contained than an entire national economy, especially if capital is capable of moving with anything like the ease suggested by the radical and neoclassical theories reviewed in Chapter 13.

Ultimately, past changes in profit as employed in this analysis may serve as a reflection of the social and economic conditions of local production, but it is not a substitute for them. Further analyses at this and smaller spatial scales would probably benefit from a more detailed and explicit consideration of the social and political issues surrounding investment, disinvestment and technological and spatial change. As a very preliminary exploration of the interface between social process and the spatial dynamics of capital mobility, it is worthwhile to recall the reasonably strong negative correlation ($R^2 = 0.50$) between the 1953 unionized proportion of state labor force and state growth rates of fixed capital between 1954 and 1976 for one of our industries, textiles, which was noted in Chapter 3.

The consistent importance of past retained earnings and depreciation allowances in all regions and industries is perhaps the most significant finding as far as policy is concerned. If this variable is regarded as representing the pool of internal savings which is directly accessible to entrepreneurs wishing to reinvest, then these findings appear to offer strong support for the argument that the lack of financing on agreeable terms is a major impediment to the realization of firms' investment plans. These findings would also appear to support quite clearly Kalecki's maxim that the most important prerequisite for the accumulation of capital is the ownership of capital itself.

Finally, the above findings indicate rather unequivocally that, once we remove replacement investment from consideration and hold constant the accelerating effect of profits, the impact of pre-existing capital stock is negative in the short run. This result strongly implies the kind of turbulent adjustment process suggested by Kalecki, in which the local business cycle becomes a series of alternating over- and under-investment phases. The fact that this process was observed to be occurring in situations of absolute decline, relative decline, and relative growth suggests that both the cumulative-causation and catastrophe models are inappropriate for explaining regional investment trends in a temporally detailed way. Furthermore, this finding is consistent with the results presented in Chapter 14 which failed to substantiate the validity of either theory in both the short and the long run. The "reversals" which have occurred regionally over the study period seem to be the outcome of the accumulation of many small adjustments over time and the varying strength of these adjustments between regions, and do not exhibit the rapid shifts postulated by Casetti (1981a).

Indeed, our model of regional capital accumulation suggests that one can discern, conceptually and empirically, two distinctly antagonistic forces at work – one which exerts expansionary influence on regional growth and one which retards it. Taken together, they suggest that the resulting time-path of capital stock in a given region is the net result of these two opposite forces, thereby underlining that the mechanisms of growth and decline are not conceptually dissimilar or discontinuous. Of course, at the level of individual communities, the actions of a single dominant employer can have immediate and direct implications for local employment opportunities and multipliers which, due to the fixity and lumpiness of invested capital, may be perceived as being catastrophic in nature. Yet such abrupt external changes as plant shutdowns belie the possibility of more continuous internal reallocation of financial capital (past profits and depreciation allowances) between places but within the firm.

The foregoing analysis has, with the exceptions noted earlier, lent considerable support to the "bottom-up" characterization of regional investment offered here. The successful use of local profit levels and changes begins to provide some definite outline to the amorphous "animal spirits" of post-Keynesian theory, while offering an alternative to the traditional output accelerator which is more appropriate for a spatial analysis. While this model is not inconsistent with the marxian theory reviewed earlier, it is clear that we have not explored within the current analysis the role of technological change which is so central to this conception of the capital accumulation process.

Capital, income distribution, and technological change

To this point we have suspended a direct consideration of technological change and its relationship to regional growth and the distribution of income. Yet this has been at our peril, for knowledge of quantitative changes in the amount of productive capacity in a region and the determinants of those changes is of little use if we are not at the same time also aware of the qualitative changes which almost always accompany them. We are again reminded of the statement by Meyer and Kuh (1957) that (to paraphrase) "like for like replacement is very rare" in the act of investing in fixed capital. Recalling also the models of Arrow (1962), Kaldor (1961) and more recently Nelson and Winter (1982) (all reviewed in Chapter 13), in which technological change is embodied in the installation of new capital, we note that this new capital may require more or less labor power per unit (ideally physical, but in practice, financial), it may require a different average level of labor skill, and it may result in more or less output per unit of labor employed. All of these potential consequences flow from the decision-making power of the owners of capital to initiate changes in production technology and, as we shall emphasize in these remaining pages, changes in the location of capital as well.

In Chapter 13 we touched on a number of determinants which may influence this "choice of technique" in an economy in which the costs of production might vary significantly over space. To begin with, it was noted that the overall possibility set of production techniques (like Joan Robinson's "book of blueprints"), as well as products, might be locally defined according to the hierarchical and nonhierarchical manner in which innovations are created and diffuse through space and time. However, the choices actually made might be influenced by a number of specific considerations. For adherents to the neoclassical school, the character of production is determined by the relative scarcity of major production inputs locally, which should also be reflected in their relative prices. Product-cycle theorists prefer to emphasize the ability of entrepreneurs, given spatially variant prices of production inputs, to select that location (along with its set of prevailing input prices) which best suits their needs. These needs are defined by the stage of development reached by the product under consideration at a particular point in time – where it is reasoned that new products require the highly skilled (but high-priced) labor which characterizes higher-order metropolitan centers, while, once the product and production techniques have been standardized, manufacturing will shift to sites offering abundant, less-skilled (and accordingly cheaper) labor power.

The restructuring school posits that technological change is driven by the imperatives of competition, the nature of which has become increasingly international and sufficiently strong so as to disturb the previously oligopolistic position of large, multilocational firms. The responses to this competitive pressure might include (a) the reallocation of private capital into new and growing product lines, abandoning older, less economical ventures, or (b) within a given product line, a switch to more efficient techniques which economize on input costs, and therefore improve profitability. In this latter case, more efficient techniques (hence higher profit rates) may or may not require more capital per man–hour of labor, since the best sort of technological improvement would hold constant (or reduce) capital and/or labor costs while enabling a greater level of output (reswitching enthusiasts take note). This process of competitively driven technological change is said to have a spatial dimension which is intimately related to the kind of technique which is ultimately chosen. Due to the inherent conflict between workers and the owners of capital over the conditions surrounding production, it is argued that such changes to technology are most easily incorporated in new capital in new locations (so much for industrial inertia and spatial cumulative causation), since the quiet reinvestment of profits in distant locations, accompanied perhaps by gradual disinvestment in initial places of production, represents a politically unobtrusive and more manageable alternative to technological change *in situ*.

This locational shift is driven not only by the "push" of obsolete capital, and perhaps, unfavorable social relations surrounding production, but also by a "pull" to particular locations which offer an eager, unsophisticated, and politically uninitiated (or, in some other sense, "vulnerable") labor force, whose lower expectations and demands concerning the division of the product and related working conditions are the result of their collective past experiences in contact with capitalist production. If such constellations of labor also tend to be lower skilled, then there may be an incentive for management to "de-skill" the requisite labor input into production when it is considering alternative techniques and locations. If so, this may indeed bias the choice of new technique in favor of more capital-intensive methods (again, especially if the labor input is measured in terms of wage-bill instead of man–hours). What is evident in this scenario however, is that the labor input will at least be "re-skilled" (see Walker & Storper 1981).

At this juncture we should also recap some general arguments concerning the tendency of the capital intensity of production to increase over time. At the heart of marxian analysis is the proposition that the capital–labor ratio will rise in the long run due to the imperative for capitalists to diminish the presence of direct labor in production, both for greater profitability and more predictable and harmonious labor relations. This tendency was, however, seen to be self-contradictory in that the increasingly diminished share of labor in total output would engender crises of underconsumption, recognized as the problem of effective demand by

Kalecki and Keynes. One way to avert this crisis would be to allow real wage rates to increase over time (Robinson 1971).

Kaldor (1961) has fashioned a similar hypothesis in his "technical progress function," which states that productivity growth is an increasing function of the rate of increase in the capital–labor ratio (see also Pasinetti 1981: Ch. 9). Piore (1968) and Nelson and Winter (1982) note the same trend currently among designers of new industrial equipment, who assume mechanization to be "a natural way to reduce costs, increase reliability and precision of production, gain more reliable control over operations, and so on" (Nelson & Winter 1982: 260). Regionally, the same tendency has been observed empirically for US metropolitan regions by Varaiya and Wiseman (1981) who note that, in spite of substantial capital investment in the northeast manufacturing sector between 1954 and 1976, employment in this region has declined significantly due to the labor-saving nature of the technology reflected in this newer capital.

Having now resummarized the relevant contending theories on the matter of regions and technological change, it is possible to note some interesting similarities and distinctions. First, we are struck by the explicitly temporal and spatial character of both the product cycle and restructuring theories. These two theories also share a common emphasis on the role of competition, although this is perhaps more integral to the latter of these two formulations. Also, they both emphasize the ability of entrepreneurs to avail themselves of more favourable production conditions (costs) in new locations. However, we can distinguish between the product-cycle conception, where the technique has been chosen first and the location (and costs of production) follow, and the restructuring scenario, in which the choice of technique will depend to an extent on the choice of location.

The description inherent in this last sentence may strike one as sounding vaguely neoclassical, since in that theory the choice of technique is a direct function of relative "factor prices." However, we must emphasize a fundamental distinction between this idea and the restructuring paradigm described above. As was pointed out in Chapter 13, the neoclassical theory is most appropriate only to an atemporal world, in which the choice of techniques and implied substitution of factors occurs along a single production function representing different equilibrium positions with technology fixed and given. In the restructuring formulation, time and space are explicitly introduced into the analysis, and "substitution of factors" is, by definition, not along "some well-behaved production function" (Pasinetti 1977, 1981). In this sense, the neoclassical contender has eliminated itself from consideration as a vehicle for understanding and explaining the empirical trends to be evaluated in this section; since we cannot hold time and space constant, we cannot prove (or disprove) the validity of the theory empirically (although, again, it is possible to challenge it on theoretical grounds; Sraffa 1960). To be sure, the goals of profit-maximization and cost-minimization (or their behavioral equivalents) are of central importance to the non–neoclassical theories reviewed here. The chief distinction is their explicit consideration of time and space (a point overlooked by Borts 1974 in his review of Richardson 1973).

From the preceding discussion there emerge a number of important questions. First, how sensitive is the regional rate of growth in capital to the costs of major inputs such as labor? Secondly, what are the major determinants of capital intensity in regional production? Thirdly, what are the interrelationships between regional growth, technological change and the distribution of the product between workers and the owners of capital?

Let us begin immediately with the first of these questions. We have already explored the relationship between capital growth and the level and rate of increase of profits, but how is this process affected by the local cost of labor? To investigate this link we tested the relationship below, again employing Beach and MacKinnon's (1978) maximum–likelihood time-series regressions for each of 74 state–industry combinations:

$$\frac{\Delta K}{K_t} = f\left[\frac{P}{K}, \frac{W}{E}, \frac{Y}{E}\right]_{t-1} \tag{15.5}$$

Hence capital growth was hypothesized to bear some relationship to previous rates of profit and the wage rate (here the annual wage-bill divided by the total number of workers). The third term was introduced to control for the possible productivity differences between workers earning the same real wage, and is simply the value of total net output (value-added) divided by the number of workers. All variables for this and subsequent analyses were deflated to 1972 dollars to correspond to the units in which capital was measured. Profits and value-added were deflated using the same BLS sector-specific producer price indices described earlier. However, where we had previously used consumer price indices to deflate wages, we are now shifting the point of view in our analysis from the worker to the entrepreneur, whose relevant real wage is arguably expressed in terms of the price of his output. Hence producer price indices were also used in the deflation of wages. The results of this analysis are summarized in Table 15.3 (see Gertler 1983 for full estimation results).

From this table we see that none of these variables was significant in greater than 30 of 74 cases. Nevertheless, within those significant cases we see that past profits tend to be positively related to current investment (which is no surprise). This effect is particularly strong in textiles (7 of 16 states) and reasonably strong in fabricated metals (8 of 27 states). Secondly, capital growth appears to be inversely related to the real wage rate seen from the producer's perspective. This effect is strongest within the fabricated metals industry (13 of 27 states) followed by electronics (6 of 17

Table 15.3 Capital growth, profit rates, real wages and productivity: summary of significant states.

	P/K_{t-1}	W/E_{t-1}	Y/E_{t-1}
positive sign			
textiles (16)	7	1	3
apparel (14)	2	1	4
fabricated metals (27)	8	4	7
electrical (17)	2	0	4
subtotal	19	6	18
negative sign			
textiles (16)	1	2	1
apparel (14)	0	3	1
fabricated metals (27)	2	13	3
electrical (17)	1	6	2
subtotal	4	24	7
total	23/74	30/74	25/74

cases), which is somewhat surprising given that these industries are of a generally more capital-intensive nature. Productivity appears to be an important determinant of capital growth, especially in apparel and fabricated metals.

While the signs of these significant parameters are in the expected directions (that is, capital growth increases with past profitability and productivity and is slowed by a larger real wage), one must acknowledge the many cases where these relationships fail to materialize at all (not to mention the few where they do, but in the opposite direction). For example, in only one southern state (Georgia) are higher wages a significant deterrent to capital growth in textiles. In apparel, only Texas exhibits this relationship in the south, and California shows a strong positive relationship. And in electronics and electrical equipment, wage rates are unimportant in the New England states of New Hampshire, Rhode Island and Connecticut, as well as in the south.

Let us now shift our attention to capital intensity and the second question posed above. By way of introduction to this topic it might be helpful to examine first some basic trends in capital–labor ratios which are revealed by our data. An earlier analysis of capital intensities (Gertler 1983) revealed that capital–labor ratios were generally increasing over the period 1954 to 1976. Textiles capital intensity grew by roughly 105%, apparel by 188%, fabricated metals by 83%, and electrical by 137%. Interestingly, the fastest increase, and the one with fewer short-run setbacks, occurred in that sector (apparel) which was least mechanized to begin with. However, both the absolute levels and the character of short-run changes in this ratio were found to exhibit tremendous intra- and inter-industry diversity across space, a diversity which has been increasing significantly in the latter years of our study period. This finding is indeed significant, for it is consistent with the claim of increasing functional (versus regional) organization of production, as well as suggesting that the nature of technology within a given industry exhibits considerable variability geographically, which makes it difficult for us to conceive of all places at a given point in time being located on the same production function.

Having now explored the basic trends within the data, we might well ask what variables in the aggregate will influence the ratio of capital to labor in production. Particularly, what are the impacts of profitability and labor costs on this variable? The various theories of "substitution in the real world" which we have reviewed do suggest a number of expectations concerning these relationships. First, if mechanization is the "natural" response to declining profitability, we ought to see a negative relationship between recent past changes in profits and current changes in capital intensity. This response we pose as a behavioral "rule of thumb" in the context of a decision which is "infinitely complicated" (Robinson 1971: 105). Since we presume the ensemble of multiregional economies to be in a state of disequilibrium, we do not interpret the rate of profit on capital in manufacturing to be equivalent to (or proportional to) the prevailing rate of interest or cost of capital.

We might also expect the capital intensity of production to respond to the relative cost of labor, although this relationship is far from straightforward. Implicit in much of the foregoing discussion is the incentive for producers to reduce their input costs, of which labor is one component. Yet it is not solely the cost of labor in simple terms which is important to entrepreneurs. Our discussion in previous chapters suggested that features such as the degree of organization or militance (and its implication for work stoppages) and the degree of certainty concerning future changes in the wage bill (as embodied in implicit or explicit contracts) are equally important. A further consideration involves the possibility that labor of equal cost may in fact be differentially productive, particularly in disequilibrium.

The observations suggest the following expression for further empirical examinations:

$$\frac{K}{L_t} = f \left[\frac{P}{K}, \frac{W}{E}, \frac{Y}{E} \right]_{t-1} \tag{15.6}$$

This relationship was estimated in a manner similar to the last test, with the capital–labor ratio computed as the dollars of capital stock per production man–hour. The results are summarized in Table 15.4. In contrast to our last test the relationships here appear to be stronger, more general and more clear cut. The negative relationship between profit rate and capital

Table 15.4 Capital intensity, profit rates, real wages, and productivity: summary of significant states.

	P/K_{t-1}	W/E_{t-1}	Y/E_{t-1}
positive sign			
textiles (16)	1	15	7
apparel (14)	0	10	8
fabricated metals (27)	0	20	17
electrical (17)	0	7	11
subtotal	1	52	43
negative sign			
textiles (16)	8	0	2
apparel (14)	8	0	0
fabricated metals (27)	14	1	1
electrical (17)	10	0	0
subtotal	40	1	3
total	41/74	53/74	46/74

intensity materializes in 40 of 74 cases. Insignificant states are in the northeast in textiles, southern states for fabricated metals, and in no particular regional concentrations in apparel and electrical (Gertler 1983). Real wage rates show a strong positive relationship, indicating that a recent rise in real wages precipitates further capital intensification in 52 of 74 cases. This relationship is particularly strong in textiles (15 of 16 states), followed by fabricated metals (20 of 27 states), apparel (10 of 14 states) and electrical (7 of 17 states). Finally, recent increases in productivity also appear to induce further mechanization of production, at least in 43 of the 74 state–industries examined here. In this case the result is strongest in electrical equipment, followed by fabricated metals, apparel and textiles.

Hence, to summarize the above findings, capital intensification is accelerated by recent increases in the real wage and productivity of labor, and encouraged in the face of recently decreased profitability. However, we must be careful to point out the potentially recursive nature of some of the relationships which we have estimated here. For example, it is likely that past increases in both productivity and the real wage are a consequence of earlier technological change, in which case these variables become "an effect, not a cause, of technical change" (Pasinetti 1981: 216). Furthermore, we may not have adequately explored longer leads and lags in these relationships.

We have now provided at least partial answers to the first two questions posed earlier in this section. Now we turn to the third and final question, which integrates the trio of phenomena of interest to us in this chapter – namely, capital accumulation, technological change and the distribution of the product between capital and labor. We do so by hypothesizing that the distribution of income between labor and capital is increasingly tilted in favor of profits as the capital growth rate and capital intensity of production increase. The influence of capital intensity (representing technological change) would appear to be fairly obvious in this relationship. The influence of the capital growth rate on income distribution (independent of technological change) is suggested by Kalecki's famous aphorism that "the capitalists get what they spend, and the workers spend what they get" (see Obrinsky 1983).

To explore these relationships we chose to estimate the following expression:

$$\frac{P}{W_t} = f\left[\frac{\Delta K}{K}, \frac{K}{L}\right]_{t-1} \tag{15.7}$$

in which all variables have been defined previously. This relationship was also estimated at time t on the right-hand side to explore the issue of lags. The results are presented in Table 15.5, and a number of interesting trends emerge. The first column indicates that, at least for 20 out of 74 cases, an increase in the rate of capital investment (in the past or current period) appears to increase the ratio of profits to wages. Although in 49 state–industries this relationship is not significant at the 0.05 level, in the case of textiles, the relationship holds in 50% of the states examined.

When it comes to the impact of the capital–labor ratio we see somewhat more definite results. In 49 of 74 state–industry combinations, a recent

Table 15.5 Regional income distribution, growth, and technological change: summary of significant states.

	$\dfrac{\Delta K}{K_{t-1\,(or\,t)}}$	$\dfrac{K}{L_{t-1}}$
positive sign		
textiles (16)	4 (4)	12
apparel (14)	3 (1)	13
fabricated metals (27)	3 (2)	10
electrical (17)	3 (0)	14
subtotal	20	49
negative sign		
textiles (16)	0	0
apparel (14)	0	0
fabricated metals (27)	0	1
electrical (17)	3 (2)	0
subtotal	5	1
total	25/74	50/74

increase in capital intensity seems to produce a corresponding rise in the share of profits to wages in total regional income. This trend is especially marked in apparel (13 of 14 states) and electrical equipment (14 of 17 states), which also happen to be two sectors which underwent the fastest overall capital growth during the 1954–76 period (see Ch. 14). Clearly, although the distribution of income between labor and capital is tending progressively in the direction of profits, it has been doing so in a context of overall growth whose employment implications are negative only in the long run. It has been through net additions to the stock of capital (and, presumably, employment) in different regions that this technological transformation has been implemented, particularly for electrical equipment. Indeed, a political–economic interpretation of this trend might suggest that this atmosphere of buoyancy and burgeoning growth in these sectors has in fact facilitated what would, in less expansionary times, be otherwise viewed as a gravely contentious decision by management to displace labor (on this, see Massey & Meegan 1982: Chs. 4, 9).

Interestingly, however, the relationship between regional capital intensity and the distribution of the product also holds reasonably well in textiles, an industry which has been racked by major locational shifts, rationalization in older centers, and market concentration in the face of increasingly stiff foreign competition. Presumably in this industry, technical change has been implemented primarily through locational change. In latter years the apparel industry has probably also come to share many of these traits.

One further point warrants illumination at this juncture. Since the overall share of labor in total income appears to be declining in the face of steadily rising capital intensity, this implies that the increases in the real wage which we have also witnessed over this period have been insufficient to offset the declining numbers of workers associated with every new dollar of investment. The result is a smaller (or more slowly increasing), better-paid workforce, but a total wage-bill which is growing more slowly than total profits. While this "smaller" workforce may be more productive, in the sense that each man–hour of labor is producing greater output, it is possibly becoming more "de-skilled" in terms of the level of training required of each position, so that individual workers have become more nearly interchangeable. However, we do not yet have direct evidence of this de-skilling trend. Furthermore, in an era of slow growth or decline, the declining share of wages in the product of industry may translate into a severe inadequacy of aggregate effective demand. While the regional dimensions of such developments would undoubtedly be important, they are beyond the realm of this study.

Bibliography

Aguado, E. 1982. A time series analysis of the Nile river low flows. *Ann. Assoc. Am. Geogs* **72**, 109–19.

Airov, J. 1963. The construction of interregional business cycle models. *J. Reg. Sci.* **5**, 1–20.

Allen, L. 1982. Regional economic stabilization and the acceleration principle. *Growth and Change* **13**, 10–17.

Alonso, W. 1968. Predicting best with imperfect data. *J. Am. Plann. Assoc.* **34**, 248–55.

Alonso, W. 1971. The economics of urban size. *Pap. Reg. Sci. Assoc.* **26**, 67–83.

Alonso, W. 1973. Problems, purposes, and implicit policies for a national strategy of urbanization. In *Population distribution and policy*, S. M. Mazie (ed.), 635–47. Washington, DC: US Government Printing Office.

Alonso, W. 1977. Surprises and rethinkings of metropolitan growth: a comment. *Int. Reg. Sci. Rev.* **2**, 171–4.

Alonso, W. 1980. Population as a system in regional development. *Pap. Proc. Am. Econ. Rev.* **70**, 405–9.

Alperovich, G. 1980. Regional elasticities of substitution. *J. Reg. Sci.* **20**, 503–12.

Alperovich, G., J. Bergman and C. Ehemann 1975. An econometric model of employment growth in metropolitan areas. *Environ. Plann. A* **7**, 833–62.

Arrow, K. J. 1962. The economic implications of learning by doing. *Rev. Econ. Stud.* **29**, 155–73.

Arrow, K. J. 1978. The future and present in economic life. *Econ. Inq.* **16**, 157–69.

Arrow, K. J. and F. Hahn 1971. *General competitive analysis*. San Francisco: Holden-Day.

Arrow, K. J., H. B. Chenery, B. S. Minhas and R. M. Solow 1961. Capital–labor substitution and economic efficiency. *Rev. Econ. Stat.* **43**, 225–50.

Atiyah, P. 1979. *The rise and fall of freedom of contract*. Oxford: Oxford University Press.

Atiyah, P. 1981. *Promises, morals and law*. Oxford: Clarendon Press.

Azariadis, C. 1975. Implicit contracts and underemployment equilibria. *J. Polit. Econ.* **83**, 1183–1202.

Azariadis, C. 1981. Implicit contracts and related topics: a survey. In *The economics of labour markets*, Z. Hornstein, J. Grice and A. Webb (eds.), 221–48. London: HMSO.

Backus, D., W. C. Brainard, G. Smith, and J. Tobin 1979. A model of U.S. financial and non-financial economic behavior. *J. Mon. Cred. Bank.* **12**, 259–93.

Baily, N. M. 1976. Contract theory and the moderation of inflation by recession and controls. *Brookings Pap. Econ. Act.* **3**, 585–622.

Baily, N. M. 1977. On the theory of layoffs and unemployment. *Econometrica* **45**, 1043–63.

Baily, N. M. 1982. Are the new economic models the answer? *Brookings Rev.* **1**, 11–14.

Ball, R. R. and E. St. Cyr 1966. Short term employment functions in British manufacturing industry. *Rev. Econ. Stud.* **33**, 179–207.

Ballard, K. P. and G. L. Clark 1981. The short-run dynamics of inter-state migration: a space–time economic adjustment model of in-migration to fast-growing states. *Reg. Stud.* **15**, 213–28.

Ballard, K. P. and R. M. Wendling 1980. The national–regional impact evaluation system: a spatial model of U.S. economic and demographic activity. *J. Reg. Sci.* **20**, 143–58.

Ballard, K. P., R. Gustely, and R. Wendling 1981. *NRIES: structure, performance and application of a bottom up interregional econometric model.* Washington, DC: US Department of Commerce.

Bartel, A. 1979. The migration decision: what role does job mobility play? *Am. Econ. Rev.* **69**, 775–86.

Bator, F. M. 1981. America's inflation: the sins of wages. *The Economist* March 21, 3–6.

Beach, C. M. and J. G. MacKinnon 1978. A maximum likelihood procedure for regression with autocorrelated errors. *Econometrica* **46**, 51–8.

Benassy, J.-P. 1982. Developments in non-Walrasian economics and micro-economic foundations of macroeconomics. In *Advances in economic theory*, W. Hildenbrand (ed.), 121–46. Cambridge: Cambridge University Press.

Bennett, R. J. 1979. *Spatial time series: analysis, forecasting, and control.* London: Pion.

Bennett, R. J. 1980. *The geography of public finance.* London: Methuen.

Berger, S. and M. J. Piore 1980. *Dualism and discontinuity in industrial societies.* Cambridge: Cambridge University Press.

Berry, B. J. L. 1970. The geography of the United States in the year 2000. *Trans Inst. Br. Geogs* **51**, 21–53.

Berry, B. J. L. 1972. Hierarchical diffusion: the basis of developmental filtering and spread in a system of cities. In *Growth centers in regional economic development*, N. M. Hansen (ed.). New York: The Free Press.

Berry, B. J. L. 1980. Urbanization and counter-urbanization in the United States. *Ann. Am. Acad. Polit. Soc. Sci.* **451**, 13–20.

Bhaduri, A. and J. Robinson 1980. Accumulation and exploitation: an analysis in the tradition of Marx, Sraffa, and Kalecki. *Camb. J. Econ.* **4**, 103–15.

Birch, D. 1979. *The job generation process.* Cambridge, Mass.: Neighborhood and Regional Change Program, MIT.

Blanchard, O. J. 1981. *Price desynchronization and price level inertia.* Discussion paper no. 899. Cambridge, Mass.: Institute of Economic Research, Harvard University.

Blinder, A. S. 1979. *Economic policy and the great stagflation.* New York: Academic Press.

Blinder, A. S. 1982. The anatomy of double-digit inflation in the 1970s. In *Inflation: causes and effects*, R. E. Hall (ed.). Chicago, Ill.: University of Chicago Press.

Blinder, A. S. and W. J. Newton 1981. The 1971–1974 controls program and the price level. *J. Mon. Econ.* **8**, 1–23.

Bluestone, B. and B. Harrison 1980. *Capital and communities.* Washington DC: The Progressive Alliance.

Bluestone, B. and B. Harrison 1982. *The deindustrialization of America.* New York: Basic Books.

Bolton, R. 1980. Multiregional models: introduction to a symposium. *J. Reg. Sci.* **20**, 131–42.

Bolton, R. 1982. *A broader view of industrial diversification.* Paper presented at the North American Annual Meeting of the Regional Science Association, Pittsburgh, Pennsylvania.

Borts, G. H. 1960. The equalization of returns and regional economic growth. *Am. Econ. Rev.* **50**, 319–47.

Borts, G. H. 1971. Growth and capital movements among U.S. regions in the postwar period. In *Essays in regional economics*, J. F. Kain and J. R. Meyer (eds.). Cambridge, Mass.: Harvard University Press.

Borts, G. H. 1974. Review of *Regional growth theory* by H. Richardson. *J. Econ. Lit.* **12**, 546–7.

Borts, G. H. and J. L. Stein 1964. *Economic growth in a free market.* New York: Columbia University Press.

Bowsher, N., J. Daane and R. Einzig 1957. The flows of funds between regions of the United States. *Pap. Reg. Sci. Assoc.* **3**, 139–65.

Box, G. and G. Jenkins 1976. *Time series analysis, forecasting, and control*, 2nd edn. San Francisco, Calif.: Holden-Day.

Brown, L. A. 1981. *Innovation diffusion: a new perspective.* New York: Methuen.

Browne, L. E. 1978a. Regional industry mix and the business cycle. *New Eng. Econ. Rev.* Nov.–Dec., 35–53.

Browne, L. E. 1978b. Regional unemployment rates – why are they so different? *New Eng. Econ. Rev.* Jul.–Aug., 5–26.

Browne, L. E., P. Mieszkowski and R. F. Syron 1980. Regional investment patterns. *New Eng. Econ. Rev.* Jul.–Aug., 5–13.

Bruno, M. and J. Sachs 1982. Input price shocks and the slowdown in economic growth: the case of UK manufacturing. *Rev. Econ. Stud.* **49**, 679–705.

Bruno, M. and J. Sachs 1985. *Economics of worldwide stagflation.* Cambridge, Mass.: Harvard University Press.

Buck, T. W. and M. H. Atkins 1976. Capital subsidies and unemployed labour: a regional production function approach. *Reg. Stud.* **10**, 215–22.

Buiter, W. H. 1980. The macroeconomics of Dr. Pangloss: a critical survey of the new classical macroeconomics. *Econ. J.* **90**, 34–50.

Bureau of Economic Analysis 1976. *Regional work force characteristics and migration data.* Washington, DC: US Department of Commerce.

Bureau of Labor Statistics 1977. *Employment and earnings, states and areas 1939–1975.* Washington, DC: US Department of Labor.

Bureau of Labor Statistics 1980. *Handbook of labor statistics.* Washington, DC: US Department of Labor.

Bureau of Labor Statistics 1982a. *CPI detailed report, June. Washington*, DC: US Department of Labor.

Bureau of Labor Statistics 1982b. *Producer prices and price indexes, supplement to data for 1981.* Washington, DC: US Department of Labor.

Cagan, P. 1979. *Persistent inflation.* New York: Columbia University Press.

Caines, P. E., C. W. Keng, and S. P. Sethi 1981. Causality analysis and multivariate autoregressive modeling with an application to supermarket sales analysis. *J. Econ. Dynamics and Control* **3**, 267–98.

Calabresi, G. and A. D. Melamed 1972. Property rules, liability rules, and inalienability: one view of the cathedral. *Harvard Law Rev.* **85**, 1089–128.

Carlino, G. A. 1983. *The growth of rural areas: a test of alternative explanations.* Philadelphia, Penn.: Federal Reserve Bank of Philadelphia.

Carr, H. C. 1960. A note on regional differences in discount rates. *J. Fin.* **15**, 62–8.

Cartwright, D. 1978. *Major limitations of CWHS files and prospects for improvement.* Washington, DC: Bureau of Economic Analysis.

Casetti, E. 1981a. A catastrophe model of regional dynamics. *Ann. Assoc. Am. Geogs* **71**, 572–9.

Casetti, E. 1981b. The transition of regional economies from growth to decline: a simulation. *Modeling and Simulation* **12**, 949–54.

Casetti, E. 1982. A reply to Vining's commentary on "A catastrophe model of regional dynamics." *Ann. Assoc. Am. Geogs* **72**, 557–8.

Casetti, E. 1983. *Manufacturing productivity and snowbelt–sunbelt shifts.* Paper presented at the Denver Annual Meeting of the Association of American Geographers.

Cassese, A. and J. R. Lothian 1982. The timing of monetary and price changes and the international transmission of inflation. *J. Mon. Econ.* **10**, 1–23.

Castells, M. 1977. *The urban question.* Cambridge, Mass.: MIT Press.

Cebula, R. J. and M. Zaharoff 1974. Interregional capital transfers and interest rate differentials: an empirical note. *Ann. Reg. Sci.* **8**, 87–94.

Chenery, H. B. 1952. Overcapacity and the acceleration principle. *Econometrica* **20**, 1–28.

Chinitz, B. 1961. Contrasts in agglomeration: New York and Pittsburgh. *Am. Econ. Rev.* **51**, 279–89.

Chinitz, B. 1978. *The declining northeast: demographic and economic analyses.* New York: Praeger.

Chow, G. 1975. *Analysis and control of dynamic economic systems.* New York: Wiley.

Christensen, L. R., D. W. Jorgenson and L. J. Lau 1973. Transcendental logarithmic production frontiers. *Rev. Econ. Stat.* **55**, 28–45.

Clark, G. L. 1980a. Capitalism and regional disparities. *Ann. Assoc. Am. Geogs* **70**, 226–37.

Clark, G. L. 1980b. Critical problems of geographical unemployment models. *Prog. Human Geog.* **4**, 157–80.

Clark, G. L. 1981a. The employment relation and the spatial division of labor: a hypothesis. *Ann. Assoc. Am. Geogs* **71**, 412–24.

Clark, G. L. 1981b. A Hicksian model of labor turnover and local wage determination. *Environ. Plann. A* **13**, 563–74.

Clark, G. L. 1982a. Dynamics of interstate labor migration. *Ann. Assoc. Am. Geogs* **72**, 297–313.

Clark, G. L. 1982b. *Urban growth and economic fluctuations.* Report of Grant 7909370. Washington DC: National Science Foundation.

Clark, G. L. 1982c. Volatility in the geographical structure of U.S. interstate migration. *Environ. Plann. A* **14**, 145–67.

Clark, G. L. 1983a. Fluctuations and rigidities in local labor markets, part I: theory and evidence. *Environ. Plann. A* **15**, 165–85.

Clark, G. L. 1983b. Fluctuations and rigidities in local labor markets, part II: reinterpreting contracts. *Environ. Plann. A* **15**, 365–77.

Clark, G. L. 1983c. *Interregional migration, national policy and social justice.* Totowa, NJ: Rowman & Allanheld.

Clark, G. L. 1984a. Does inflation vary between cities? *Environ. Plann. A* **16**, 513–27.

Clark, G. L. 1984b. Labor demand and economic development policy. *Environ. Plann. C: Gov. Policy.* **2**, 45–55.

Clark, G. L. 1986. The crisis of the midwest auto industry. In *Production, work, and territory,* A. Scott and M. Storper (eds.). London: Allen & Unwin.

Clark, G. L. and K. P. Ballard 1980. Modelling out-migration from depressed regions: the significance of origin and destination characteristics. *Environ. Plann. A* **12**, 799–812.

Clark, G. L. and K. P. Ballard 1981. The demand and supply of labor and interstate relative wages: an empirical analysis. *Econ. Geog.* **57**, 95–112.

Clark, G. L. and M. Dear 1984. *State apparatus: structures and language of legitimacy*. London: Allen & Unwin.

Clark, G. L. and M. S. Gertler 1983. Migration and capital. *Ann. Assoc. Am. Geogs* **73**, 18–34.

Clark, G. L. and M. S. Gertler 1985. An adjustment model of regional production. *Environ. Plann. A* **17**, 231–52.

Clark, G. L. and T. Tabuchi 1984. Regional wage and price dynamics. *Geog. Anal.* **16**, 223–43.

Clark, G. L. and J. Whiteman 1983. Why poor people don't move: job search behavior and disequilibrium amongst local labor markets. *Environ. Plann. A* **15**, 85–104.

Clark, J. M. 1917. Business acceleration and the law of demand: a technological factor in economic cycles. *J. Polit. Econ.* **25**, 217–35.

Clark, P. K. 1979. Investment in the 1970s: theory, performance, and prediction. *Brookings Pap. Econ. Act.* **1**, 73–113.

Cliff, A. D., P. Haggett, J. K. Ord, K. Bassett, and R. Davies 1975. *Elements of spatial structure*. Cambridge: Cambridge University Press.

Coase, R. 1960. The problem of social cost. *J. Law Econ.* **3**, 1–44.

Cobb, C. W. and P. H. Douglas 1928. A theory of production. *Am. Econ. Rev.* **18**, 139–65.

Cochrane, D. and G. H. Orcutt 1949. Application of least squares regressions to relationships containing autocorrelated error terms. *J. Am. Statist. Assoc.* **44**, 32–61.

Coleman, J. 1980. Efficiency, utility, and wealth maximization. *Hofstra Law Rev.* **8**, 509–51.

Dahlman, C. J. 1979. The problem of externality. *J. Law. Econ.* **22**, 141–62.

Daniels, B. 1981. *An investigation of the impact of acquisition on the acquired firm*. Cambridge, Mass.: Counsel for Community Development Inc.

Davis, L. 1966. The capital market and industrial concentration. *Econ. Hist. Rev.* **19**, 255–72.

DeBruyne, G. and P. Van Rompuy 1982. The impact of interest subsidies on the interregional allocation of capital: an econometric analysis for Belgium. *Reg. Sci. Urb. Econ.* **12**, 121–31.

Denison, E. F. 1979. *Accounting for slower economic growth*. Washington, DC: Brookings Institution.

Department of Commerce (various years). *Census of manufactures*. Washington, DC: USGPO.

Department of Commerce 1981. *Industrial outlook*. Washington, DC: USGPO.

Doeringer, P. and M. Piore 1971. *Internal labor markets and manpower*. Lexington, Mass.: D. C. Heath.

Dunford, M. F. 1977. *Regional policy and the restructuring of capital*. Working paper no. 4, Urban and Regional Studies. Brighton: Sussex University.

Dunlop, J. T. 1944. *Wage determination under trade unions*. New York: Augustus Kelley.

Dworkin, R. 1972. Social rules and legal theory. *Yale Law J.* **81**, 855–90.

Dworkin, R. 1981. What is equality? *Phil. Publ. Aff.* **10**, 185–246; 283–345.

Eckstein, O. 1981. *Core inflation*. Englewood Cliffs, NJ: Prentice-Hall.

Edel, M. 1980. People versus places in urban impact analysis. In *The urban impacts of federal policies*, N. J. Glickman (ed.). Baltimore, Md.: Johns Hopkins University Press.

Edwards, R. C., M. Reich and D. M. Gordon (eds.) 1975. *Labor market segmentation.* Lexington, Mass.: D. C. Heath.

Emmer, R. 1957. Influences on regional credit expansion. *Pap. Reg. Sci. Assoc.* **3**, 166–79.

Engle, R. F. 1974. A disequilibrium model of regional investment. *J. Reg. Sci.* **14**, 367–76.

Erickson, R. A. and T. R. Leinbach 1979. Characteristics of branch plants attracted to nonmetropolitan areas. In *Non-metropolitan industrialization*, R. E. Lonsdale and L. Seyler (eds.). New York: Halsted Press.

Estall, R. C. 1972. Some observations on the internal mobility of investment capital. *Area* **4**, 193–8.

Farber, H. S. 1984. Right-to-work laws and the extent of unionization. *J. Lab. Econ.* **2**, 319–52.

Fielding, A. J. 1982. Counterurbanization in Western Europe. *Progr. Plann.* **17**, 1–52.

Fischer, S. 1981. Towards an understanding of the costs of inflation II. *Carnegie-Rochester Conference Series on Public Policy* **15**, 5–42.

Fisher, F. 1983. *Disequilibrium foundations of equilibrium economics.* Cambridge: Cambridge University Press.

Fried, C. 1981. *Contract as promise.* Cambridge, Mass.: Harvard University Press.

Friedmann, J. 1966. *Regional development policy: a case study of Venezuela.* Cambridge, Mass.: MIT Press.

Gandolfo, G. 1971. *Mathematical methods and models in economic dynamics.* Amsterdam: North-Holland.

Garnick, D. H. 1983. Shifting balances in metropolitan and non-metropolitan area growth. Washington, DC: US Department of Commerce.

Garnick, D. H. and H. L. Friedenberg 1982. Accounting for regional differences in per capita personal income growth, 1929–1979. *Surv. Cur. Bus.* **62**, 24–34.

Genberg, H. 1977. The concept and measurement of the world price level and rate of inflation. *J. Mon. Econ.* **3**, 231–52.

Gerking, S. and A. Isserman 1981. Bifurcation and the time pattern of impacts in the economic base model. *J. Reg. Sci.* **21**, 451–67.

Gersovitz, M. 1980. Mis-specification and cyclical models: the real wage and the Phillips curve. *Economica* **47**, 433–41.

Gertler, Mark 1982. Imperfect information and wage inertia in the business cycle. *J. Polit. Econ.* **90**, 967–87.

Gertler, M. S. 1983. *Capital dynamics and regional development.* Unpublished PhD thesis. Cambridge, Mass.: Graduate School of Arts and Sciences, Harvard University.

Gertler, M. S. 1984a. The dynamics of regional capital accumulation. *Econ. Geog.* **60**, 150–74.

Gertler, M. S. 1984b. Regional capital theory. *Prog. Human Geog.* **8**, 50–81.

Gertler, M. S. 1986a. Discontinuities in regional development. *Environ. Plann. D: Soc. Space* **3**.

Gertler, M. S. 1986b. Profits and the regional accumulation of capital. Toronto, Ontario: Discussion paper, Department of Geography, University of Toronto. **76**.

Geweke, J. 1982. Causality, exogeneity and inference. In *Advances in econometrics*, W. Hildenbrand (ed.). Cambridge: Cambridge University Press.

Giddens, A. 1981. *A contemporary critique of historical materialism.* Berkeley, Calif.: University of California Press.

Gleave, D. and M. Cordey-Hayes 1977. Migration dynamics and labor market turnover. *Prog. Plann.* **8**, 1–95.

Glickman, N. J. 1977. *Econometric analysis of regional systems*. New York: Academic Press.

Goodwin, R. W. 1951. The non-linear accelerator and the persistence of business cycles. *Econometrica* **19**, 1–17.

Gordon, D. M. 1978. Capitalist development and the history of American cities. In *Marxism and the metropolis: new perspectives in urban political economy*, W. K. Tabb and L. Sawers (eds.). New York: Oxford University Press.

Gordon, D. M., R. C. Edwards and M. Reich 1982. *Segmented work, divided workers: the historical transformation of labor in the United States*. Cambridge: Cambridge University Press.

Gordon, I. R. and D. Lamont 1982. A model of labor-market interdependencies in the London region. *Environ. Plann. A* **14**, 237–64.

Gordon, R. J. 1980a. Comment on "Unanticipated money and economic activity" by R. Barro and M. Rush. In *Rational expectations and economic policy*, S. Fischer (ed.). Chicago, Ill.: University of Chicago Press.

Gordon, R. J. 1980b. A consistent characterization of a near-century of price behavior. *Pap. Proc. Am. Econ. Rev.* **70**, 243–9.

Gordon, R. J. 1981. Output fluctuations and gradual price adjustment. *J. Econ. Lit.* **19**, 493–530.

Granger, C. W. J. 1977. Comment. *J. Am. Statist. Assoc.* **72**, 22–3.

Granger, C. W. J. 1982. Generating mechanisms, models, and causality. In *Advances in econometrics*, W. Hildenbrand (ed.). Cambridge: Cambridge University Press.

Granger, C. W. J. and P. Newbold 1975. Economic forecasting: the atheist's viewpoint. In *Modelling the economy*, G. Renton (ed.). London: Heinemann.

Granger, C. W. J. and P. Newbold 1977. *Forecasting economic time series*. New York: Academic Press.

Gray, J. A. 1978. On indexation and contract length. *J. Polit. Econ.* **86**, 1–18.

Green, R. J. and G. R. Albrecht 1979. Testing for causality in regional econometric models. *Int. Reg. Sci. Rev.* **4**, 155–63.

Greenwood, M. J. 1975. Research on internal migration in the United States: a survey. *J. Econ. Lit.* **13**, 397–433.

Greenwood, M. J. 1981. *Migration and economic growth in the United States*. New York: Academic Press.

Grossman, S. and J. E. Stiglitz 1980. On the impossibility of informationally efficient markets. *Am. Econ. Rev.* **70**, 393–408.

Guccione, A. and W. J. Gillen 1972. A simple disaggregation of a neoclassical investment function. *J. Reg. Sci.* **12**, 279–94.

Guckenheimer, J. 1978. The catastrophe controversy. *Math. Intell.* **1**, 15–20.

Hahn, F. 1970. Some adjustment problems. *Econometrica* **38**, 1–17.

Hahn, F. 1982. *Money and inflation*. Oxford: Blackwell.

Hahn, F. 1984. *Equilibrium and macroeconomics*. Oxford: Blackwell.

Hall, R. E. 1980. Employment fluctuations and wage rigidity. *Brookings Pap. Econ. Act.* **1**, 91–123.

Hall, R. E. 1981. *The importance of lifetime jobs in the U.S. economy*. Working Paper no. 560. Cambridge, Mass.: National Bureau of Economic Research.

Hamermesh, D. S. 1975. Interdependence in the labor market. *Economica* **42**, 420–9.

Hansen, N. M. 1980. Dualism, capital–labor ratios and the regions of the U.S.: a comment. *J. Reg. Sci.* **20**, 401–3.

Harcourt, G. C. 1979. Non-neoclassical capital theory. *World Dev*. **7**, 923–32.

Harris, D. J. 1981. On the timing of wage payments. *Camb. J. Econ*. **5**, 369–81.

Harrison, B. 1982a. *Rationalization, restructuring, and industrial reorganization in older regions: the economic transformation of New England since World War II*. Cambridge, Mass.: Joint Center for Urban Studies of the Massachusetts Institute of Technology and Harvard University.

Harrison, B. 1982b The tendency toward instability and inequality underlying the "revival" of New England. *Pap. Reg. Sci. Assoc*. **50**, 41–65.

Harrison, B. 1984. The international movement for prenotification of plant closures. *Ind. Relations* **23**, 387–409.

Harrison, B. and B. Bluestone 1984. The incidence and regulation of plant closings. In *Sunbelt/snowbelt: urban development and regional restructuring*, L. Sawers and W. Tabb (eds.). Oxford: Oxford University Press.

Hart, H. L. A. 1961. *The concept of law*. Oxford: Oxford University Press.

Hartman, L. M. and D. Seckler 1967. Towards the application of dynamic growth theory to regions. *J. Reg. Sci*. **7**, 167–73.

Harvey, D. 1973. *Social justice and the city*. London: Edward Arnold.

Harvey, D. 1982. *The limits to capital*. Chicago, Ill.: University of Chicago Press.

Hayes, S. L. 1979. The transformation of investment banking. *Harvard Bus. Rev*. **57**, 153–70.

Hayes, S. L., A. M. Spence, and D. V. P. Marks 1983. *Competition in the investment banking industry*. Cambridge, Mass.: Harvard University Press.

Hazledine, T. 1978. New specifications for employment and hours functions. *Economica* **45**, 179–93.

Hazledine, T. 1981. "Employment functions" and the demand for labor in the short-run. In *The economics of the labour market*, Z. Hornstein, J. Grice, and A. Webb (eds.). London: HMSO.

Heilbrun, J. 1981. *Urban economics and public policy*, 2nd ed. New York: St. Martin's Press.

Hicks, J. R. 1932. *The theory of wages*. London: Macmillan.

Hicks, J. R. 1965. *Capital and growth*. Oxford: Oxford University Press.

Hicks, J. R. 1979. *Causality in economics*. Oxford: Blackwell.

Hildreth, C. and J. Y. Lu 1960. *Demand relations with autocorrelated disturbances*. AES Technical Bulletin no. 276. East Lansing, Mich.: Michigan State University.

Hirschman, A. O. 1958. *The strategy of economic development*. New Haven, Conn.: Yale University Press.

Holland, S. 1976. *Capital versus the regions*. London: Macmillan.

Holmes, J. 1983. Industrial reorganization, capital restructuring and locational change: an analysis of the Canadian automobile industry in the 1960s. *Econ. Geog*. **59**, 251–71.

Hoover, E. M. 1948. *The location of economic activity*. New York: McGraw-Hill.

Hoover, E. M. and R. A. Vernon 1959. *Anatomy of a metropolis*. Cambridge, Mass.: Harvard University Press.

Horiba, Y. and R. C. Kirkpatrick 1981. Factor endowments, factor proportions, and the allocative efficiency of U.S. interregional trade. *Rev. Econ. Stat*. **63**, 178–87.

Hudson, J. 1982. *Inflation: a theoretical survey and synthesis*. London: Allen & Unwin.

Irwin, R. 1977. Use of the cohort-component method in population projections for small areas. *Population forecasting for small areas*. Proceedings of the conference. Oak Ridge, Tenn.: Oak Ridge Associated Universities.

Iwai, K. 1981. *Disequilibrium dynamics: a theoretical analysis of inflation and unemployment*. New Haven, Conn.: Yale University Press.

Jackson, G., G. Masnick, R. Bolton, S. Bartlett and J. Pitkin 1981. *Regional diversity: growth in the United States, 1960–1990.* Boston, Mass.: Auburn House.

Jacobs, R. L. and R. A. Jones 1980. Price expectations in the United States: 1947–75. *Am. Econ. Rev.* **70**, 269–77.

Johansen, L. 1959. Substitution versus fixed production coefficients in the theory of economic growth: a synthesis. *Econometrica* **27**, 157–76.

Johnson, G. 1983. Intermetropolitan wage differentials in the United States. In *The measurement of labor cost*, J. Triplet (ed.). Chicago, Ill.: University of Chicago Press.

Johnston, K. 1986. Contract rights, judicial interpretation, and the spatial structure of production: a study of recent decisions by the NLRB. *Environ. Plann. A* **18**.

Johnston, R. J. 1979. On the relationships between regional and national unemployment trends. *Reg. Stud.* **13**, 453–64.

Jones, D. 1976. Conceptual and definitional problems associated with the subnational analysis of inflation and balance of payments. In *Geographical aspects of inflationary processes*, P. Corbin and M. Sabrin (eds.). Pleasantville, NY: Redgrave Publishing.

Jones, D. 1981. A geography of money. *Prog. Human Geog.* **5**, 342–69.

Jones, D. 1983. Mechanisms for geographical transmission of economic fluctuations. *Ann. Assoc. Am. Geogs* **73**, 35–50.

Jorgenson, D. W. 1971. Econometric studies of investment behavior: a survey. *J. Econ. Lit.* **9**, 1111–47.

Kaldor, N. 1961. Capital accumulation and economic growth. In *The theory of capital*, F. A. Lutz and D. C. Hague (eds.). New York: St. Martin's Press.

Kaldor, N. 1970. The case for regional policies. *Scott. J. Polit. Econ.* **17**, 337–48.

Kalecki, M. 1935. A macro-dynamic theory of business cycles. *Econometrica* **3**, 327–44.

Kalecki, M. 1937. Principle of increasing risk. *Economica* **4**, 440–7.

Kalecki, M. 1943. The determinants of investment. In *Studies in economic dynamics*. London: Allen & Unwin.

Kalecki, M. 1971. *Selected essays on the dynamics of the capitalist economy, 1933–1970.* Cambridge: Cambridge University Press.

Kaplan, W. 1958. *Ordinary differential equations.* Reading, Mass.: Addison-Wesley.

Kennedy, D. 1976. Form and substance in private law adjudication. *Harvard Law Rev.* **89**, 685–778.

Kennedy, D. and F. Michelman 1980. Are property and contract efficient? *Hofstra Law Rev.* **8**, 711–70.

Keyfitz, N. 1977. *Introduction to the mathematics of population.* Reading, Mass.: Addison-Wesley.

Keynes, J. M. 1936. *The general theory of employment, interest and money.* London: Macmillan.

King, L. J. 1976. Alternatives to a positive economic geography. *Ann. Assoc. Am. Geogs* **66**, 293–308.

King, L. J. and G. L. Clark 1978. Regional unemployment patterns and the spatial dimensions of macroeconomic policy. *Reg. Stud.* **12**, 283–96.

Klein, L. R. 1950. *Economic fluctuations in the United States, 1921–1941.* New York: Wiley.

Kolata, G. B. 1977. Catastrophe theory: the emperor has no clothes. *Science* **196**, 287, 350–1.

Koyck, L. M. 1954. *Distributed lags and investment analysis.* Amsterdam: North Holland.

Kurihara, K. K. 1972. *Essays in macrodynamic economics.* London: Allen & Unwin.

Lande, P. S. 1978. The interregional comparison of production functions. *Reg. Sci. Urb. Econ.* **8**, 339–53.

Lawrence, R. Z. 1979. Within and between-country variances in inflation rates: are they similar? *J. Mon. Econ.* **5**, 145–52.

Leone, R. A. and R. Struyk 1976. The incubator hypothesis: evidence from five SMSAs. *Urb. Stud.* **13**, 325–31.

Leontief, W. 1956. Factor proportions and the structure of American trade: further theoretical and empirical analysis. *Rev. Econ. Stat.* **38**, 386–407.

Leontief, W. 1981. *Theory and evidence.* Paper presented at the North-American Annual Meeting of the Regional Science Association, Pittsburgh, Pennsylvania.

L'Esperance, W. L. 1979a. Comment. *Int. Reg. Sci. Rev.* **4**, 164–6.

L'Esperance, W. L. 1979b. Commercial banking and the economic development of Ohio and Columbus. *Bull. Bus. Res.* **54** (12). Columbus, Ohio: Center for Business and Economic Research, Ohio State University.

L'Esperance, W. L. 1981a. *Modelling the regional monetary system.* Paper presented at the Twenty-Eighth North American Meeting of the Regional Science Association, Montreal, Canada.

L'Esperance, W. L. 1981b. *The structure and control of a state economy.* London: Pion.

Light, J. O. and W. L. White 1979. *The financial system.* Homewood, Ill.: R. D. Irwin.

Lipietz, A. 1977. *Le capital et son espace.* Paris: F. Maspéro.

Litvak, L. and B. H. Daniels 1979. *Innovations in development finance.* Washington, DC: Council of State Planning Agencies.

Lloyd, P. E. and P. Dicken 1972. *Location in space: a theoretical approach to economic geography.* New York: Harper & Row.

Lösch, A. 1954. *The economics of location.* New Haven, Conn.: Yale University Press.

Lowry, I. 1966. *Migration and metropolitan growth.* San Francisco, Calif.: Chandler.

Lucas, R. E. 1981. *Studies in business-cycle theory.* Cambridge, Mass.: MIT Press.

McKay, J. and J. Whitelaw 1977. The role of large private and government organizations in generating flows of interregional migrants: the case of Australia. *Econ. Geog.* **53**, 28–44.

McKay, J. and J. Whitelaw 1978. Internal migration and the Australian urban system. *Prog. Plann.* **10**, 1–84.

McKenzie, R. B. 1981. The case for plant closures. *Policy Rev.* **15**, 119–34.

McMahon, W. and C. Melton 1978. Measuring cost of living variation. *Indust. Rel.* **17**, 324–32.

Mackness, W. 1984. The need for equity capital. *Policy Options* **5**, 24–7.

MacNeil, I. R. 1980. *The new social contract.* New Haven: Yale University Press.

MacNeil, I. R. 1981. Economic analysis of contractual relations: its shortfalls and the need for a rich classificatory apparatus. *Northwestern Univ. Law Rev.* **75**, 1018–63.

Maddala, G. S. 1977. *Econometrics.* New York: McGraw-Hill.

Malecki, E. J. 1981. Recent trends in the location of industrial research and development: regional development implications for the United States. In *Industrial location and regional systems: spatial organization in the economic sector,* J. Rees, G. J. D. Hewings, and H. A. Stafford (eds.). Brooklyn, NY: Bergin.

Marchand, C. 1981. Maximum entropy spectra and the spatial and temporal dimensions of economic fluctuations in an urban system. *Geog. Anal.* **13**, 95–116.

Marglin, S. 1984. *Growth, distribution, and prices.* Cambridge, Mass.: Harvard University Press.

Markusen, A. 1978a. Class, rent, and sectoral conflict: uneven development in western boomtowns. *Rev. Rad. Polit. Econ.* **10**, 117–29.

Markusen, A. R. 1978b. Regionalism and the capitalist state: the case of the United States. *Kapitalistate* **7**, 39–62.

Markusen, A. R. 1985. *Profit cycles, oligopoly, and regional development.* Cambridge, Mass.: MIT Press.

Marquardt, D. W. 1963. An algorithm for least squares estimation of nonlinear parameters. *J. Soc. Ind. Appl. Math.* **11**, 431–41.

Marshall, A. 1920. *Principles of economics,* 8th edn. London: Macmillan.

Martin, F., N. Swan, I. Banks, G. Barker, and R. Beaudry 1979. *The interregional diffusion of innovations in Canada.* Ottawa, Canada: Economic Council of Canada.

Martin, R. L. 1981. Wage-change interdependence amongst regional labor markets: conceptual issues and some empirical evidence from the United States. In *Regional wage inflation and unemployment,* R. L. Martin (ed.). London: Pion.

Martin, R. L. and J. E. Oeppen 1975. The identification of regional forecasting models using space–time correlation functions. *Trans. Inst. Br. Geogs* **66**, 95–118.

Massey, D. 1975. *Restructuring and regionalism: some spatial effects of the crisis.* Working note no. 449. London: Centre for Environmental Studies.

Massey, D. 1978a. Capital and location change: the UK electrical engineering and electronics industry. *Rev. Rad. Polit. Econ.* **10**, 39–54.

Massey, D. 1978b. Regionalism: some current issues. *Cap. Class* **6**, 106–25.

Massey, D. 1984. *Spatial divisions of labor.* London: Macmillan.

Massey, D. and R. Meegan 1982. *The anatomy of job loss.* New York: Methuen.

Medoff, J. 1979. Layoffs and alternatives under trade unions in U.S. manufacturing. *Am. Econ. Rev.* **69**, 380–95.

Medoff, J. 1983. *Labor markets in imbalance.* Working paper. Cambridge, Mass.: National Bureau of Economic Research.

Mera, K. 1969. *Regional production functions and redistribution policies: the case of Japan.* Cambridge, Mass.: Program on Regional and Urban Economics, Harvard University.

Mera, K. 1975. *Income distribution and regional development.* Tokyo: University of Tokyo Press.

Meyer, J. R. and E. Kuh 1957. *The investment decision: an empirical study.* Cambridge, Mass.: Harvard University Press.

Meyer, J. R., R. Schmenner and L. Meyer 1980. *Business location decisions, capital market imperfections and development of central city employment.* Cambridge, Mass.: Joint Center for Urban Studies of MIT and Harvard University.

Meyer, P. A. 1967. Price discrimination, regional loan rates and the structure of the banking industry. *J. Fin.* **22**, 37–48.

Miernyk, W. H. 1979. A note on recent regional growth theories. *J. Reg. Sci.* **19**, 303–8.

Miernyk, W. H. 1982. *Regional analysis and regional policy.* Cambridge Mass.: Oelgeschlager, Gunn and Hain.

Miller E. M. 1983. A difficulty in measuring productivity with a perpetual inventory capital stock measure. *Oxford Bull. Econ. Statis.* **45**, 297–306.

Miller, R. E. 1979. *Dynamic optimization and economic applications.* New York: McGraw-Hill.

Milne, W. J., N. J. Glickman, and F. G. Adams 1980. A framework for analyzing regional growth and decline: a multiregional econometric model of the United States. *J. Reg. Sci.* **20**, 173–89.

Moriarty, B. 1976. The distributed lag between metropolitan-area employment and population growth. *J. Reg. Sci.* **16**, 195–212.

Morishima, M. 1976. *The economic theory of modern society*. Cambridge: Cambridge University Press.

Morishima, M. 1977. *Walras' economics: a pure theory of capital and money*. Cambridge: Cambridge University Press.

Morishima, M. and G. Catephores 1978. *Value, exploitation, and growth*. New York: Wiley.

Murg, G. E. and C. Scharman, 1982. "Employment at will": do the exceptions overwhelm the rule? *Boston Coll. Law Rev.* **23**, 329–84.

Muth, J. R. 1961. Rational expectations and the theory of price movements. *Econometrica* **29**, 315–35.

Muth, R. 1971. Migration: chicken or egg. *South Econ. J.* **37**, 295–306.

Myrdal, G. 1957. *Rich lands and poor*. New York: Harper & Row.

Nadji, M. and C. C. Harris Jr. 1984. A note on regional investment functions. *J. Reg. Sci.* **24**, 271–5.

National Academy of Sciences 1982. *Critical issues for national urban policy*. Washington, DC: National Research Council.

National Association of Securities Dealers 1979. *Small business financing: the current environment and suggestions for improvement*. Special report, Washington, DC.

Nelson, R. R. and S. G. Winter 1982. *An evolutionary theory of economic change*. Cambridge, Mass.: Harvard University Press.

Newman, R. 1984. *Growth in the American south*. New York: New York University Press.

Nickell, S. J. 1978. Fixed costs employment and labor demand over the cycle. *Economica* **45**, 329–45.

Norcliffe, G. B. 1975. A theory of manufacturing places. In *Locational dynamics of manufacturing*, L. Collins and D. F. Walker (eds.). New York: Wiley.

Obrinsky, M. 1983. *Profit theory and capitalism*. Philadelphia, Penn.: University of Pennsylvania Press.

Ohlin, B. 1933. *Interregional and international trade*. Cambridge, Mass.: Harvard University Press.

Oi, W. 1962. Labor as a quasi-fixed factor. *J. Polit. Econ.* **70**, 538–55.

Okun, A. 1981. *Prices and quantities: a macroeconomic analysis*. Washington, DC: Brookings Institution.

Olsen, E. 1971. *International trade theory and regional income differences*. Amsterdam: North-Holland.

Osborne, A. E. Jr. 1980. Financing small and high-risk enterprises. In *Cities and firms*, H. J. Bryce (ed.). Lexington, Mass.: Lexington Books.

O'Sullivan, P. 1981. *Geographical economics*. London: Penguin.

Pasinetti, L. L. 1977. On non-substitution in production models. *Camb. J. Econ.* **1**, 389–94.

Pasinetti, L. L. 1981. *Structural change and economic growth: a theoretical essay on the dynamics of the wealth of nations*. Cambridge: Cambridge University Press.

Peel, D. A. and I. Walker 1978. Short-run employment functions, excess supply and the speed of adjustment: a note. *Economica* **45**, 195–202.

Perry, D. and A. Watkins (eds.) 1978. *The rise of the sunbelt cities*. Beverly Hills: Sage.

Persky, J. 1978. Dualism, capital–labor ratios and the regions of the U.S. *J. Reg. Sci.* **18**, 373–81.

Persky, J. and W. Klein 1975. Regional capital growth and some of those other things we never talk about. *Pap. Reg. Sci. Assoc.* **35**, 181–90.

Pesaran, M. H. 1982. A critique of the proposed tests of the natural rate–rational expectations hypothesis. *Econ. J.* **92**, 529–54.

Phelps, E. 1979. *Studies in macroeconomic theory.* Vol. 1: *Employment and inflation.* New York: Academic Press.

Phillips, A. W. 1958. The relationship of unemployment and the rate of change of money wage rates in the United Kingdom, 1861–1957. *Economica* **25**, 283–99.

Pierce, D. A. 1977. Relationships – and the lack thereof – between economic time series, with special reference to money and interest rates. *J. Am. Statist. Assoc.* **72**, 11–22.

Piore, M. 1968. The impact of the labor market upon the design and selection of productive technology within the manufacturing plant. *Q. J. Econ.* **82**, 602–20.

Piore, M. 1979a. *Birds of passage.* Cambridge: Cambridge University Press.

Piore, M. (ed.) 1979b. *Unemployment and inflation: institutionalist and structuralist views.* New York: M. E. Sharpe.

Piore, M. 1981. *The theory of economic regulation and the current economic crisis in the US.* Cambridge, Mass.: Working Paper, Department of Economics, MIT.

Pittenger, D. 1976. *Projecting state and local populations.* Cambridge, Mass.: Ballinger.

Plane, D. 1981. *A minimum information approach to the spatial modeling of human migration flows.* Ph.D. dissertation. Philadelphia, Penn.: University of Pennsylvania.

Plaut, T. R. 1981. An econometric model for forecasting regional population growth. *Int. Reg. Sci. Rev.* **6**, 53–70.

Pollard, J. H. 1973. *Mathematical models for the growth of human populations.* Cambridge: Cambridge University Press.

Pred, A. R. 1966. *The spatial dynamics of U.S. urban-industrial growth, 1800–1914: interpretative and theoretical essays.* Cambridge: Mass.: MIT Press.

Pred, A. R. 1973. *Urban growth and the circulation of information: the United States system of cities, 1790–1840.* Cambridge, Mass.: Harvard University Press.

Pred, A. R. 1977. *City-systems in advanced economies.* New York: Halsted/Wiley.

Pred, A. R. 1980. *Urban growth and city-systems in the United States, 1840–1860.* Cambridge, Mass.: Harvard University Press.

Pred, A. R. 1981. Social reproduction and the time-geography of everyday life. *Geografiska Annaler* **63B**, 5–22.

Pred, A. R. 1983. Structuration and place: on the becoming of sense of place and structure of feeling. *J. Theory Soc. Behav.* **13**, 45–68.

Pred, A. R. 1984. Place as historically contingent process: structuration and the time-geography of becoming places. *Ann. Assoc. Am. Geogs* **74**, 279–97.

President's Commission for a National Agenda for the Eighties. 1980. *Urban America in the eighties: perspectives and prospects.* Washington, DC: USGPO.

Radner, R. 1982. The role of private information in markets and other organizations. In *Advances in economic theory*, W. Hildenbrand (ed.). Cambridge: Cambridge University Press.

Rees, J. 1979. Technological change and regional shifts in American manufacturing. *Prof. Geogr.* **31**, 45–54.

Rees, P. M. 1977. The measurement of migration, from census data and other sources. *Environ. Plann. A* **9**, 247–72.

Renshaw, V. 1978. *The impact of reporting and clerical errors on migration data tabulated from the CWHS of the Social Security Administration.* Washington, DC: Bureau of Economic Analysis.

Richardson, H. W. 1973. *Regional growth theory.* London: Macmillan.

Rives, N. W. 1981. *The use of population projections to allocate public funds*. Report number P-6584. Santa Monica, Calif.: Rand Corporation.

Robinson, J. 1953. The production function and the theory of capital. *Rev. Econ. Stud.* **21**, 81–106.

Robinson, J. 1962. *Essays in the theory of economic growth*. London: Macmillan.

Robinson, J. 1971. *Economic heresies: some old-fashioned questions in economic theory*. New York: Basic Books.

Robinson, J. 1974a. The abdication of neoclassical economics. In *Economic theory and planning: essays in honor of A. K. Das Gupta*, A. Mitra (ed.). Calcutta: Oxford University Press.

Robinson, J. 1974b. *History versus equilibrium*. London: Thames Polytechnic.

Robinson, J. 1975. The unimportance of reswitching. *Q. J. Econ.* **89**, 76–89.

Robinson, J. 1979. The meaning of capital. In *Contributions to modern economics*, J. Robinson (ed.). 114–25. Oxford: Basil Blackwell.

Rogers, A. 1979. *Essays in the formal demography of migration and population redistribution*. Laxenburg, Austria: International Institute for Applied Systems Analysis.

Rogerson, P. and R. MacKinnon 1981. A geographical model of job search, migration and unemployment. *Pap. Reg. Sci. Assoc.* **48**, 89–102.

Rogerson, P. and R. MacKinnon 1982. Interregional migration models with source and interaction information. *Environ. Plann. A* **14**, 445–54.

Romans, J. T. 1965. *Capital exports and growth among U.S. regions*. Middletown, Conn.: Wesleyan University Press.

Rosenberg, S. and T. E. Weisskopf 1981. A conflict theory approach to inflation in the postwar U.S. economy. *Pap. Proc. Am. Econ. Rev.* **71**, 42–47.

Ross, A. M. 1948. *Trade union wage policy*. Berkeley, Calif.: University of California Press.

Rotemberg, J. J. 1982. Sticky prices in the United States. *J. Polit. Econ.* **90**, 1187–211.

Rothschild, M. 1973. Models of market information with imperfect information. *J. Polit. Econ.* **81**, 1283–308.

Rowthorn, B. 1980. *Capitalism, conflict and inflation*. London: Lawrence and Wishart.

Samuelson, P. A. 1947. *Foundations of economic analysis*. Cambridge, Mass.: Harvard University Press.

Samuelson, P. A. 1966. A summing up. *Q. J. Econ.* **80**, 444–8.

Saxenian, A. L. 1984. The urban contradictions of Silicon Valley: regional growth and the restructuring of the semiconductor industry. In *Sunbelt/snowbelt: urban development and regional restructuring*, L. Sawers and W. Tabb (eds.). Oxford: Oxford University Press.

Schelling, T. 1961. *The strategy of conflict*. Cambridge, Mass.: Harvard University Press.

Schumpeter, J. A. 1934. *The theory of economic development*. Cambridge, Mass.: Harvard University Press.

Scott, A. 1982. Production system dynamics and metropolitan development. *Ann. Assoc. Am. Geogs* **72**, 185–200.

Sen, A. and B. Williams (eds.). 1982. *Utilitarianism and beyond*. Cambridge: Cambridge University Press.

Sheppard, E. and L. Curry 1982. Spatial price equilibria. *Geog. Anal.* **14**, 279–304.

Simmons, J. W. 1980. Changing migration patterns in Canada: 1966–1971 and 1971–1976. *Can. J. Reg. Sci.* **3**, 139–62.

Simon, H. A. 1951. A formal theory of the employment relationship. *Econometrica* **19**, 293–305.

Sims, C. 1977. Comment. *J. Am. Statist. Assoc.* **72**, 23–4.

Sims, C. 1980 Macroeconomics and reality. *Econometrica* **48**, 1–48.

Smale, S. 1978. Review of "Catastrophe theory: selected papers" by E. C. Zeeman. *Bull. Am. Math. Soc.* **84**, 1360–8.

Smith, D. M. 1971. *Industrial location: an economic geographical analysis.* New York: Wiley.

Smith, L. A. 1983. *The effect of right-to-work laws on the level of unionization in regional economies.* Bevea, Ohio.: Baldwin-Wallace College.

Solo, V. 1982. *Topics in advanced time series analysis.* Cambridge, Mass.: Department of Statistics, Harvard University.

Spence, M. 1973. *Market signaling.* Cambridge, Mass.: Harvard University Press.

Sraffa, P. 1960. *Production of commodities by means of commodities.* Cambridge: Cambridge University Press.

Stone, K. 1981. The post-war paradigm in American labor law. *Yale Law J.* **90**, 1509–80.

Storper, M. and R. A. Walker 1983. The theory of labor and the theory of location. *Int. J. Urb. Reg. Res.* **7**, 1–41.

Storper, M. and R. A. Walker 1984. The spatial division of labor: labor and the location of industries. In *Sunbelt/snowbelt: urban development and regional restructuration,* L. Sawers and W. Tabbs (eds.). Oxford: Oxford University Press.

Straszheim, M. R. 1971. An introduction and overview of regional money capital markets. In *Essays in regional economics,* J. Kain and J. Meyer (eds.). Cambridge, Mass.: Harvard University Press.

Strong, J. 1983. Regional variations in industrial performance. *Reg. Stud.* **17**, 429–44.

Sullivan T. G. 1978. The cost of capital and the market power of firms. *Rev. Econ. Stat.* **60**, 209–17.

Sussman, H. J. and R. S. Zahler 1978. Catastrophe theory as applied to the social and biological sciences: a critique. *Synthèse* **37**, 1–216.

Syron, R. 1978. Regional experiences during business cycles: are we becoming more or less alike? *New Eng. Econ. Rev.* Nov.–Dec., 25–34.

Tabuchi, T. 1983. *Interregional migration and development in Japan and in the United States.* Unpublished Ph.D. thesis, Cambridge, Mass.: Graduate School of Arts and Sciences, Harvard University.

Tannenwald, R. 1982. Are wage and training subsidies cost effective? – some evidence from the new jobs tax credit. *New Eng. Econ. Rev.* Sept.–Oct. 25–34.

Taylor, J. B. 1980. Aggregate dynamics and staggered contracts. *J. Polit. Econ.* **88**, 1–23.

Taylor, J. B. 1981. On the relation between the variability of inflation and the average inflation rate. *Carnegie–Rochester Conference Series on Public Policy* **15**, 57–86.

Taylor, M. and N. J. Thrift 1983. Business organization, segmentation and location. *Reg. Stud.* **17**, 445–66.

Thom, R. 1975. *Structural stability and morphogenesis.* Reading, Mass.: Benjamin Cumming.

Thompson, W. R. 1965. *A preface to urban economics.* Baltimore, Md.: Johns Hopkins University Press.

Thompson, W. R. 1975. Internal and external factors in the development of urban economies. In *Regional policy: readings in theory and applications,* J. Friedmann and W. Alonso (eds.). Cambridge, Mass.: MIT Press.

Thrall G. I. and C. Erol 1983. A dynamic equilibrium model of regional capital investment with supporting evidence from Canada and the United States. *Econ. Geog.* **53**, 272–81.

Thrift, N. J. 1983. On the determination of social action in time and space. *Environ. Plann. D: Soc. Sp.* **1**, 23–57.

Thrift, N. J. and A. Pred 1981. Time geography: a new beginning. *Prog. Human Geog.* **5**, 277–86.

Thurow, L. 1984. The disappearance of the middle class: it's not just demographics. *The New York Times,* February 5.

Tiao, G. C. *et al.* 1981. *The Wisconsin multiple time series program.* Madison, Wisc.: Department of Statistics, University of Wisconsin.

Tobin, J. 1980. *Asset accumulation and economic activity.* Oxford: Basil Blackwell.

Tooze, M. J. 1976. Regional elasticities of substitution in the United Kingdom in 1968. *Urban Stud.* **13**, 35–44.

Treyz, G. I. 1980. Design of a multiregional policy analysis model. *J. Reg. Sci.* **20**, 191–206.

US Department of Housing and Urban Development 1982. *President's national urban policy report.* Washington, DC: US Government Printer.

Varaiya, P. and M. Wiseman 1978. The age of cities and the movement of manufacturing employment, 1947–1972. *Pap. Reg. Sci. Assoc.* **41**, 127–40.

Varaiya, P. and M. Wiseman 1981. Investment and employment in manufacturing in the US metropolitan areas 1960–1976. *Reg. Sci. Urban Econ.* **11**, 431–69.

Vaughan, R. J. 1980a. Capital needs of the business sector and the future economy of the city. In *Cities and firms,* H. J. Bryce (ed.). Lexington, Mass.: Lexington Books.

Vaughan, R. J. 1980b. The urban impacts of federal policies. In *The prospective city,* A. Solomon (ed.). Cambridge, Mass.: MIT Press.

Veblen, T. 1908. Professor Clark's economics. *Q. J. Econ.* **22**, 147–95.

Verdoorn, P. J. 1949. Fattori che regolano lo sviluppo della produttivita del lavoro. *L'Industria* **1**, 43–53.

Verdoorn, P. J. 1956. Complementary and long-range projections. *Econometrica* **24**, 429–50.

Vernez, G., R. Vaughan, B. Burright and S. Coleman 1977. *Regional cycles and employment effects of public works investments.* Report number R-2052-EDA. Santa Monica, Calif.: Rand Corporation.

Vernon, R. A. 1966. International investment and international trade in the product cycle. *Q. J. Econ.* **18**, 190–206.

Vietorisz, T. 1967. Locational choices in planning. In *National economic planning.* Princeton, NJ: Princeton University Press.

Vining, D. R. 1981. Review of *Interregional movements and regional growth,* W. Wheaton (ed.). *Environ. Plann. A* **13**, 1177–80.

Vining, D. R. 1982. On "A catastrophe model of regional dynamics." *Ann. Assoc. Am. Geogs* **72**, 554–5.

Vining, D. and A. Strauss 1977. A demonstration that the current deconcentration of population in the United States is a clean break with the past. *Environ. Plann. A* **9**, 751–8.

Wahl, R. W. 1982. Is the consumer price index a fair measure of inflation? *J. Policy Anal. Mgmt.* **1**, 496–511.

Walker, R. A. 1978. Two sources of uneven development under advanced capitalism: spatial differentiation and capital mobility. *Rev. Rad. Polit. Econ.* **10**, 28–38.

Walker, R. A. and M. Storper 1981. Capital and industrial location. *Prog. Human Geog.* **5**, 473–509.

Wallace, M. and A. L. Kalleberg 1982. Industrial transformation and the decline of craft. *Am. Soc. Rev.* **47**, 307–24.

Walras, L. 1874. *Eléments d'économie politique pure.* Lausanne: F. Rouge.

Webber, M. J. 1972. *The impact of uncertainty upon location.* Cambridge, Mass.: MIT Press.

Westaway, J. 1974. The spatial hierarchy of business organizations and its implications for the British urban system. *Reg. Stud.* **8**, 145–55.

Wheaton, W. 1979. Metropolitan growth, unemployment, and interregional factor mobility. In *Interregional movements and regional growth*, W. Wheaton (ed.). Washington, DC: Urban Institute.

Whiteman, J. 1985. *The vicissitudes of economic life: a study of employment fluctuations in American cities.* Unpublished Ph.D. thesis. Cambridge, Mass.: Graduate School of Arts and Sciences, Harvard University.

Whitman, M. v. N. 1979. *Reflections of interdependence.* Pittsburgh, Penn.: University of Pittsburgh Press.

Willekins, F. 1976. *Sensitivity analysis.* RM-76-49. Laxenburg, Austria: International Institute for Applied Systems Analysis.

Williamson, O. 1975. *Markets and hierarchies.* New York: Free Press.

Williamson, O. Transaction-cost economics: the governance of contractual relations. *J. Law Econ.* **22**, 233–60.

Wilson, A. G. 1981. *Catastrophe theory and bifurcation: applications to urban and regional systems.* London: Croom Helm.

Wood, A. 1978. *A theory of pay.* Cambridge: Cambridge University Press.

Zeeman, E. C. 1977. *Catastrophe theory.* Reading, Mass.: Addison-Wesley.

Zelinsky, W. 1977. Coping with the migration turnaround: the theoretical challenge. *Int. Reg. Sci. Rev.* **2**, 175–8.

Index

334